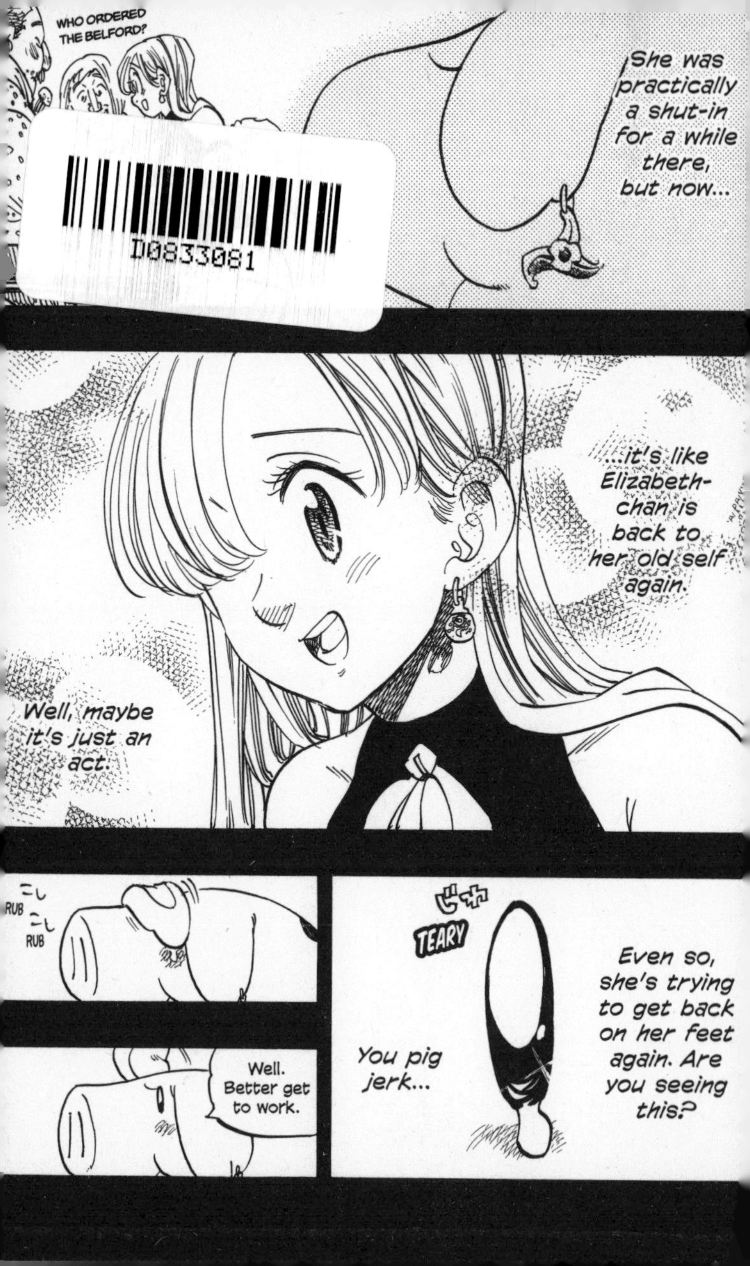

She was practically a shut-in for a while there, but now...
WHO ORDERED THE BELFORD?
...it's like Elizabeth-chan is back to her old self again.
Well, maybe it's just an act.
じわ
TEARY
Even so, she's trying to get back on her feet again. Are you seeing this?
You pig jerk...
こし RUB
こし RUB
Well. Better get to work.

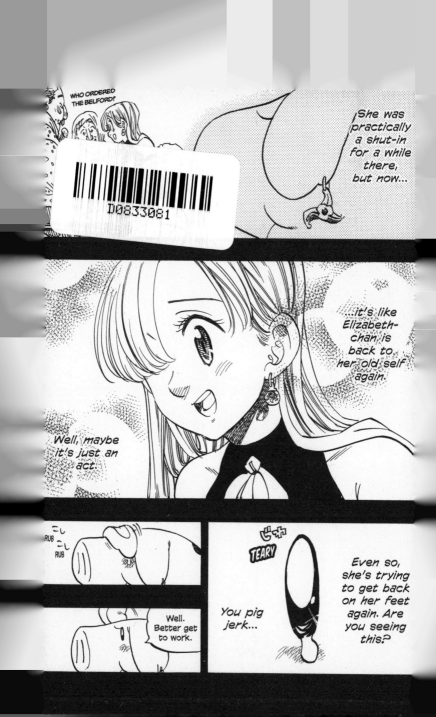

CONTENTS

BOAR HAT

The Seven Deadly Sins

Chapter 180 - The Wandering Knight

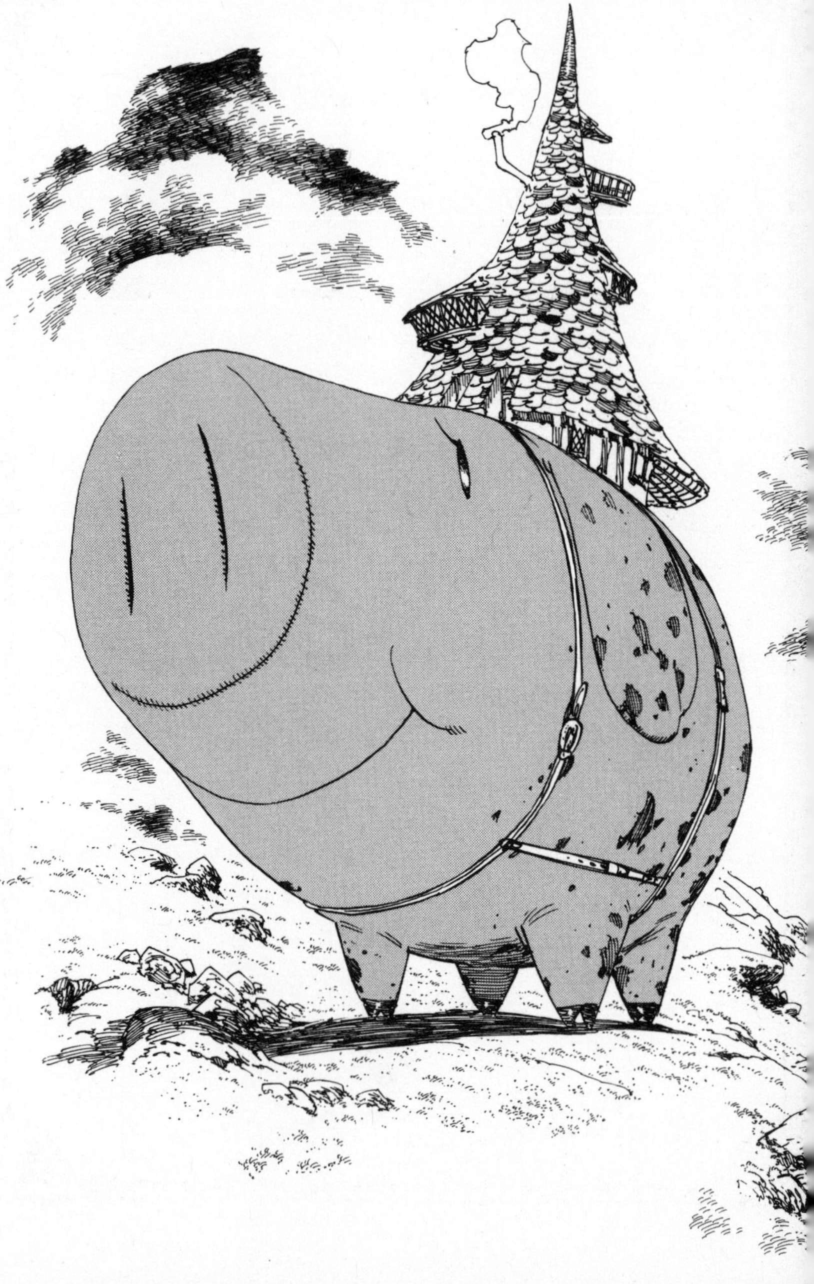

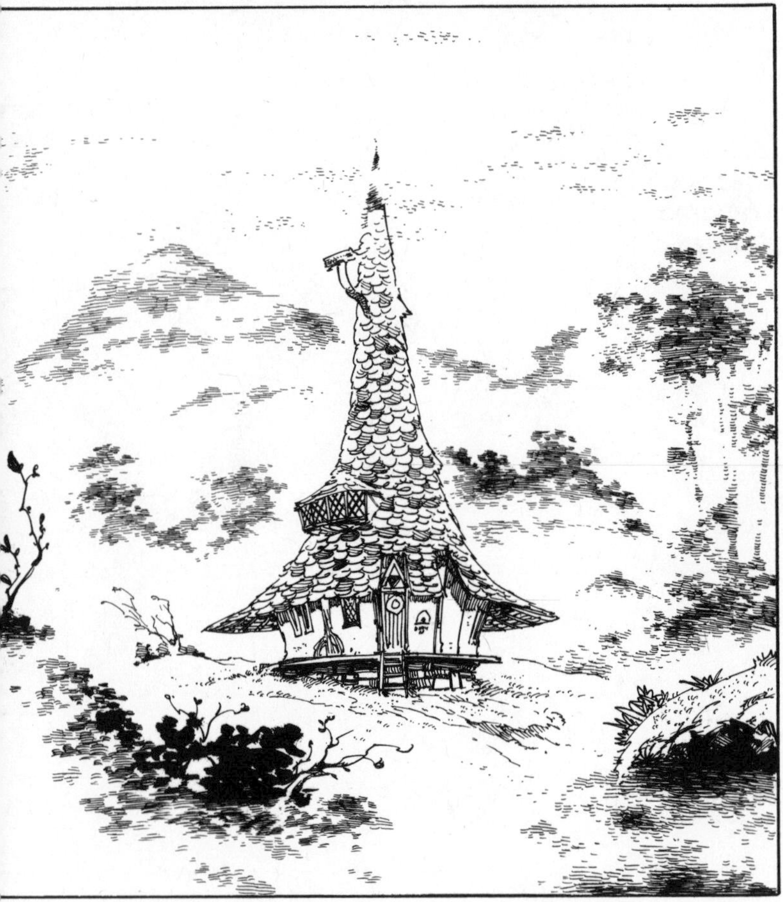

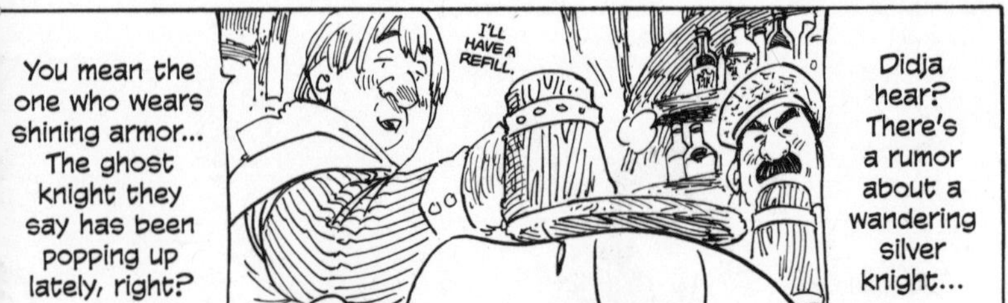
Didja hear? There's a rumor about a wandering silver knight...
I'LL HAVE A REFILL.
You mean the one who wears shining armor... The ghost knight they say has been popping up lately, right?
I'M COLLECTING EMPTY STEINS.

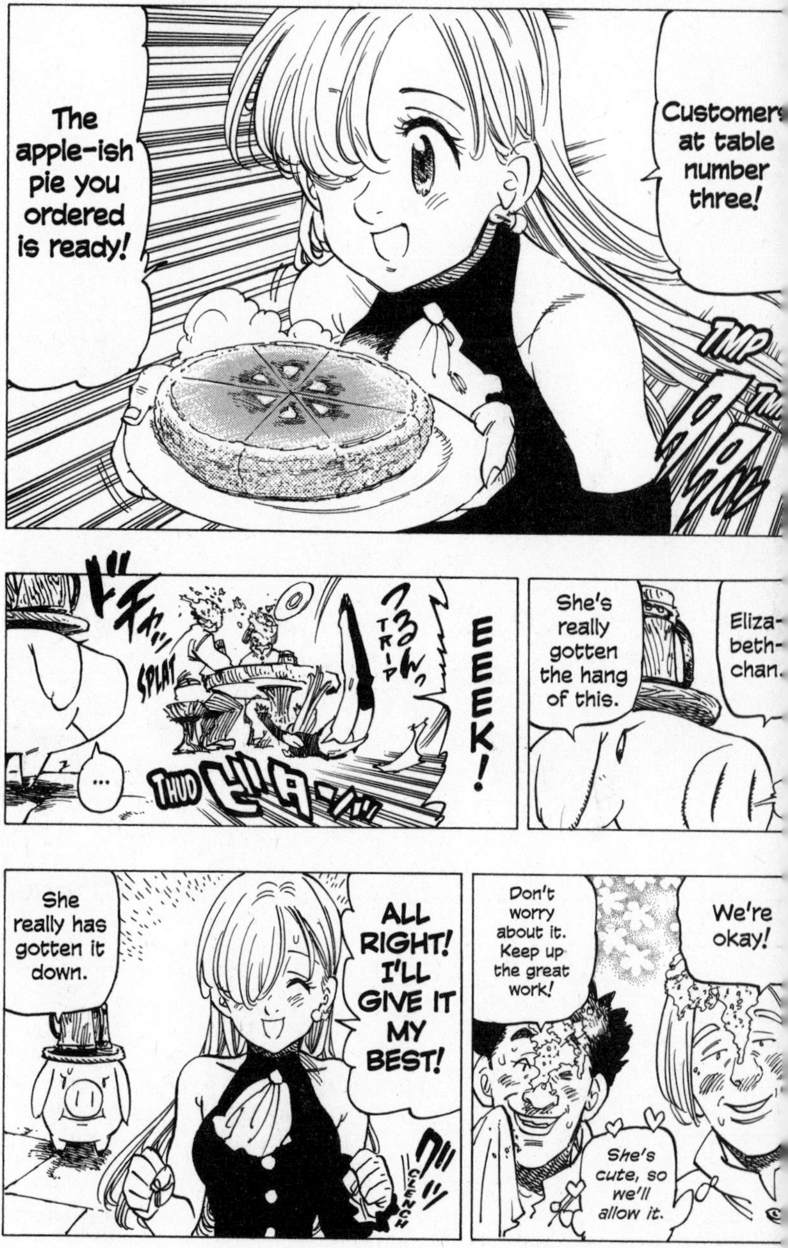

Customers at table number three!
The apple-ish pie you ordered is ready!
TMP
Eliza-beth-chan.
She's really gotten the hang of this.
EEEEK!
TRIP
SPLAT
THUD
...
We're okay!
Don't worry about it. Keep up the great work!
She's cute, so we'll allow it.
ALL RIGHT! I'LL GIVE IT MY BEST!
CLENCH
She really has gotten it down.

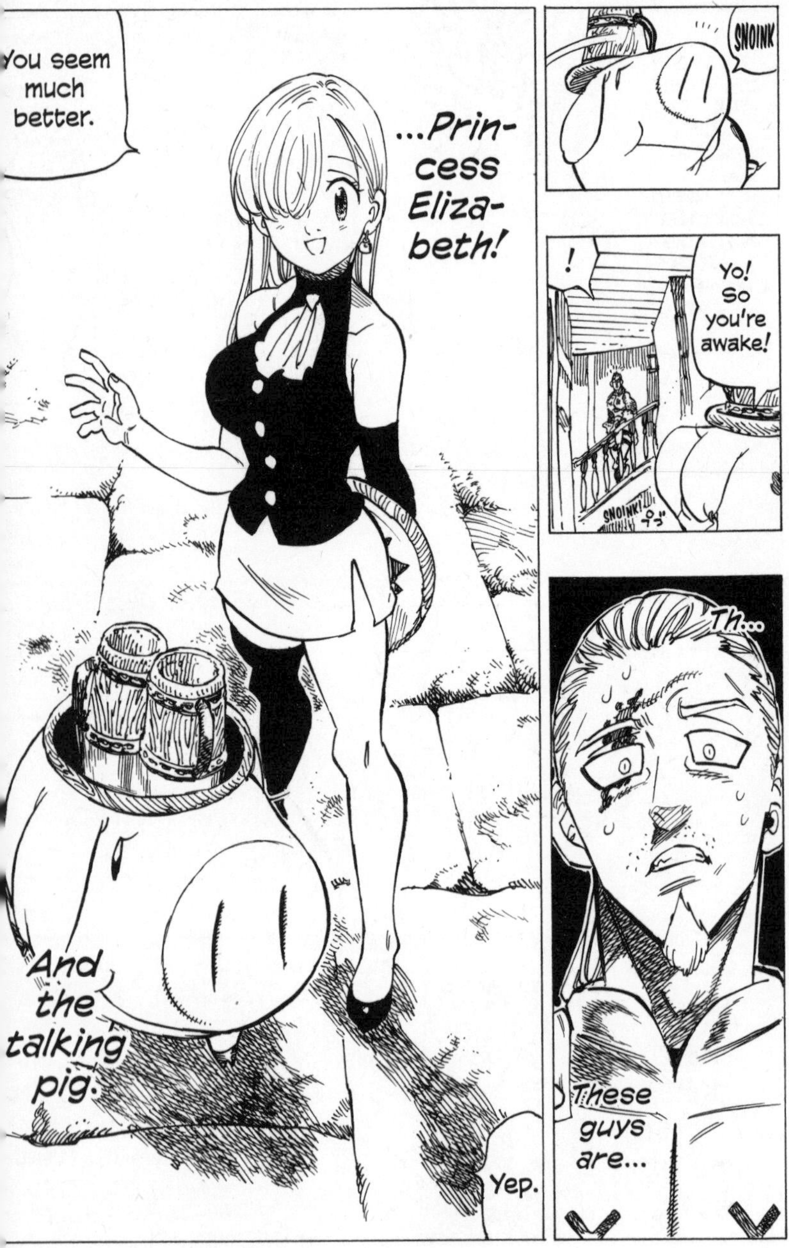
SNOINK
!
Yo! So you're awake!
SNOINK!
Th...
These guys are...
You seem much better.
...Prin-cess Eliza-beth!
And the talking pig.
Yep.

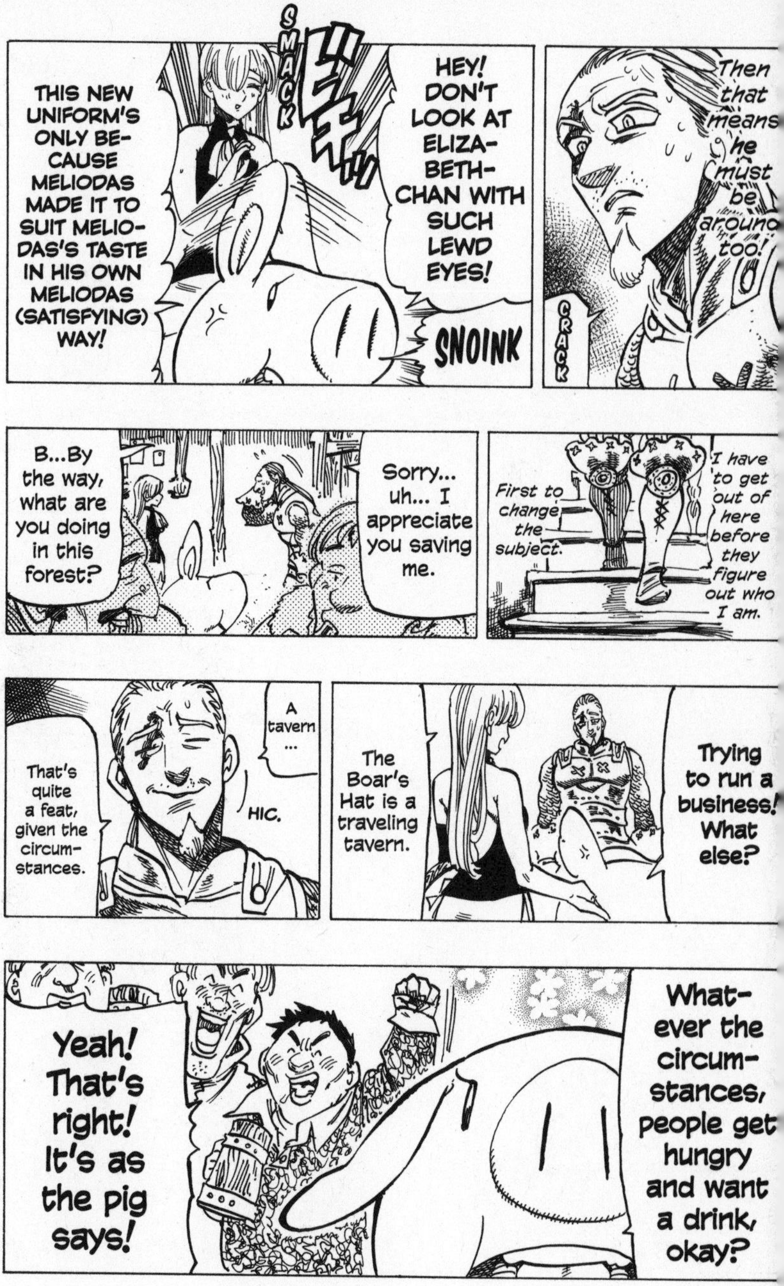
Then that means he must be around too!
CRACK
SMACK
HEY! DON'T LOOK AT ELIZABETH-CHAN WITH SUCH LEWD EYES!
THIS NEW UNIFORM'S ONLY BECAUSE MELIODAS MADE IT TO SUIT MELIODAS'S TASTE IN HIS OWN MELIODAS (SATISFYING) WAY!
SNOINK
I have to get out of here before they figure out who I am.
First to change the subject.
Sorry... uh... I appreciate you saving me.
B...By the way, what are you doing in this forest?
Trying to run a business! What else?
The Boar's Hat is a traveling tavern.
A tavern...
HIC.
That's quite a feat, given the circumstances.
Whatever the circumstances, people get hungry and want a drink, okay?
Yeah! That's right! It's as the pig says!

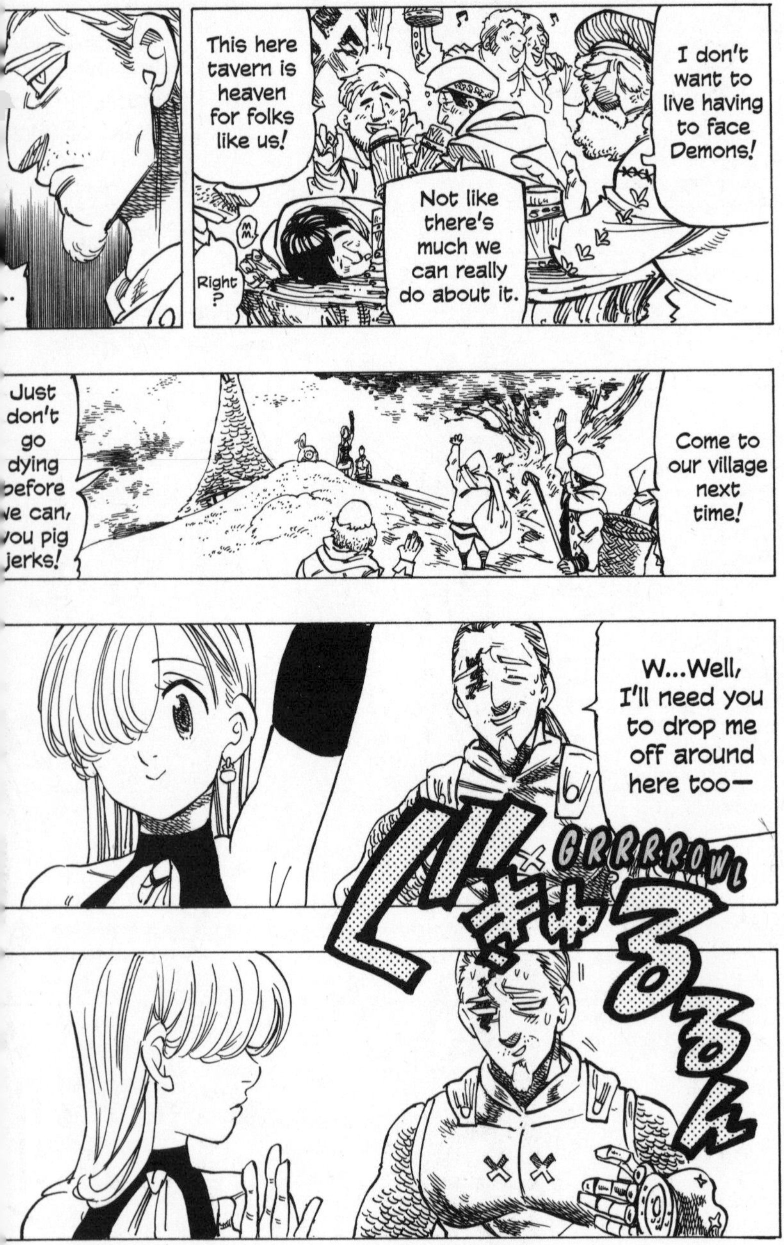
I don't want to live having to face Demons!
This here tavern is heaven for folks like us!
Not like there's much we can really do about it.
Mm.
Right?
Come to our village next time!
Just don't go dying before we can, you pig jerks!
W...Well, I'll need you to drop me off around here too—
GRRRRROWL

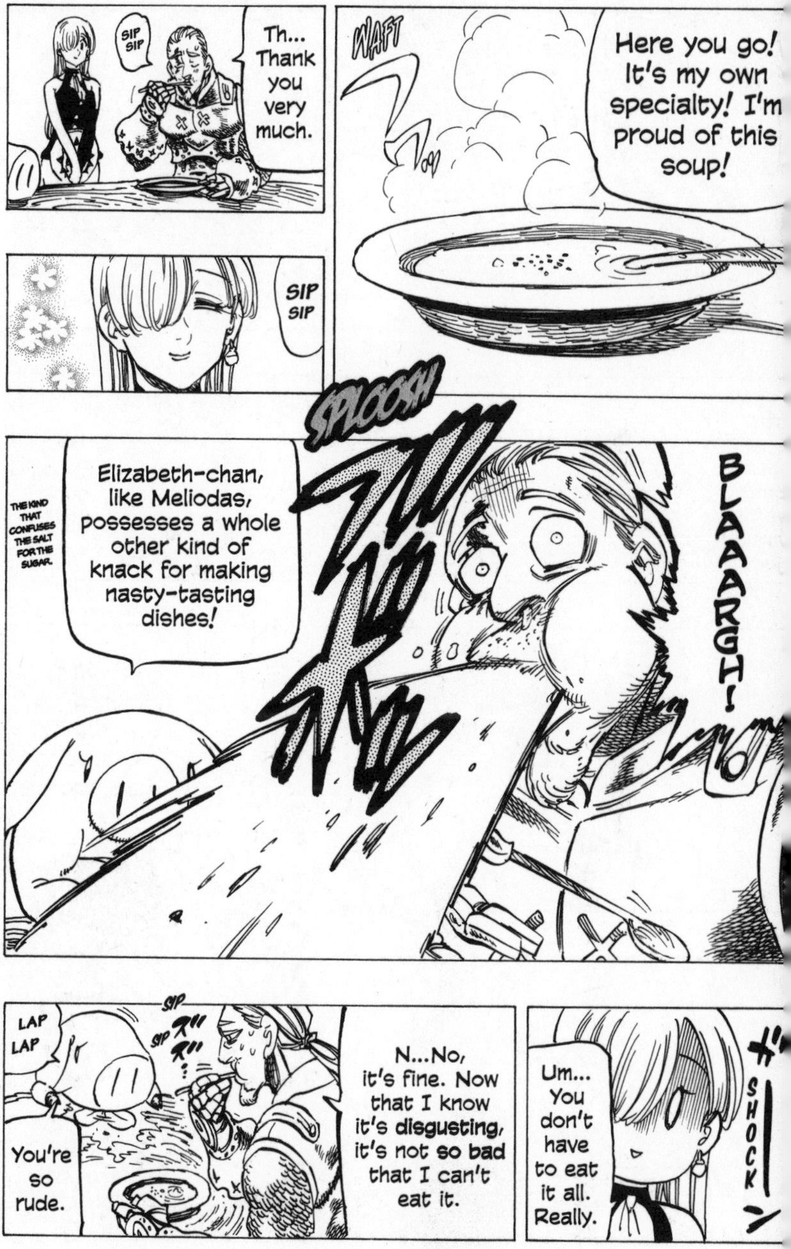
WAFT
Here you go! It's my own specialty! I'm proud of this soup!
SIP SIP
Th... Thank you very much.
SIP SIP
SPLOOSH
BLAAARGH!
Elizabeth-chan, like Meliodas, possesses a whole other kind of knack for making nasty-tasting dishes!
THE KIND THAT CONFUSES THE SALT FOR THE SUGAR.
SHOCK
Um... You don't have to eat it all. Really.
N...No, it's fine. Now that I know it's disgusting, it's not so bad that I can't eat it.
SIP SIP
LAP LAP
You're so rude.

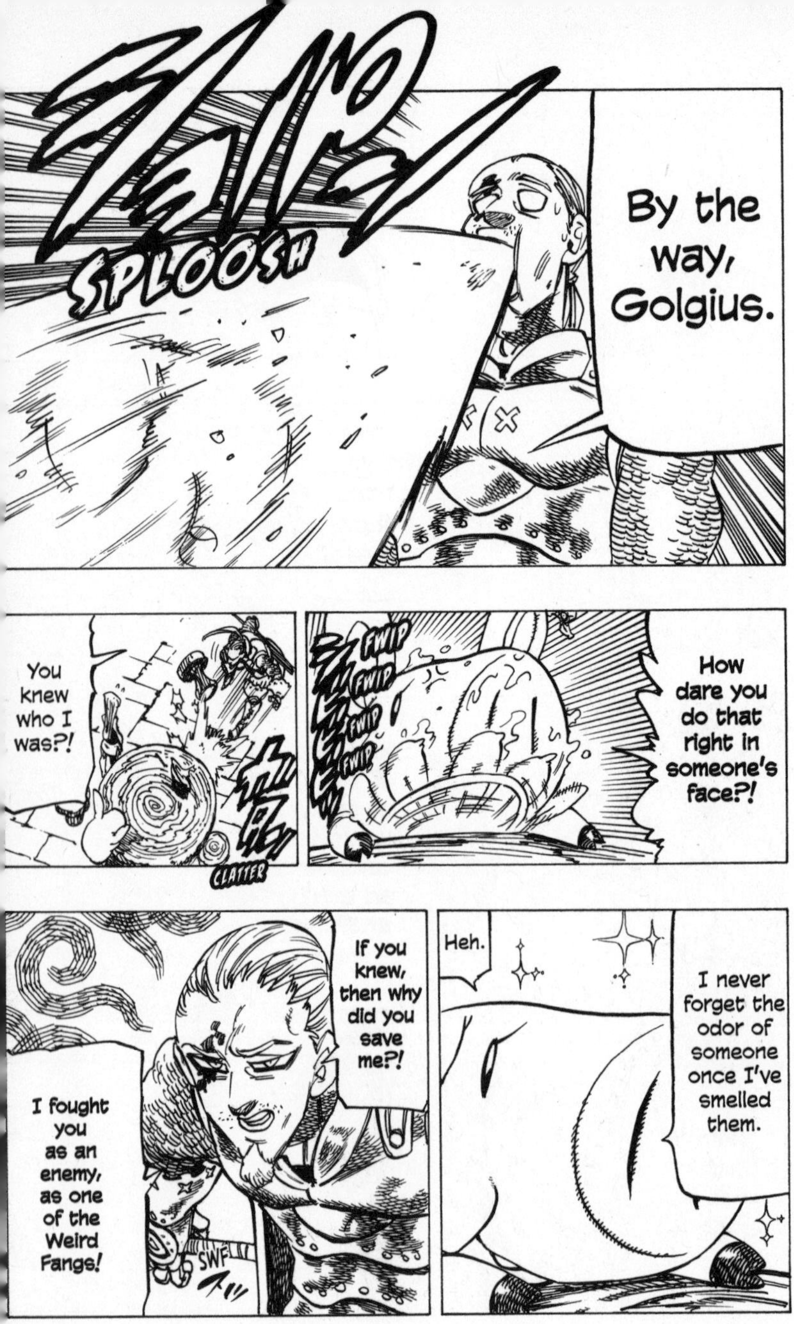
By the way, Golgius.
SPLOOSH
How dare you do that right in someone's face?!
FWIP FWIP FWIP FWIP
You knew who I was?!
CLATTER
Heh.
I never forget the odor of someone once I've smelled them.
If you knew, then why did you save me?!
I fought you as an enemy, as one of the Weird Fangs!
SWF

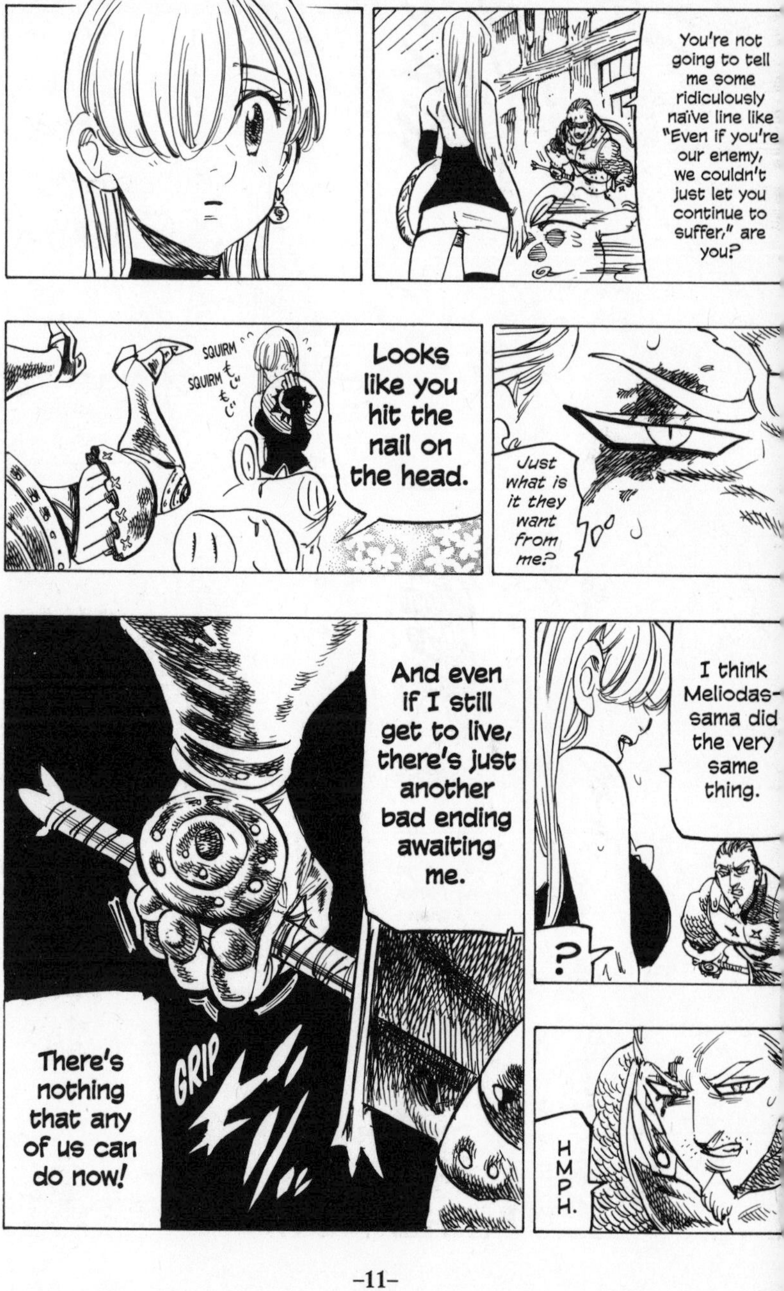

You're not going to tell me some ridiculously naïve line like "Even if you're our enemy, we couldn't just let you continue to suffer," are you?
Just what is it they want from me?
Looks like you hit the nail on the head.
SQUIRM SQUIRM
もじ もじ
I think Meliodas-sama did the very same thing.
?
HMPH.
And even if I still get to live, there's just another bad ending awaiting me.
GRIP
There's nothing that any of us can do now!

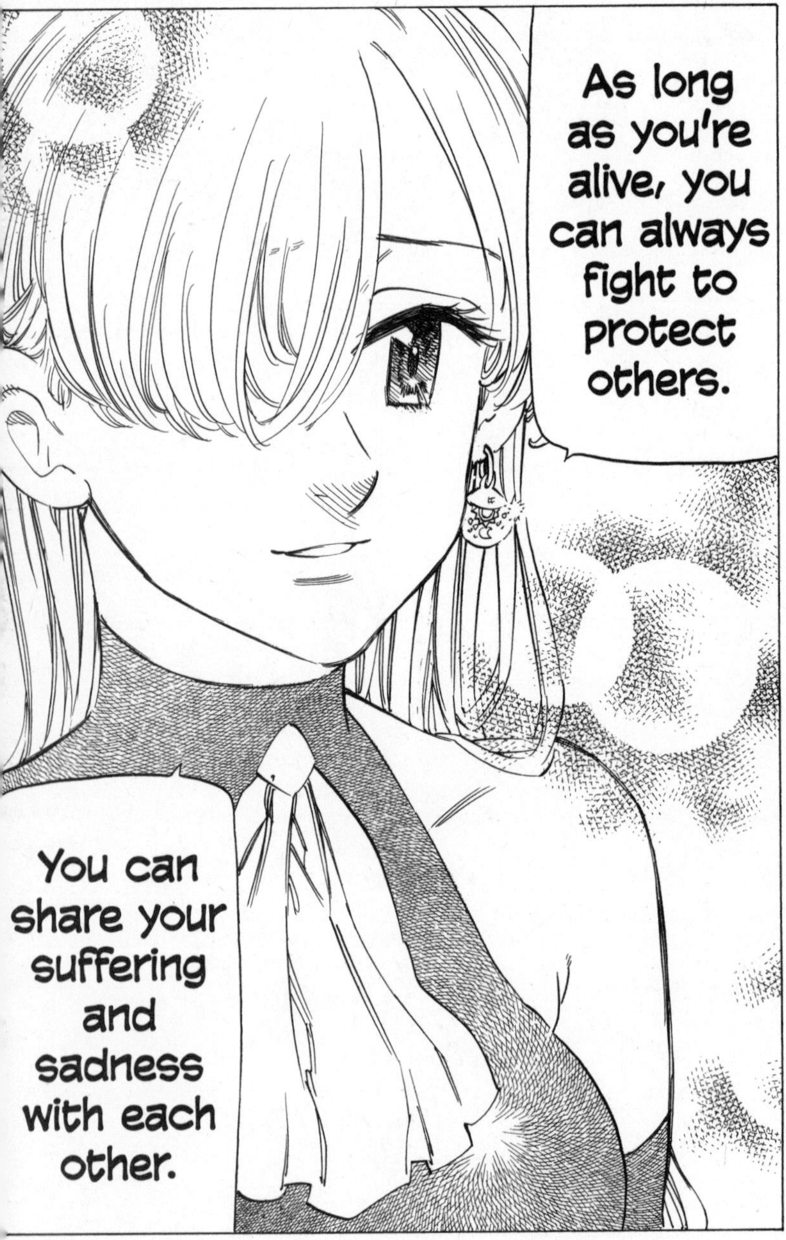
As long as you're alive, you can always fight to protect others.
You can share your suffering and sadness with each other.

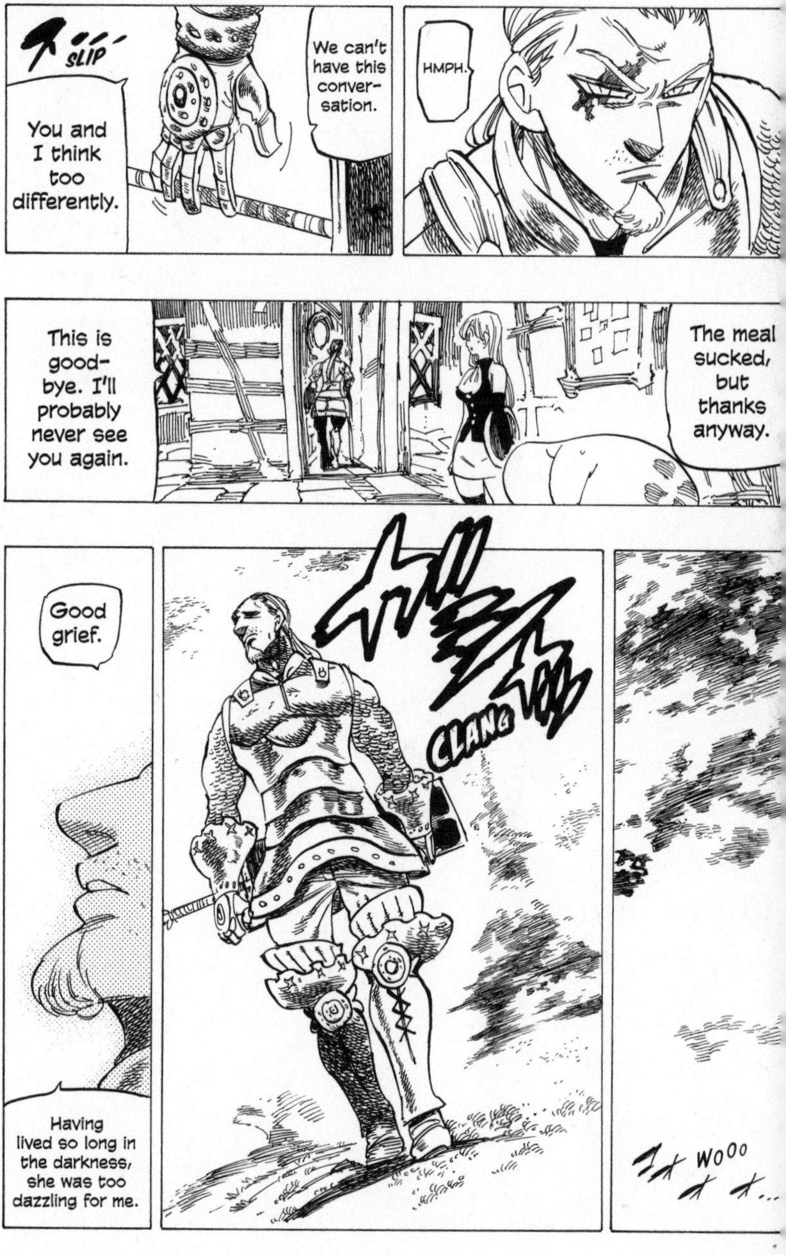
HMPH.
We can't have this conversation.
SLIP
You and I think too differently.
The meal sucked, but thanks anyway.
This is good-bye. I'll probably never see you again.
WOOO
CLANG
Good grief.
Having lived so long in the darkness, she was too dazzling for me.

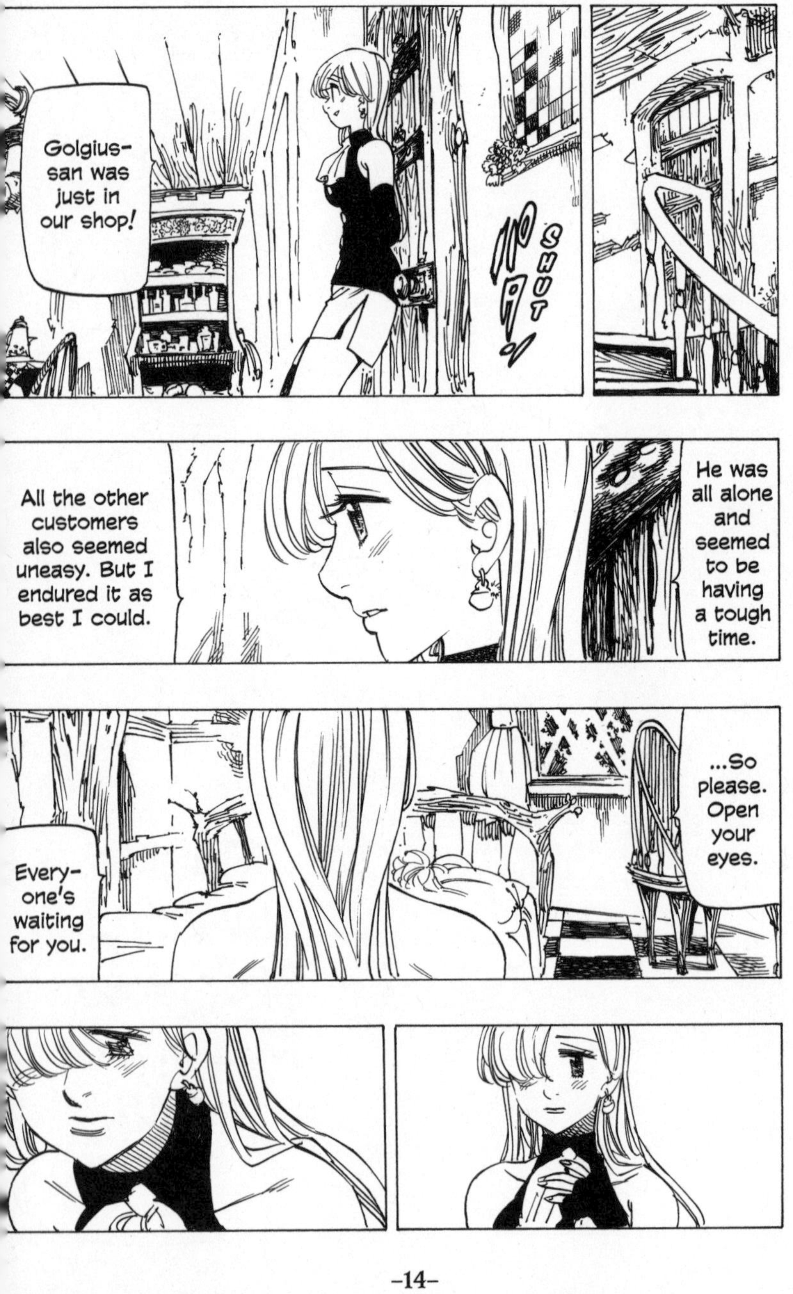
SHUT
Golgius-san was just in our shop!
He was all alone and seemed to be having a tough time.
All the other customers also seemed uneasy. But I endured it as best I could.
...So please. Open your eyes.
Everyone's waiting for you.

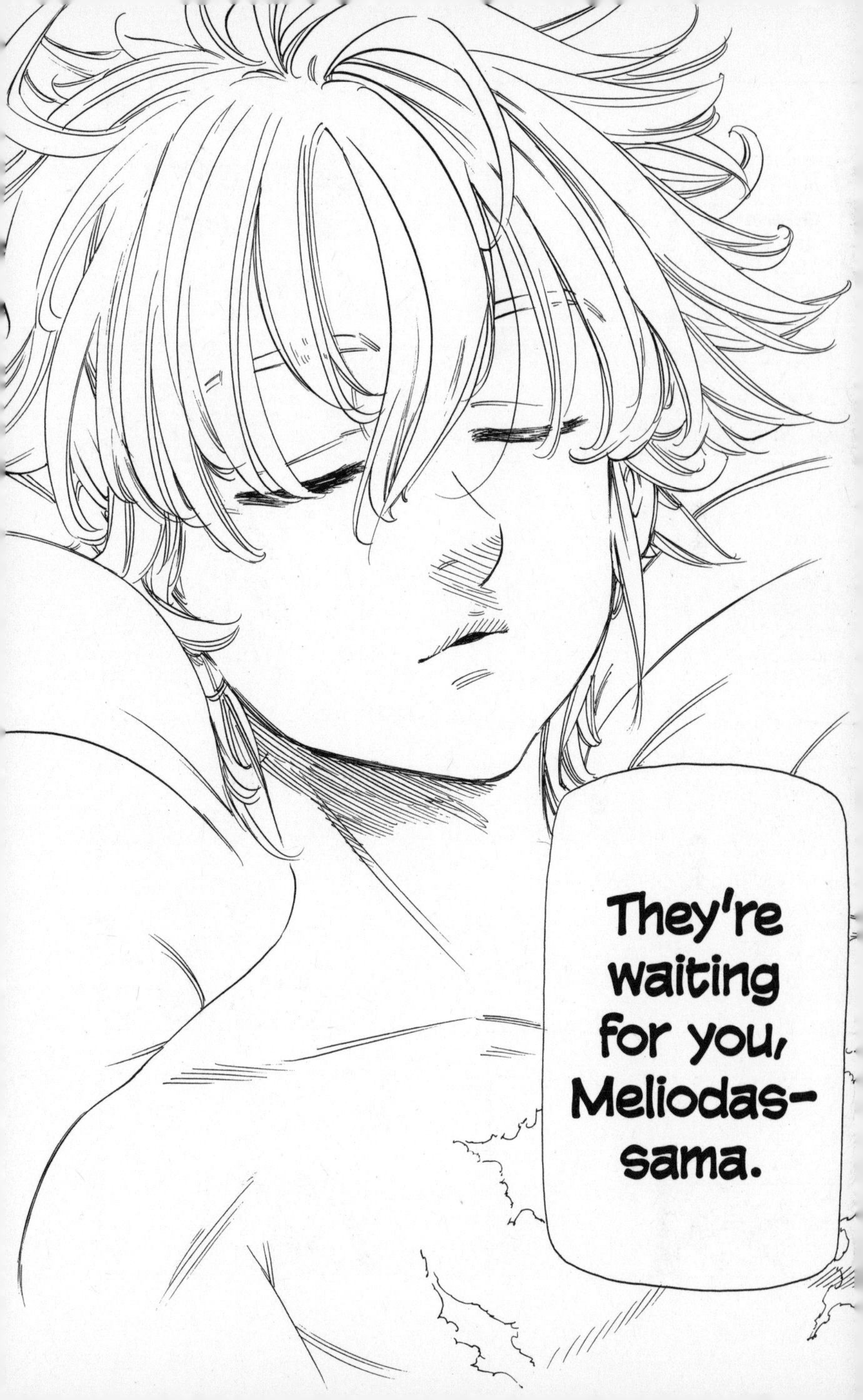
They're waiting for you, Meliodas-sama.

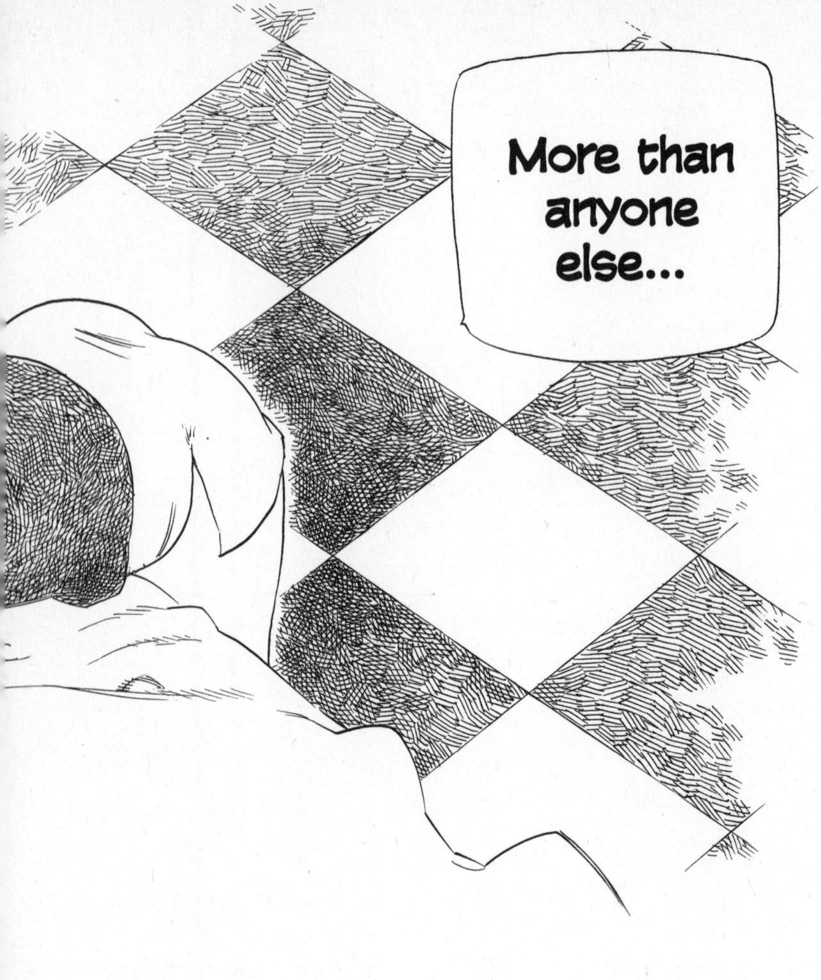
More than anyone else...

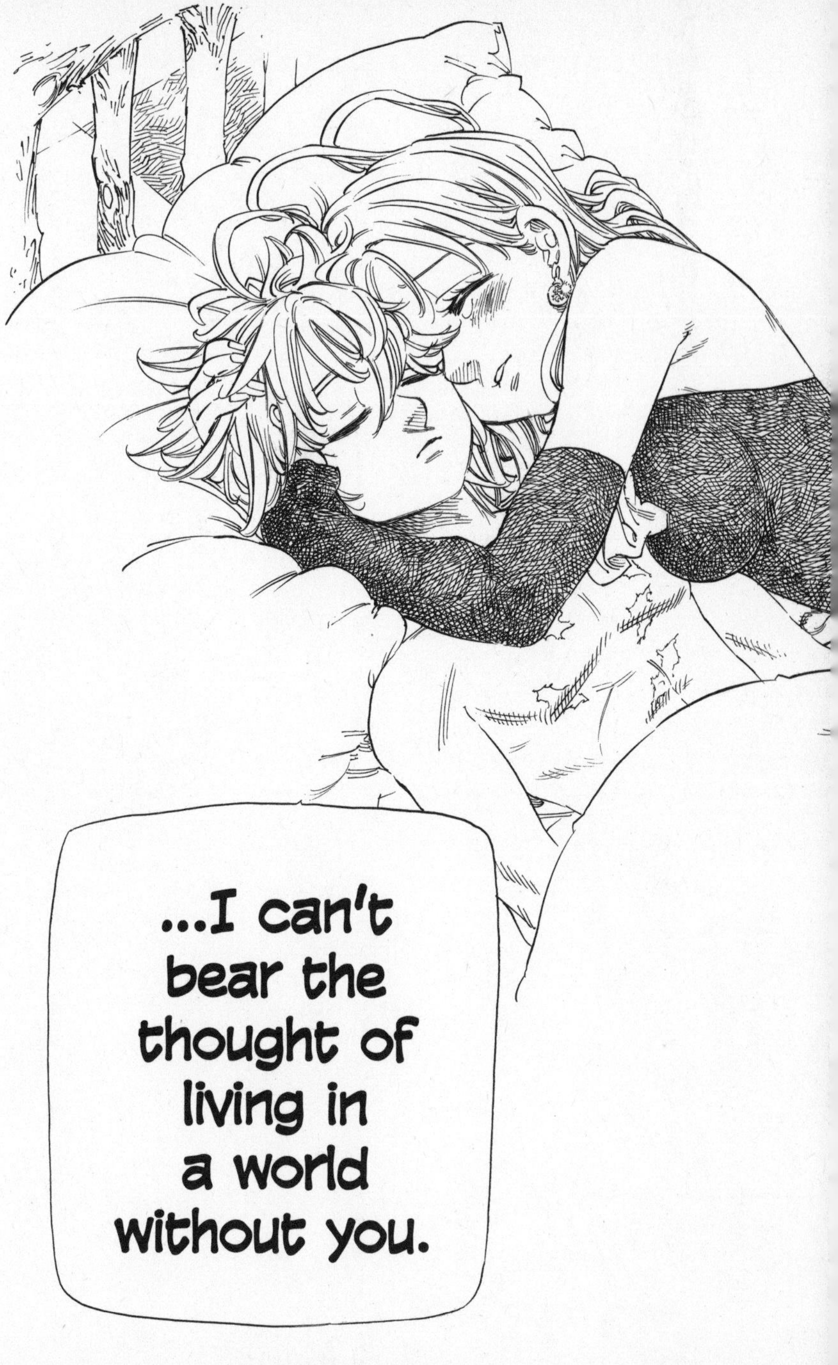
...I can't bear the thought of living in a world without you.

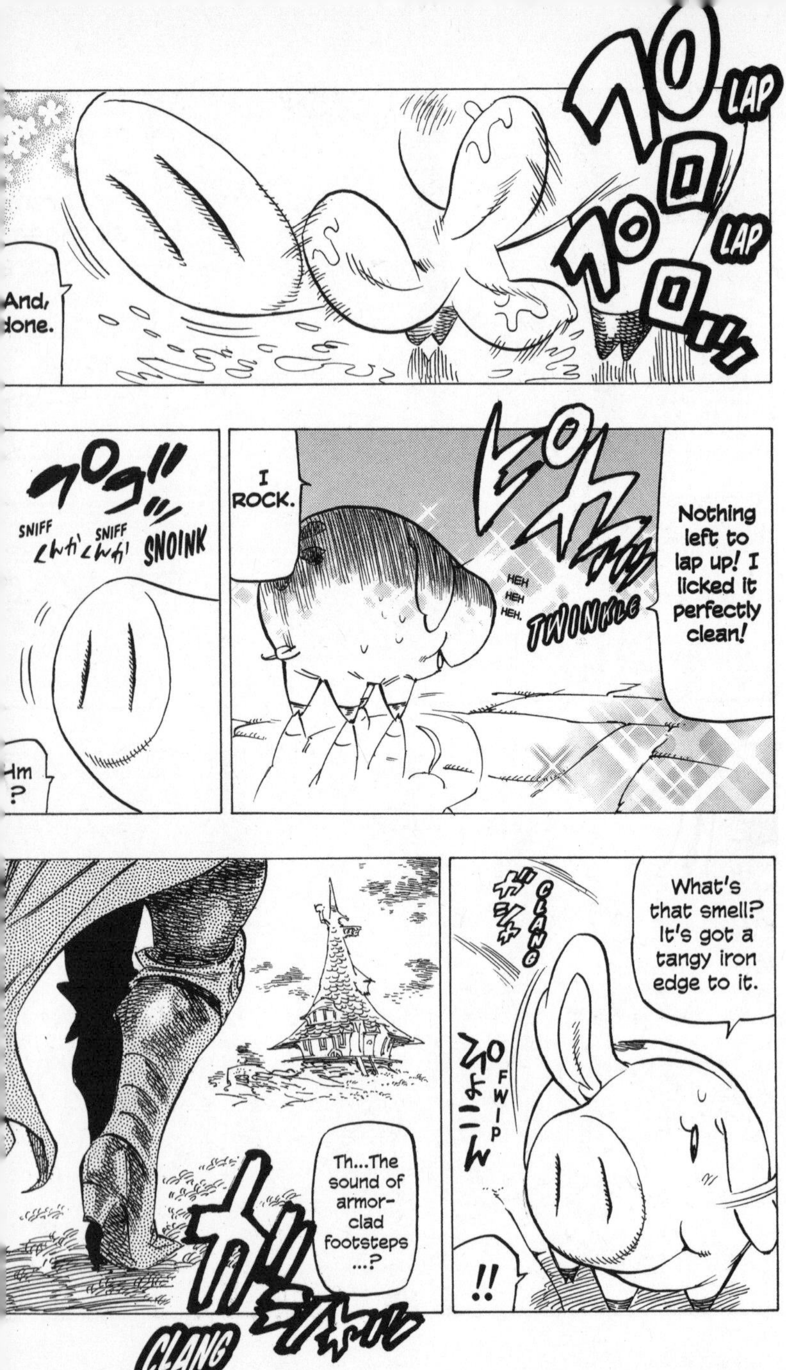
LAP
LAP
And, done.
Nothing left to lap up! I licked it perfectly clean!
TWINKLE
HEH HEH HEH.
I ROCK.
SNIFF
SNIFF
SNOINK
Hm?
CLANG
What's that smell? It's got a tangy iron edge to it.
FWIP
!!
Th...The sound of armor-clad footsteps ...?
CLANG

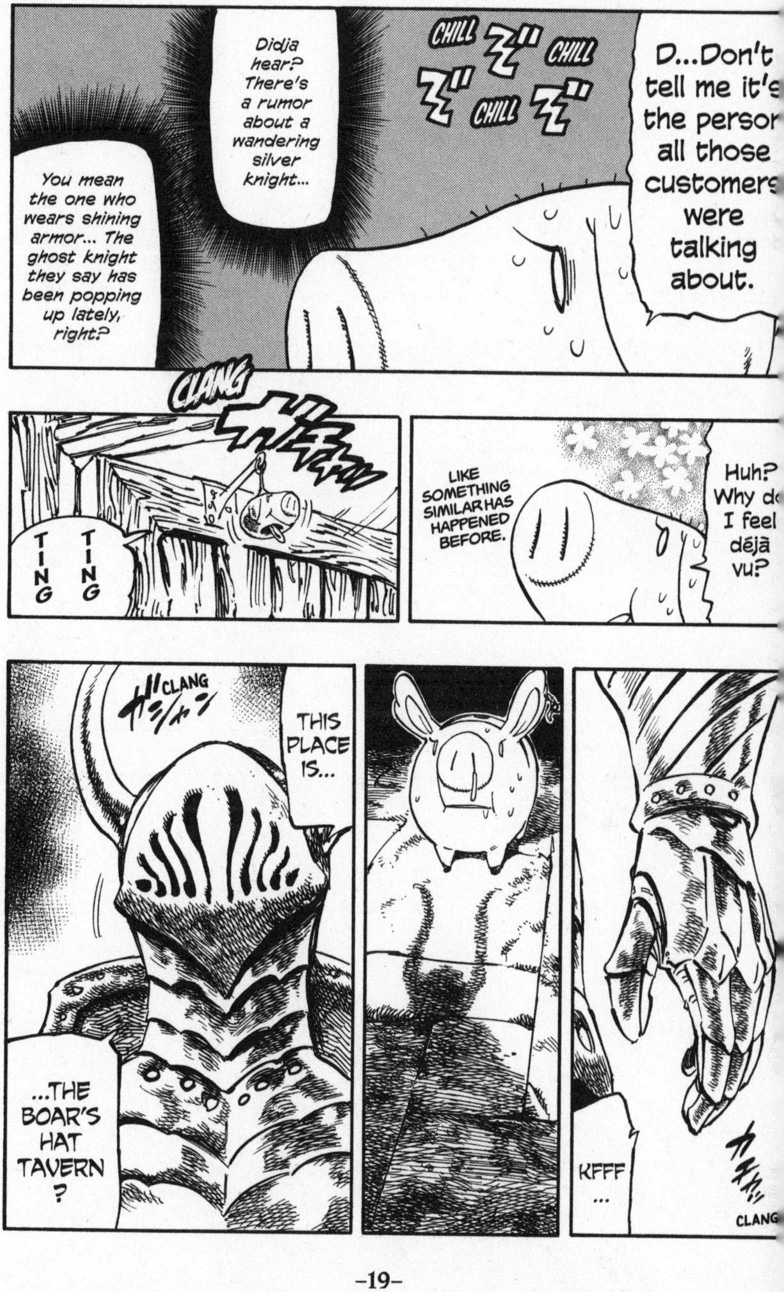
D...Don't tell me it's the person all those customers were talking about.
CHILL CHILL CHILL
Didja hear? There's a rumor about a wandering silver knight...
You mean the one who wears shining armor... The ghost knight they say has been popping up lately, right?
Huh? Why do I feel déjà vu?
LIKE SOMETHING SIMILAR HAS HAPPENED BEFORE.
CLANG
TING TING
CLANG
KFFF...
CLANG
THIS PLACE IS...
...THE BOAR'S HAT TAVERN?

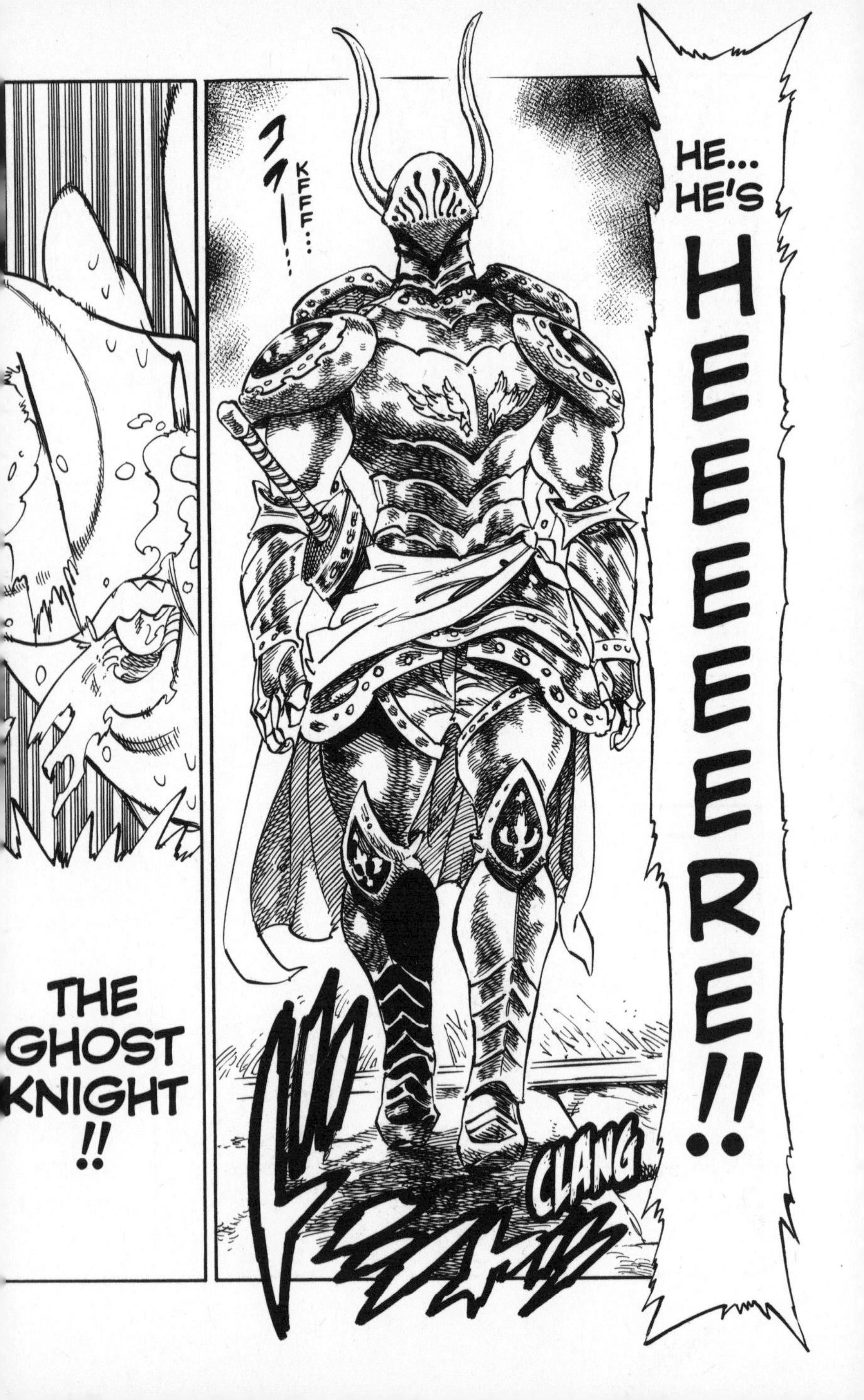
HE... HE'S HEEEEERE!!
KFFF...
CLANG
THE GHOST KNIGHT!!

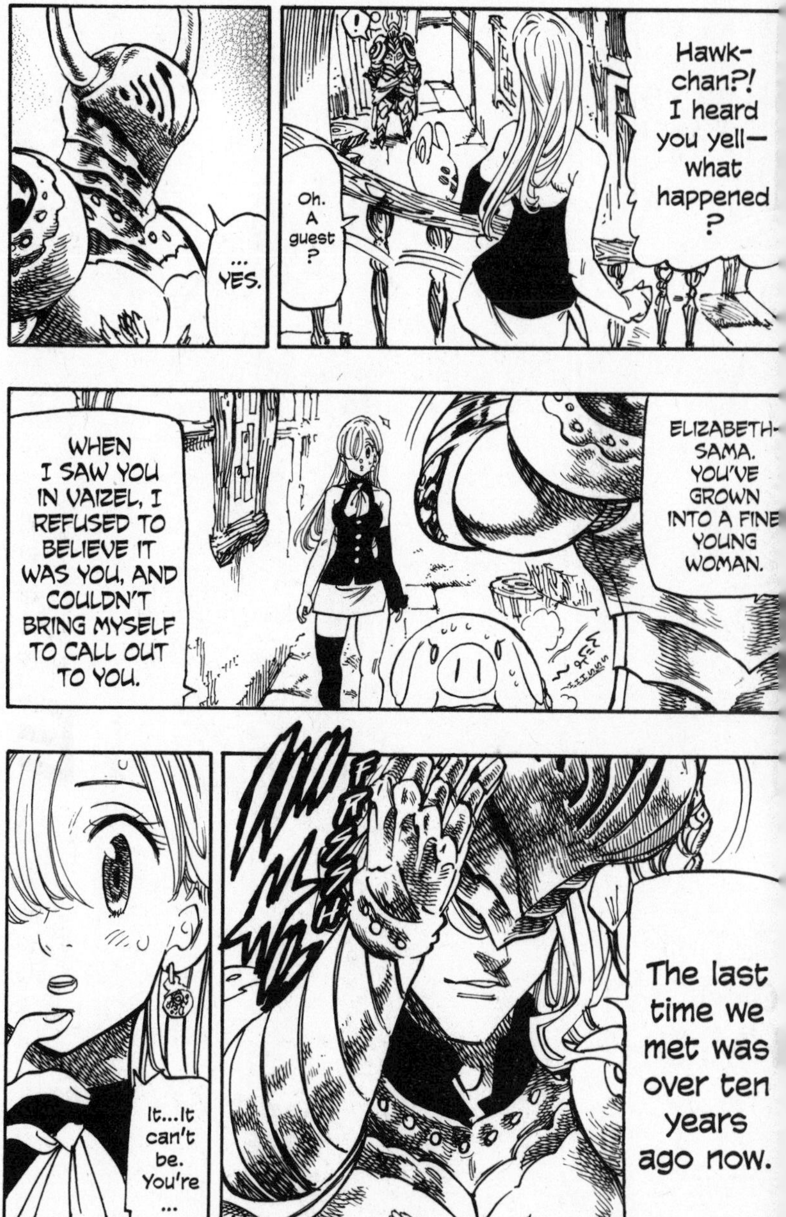
Hawk-chan?! I heard you yell—what happened?
Oh. A guest?
... YES.
ELIZABETH-SAMA. YOU'VE GROWN INTO A FINE YOUNG WOMAN.
WHEN I SAW YOU IN VAIZEL, I REFUSED TO BELIEVE IT WAS YOU, AND COULDN'T BRING MYSELF TO CALL OUT TO YOU.
FRSSSH
The last time we met was over ten years ago now.
It...It can't be. You're ...

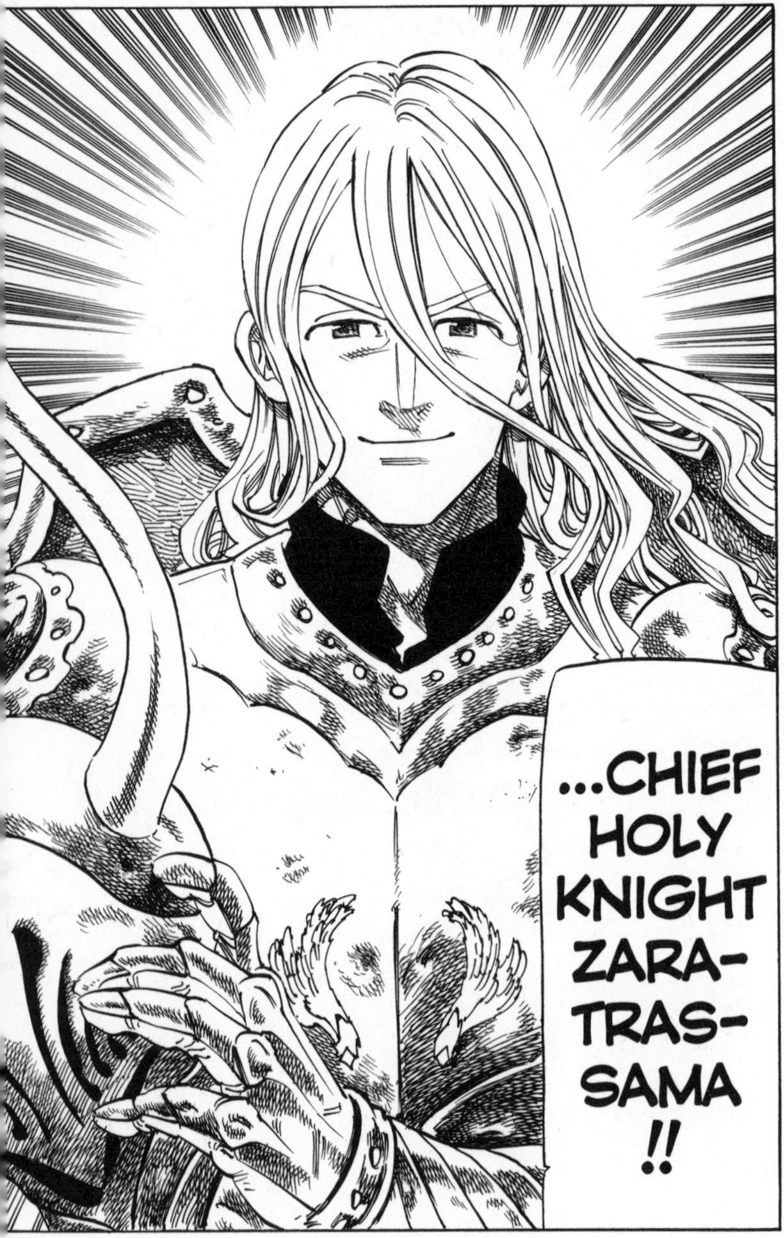
...CHIEF HOLY KNIGHT ZARA-TRAS-SAMA !!

Chapter 181 - Chief Holy Knight Zaratras

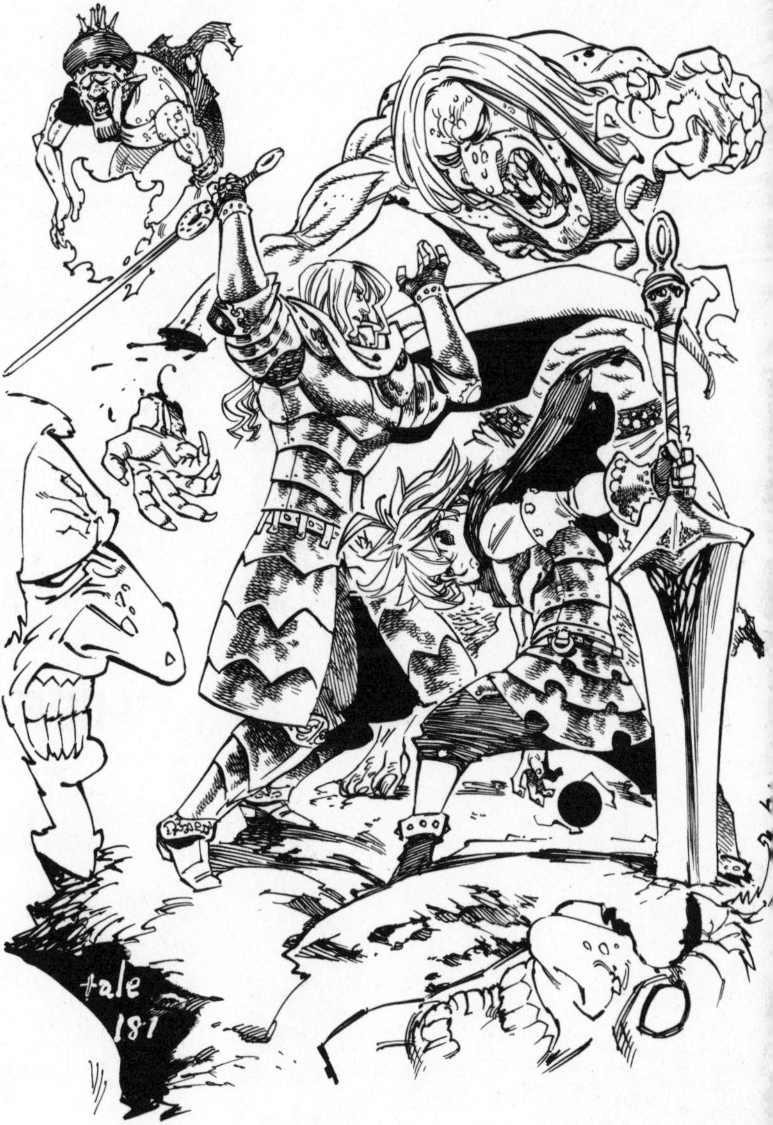
tale 181

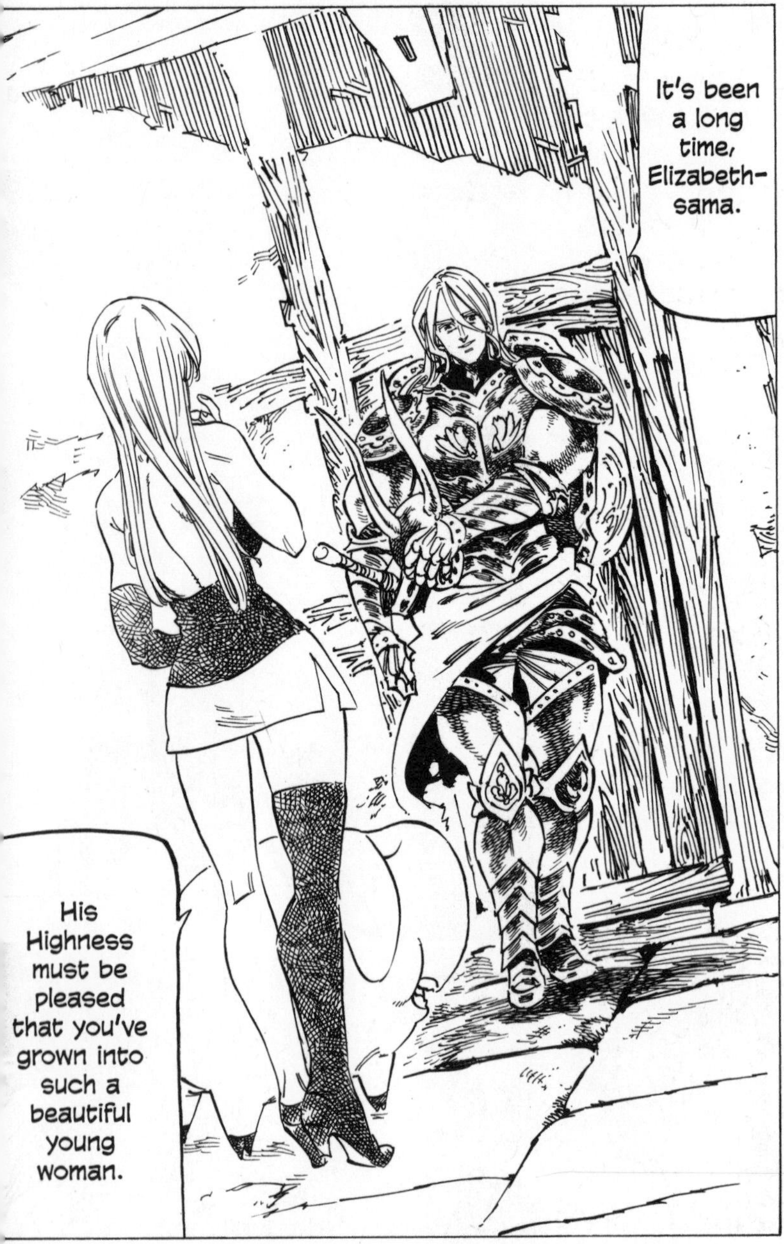
It's been a long time, Elizabeth-sama.
His Highness must be pleased that you've grown into such a beautiful young woman.

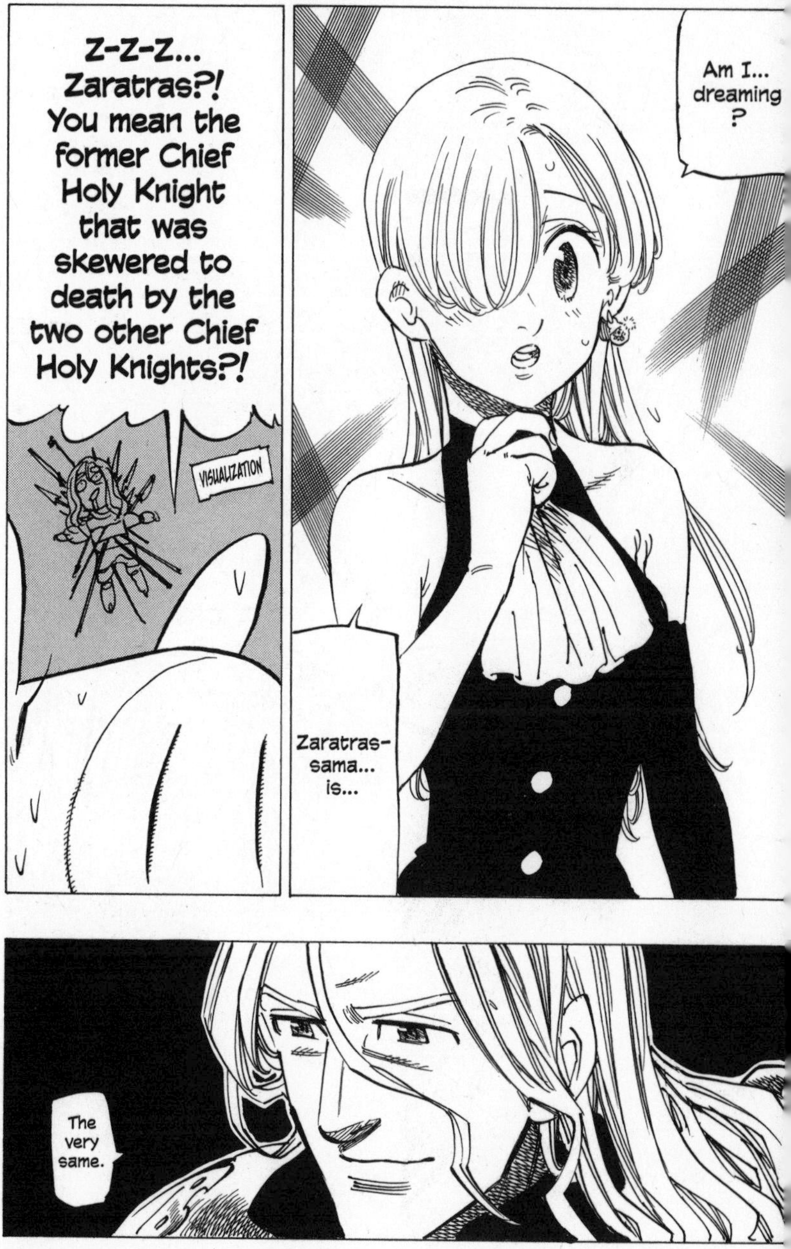
Am I... dreaming?
Zaratras-sama... is...
Z-Z-Z... Zaratras?! You mean the former Chief Holy Knight that was skewered to death by the two other Chief Holy Knights?!
VISUALIZATION
The very same.

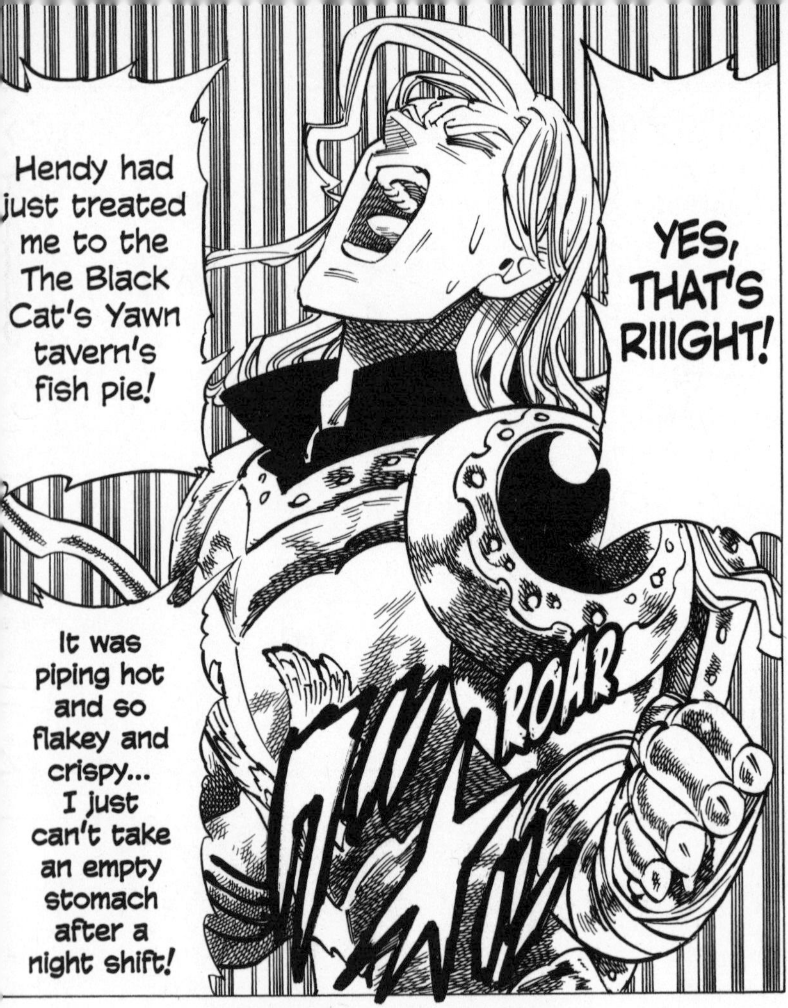
YES, THAT'S RIIIGHT!
Hendy had just treated me to the The Black Cat's Yawn tavern's fish pie!
It was piping hot and so flakey and crispy... I just can't take an empty stomach after a night shift!
ROAR

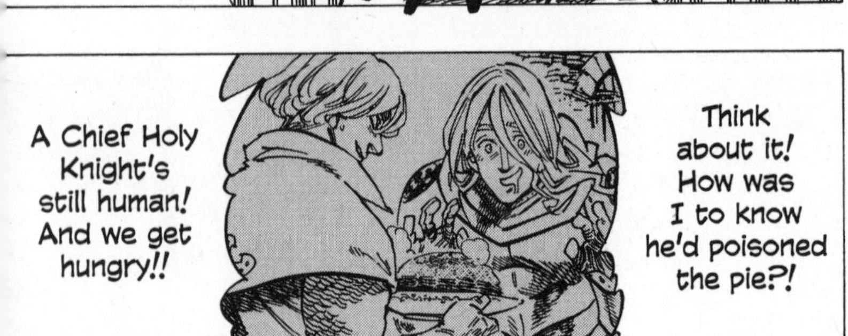
Think about it! How was I to know he'd poisoned the pie?!
A Chief Holy Knight's still human! And we get hungry!!

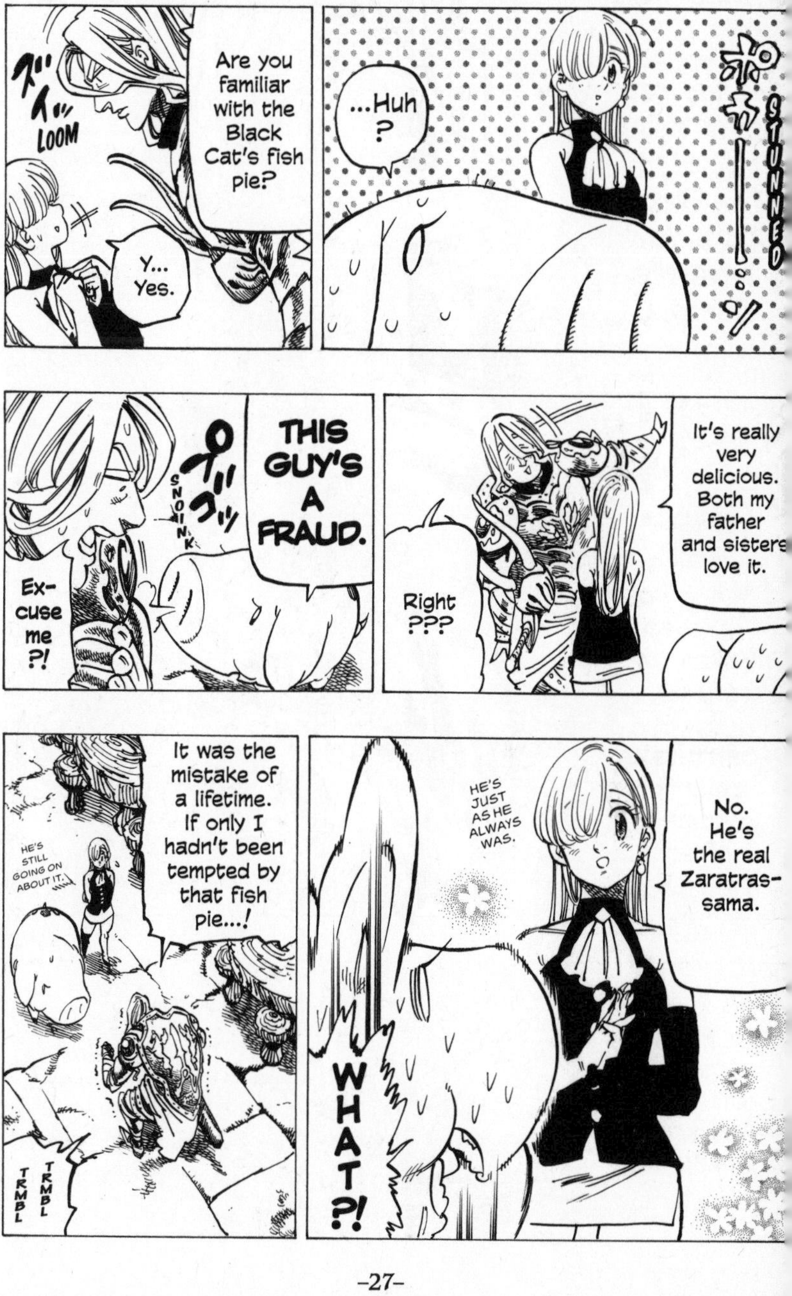
STUNNED
...Huh?
Are you familiar with the Black Cat's fish pie?
LOOM
Y... Yes.
It's really very delicious. Both my father and sisters love it.
Right???
THIS GUY'S A FRAUD.
SNOINK
Excuse me?!
No. He's the real Zaratras-sama.
HE'S JUST AS HE ALWAYS WAS.
WHAT?!
It was the mistake of a lifetime. If only I hadn't been tempted by that fish pie...!
HE'S STILL GOING ON ABOUT IT.
TRMBL TRMBL

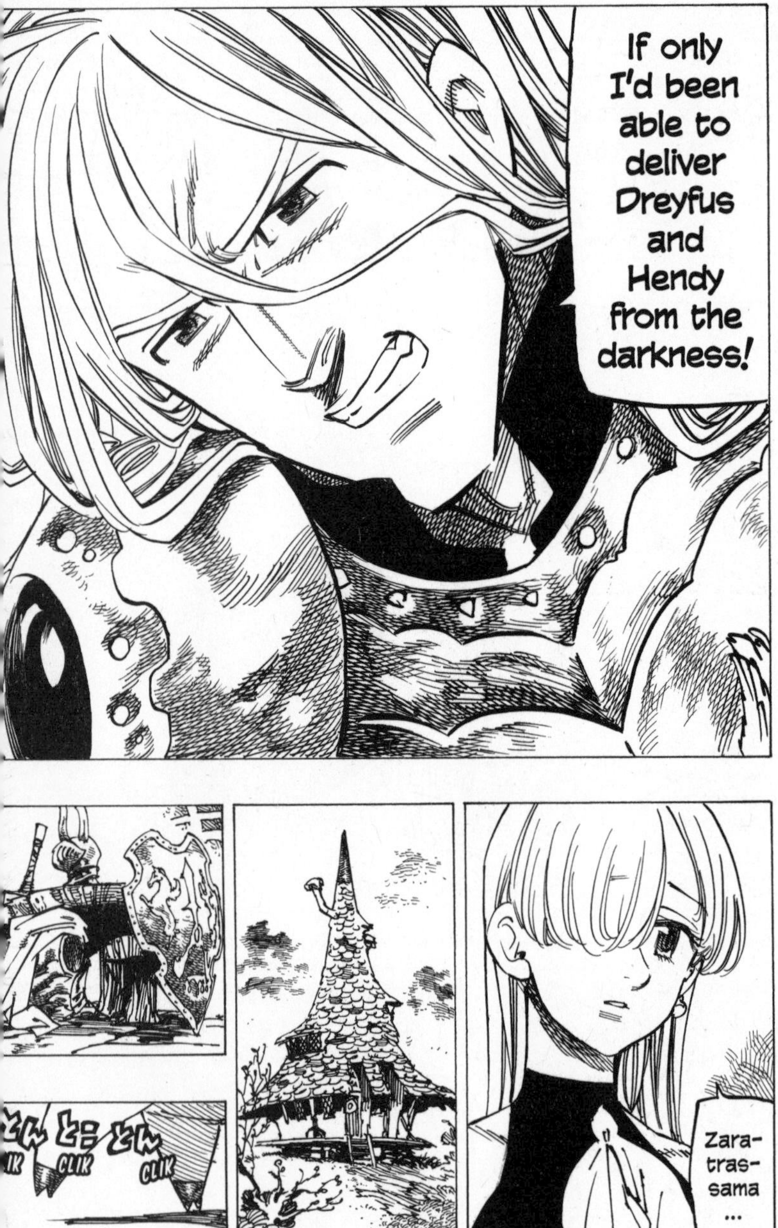
If only I'd been able to deliver Dreyfus and Hendy from the darkness!
Zara-tras-sama ...
CLIK
CLIK

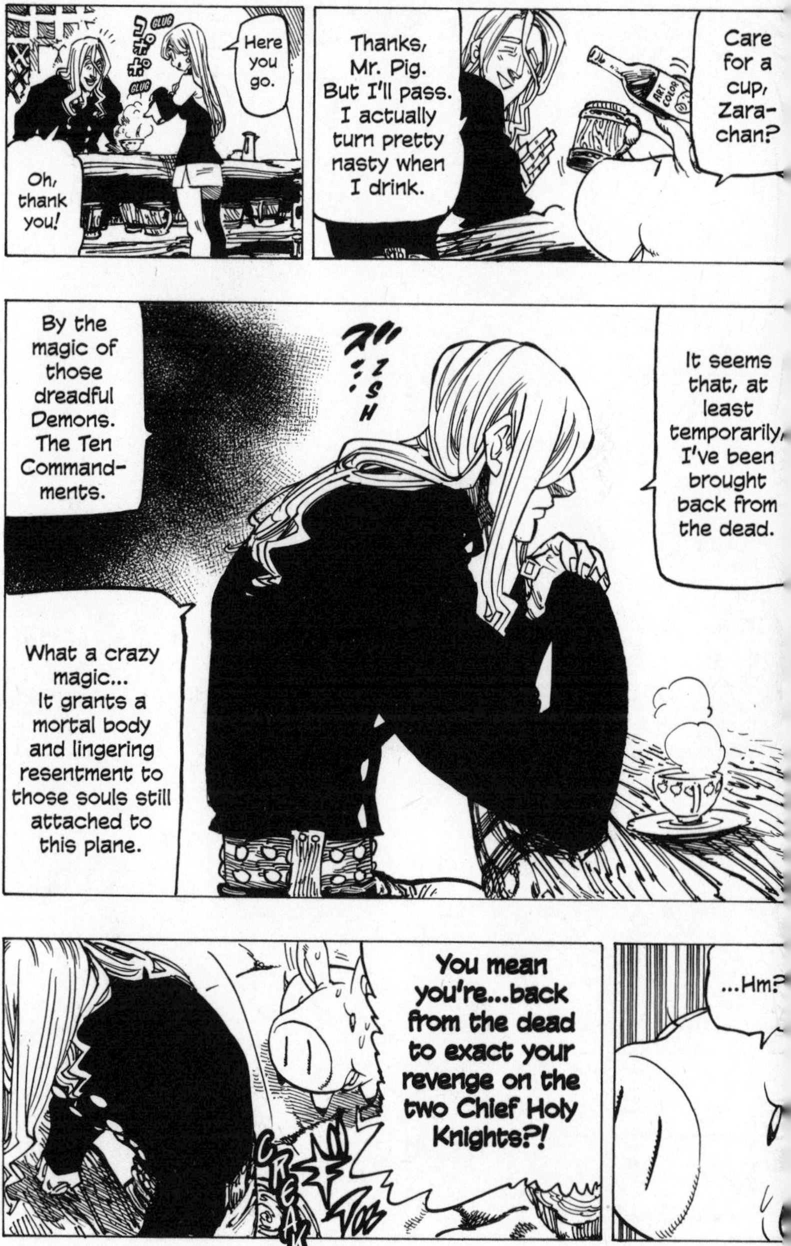

Care for a cup, Zara-chan?
Thanks, Mr. Pig. But I'll pass. I actually turn pretty nasty when I drink.
Here you go.
GLUG
GLUG
Oh, thank you!
It seems that, at least temporarily, I've been brought back from the dead.
ZZSH
By the magic of those dreadful Demons. The Ten Commandments.
What a crazy magic... It grants a mortal body and lingering resentment to those souls still attached to this plane.
...Hm?
You mean you're...back from the dead to exact your revenge on the two Chief Holy Knights?!
CREAK

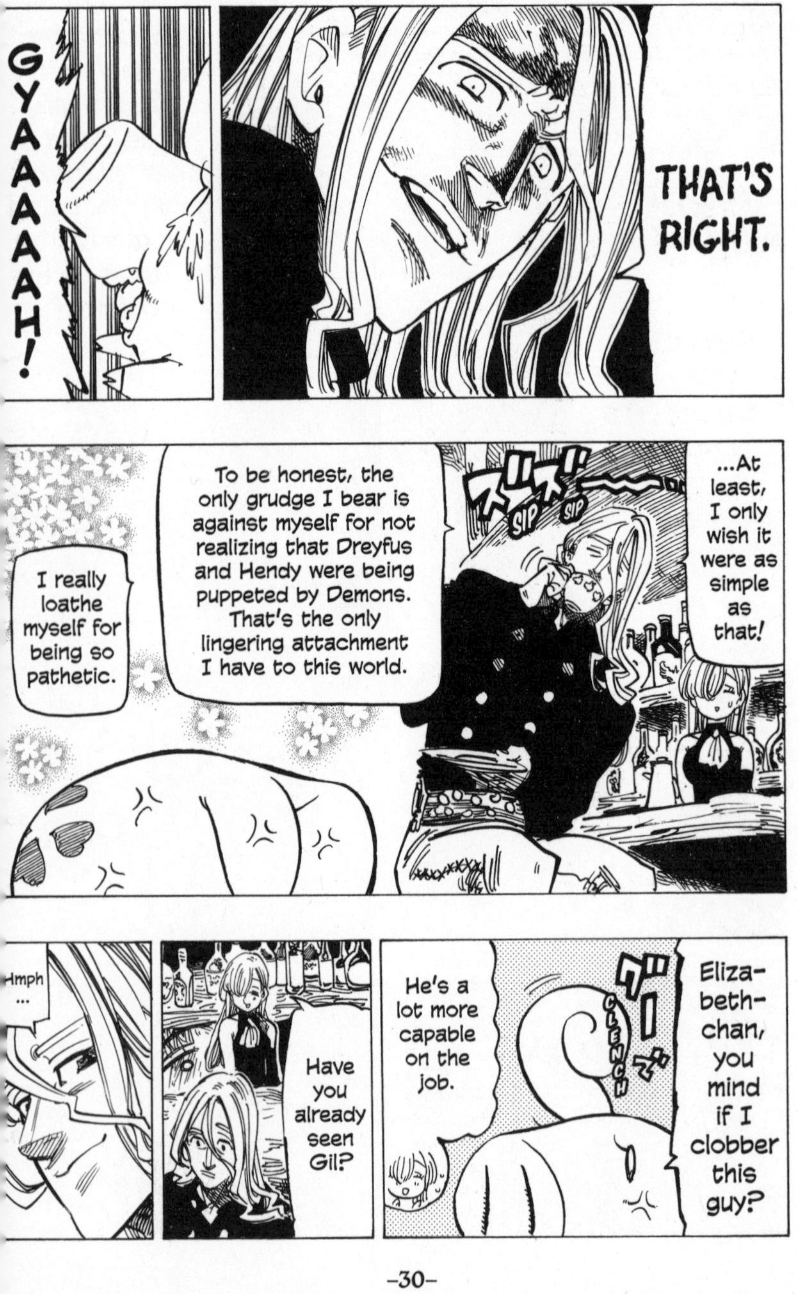
THAT'S RIGHT.
GYAAAAAH!
...At least, I only wish it were as simple as that!
SIP SIP
To be honest, the only grudge I bear is against myself for not realizing that Dreyfus and Hendy were being puppeted by Demons. That's the only lingering attachment I have to this world.
I really loathe myself for being so pathetic.
Eliza-beth-chan, you mind if I clobber this guy?
CLENCH
He's a lot more capable on the job.
Have you already seen Gil?
Hmph ...

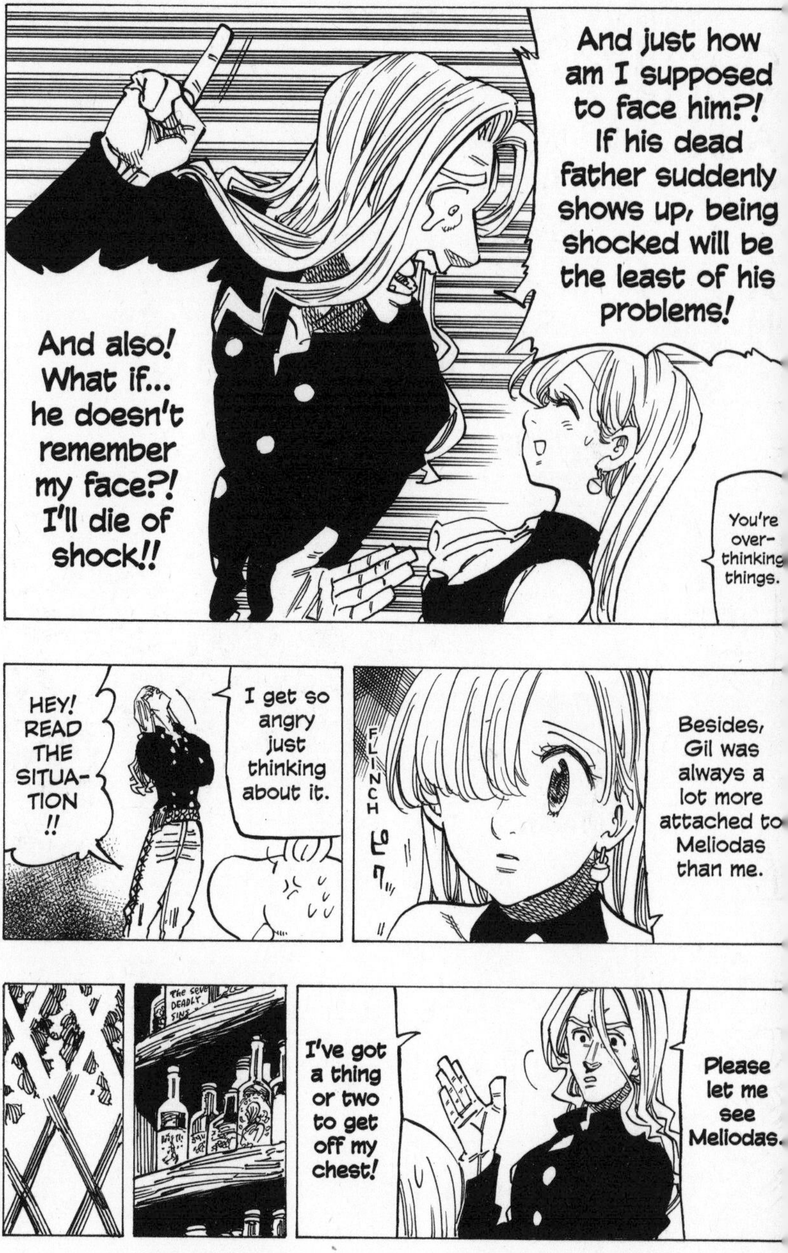
And just how am I supposed to face him?! If his dead father suddenly shows up, being shocked will be the least of his problems!
And also! What if... he doesn't remember my face?! I'll die of shock!!
You're over-thinking things.
FLINCH
Besides, Gil was always a lot more attached to Meliodas than me.
I get so angry just thinking about it.
HEY! READ THE SITUA-TION!!
Please let me see Meliodas.
I've got a thing or two to get off my chest!

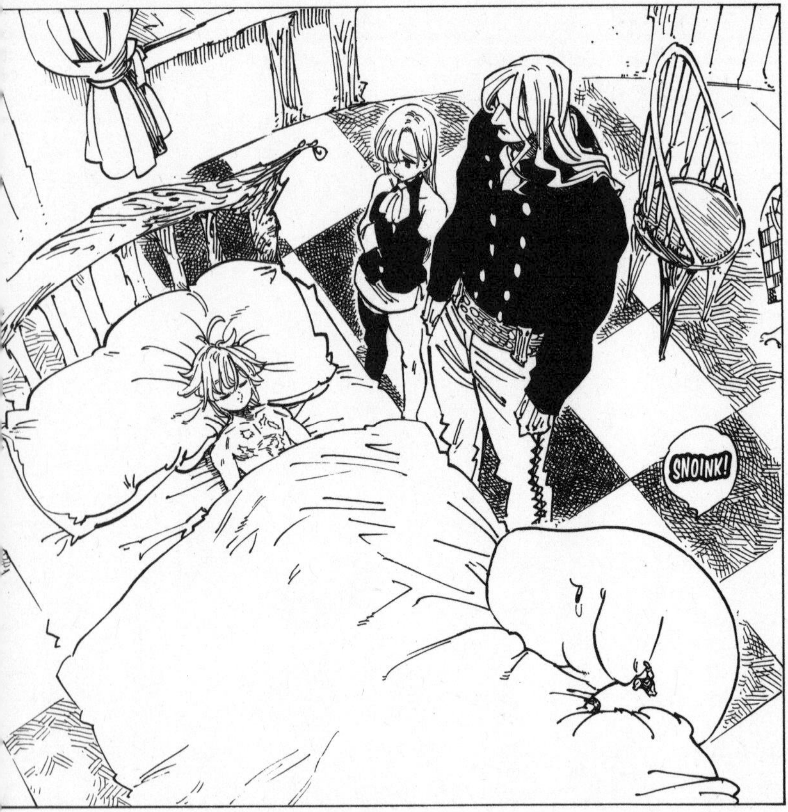
SNOINK!

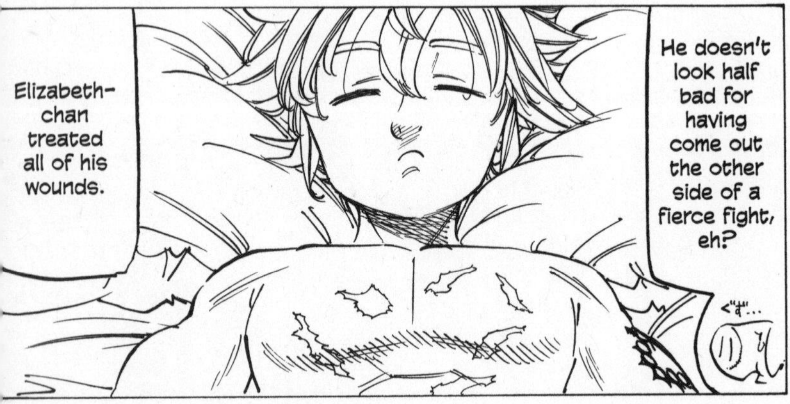
He doesn't look half bad for having come out the other side of a fierce fight, eh?
Elizabeth-chan treated all of his wounds.

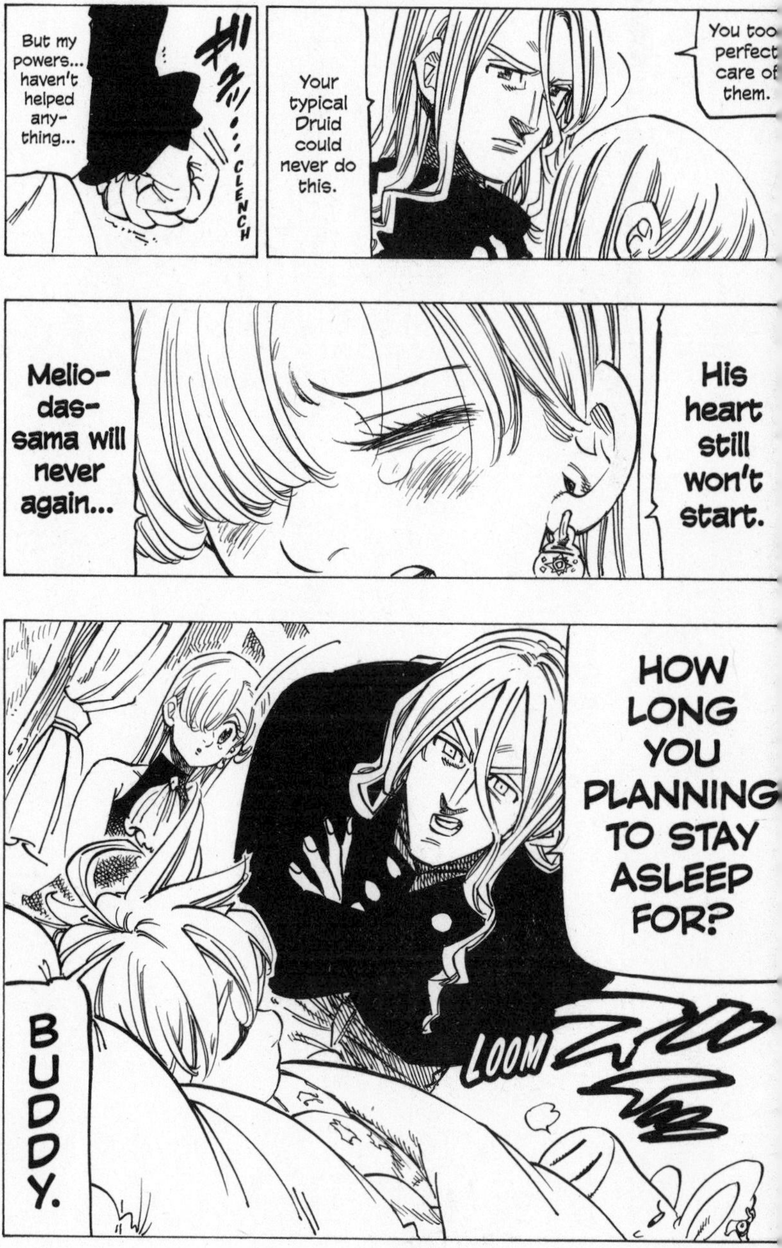
You too perfect care of them.
Your typical Druid could never do this.
But my powers... haven't helped anything...
CLENCH
His heart still won't start.
Meliodas-sama will never again...
HOW LONG YOU PLANNING TO STAY ASLEEP FOR?
LOOM
BUDDY.

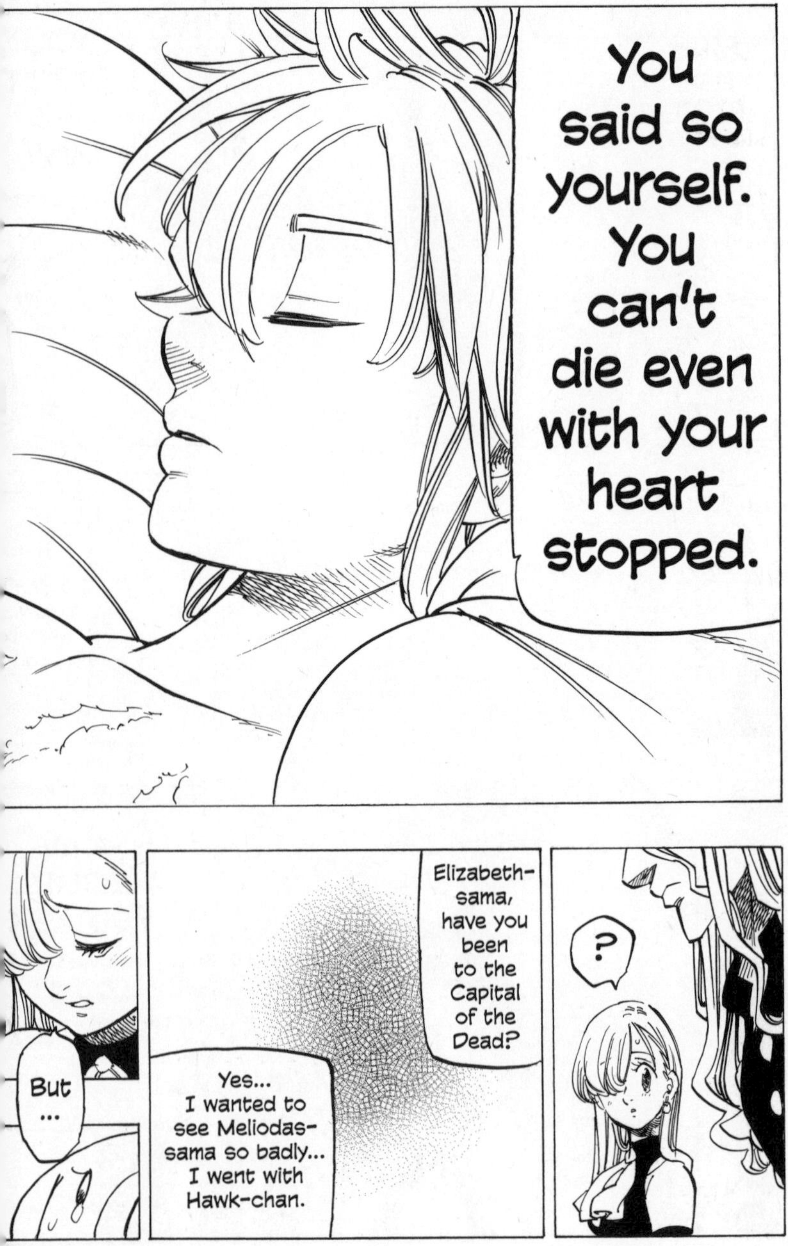
You said so yourself. You can't die even with your heart stopped.
?
Elizabeth-sama, have you been to the Capital of the Dead?
Yes... I wanted to see Meliodas-sama so badly... I went with Hawk-chan.
But ...

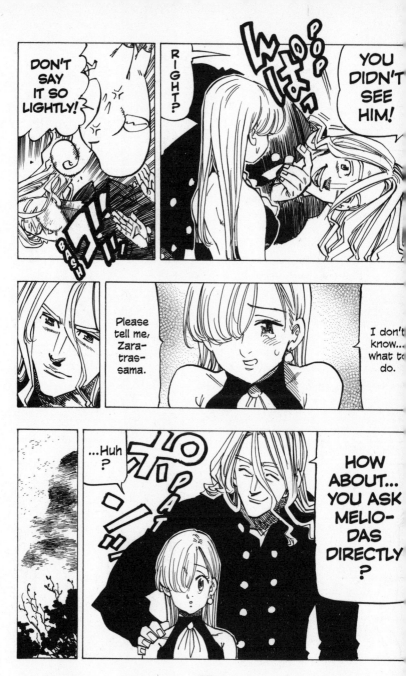

POP
YOU DIDN'T SEE HIM!
RIGHT?
DON'T SAY IT SO LIGHTLY!
BASH
I don't know... what to do.
Please tell me, Zaratras-sama.
HOW ABOUT... YOU ASK MELIODAS DIRECTLY?
PAT
...Huh?

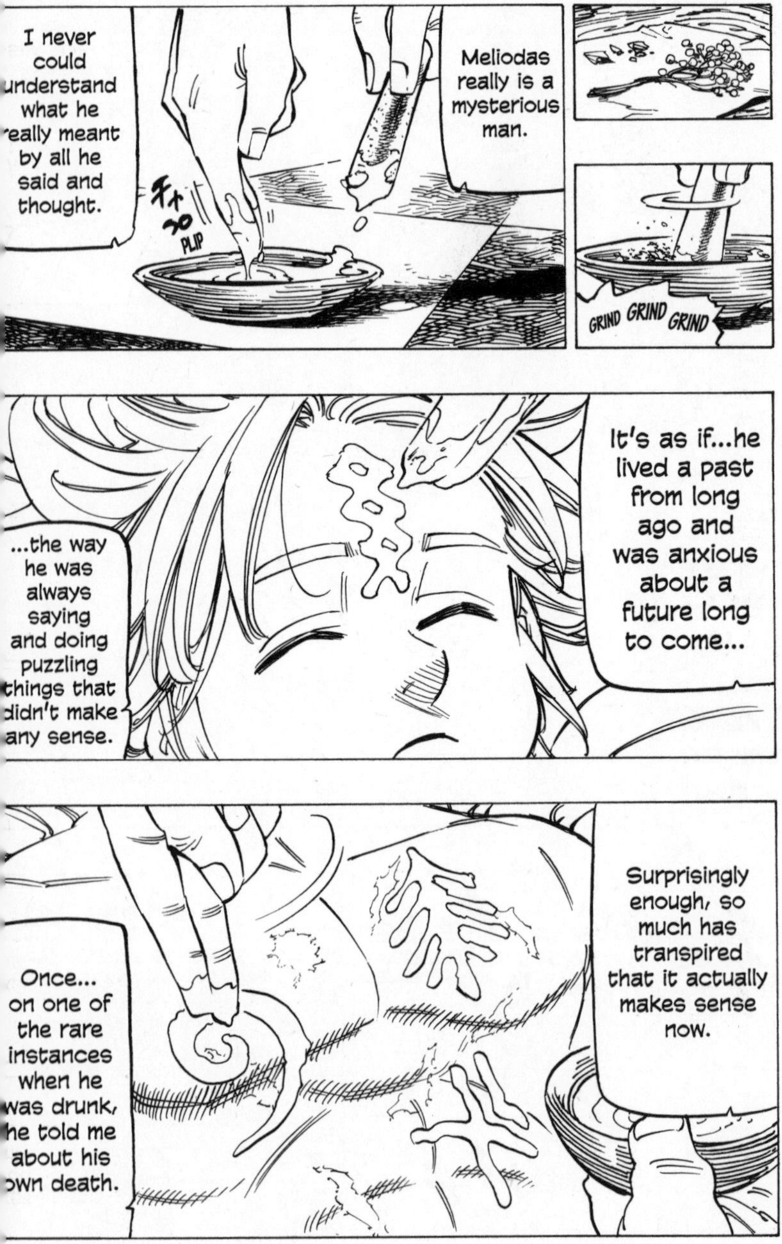

GRIND GRIND GRIND
Meliodas really is a mysterious man.
I never could nderstand what he eally meant by all he said and thought.
PLIP
It's as if...he lived a past from long ago and was anxious about a future long to come...
...the way he was always saying and doing puzzling hings that idn't make ny sense.
Surprisingly enough, so much has transpired that it actually makes sense now.
Once... on one of the rare instances when he vas drunk, he told me about his wn death.

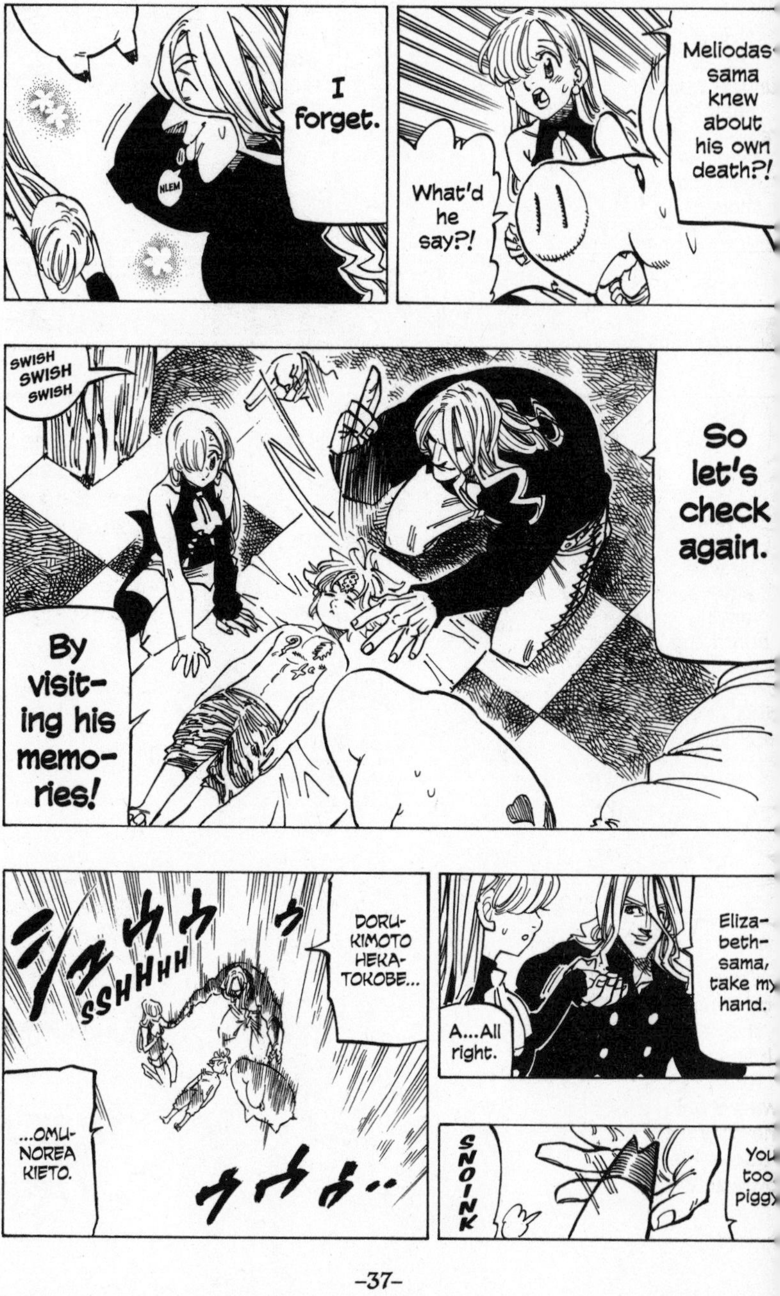
Meliodas-sama knew about his own death?!
What'd he say?!
I forget.
NLEM
So let's check again.
SWISH SWISH SWISH
By visiting his memories!
Eliza-beth-sama, take my hand.
A...All right.
You too piggy
SNOINK
DORU-KIMOTO HEKA-TOKOBE...
SSHHHH
...OMU-NOREA KIETO.

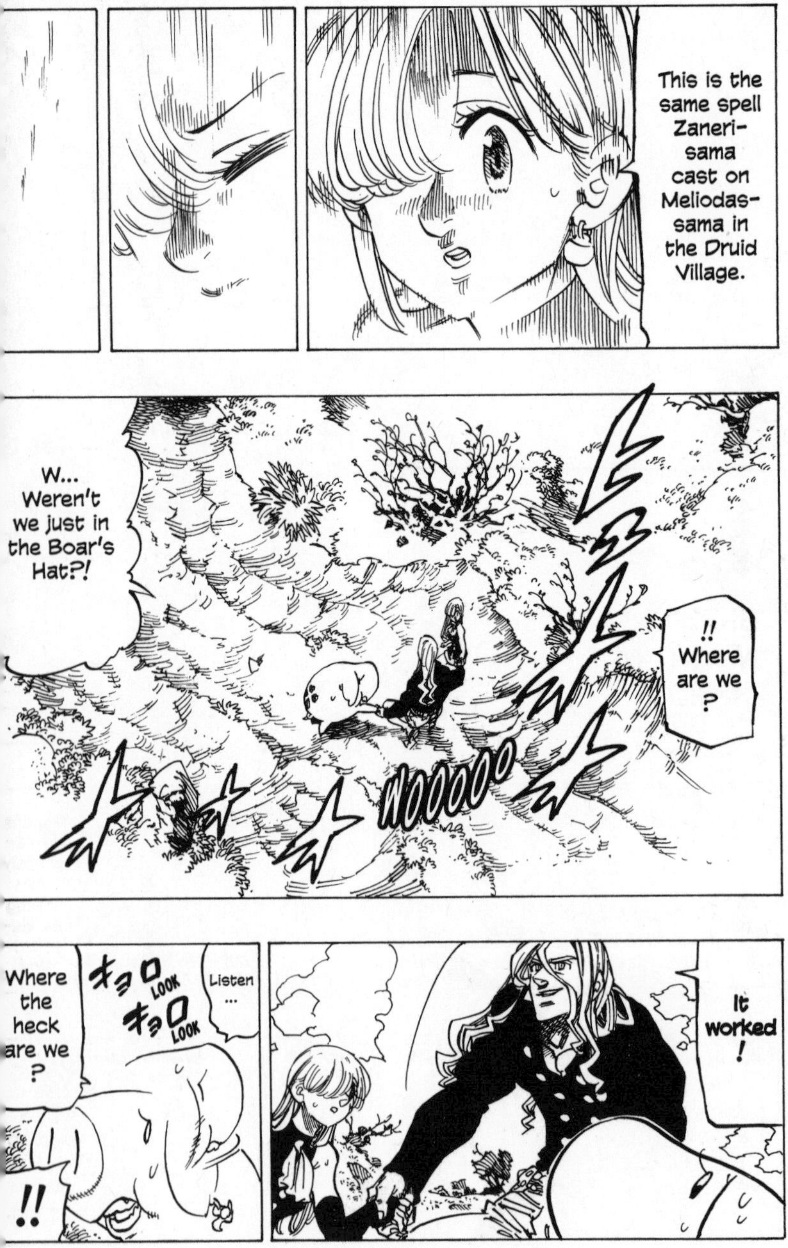
This is the same spell Zaneri-sama cast on Meliodas-sama in the Druid Village.
!! Where are we ?
WOOOOO
W... Weren't we just in the Boar's Hat?!
It worked!
Listen ...
キョロ LOOK
キョロ LOOK
Where the heck are we ?
!!

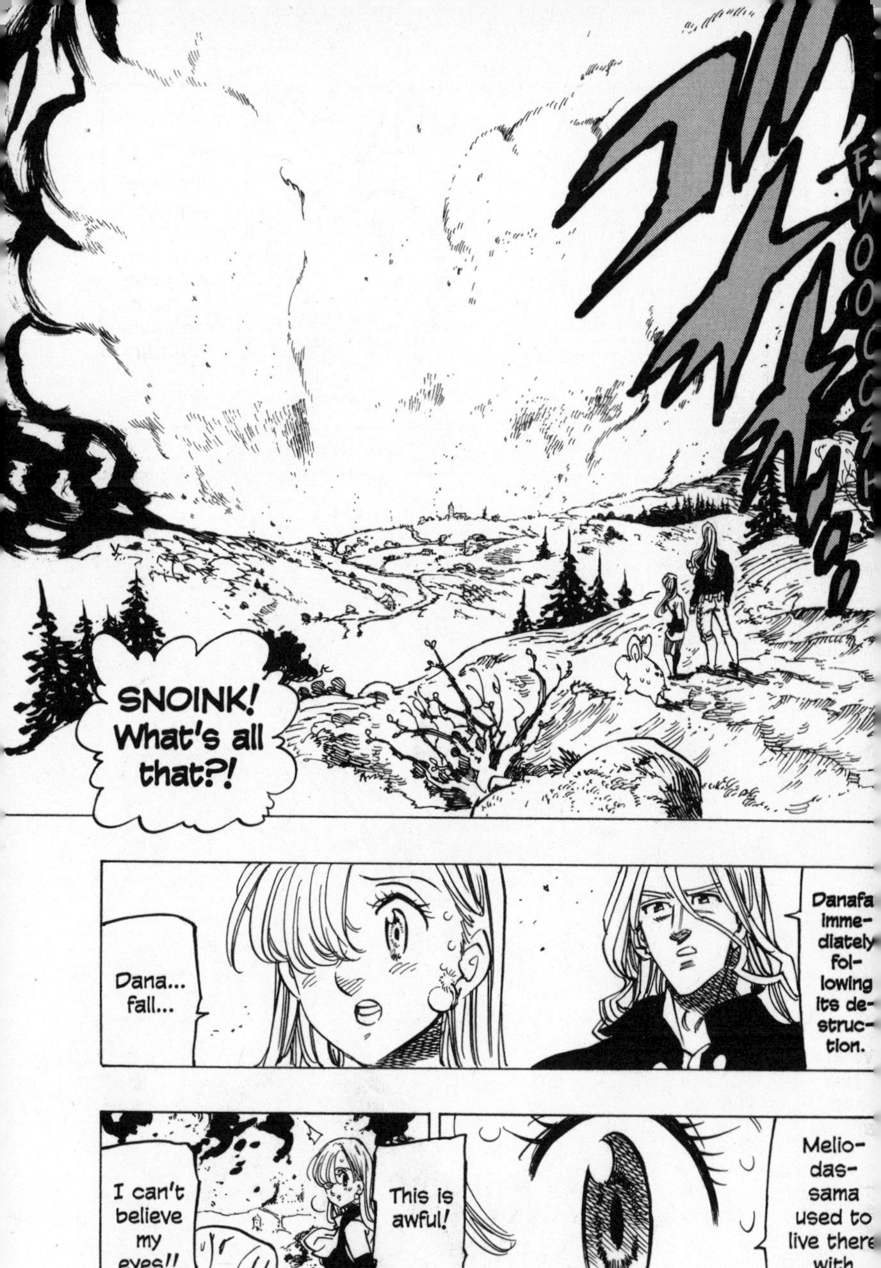
FWOOOOSH
SNOINK! What's all that?!
Danafa immediately following its destruction.
Dana... fall...
Meliodas-sama used to live there with Liz-san.
This is awful!
I can't believe my eyes!!

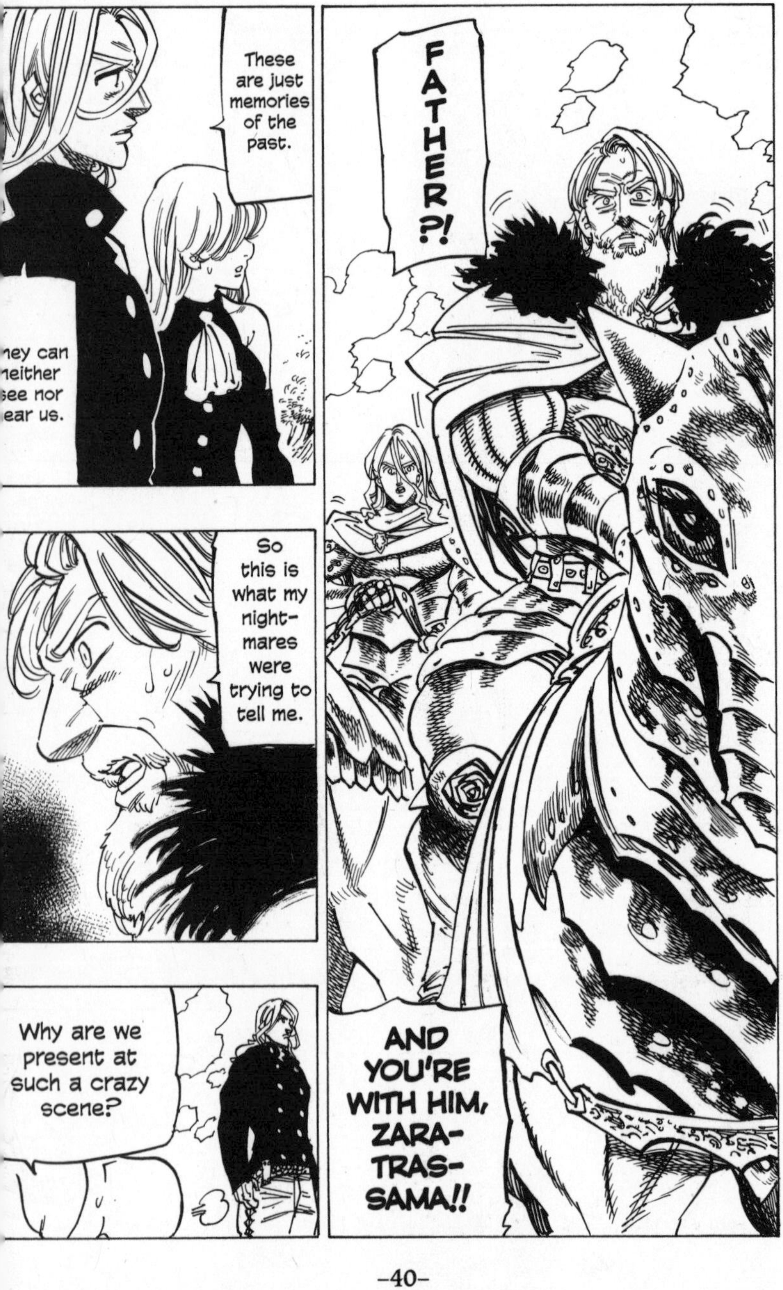
FATHER?!
AND YOU'RE WITH HIM, ZARA-TRAS-SAMA!!
These are just memories of the past.
ney can neither see nor ear us.
So this is what my night-mares were trying to tell me.
Why are we present at such a crazy scene?

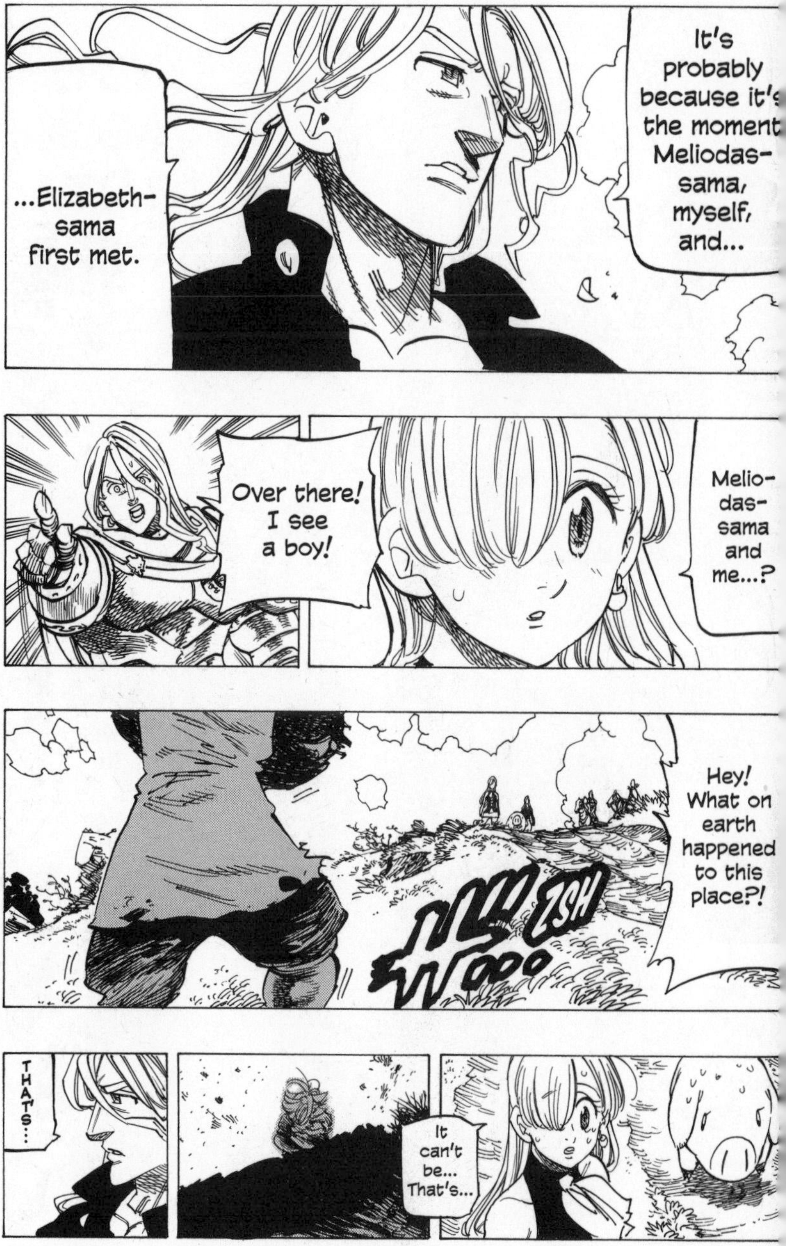

It's probably because it's the moment Meliodas-sama, myself, and...
...Elizabeth-sama first met.
Melio-das-sama and me...?
Over there! I see a boy!
Hey! What on earth happened to this place?!
It can't be... That's...
THAT'S...

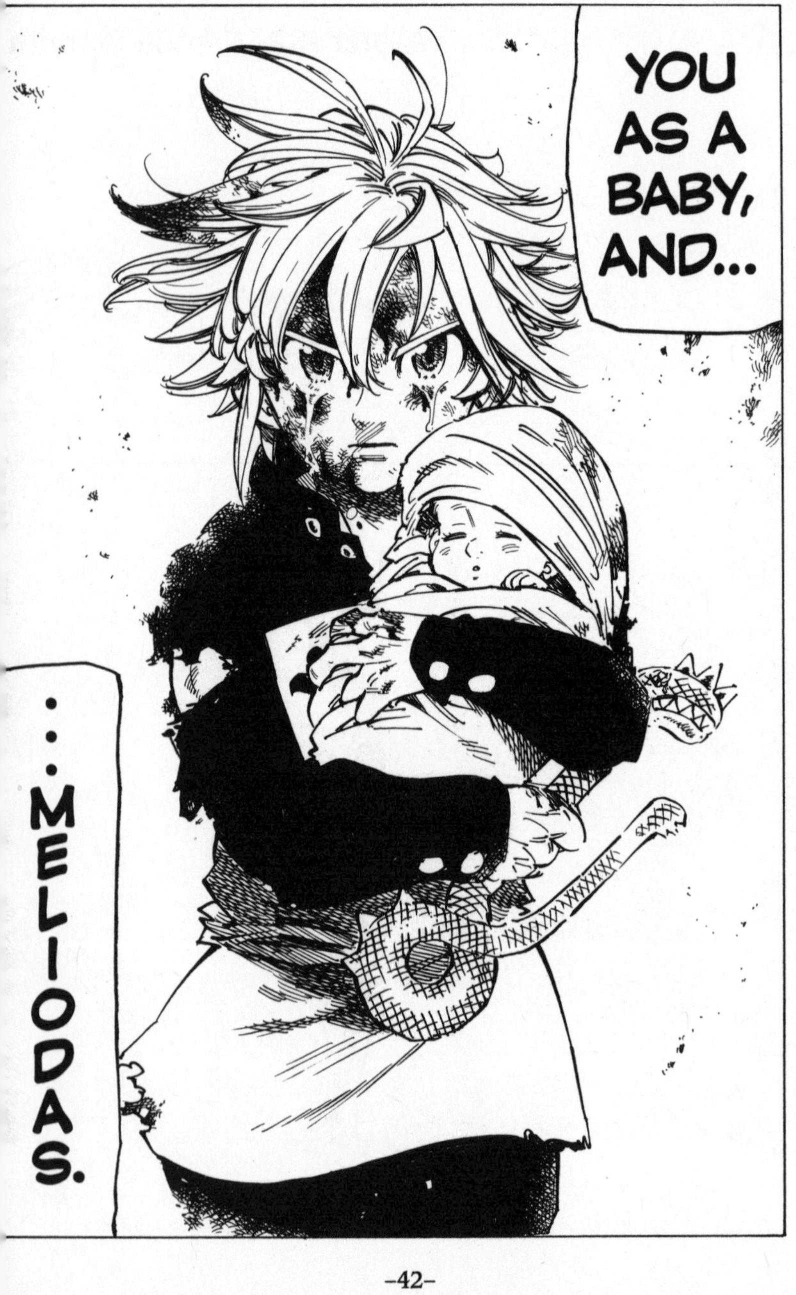
YOU AS A BABY, AND...
...MELIODAS.

Chapter 182 - Certain Warmth

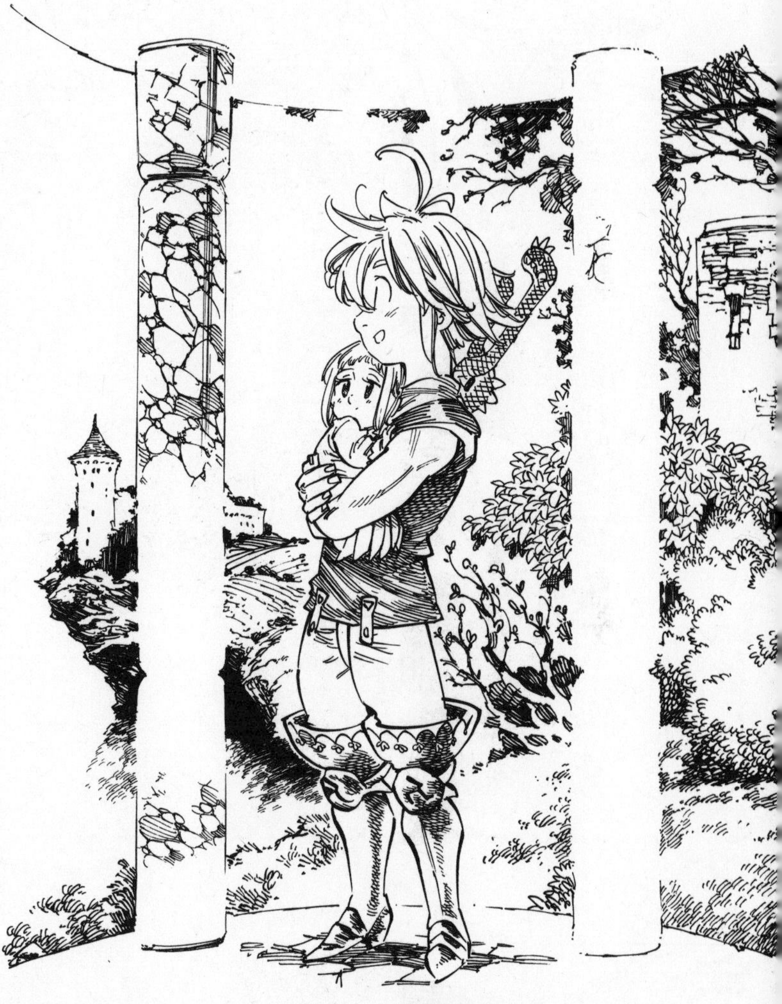

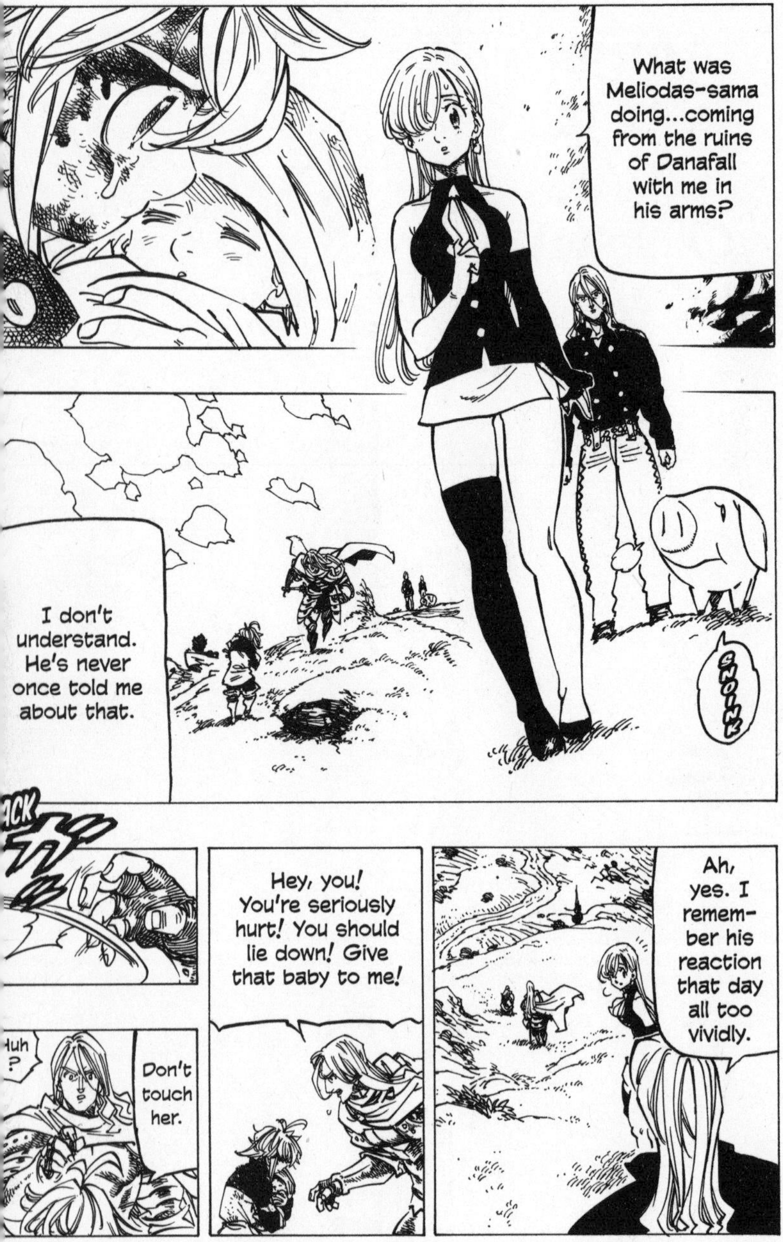
What was Meliodas-sama doing...coming from the ruins of Danafall with me in his arms?
SNOINK
I don't understand. He's never once told me about that.
Ah, yes. I remember his reaction that day all too vividly.
Hey, you! You're seriously hurt! You should lie down! Give that baby to me!
ACK
Don't touch her.
Huh?

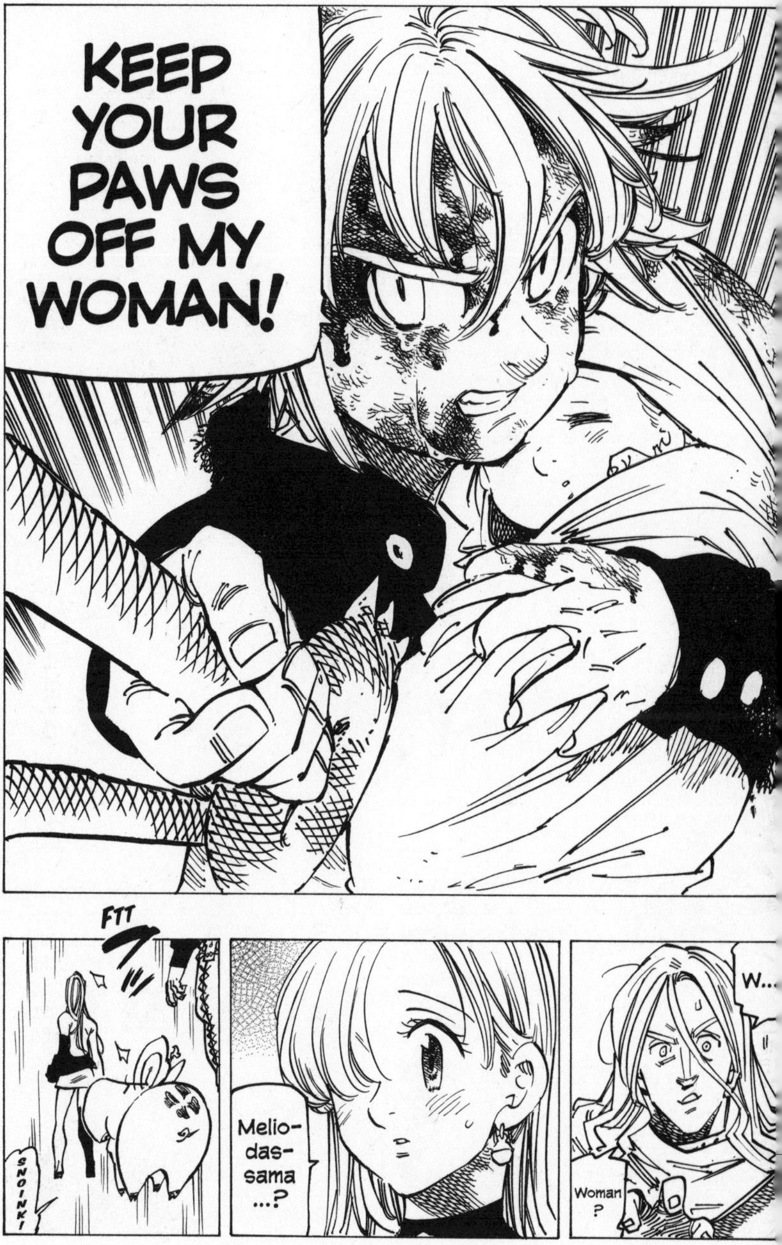
KEEP YOUR PAWS OFF MY WOMAN!
W...
Woman ?
Melio-das-sama ...?
FTT
SNOINK!

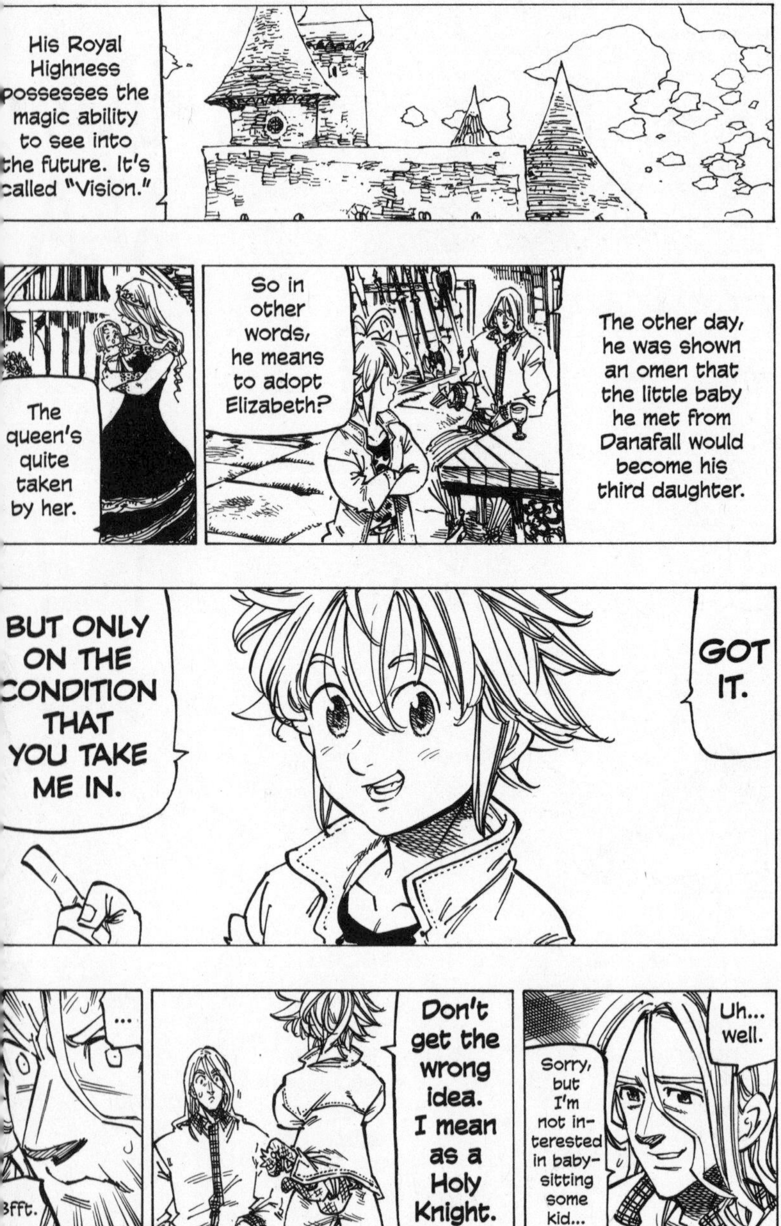
His Royal Highness possesses the magic ability to see into the future. It's called "Vision."
The other day, he was shown an omen that the little baby he met from Danafall would become his third daughter.
So in other words, he means to adopt Elizabeth?
The queen's quite taken by her.
GOT IT.
BUT ONLY ON THE CONDITION THAT YOU TAKE ME IN.
Uh... well.
Sorry, but I'm not interested in baby-sitting some kid...
Don't get the wrong idea. I mean as a Holy Knight.
...
fft.

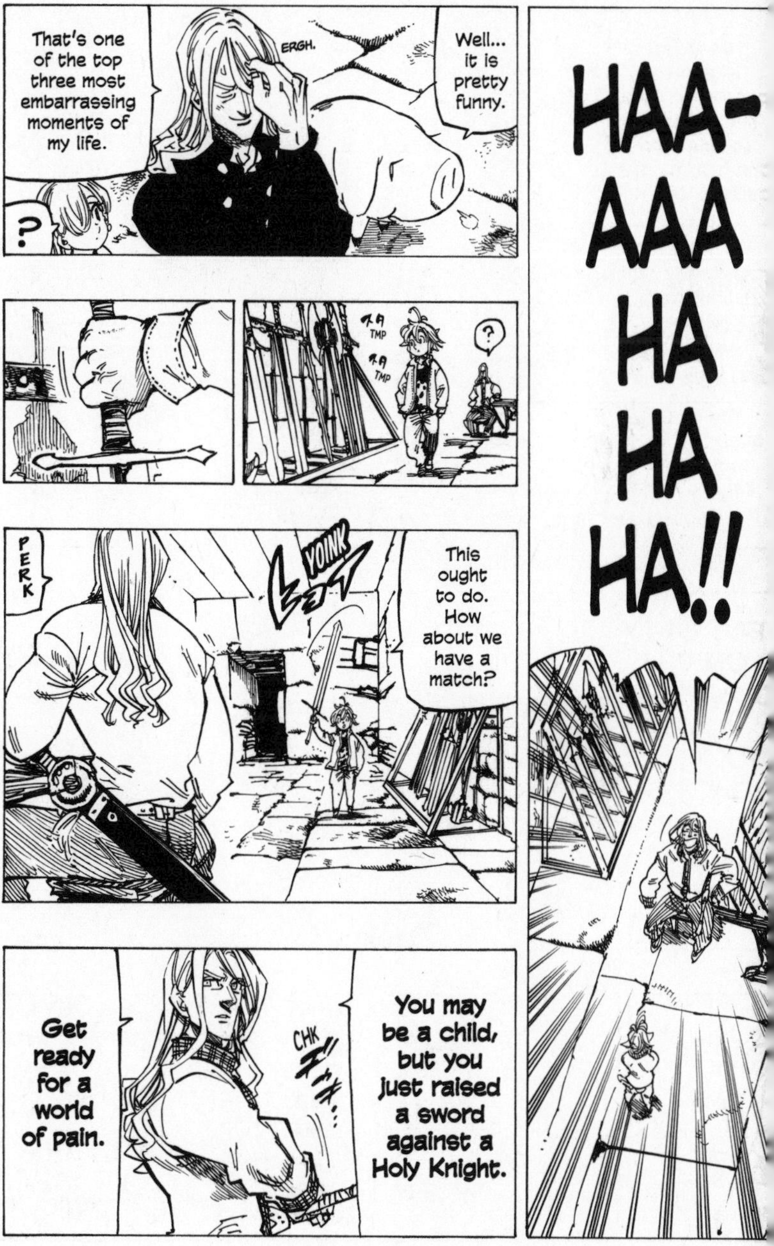
HAA-AAA HA HA HA!!
Well... it is pretty funny.
ERGH.
That's one of the top three most embarrassing moments of my life.
?
TMP
TMP
?
This ought to do. How about we have a match?
YOINK
PERK
You may be a child, but you just raised a sword against a Holy Knight.
CHK
Get ready for a world of pain.

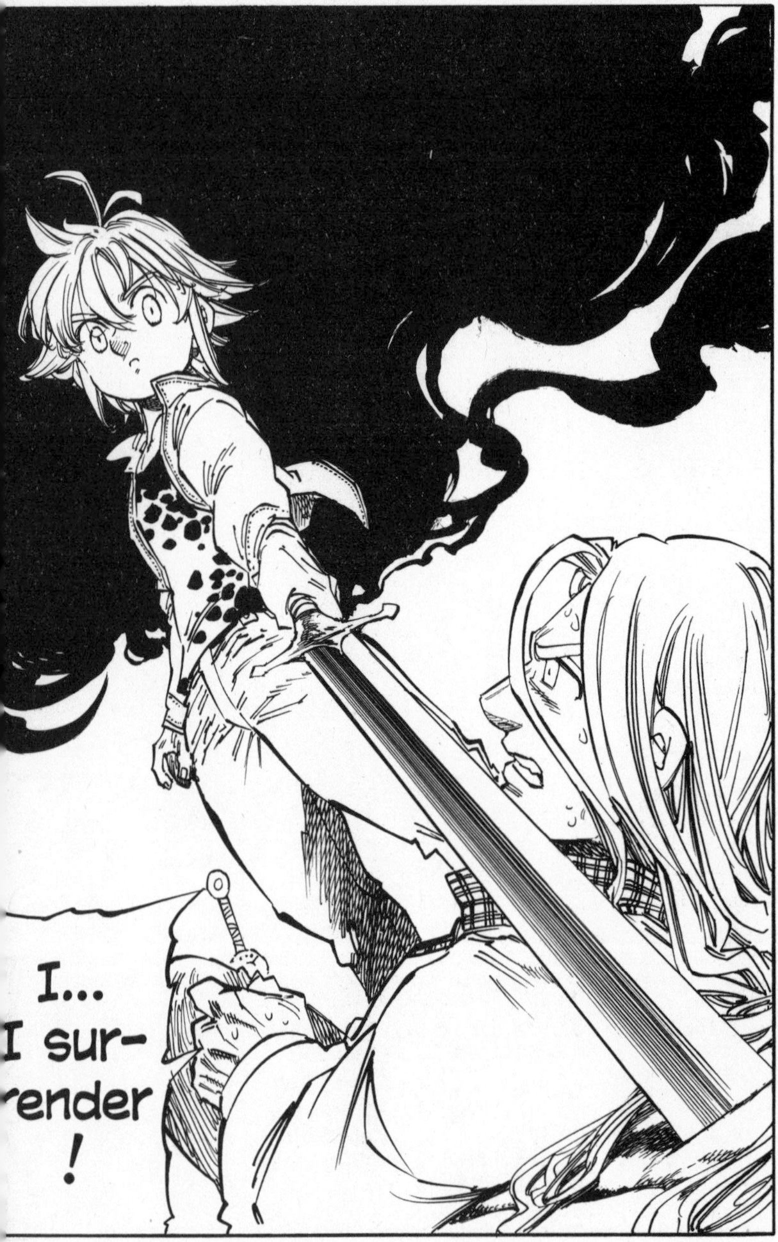
I...
I sur-
render
!

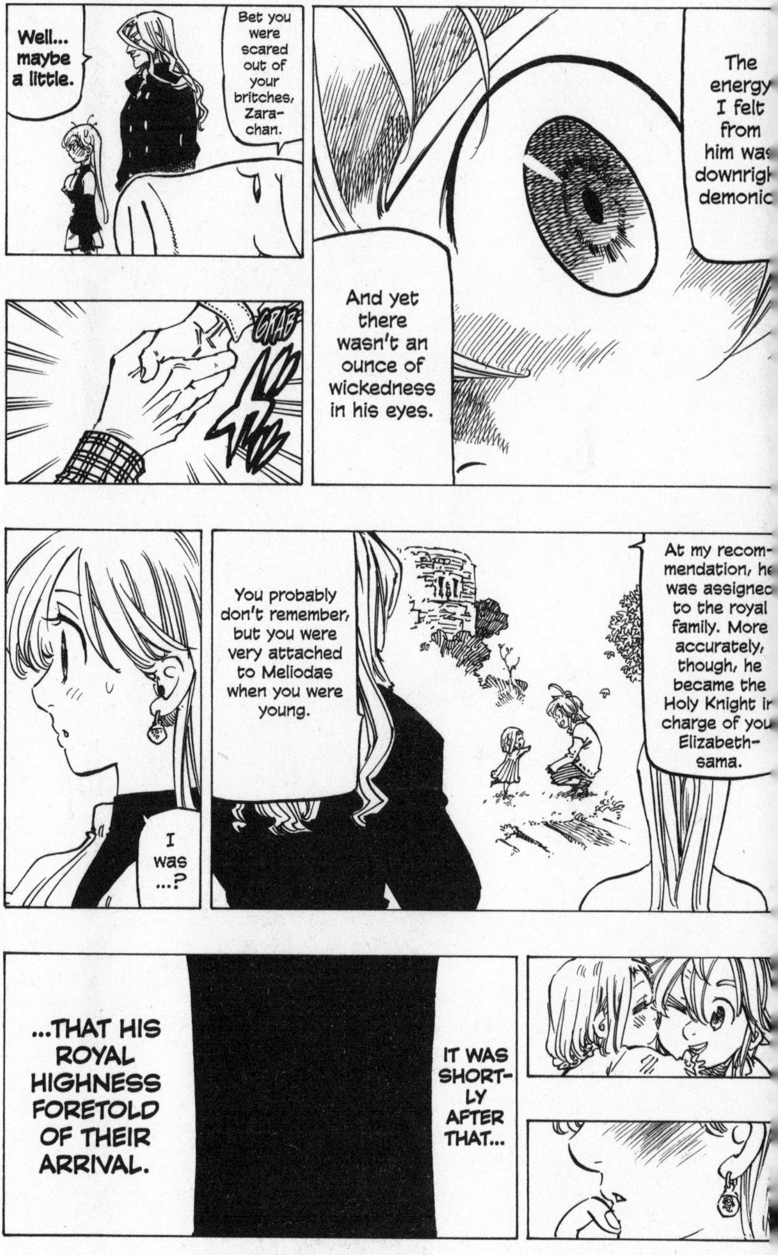
The energy I felt from him was downrigh demonic
And yet there wasn't an ounce of wickedness in his eyes.
Bet you were scared out of your britches, Zara-chan.
Well... maybe a little.
GRAB
At my recommendation, he was assigned to the royal family. More accurately, though, he became the Holy Knight in charge of you Elizabeth-sama.
You probably don't remember, but you were very attached to Meliodas when you were young.
I was ...?
IT WAS SHORTLY AFTER THAT...
...THAT HIS ROYAL HIGHNESS FORETOLD OF THEIR ARRIVAL.

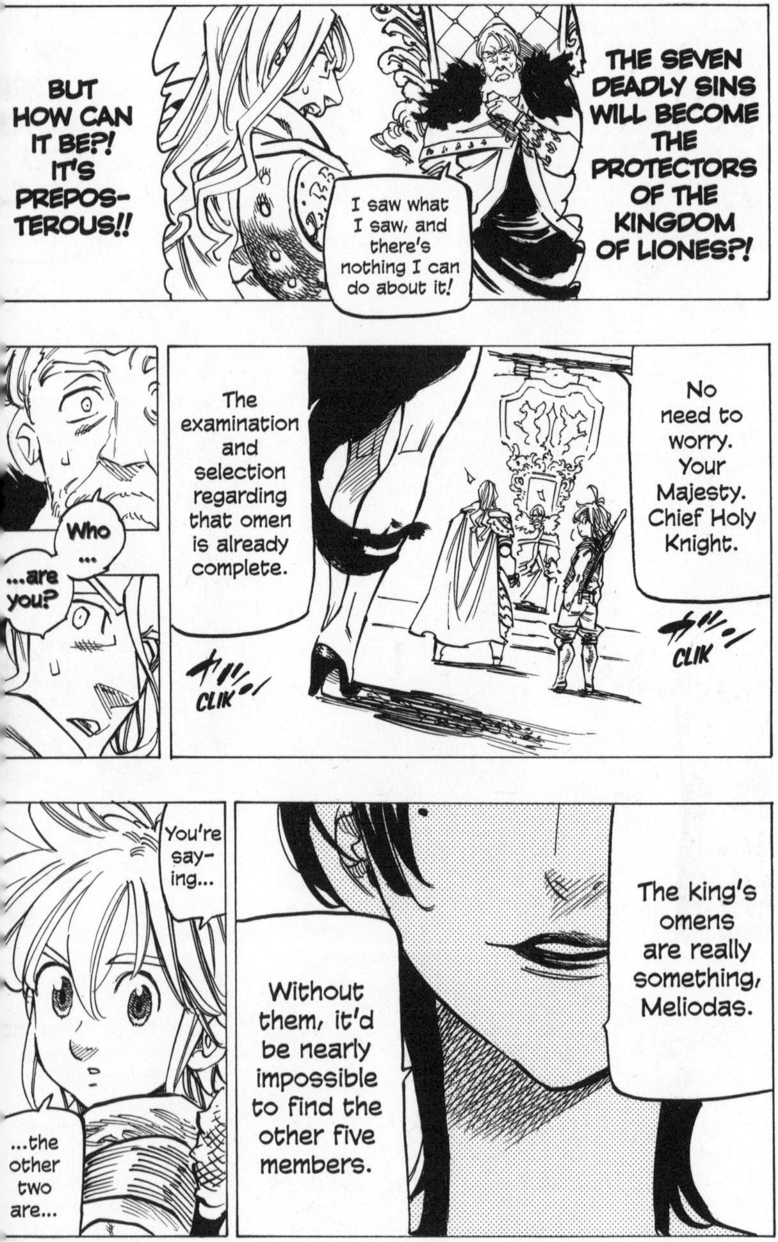
THE SEVEN DEADLY SINS WILL BECOME THE PROTECTORS OF THE KINGDOM OF LIONES?!
BUT HOW CAN IT BE?! IT'S PREPOS-TEROUS!!
I saw what I saw, and there's nothing I can do about it!
No need to worry. Your Majesty. Chief Holy Knight.
CLIK
The examination and selection regarding that omen is already complete.
CLIK
Who ...
...are you?
The king's omens are really something, Meliodas.
Without them, it'd be nearly impossible to find the other five members.
You're say-ing...
...the other two are...

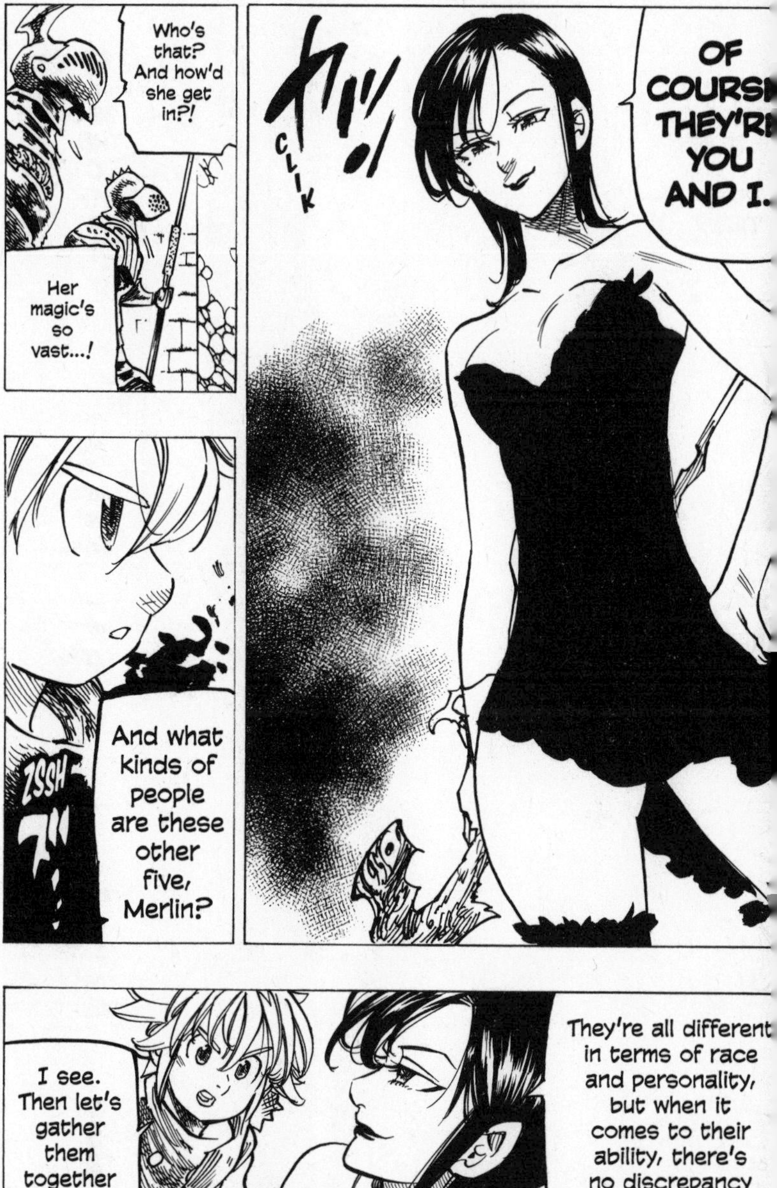
CLIK
OF COURS THEY'R YOU AND I.
Who's that? And how'd she get in?!
Her magic's so vast...!
ZSSH
And what kinds of people are these other five, Merlin?
They're all different in terms of race and personality, but when it comes to their ability, there's no discrepancy between them.
I see. Then let's gather them together at once.

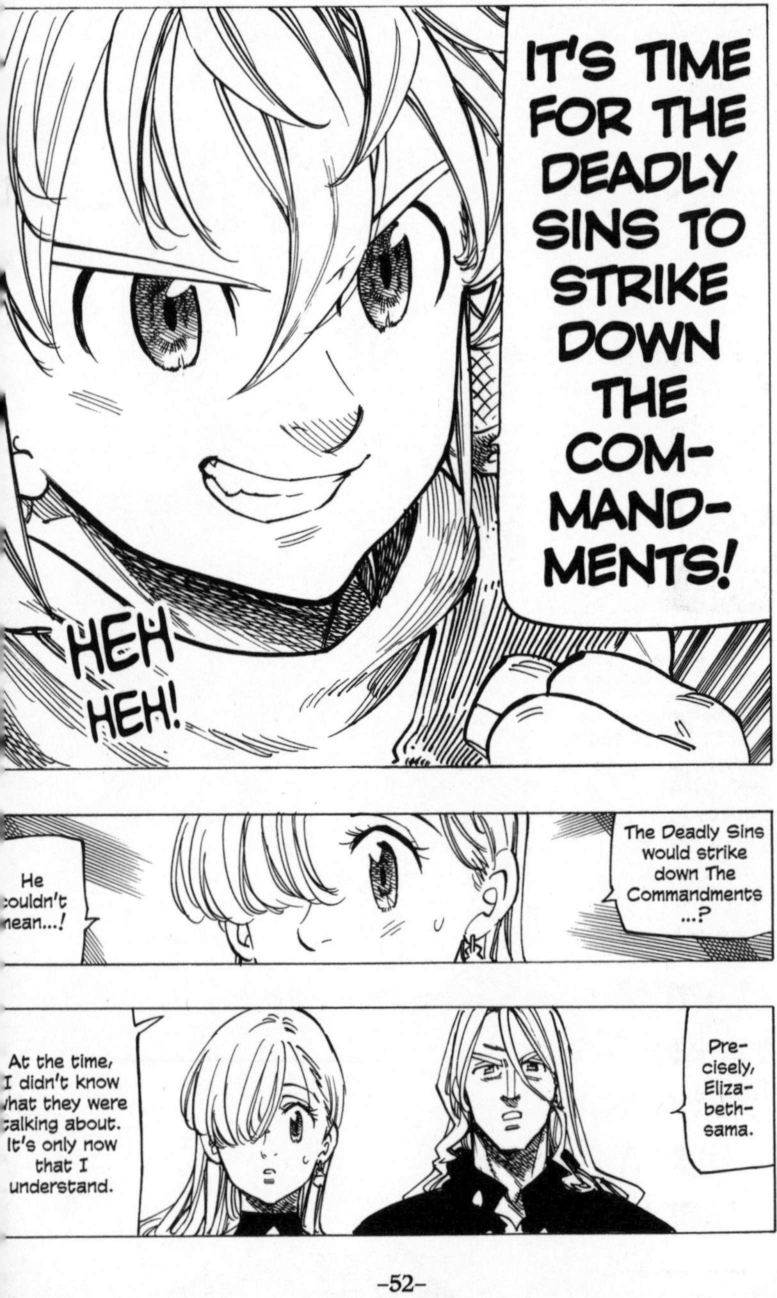
IT'S TIME FOR THE DEADLY SINS TO STRIKE DOWN THE COMMANDMENTS!
HEH HEH!
The Deadly Sins would strike down The Commandments ...?
He couldn't mean...!
Precisely, Elizabeth-sama.
At the time, I didn't know what they were talking about. It's only now that I understand.

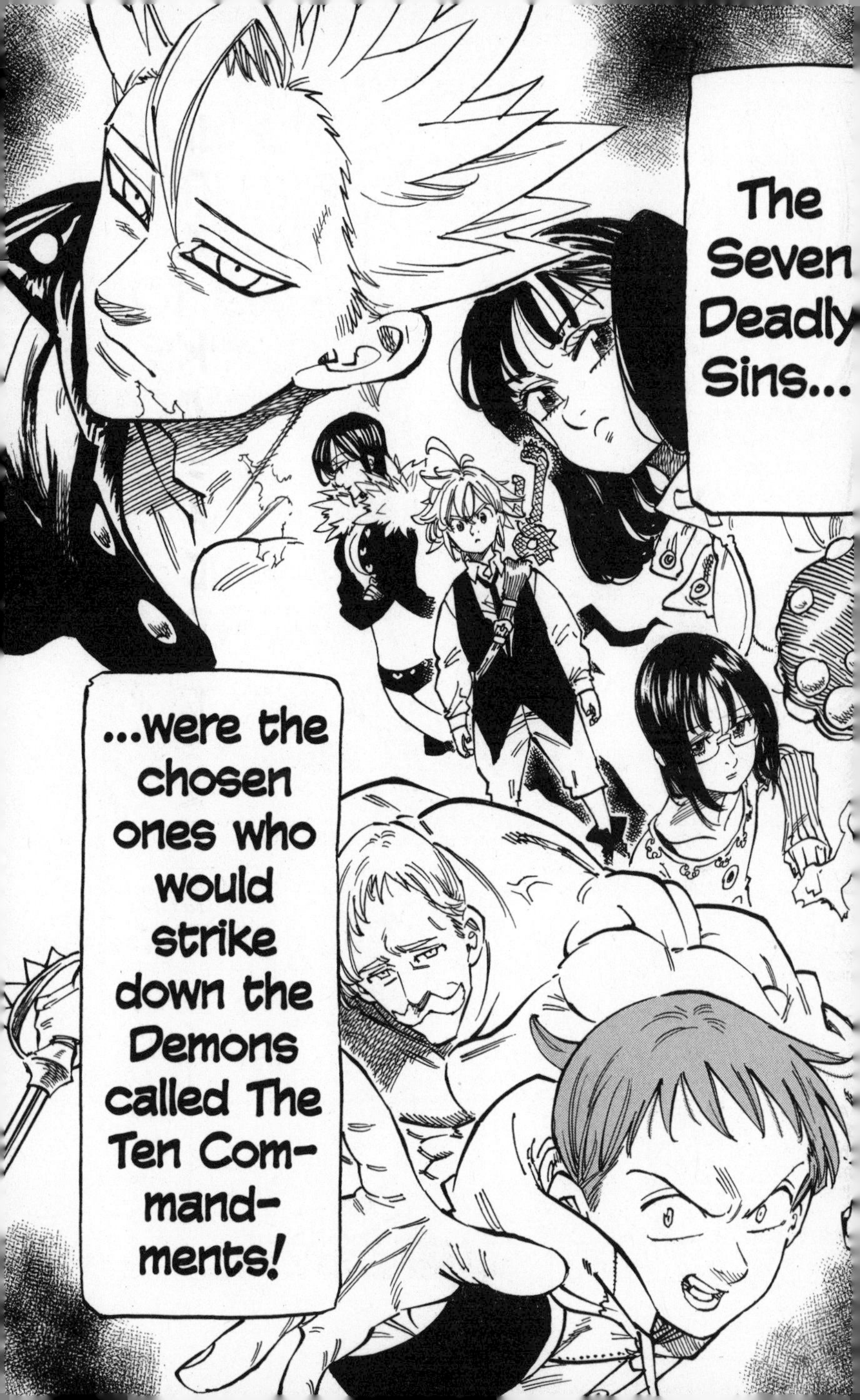
The Seven Deadly Sins...
...were the chosen ones who would strike down the Demons called The Ten Commandments!

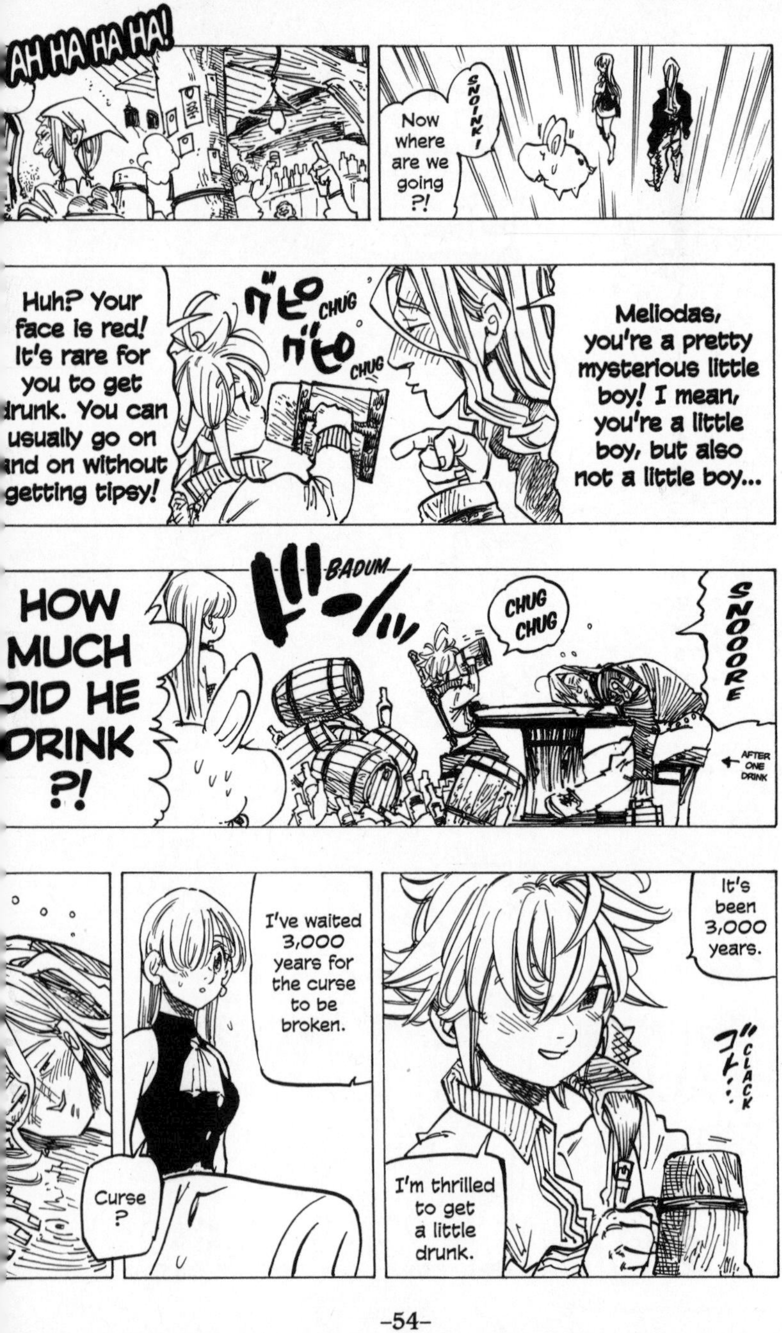
SNOINK!
Now where are we going?!
AH HA HA HA!
Meliodas, you're a pretty mysterious little boy! I mean, you're a little boy, but also not a little boy...
CHUG
CHUG
Huh? Your face is red! It's rare for you to get drunk. You can usually go on and on without getting tipsy!
SNOOORE
AFTER ONE DRINK
CHUG CHUG
BADUM
HOW MUCH DID HE DRINK?!
It's been 3,000 years.
CLACK
I'm thrilled to get a little drunk.
I've waited 3,000 years for the curse to be broken.
Curse?

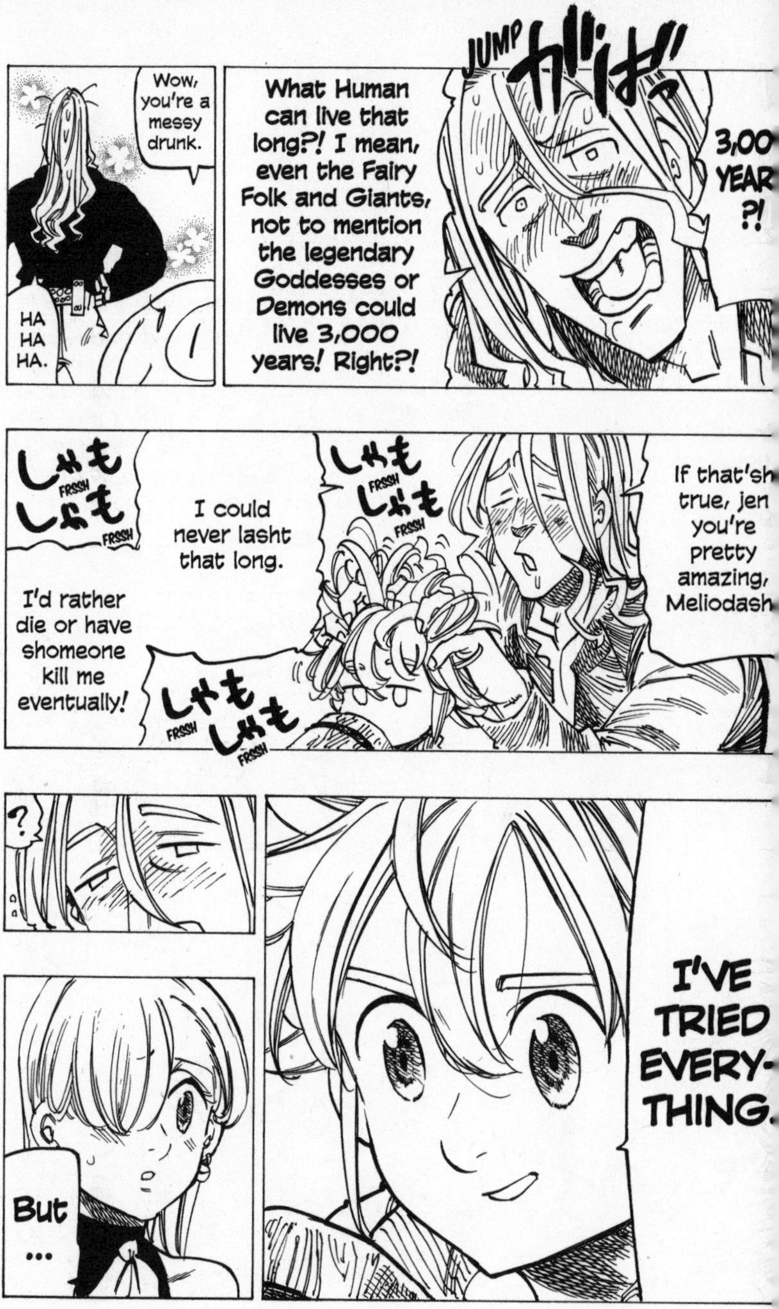

JUMP
3,00
YEAR
?!
What Human can live that long?! I mean, even the Fairy Folk and Giants, not to mention the legendary Goddesses or Demons could live 3,000 years! Right?!
Wow, you're a messy drunk.
HA HA HA.
If that'sh true, jen you're pretty amazing, Meliodash
FRSSH
FRSSH
I could never lasht that long.
FRSSH
FRSSH
I'd rather die or have shomeone kill me eventually!
FRSSH
FRSSH
I'VE TRIED EVERY-THING.
?
But ...

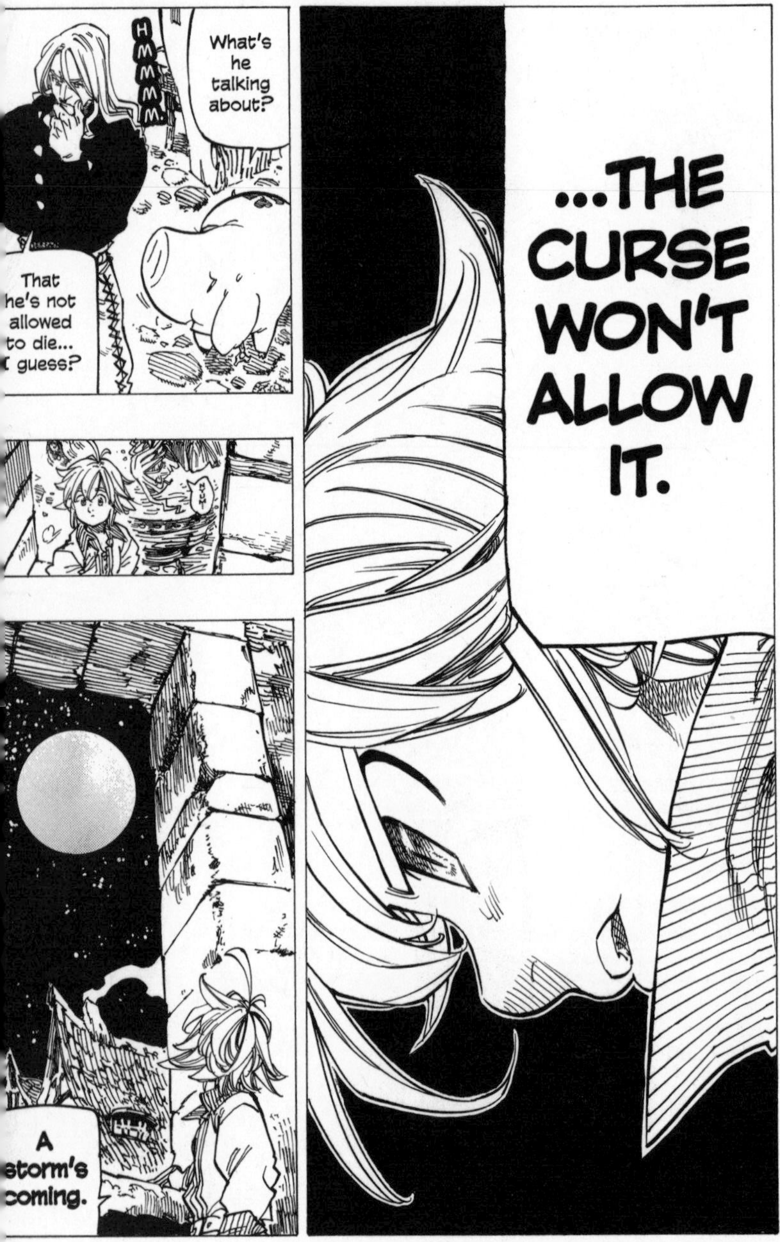
...THE CURSE WON'T ALLOW IT.
What's he talking about?
HMMMM.
That he's not allowed to die... I guess?
A storm's coming.

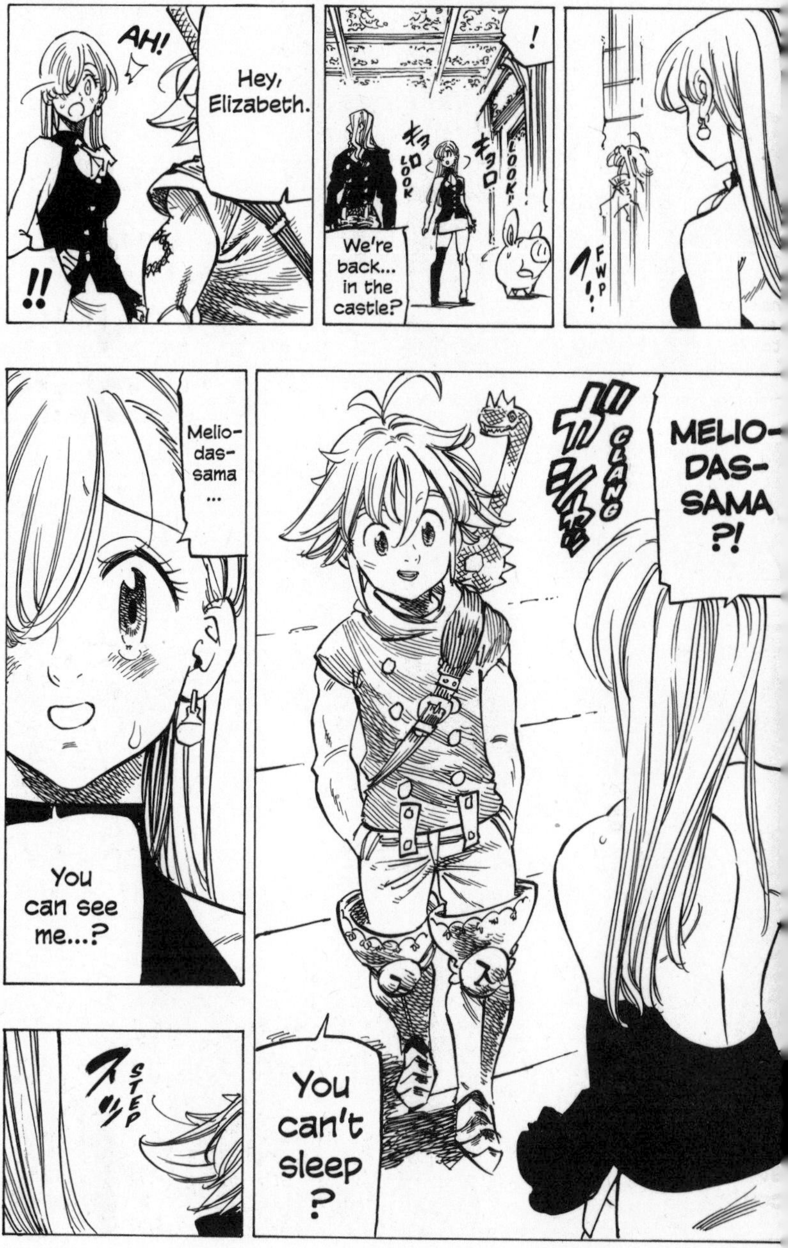
FWP
!
LOOK
LOOK
We're back... in the castle?
Hey, Elizabeth.
AH!
!!
MELIO-DAS-SAMA?!
CLANG
You can't sleep?
Melio-das-sama...
You can see me...?
STEP

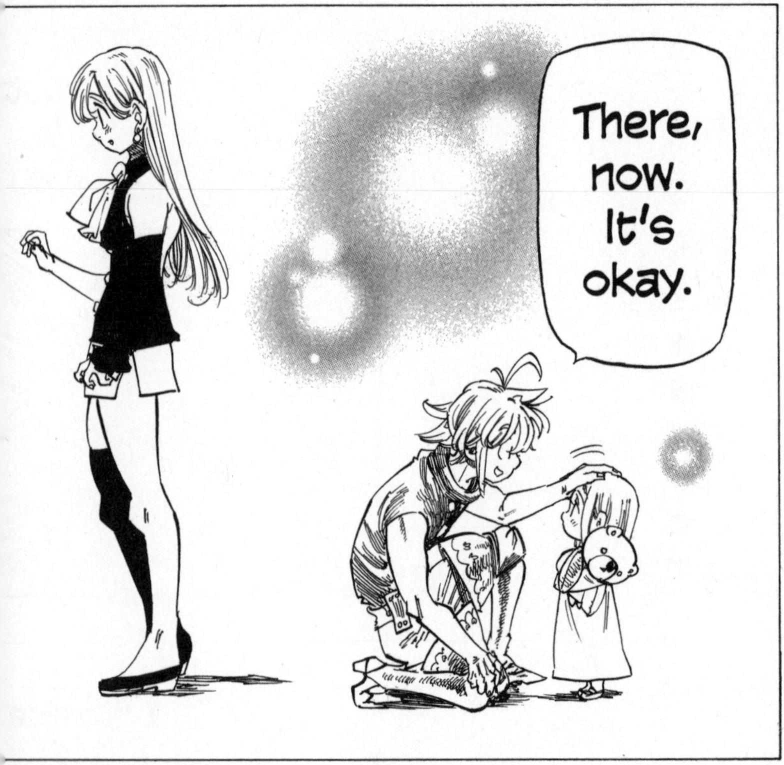
There, now. It's okay.
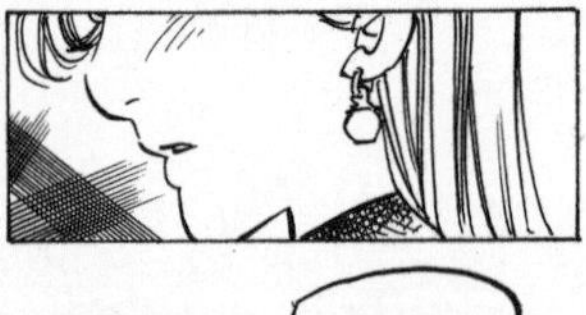
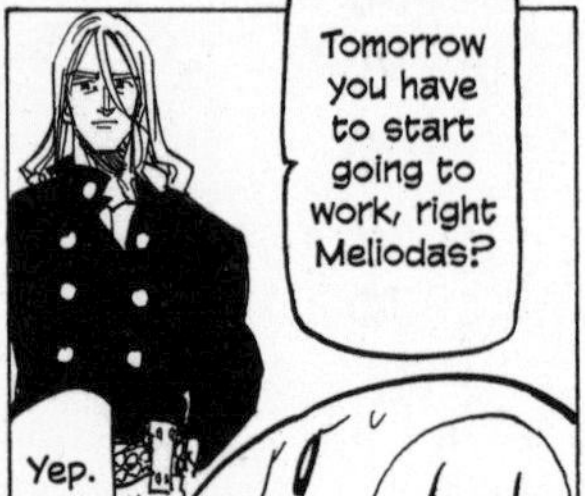
Tomorrow you have to start going to work, right Meliodas?
Yep.
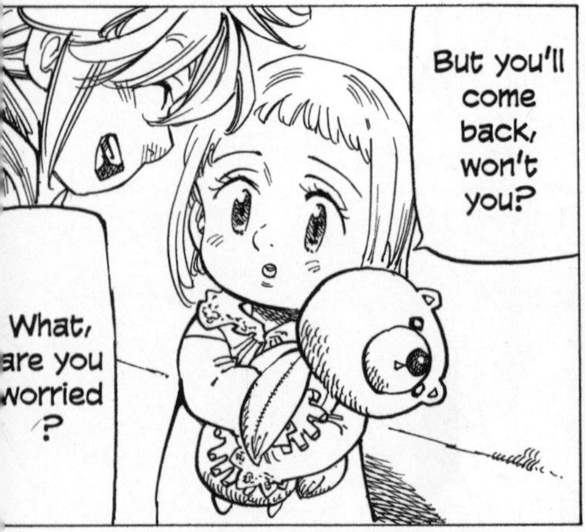
But you'll come back, won't you?
What, are you worried?

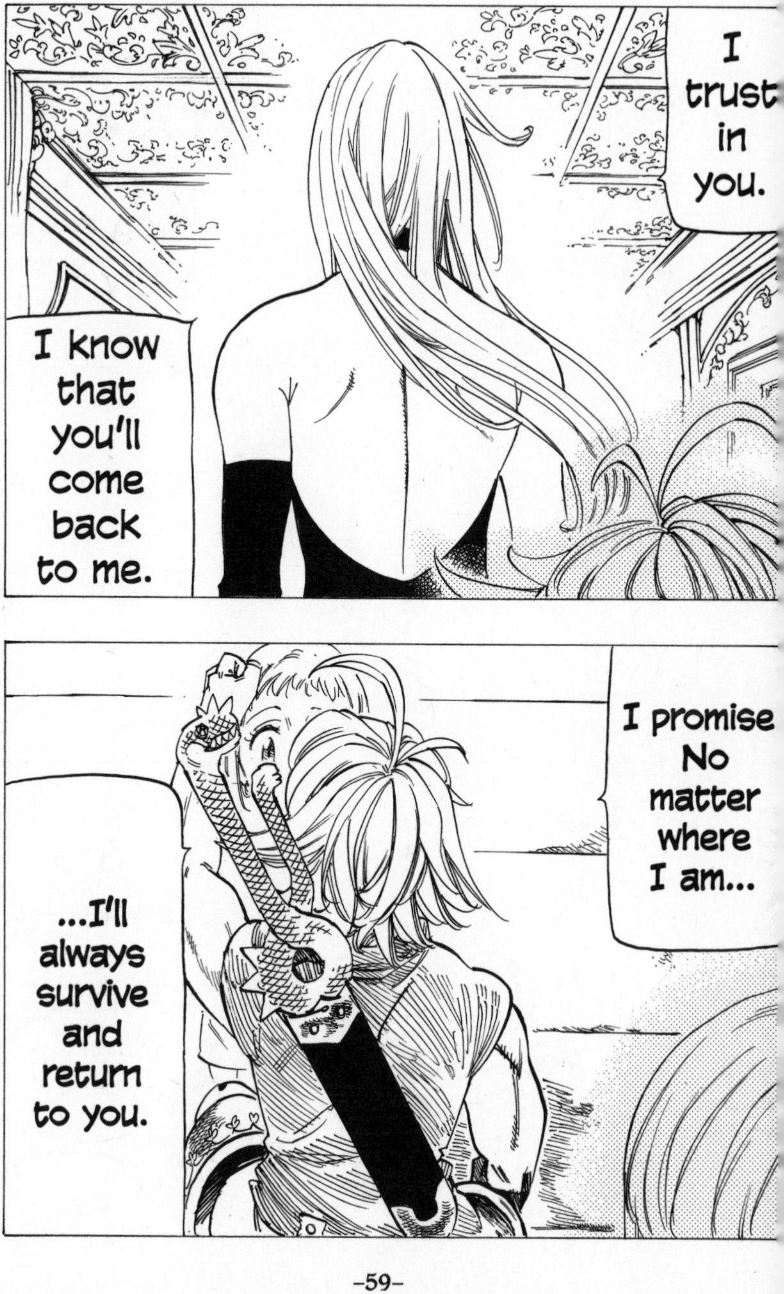
I trust in you.
I know that you'll come back to me.
I promise No matter where I am...
...I'll always survive and return to you.

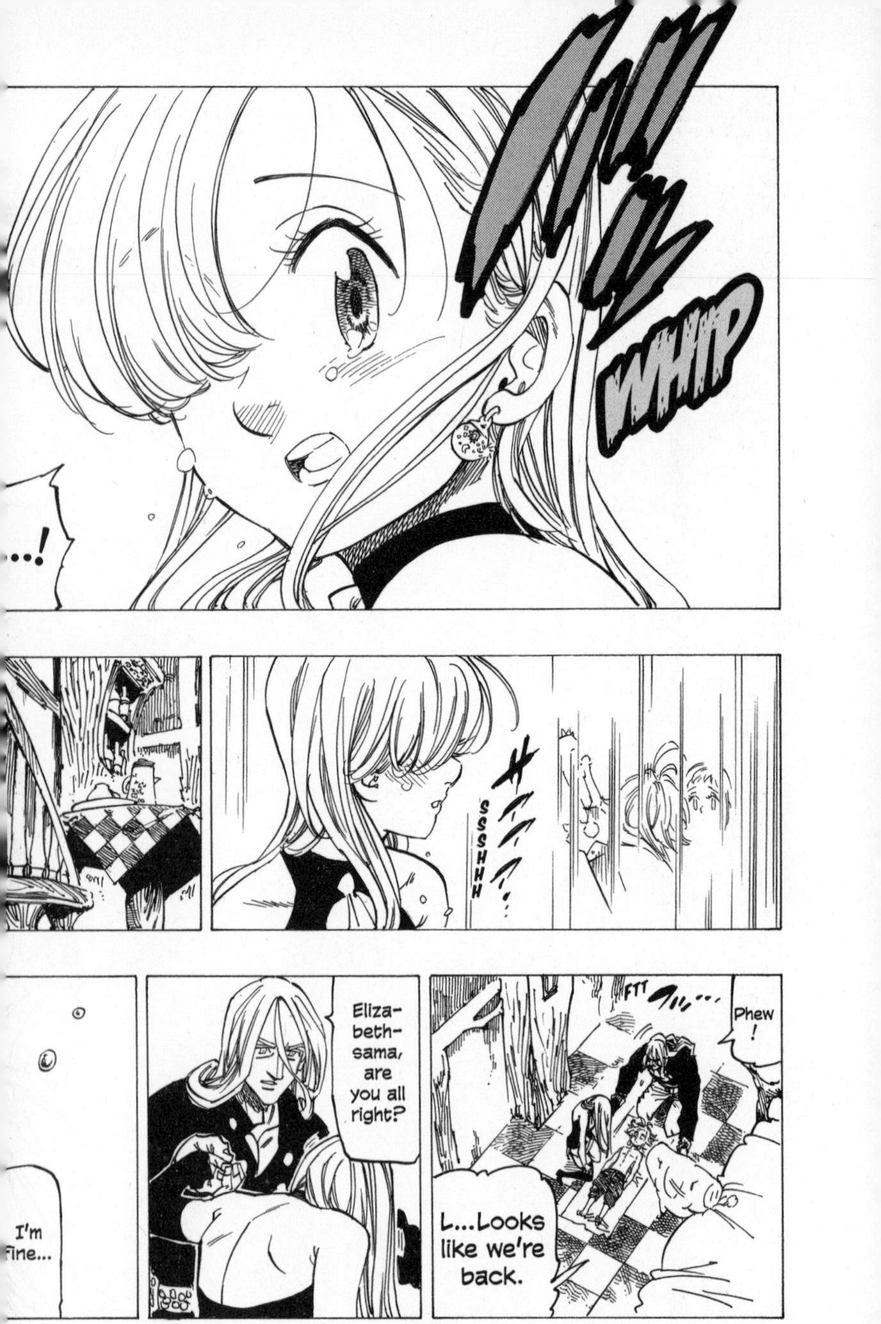
WHIP
...!
SSSHHH
Phew!
FTT
L...Looks like we're back.
Eliza-beth-sama, are you all right?
I'm Fine...

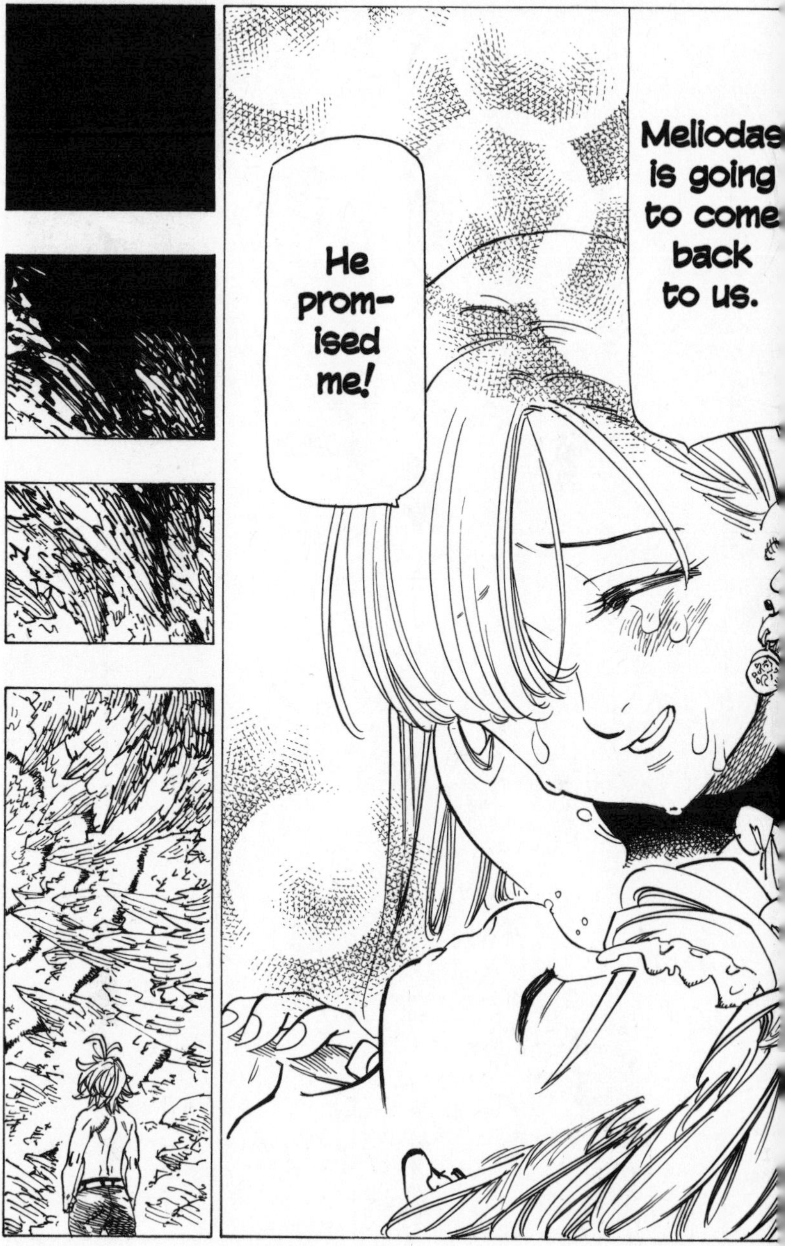
Meliodas is going to come back to us.
He prom- ised me!

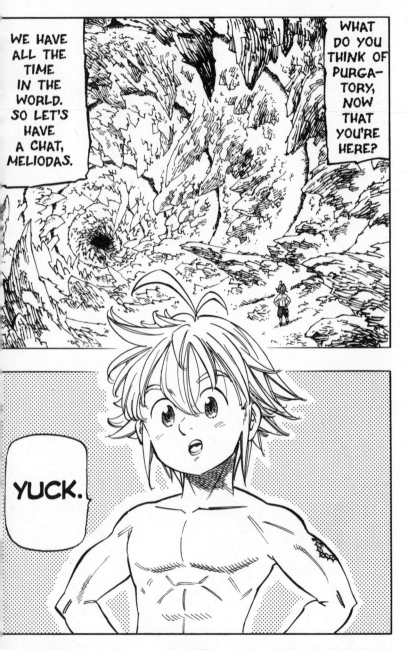

WHAT DO YOU THINK OF PURGATORY, NOW THAT YOU'RE HERE?
WE HAVE ALL THE TIME IN THE WORLD. SO LET'S HAVE A CHAT, MELIODAS.
YUCK.

Chapter 183 - Danger Zon

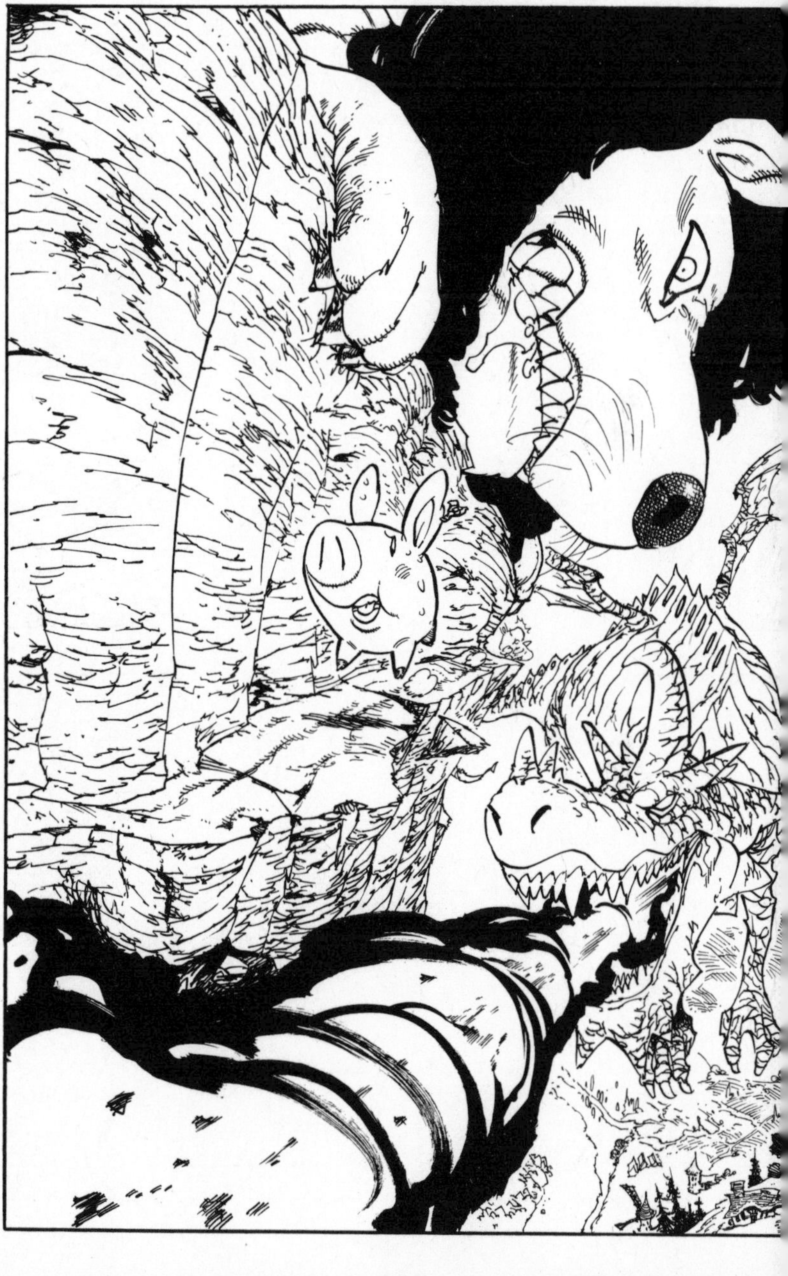

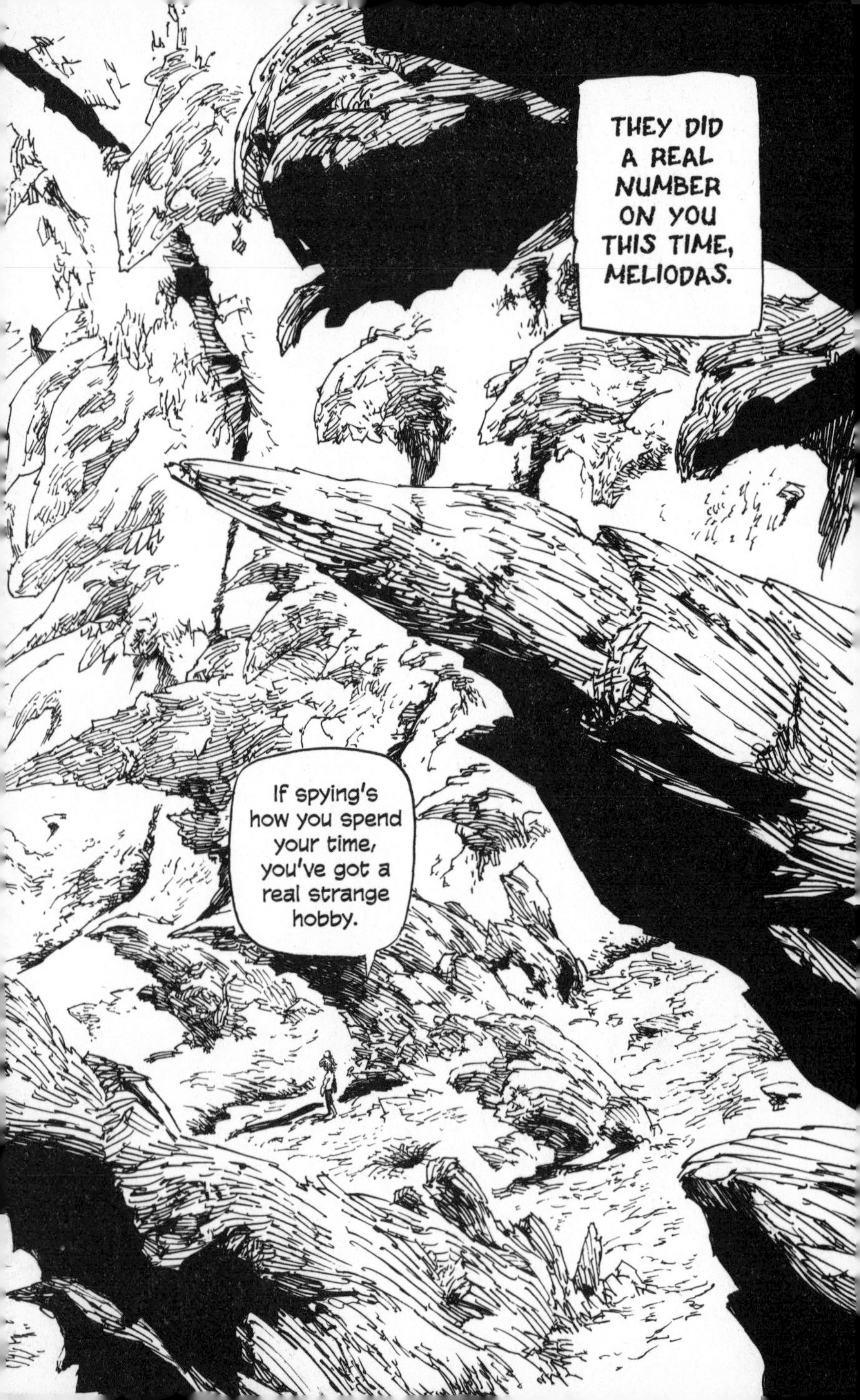
THEY DID A REAL NUMBER ON YOU THIS TIME, MELIODAS.
If spying's how you spend your time, you've got a real strange hobby.

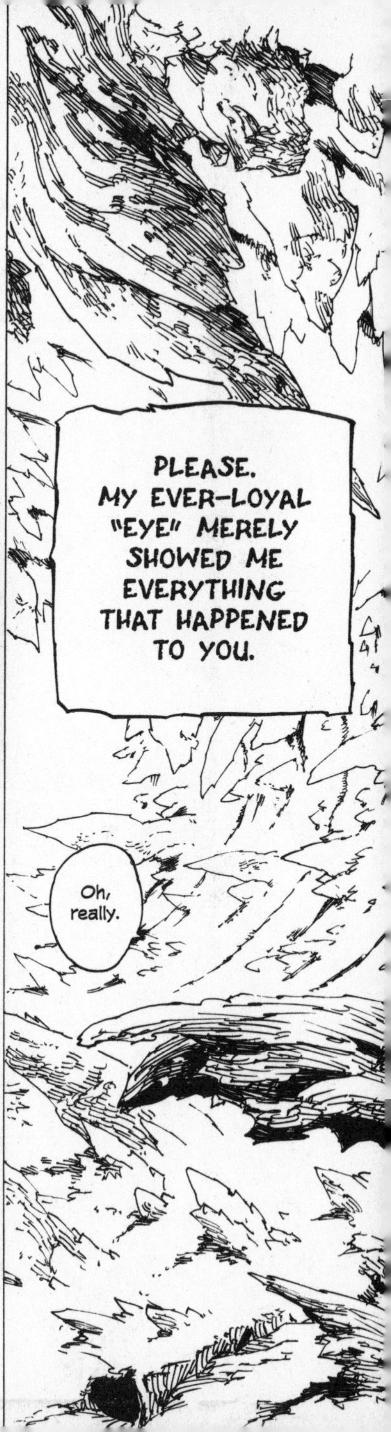
PLEASE. MY EVER-LOYAL "EYE" MERELY SHOWED ME EVERYTHING THAT HAPPENED TO YOU.
Oh, really.
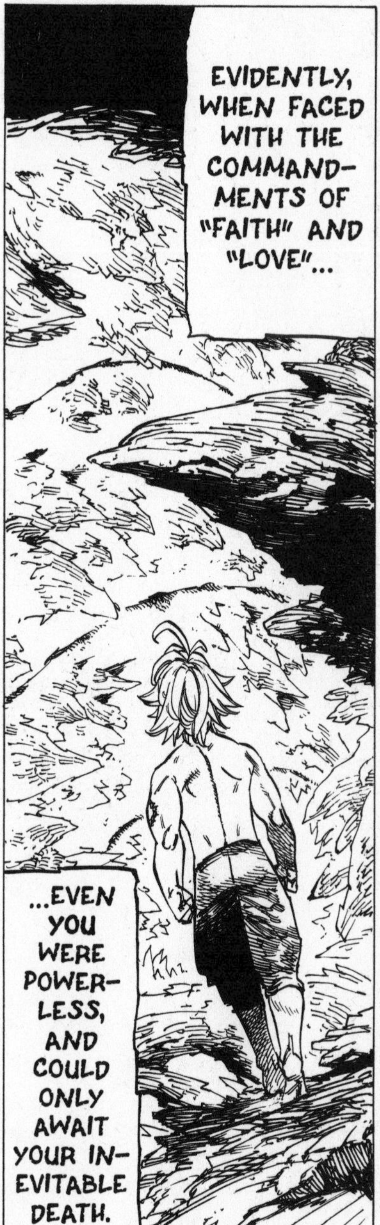
EVIDENTLY, WHEN FACED WITH THE COMMAND-MENTS OF "FAITH" AND "LOVE"...
...EVEN YOU WERE POWER-LESS, AND COULD ONLY AWAIT YOUR IN-EVITABLE DEATH.

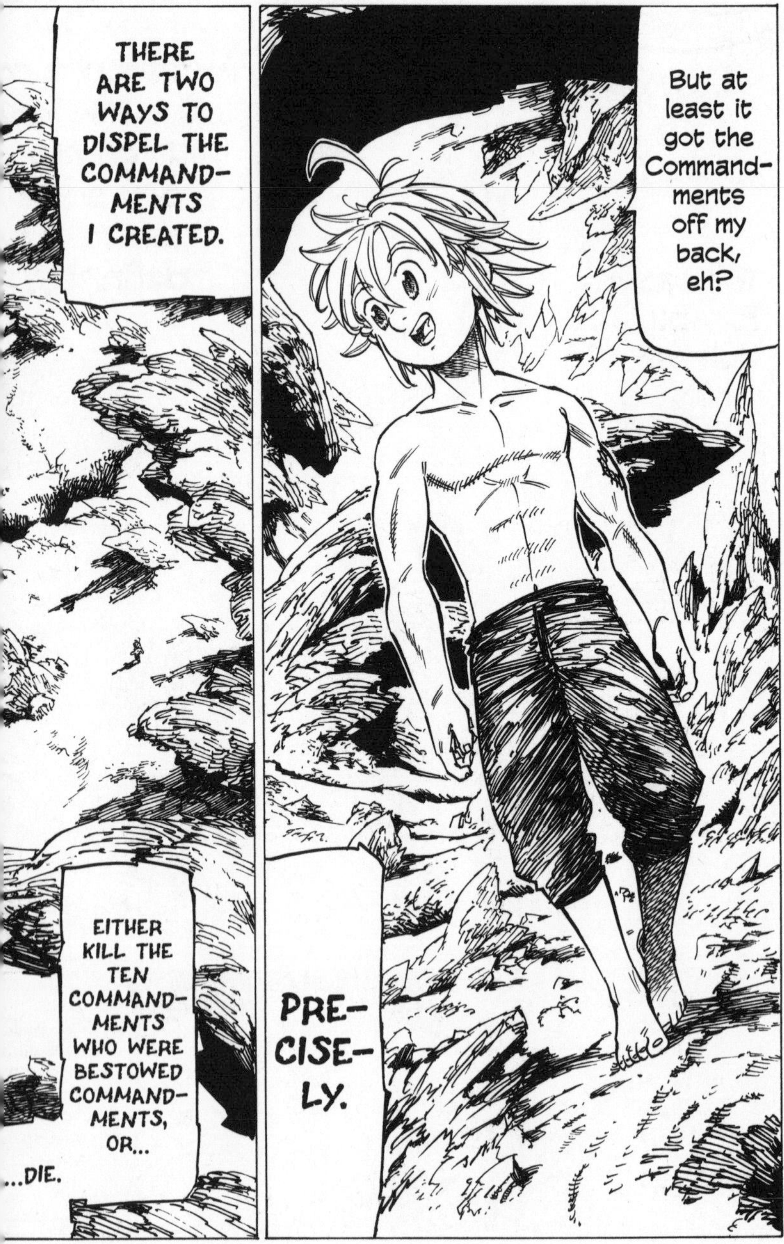
But at least it got the Command-ments off my back, eh?
PRE-CISE-LY.
THERE ARE TWO WAYS TO DISPEL THE COMMAND-MENTS I CREATED.
EITHER KILL THE TEN COMMAND-MENTS WHO WERE BESTOWED COMMAND-MENTS, OR...
...DIE.

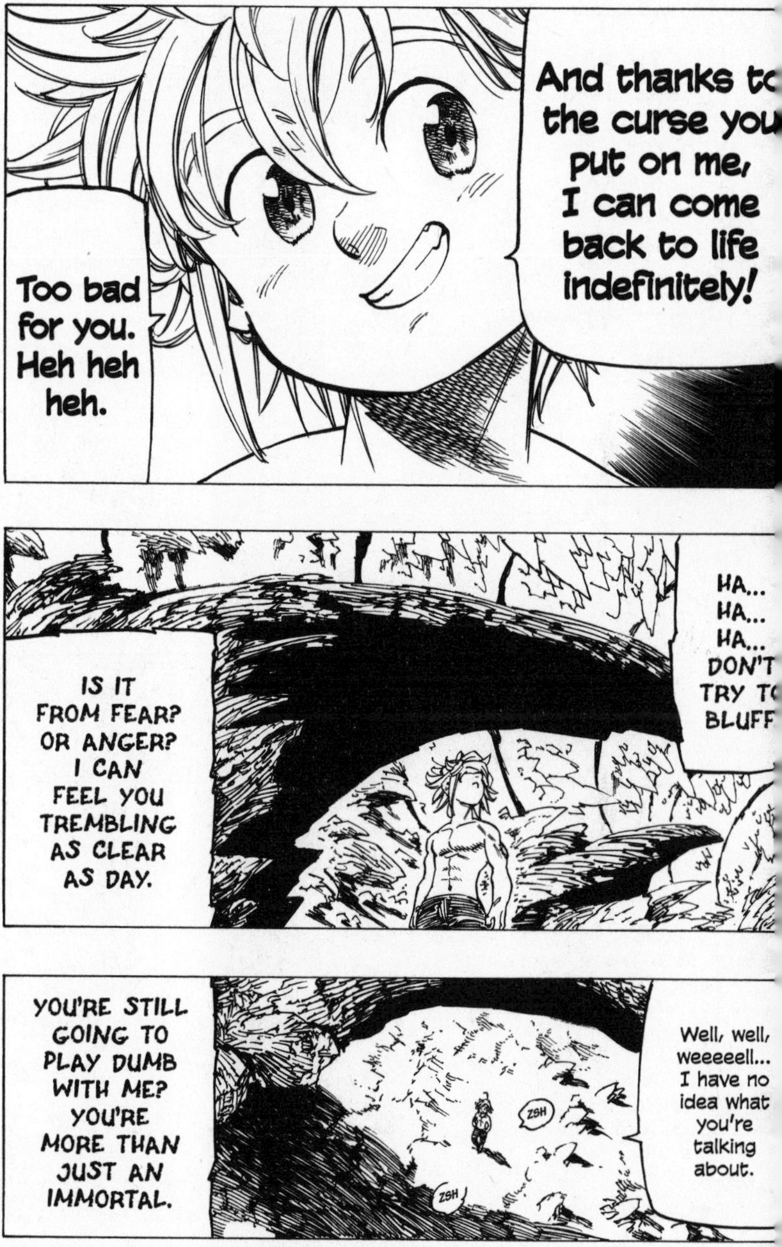
And thanks to the curse you put on me, I can come back to life indefinitely!
Too bad for you. Heh heh heh.
HA... HA... HA... DON'T TRY T BLUFF
IS IT FROM FEAR? OR ANGER? I CAN FEEL YOU TREMBLING AS CLEAR AS DAY.
Well, well, weeeeell... I have no idea what you're talking about.
ZSH
ZSH
YOU'RE STILL GOING TO PLAY DUMB WITH ME? YOU'RE MORE THAN JUST AN IMMORTAL.

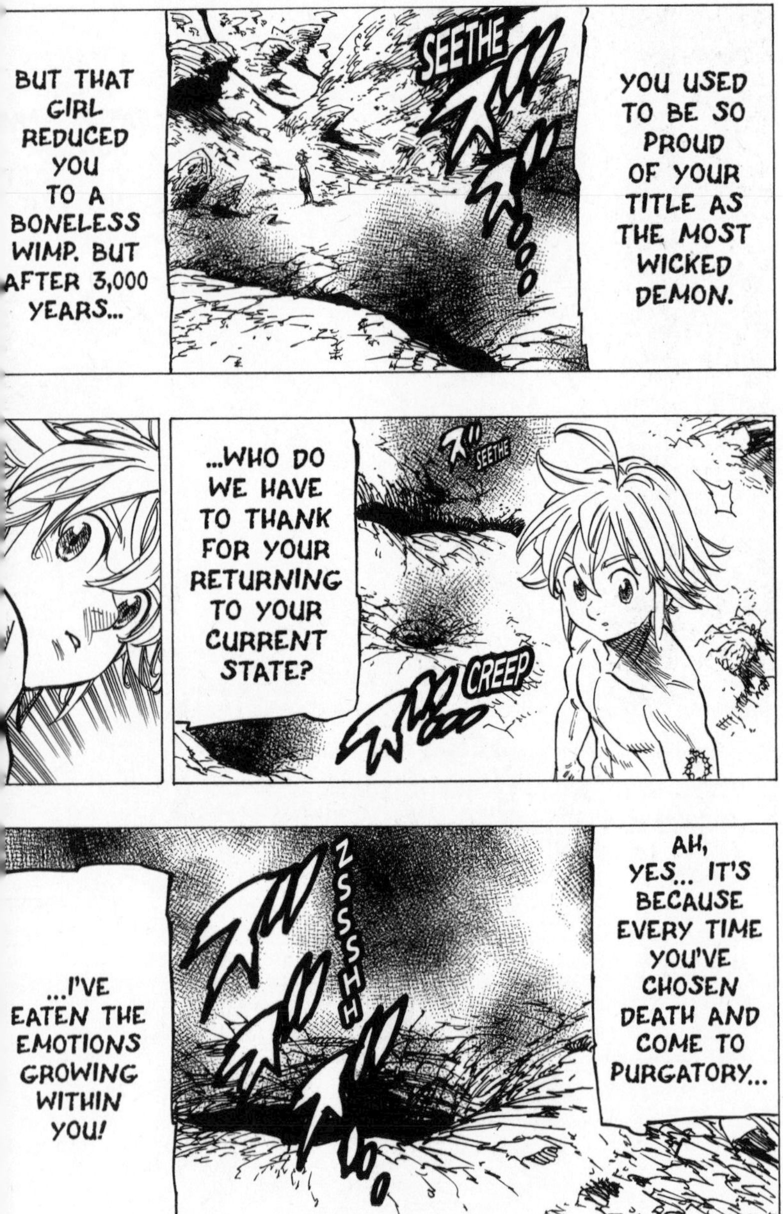
YOU USED TO BE SO PROUD OF YOUR TITLE AS THE MOST WICKED DEMON.
SEETHE
BUT THAT GIRL REDUCED YOU TO A BONELESS WIMP. BUT AFTER 3,000 YEARS...
SEETHE
...WHO DO WE HAVE TO THANK FOR YOUR RETURNING TO YOUR CURRENT STATE?
CREEP
AH, YES... IT'S BECAUSE EVERY TIME YOU'VE CHOSEN DEATH AND COME TO PURGATORY...
ZSSSHH
...I'VE EATEN THE EMOTIONS GROWING WITHIN YOU!

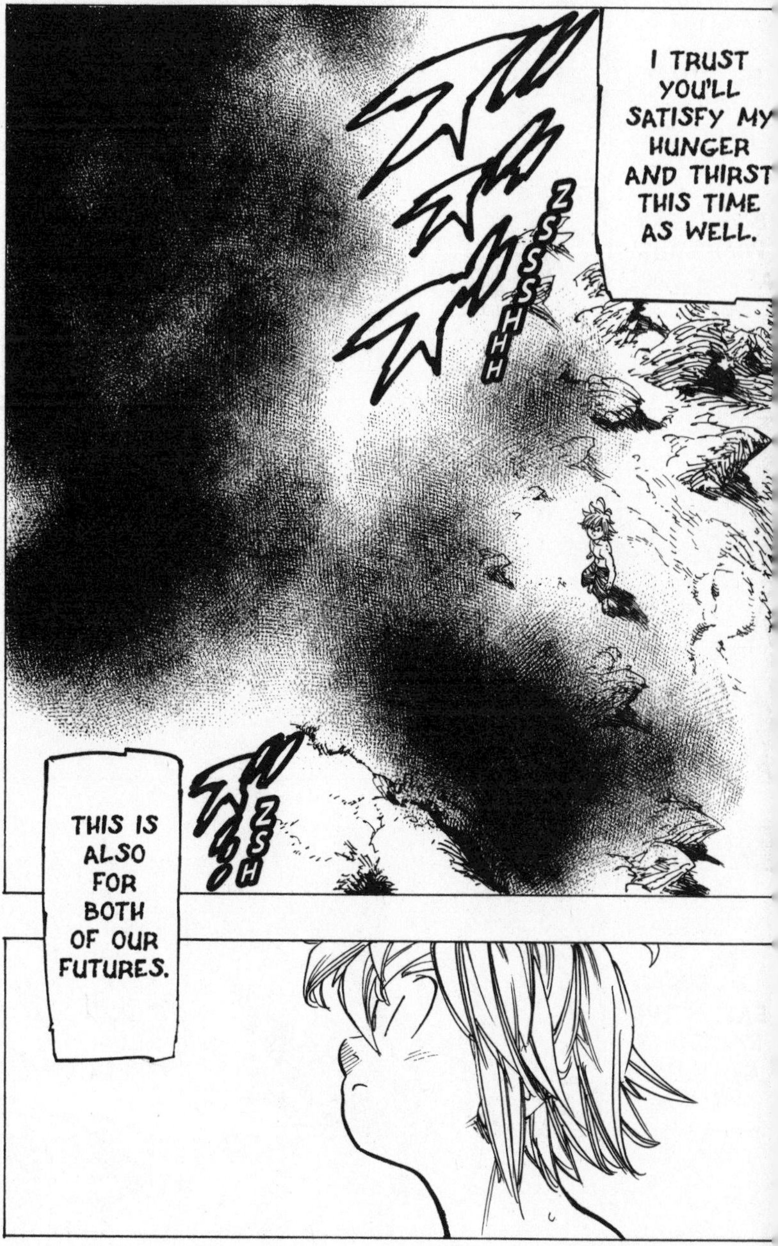
I TRUST YOU'LL SATISFY MY HUNGER AND THIRST THIS TIME AS WELL.
ZSSSHHH
ZSH
THIS IS ALSO FOR BOTH OF OUR FUTURES.

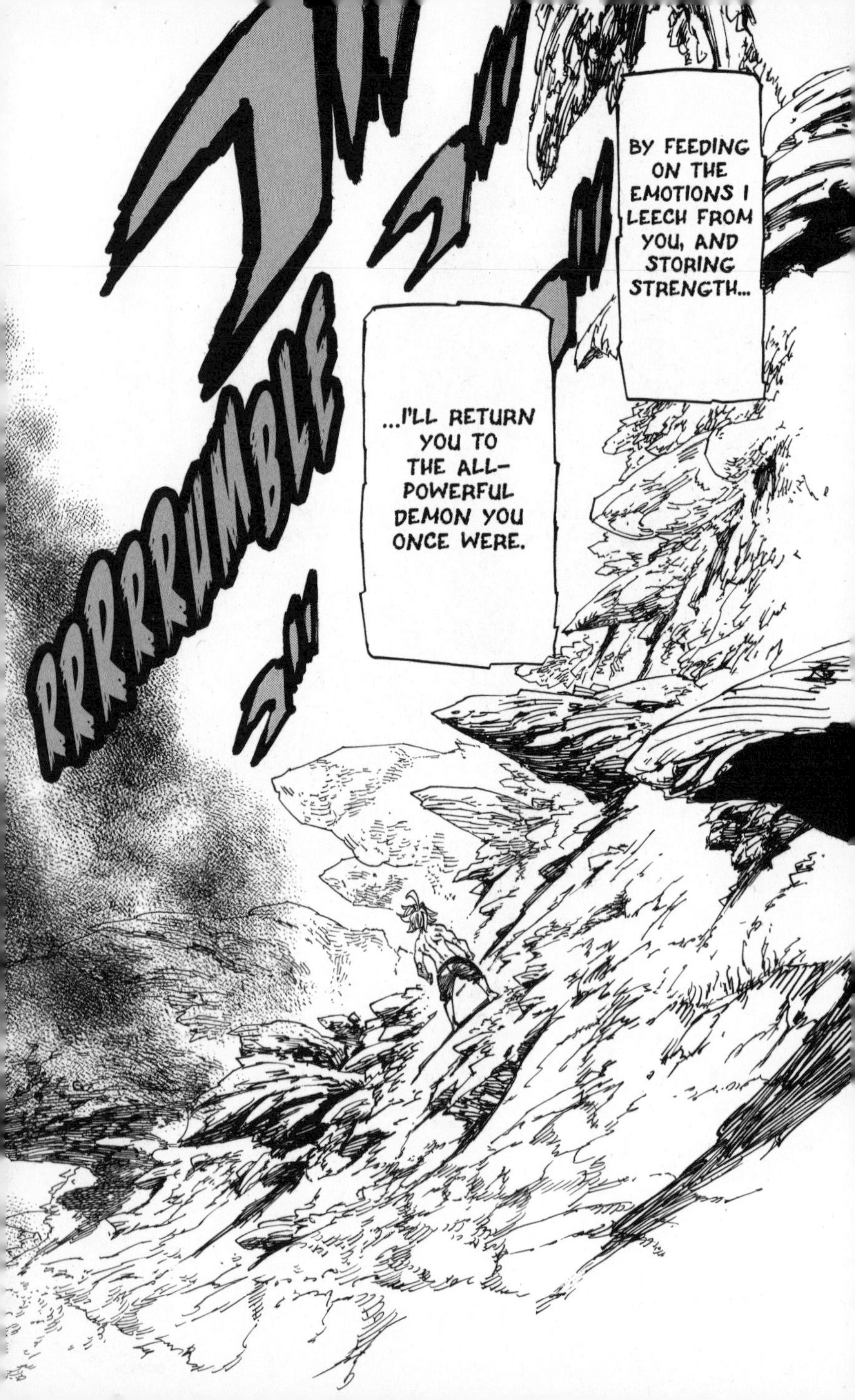
BY FEEDING ON THE EMOTIONS I LEECH FROM YOU, AND STORING STRENGTH...
...I'LL RETURN YOU TO THE ALL-POWERFUL DEMON YOU ONCE WERE.
RRRRUMBLE

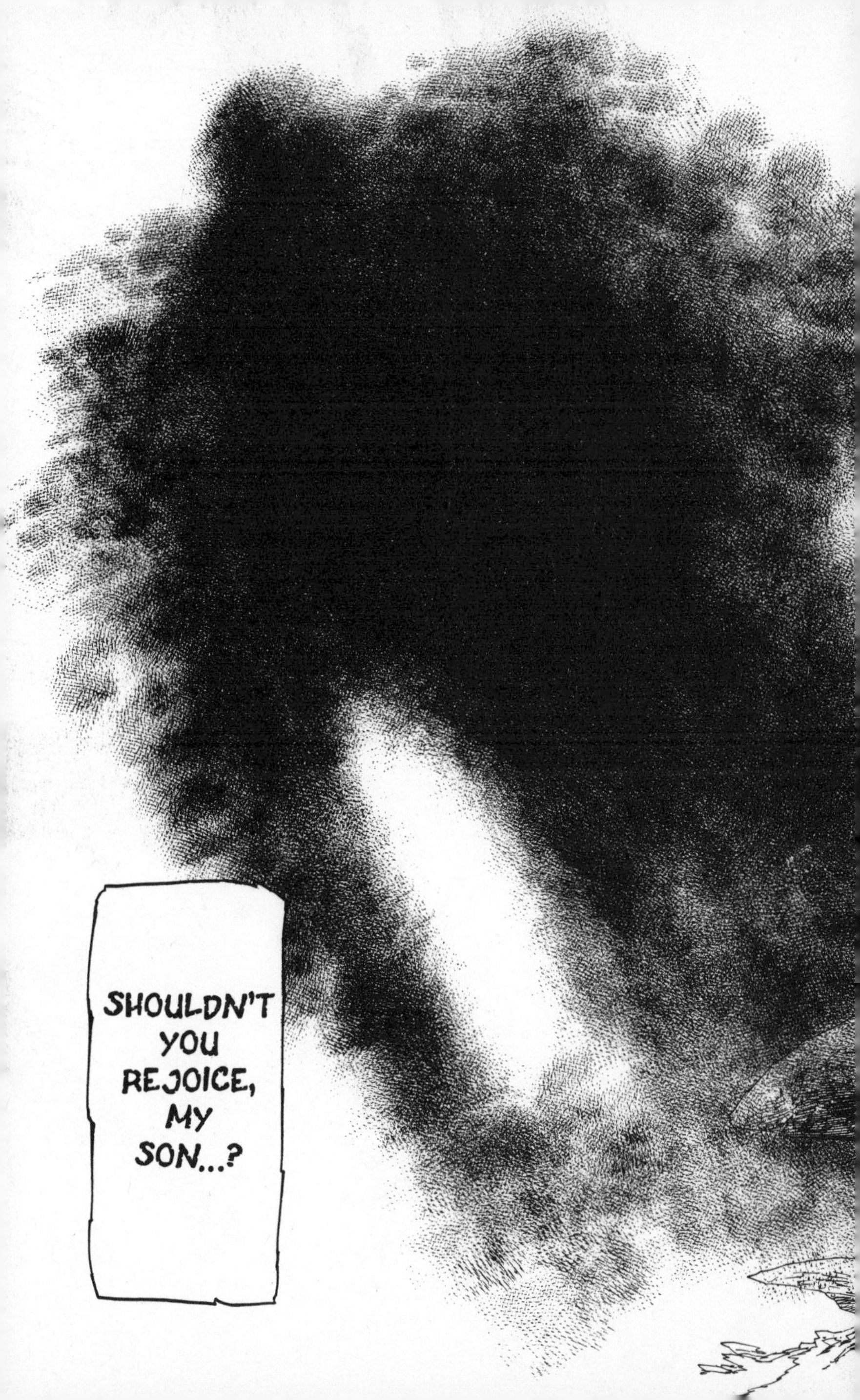
SHOULDN'T YOU REJOICE, MY SON...?

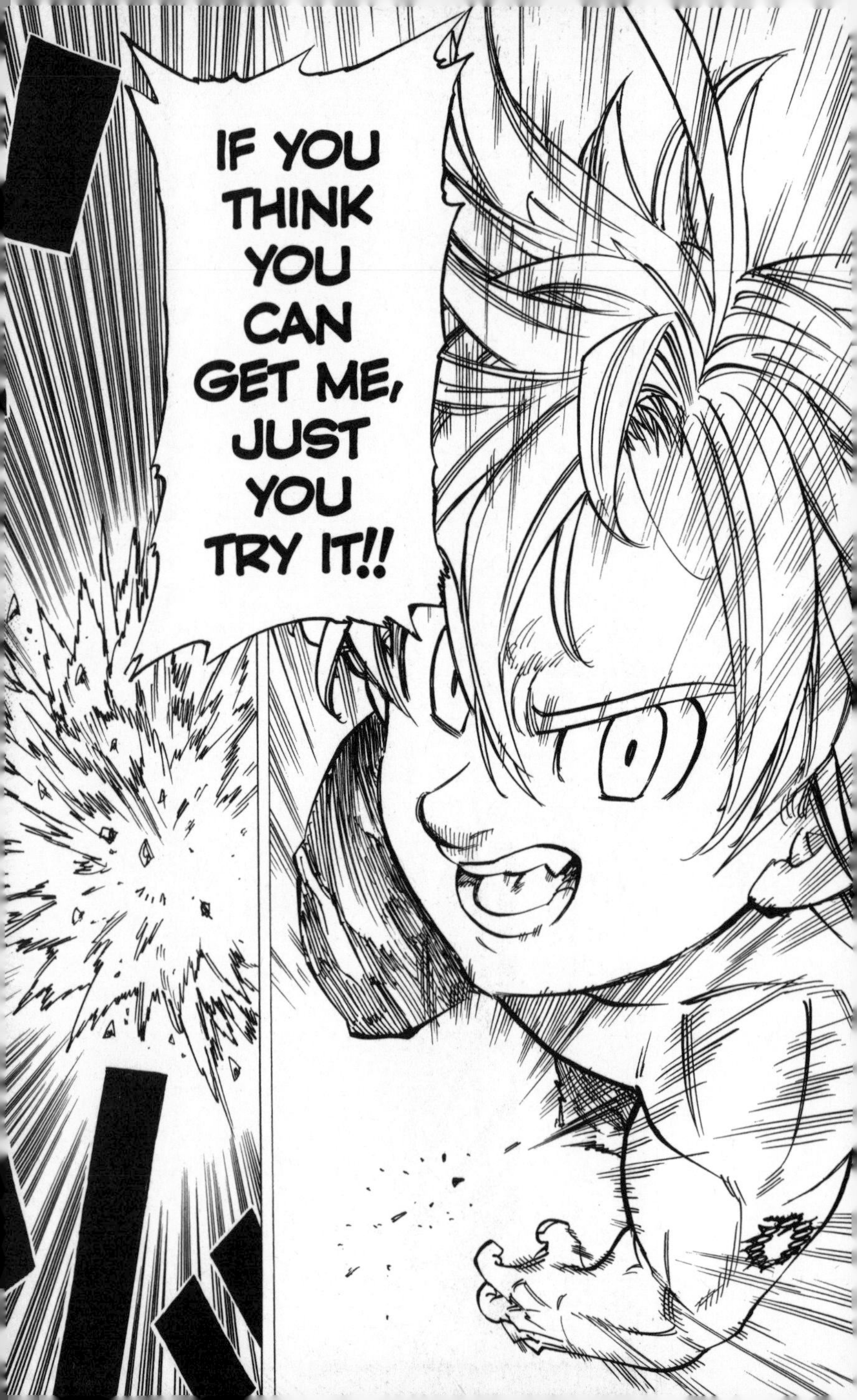
IF YOU THINK YOU CAN GET ME, JUST YOU TRY IT!!

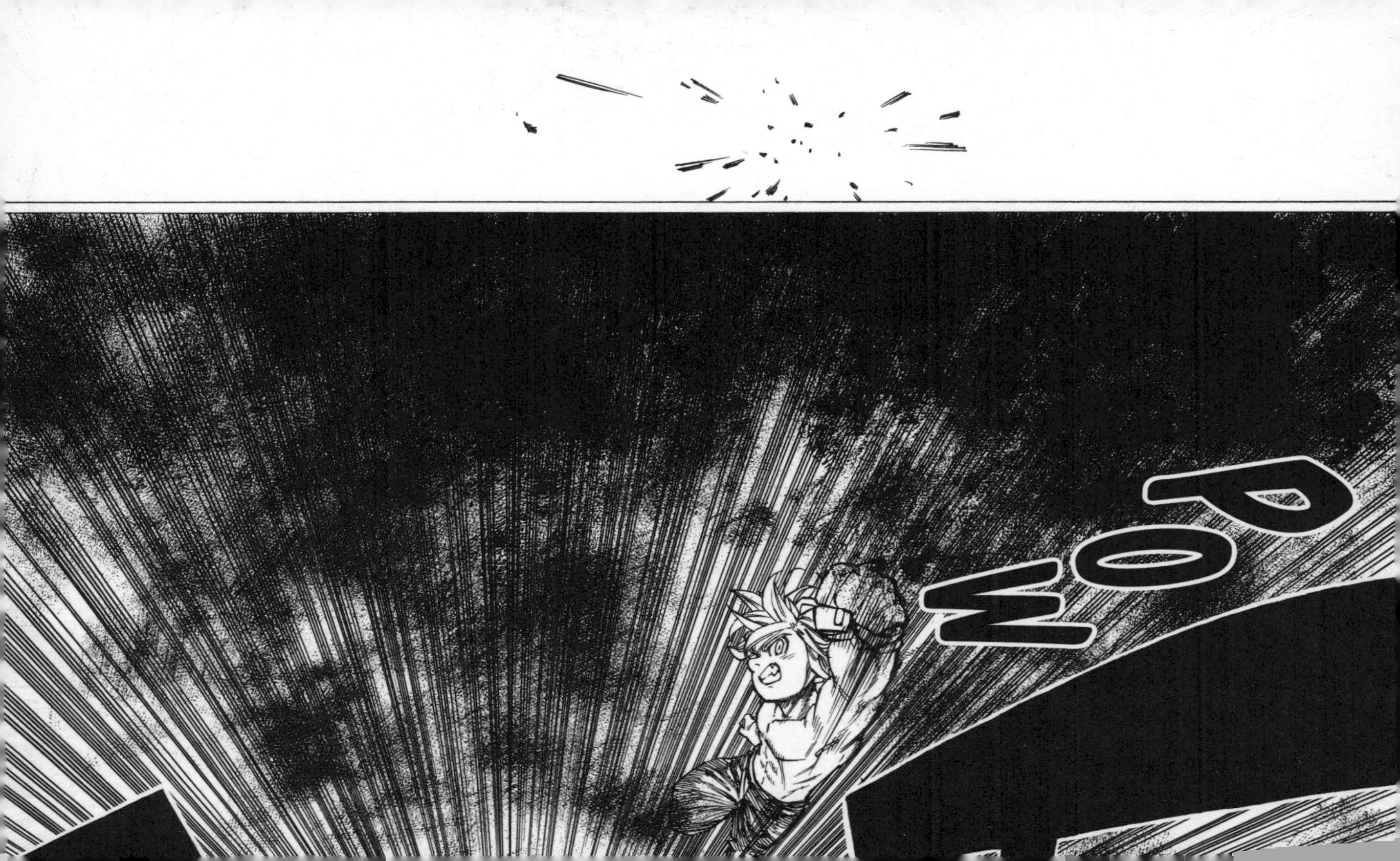
POW

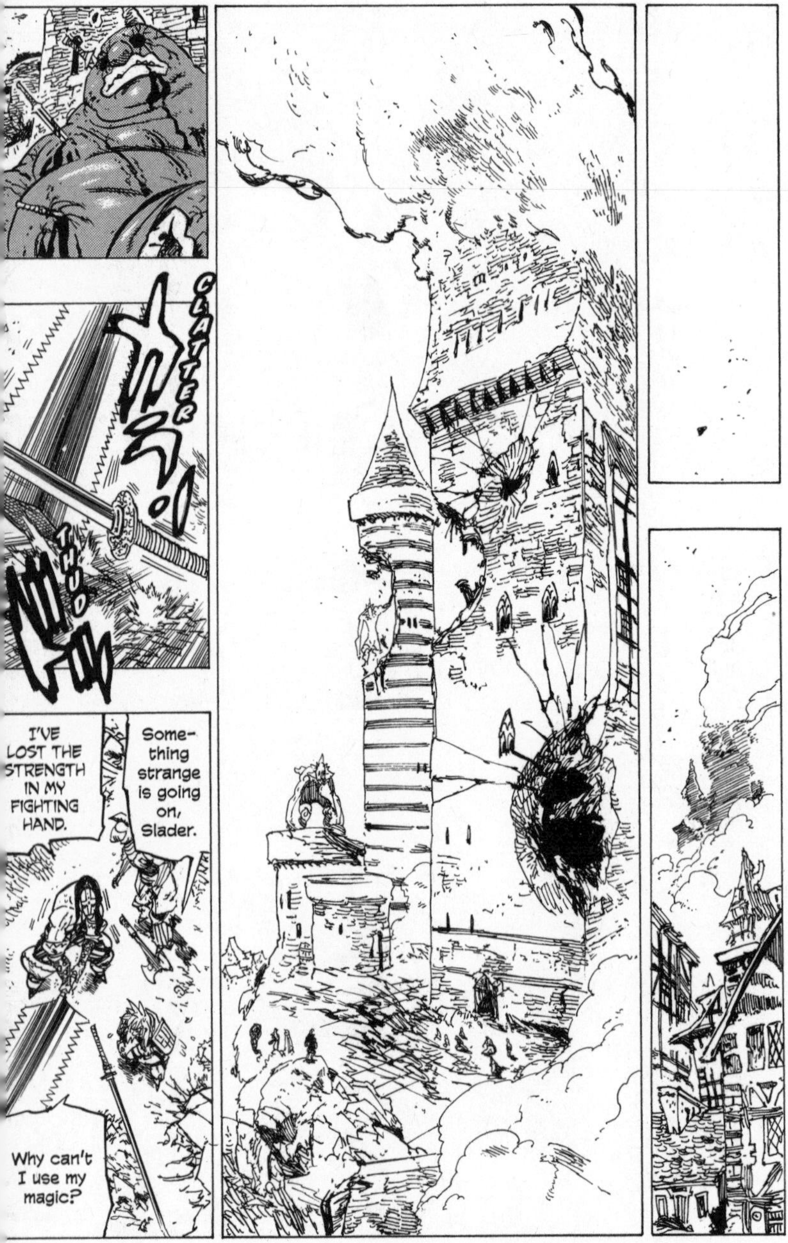
CLATTER
THUD
Some-thing strange is going on, Slader.
I'VE LOST THE STRENGTH IN MY FIGHTING HAND.
Why can't I use my magic?

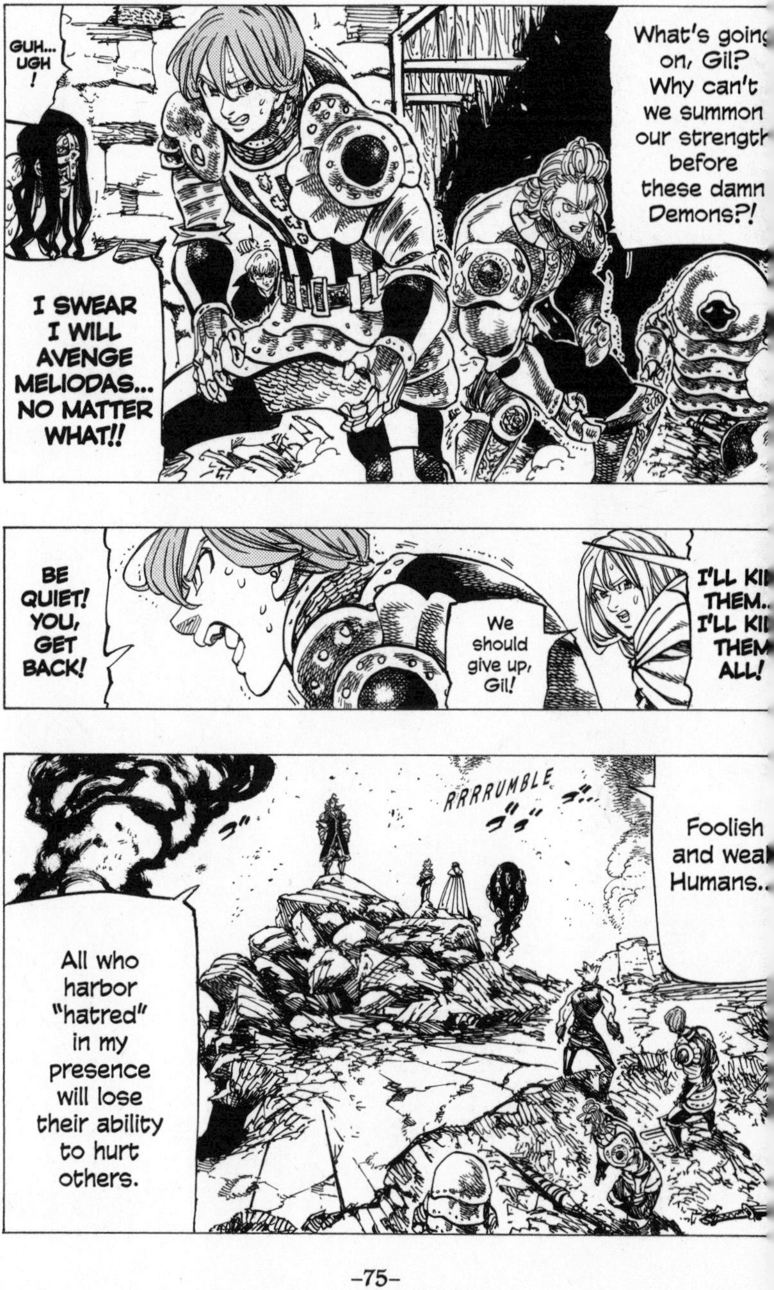
What's goin on, Gil? Why can't we summon our strengt before these damn Demons?!
GUH... UGH!
I SWEAR I WILL AVENGE MELIODAS... NO MATTER WHAT!!
I'LL KI THEM.. I'LL KI THEM ALL!
We should give up, Gil!
BE QUIET! YOU, GET BACK!
RRRRUMBLE
Foolish and wea Humans..
All who harbor "hatred" in my presence will lose their ability to hurt others.

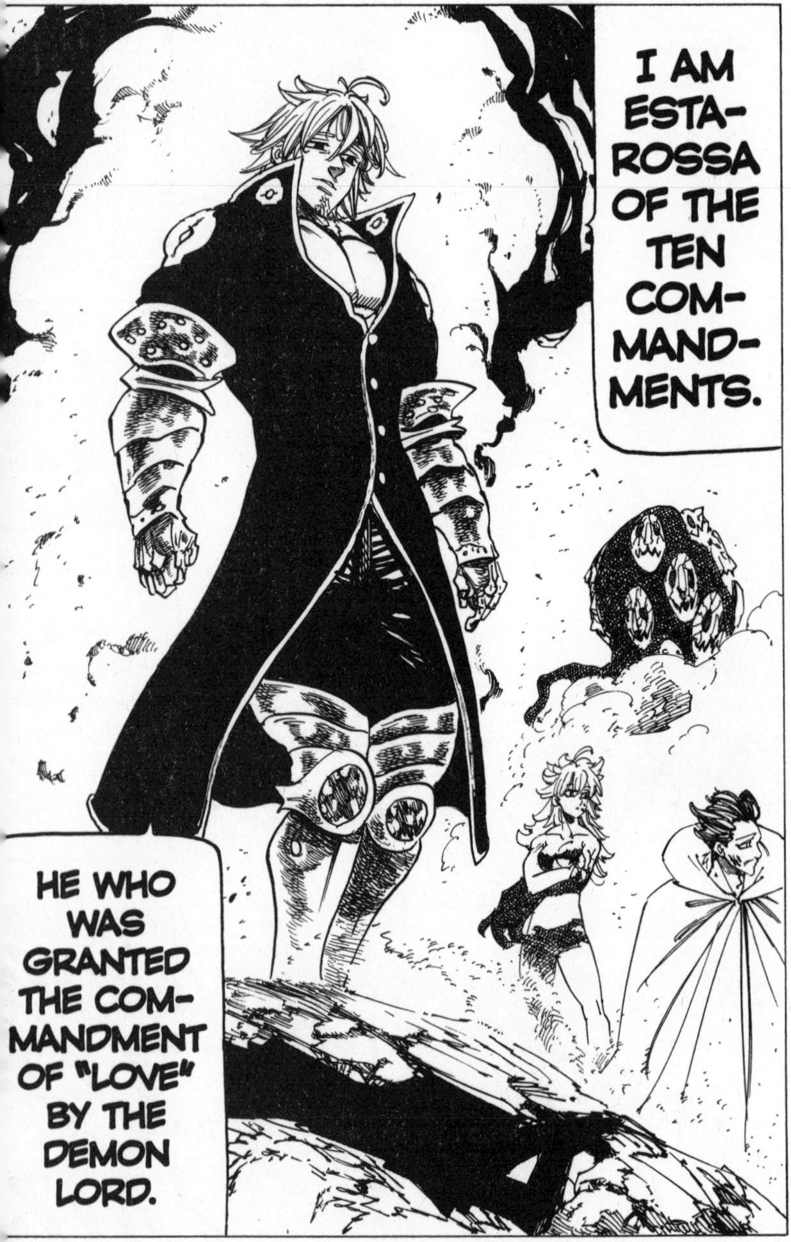
I AM ESTA-ROSSA OF THE TEN COM-MAND-MENTS.
HE WHO WAS GRANTED THE COM-MANDMENT OF "LOVE" BY THE DEMON LORD.

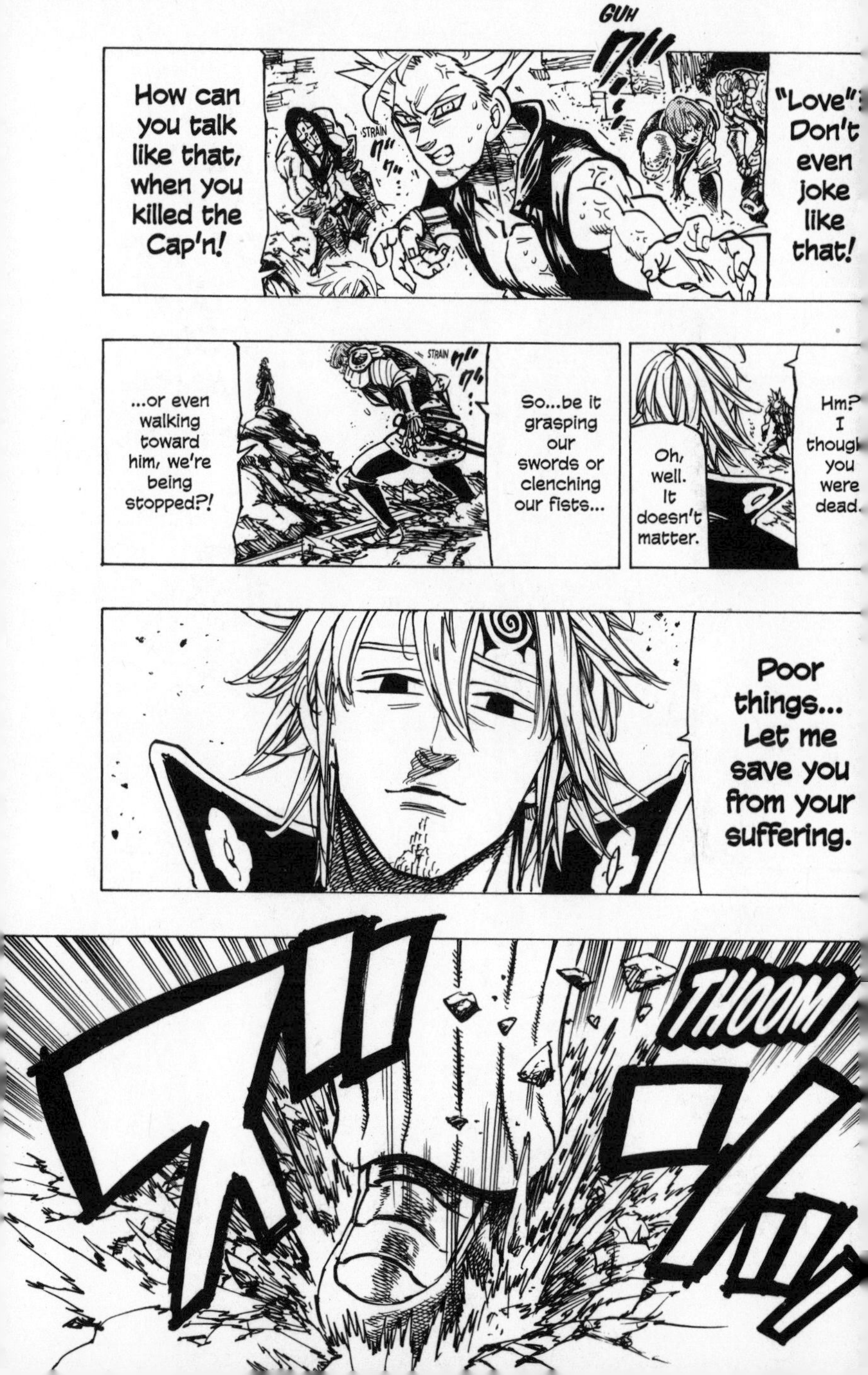

GUH
"Love"?
Don't even joke like that!
STRAIN
How can you talk like that, when you killed the Cap'n!
Hm? I thoug you were dead.
Oh, well. It doesn't matter.
STRAIN
So...be it grasping our swords or clenching our fists...
...or even walking toward him, we're being stopped?!
Poor things... Let me save you from your suffering.
THOOM

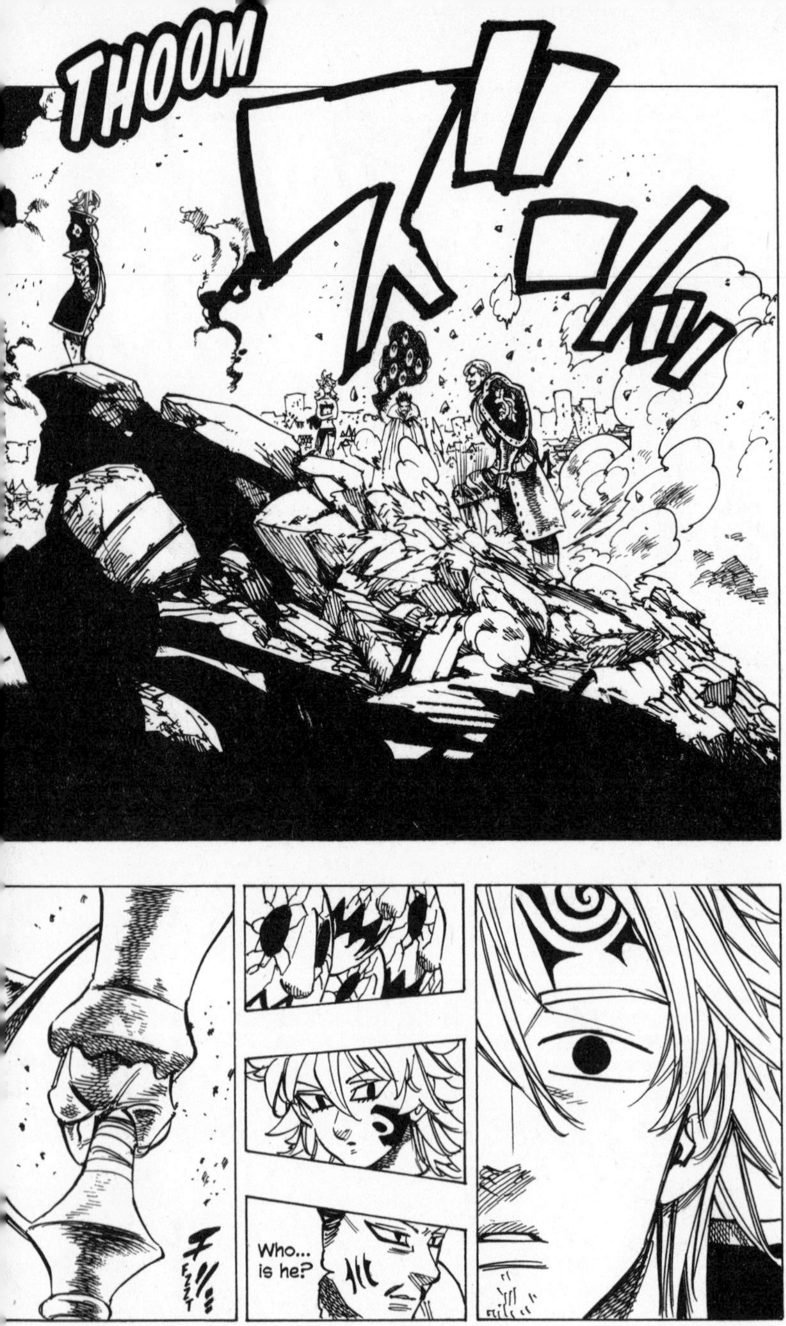
THOOM
Who... is he?
FZZT

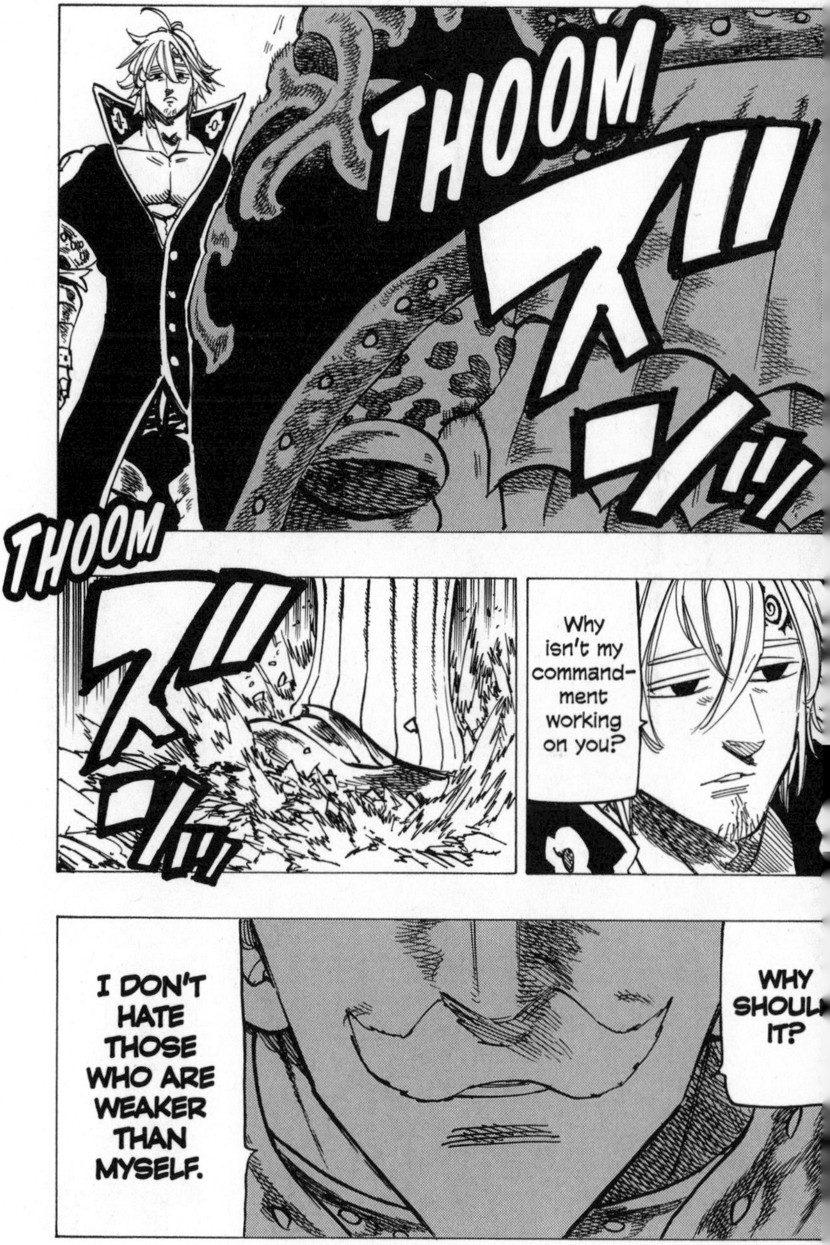
THOOM
Why isn't my command-ment working on you?
THOOM
WHY SHOUL IT?
I DON'T HATE THOSE WHO ARE WEAKER THAN MYSELF.

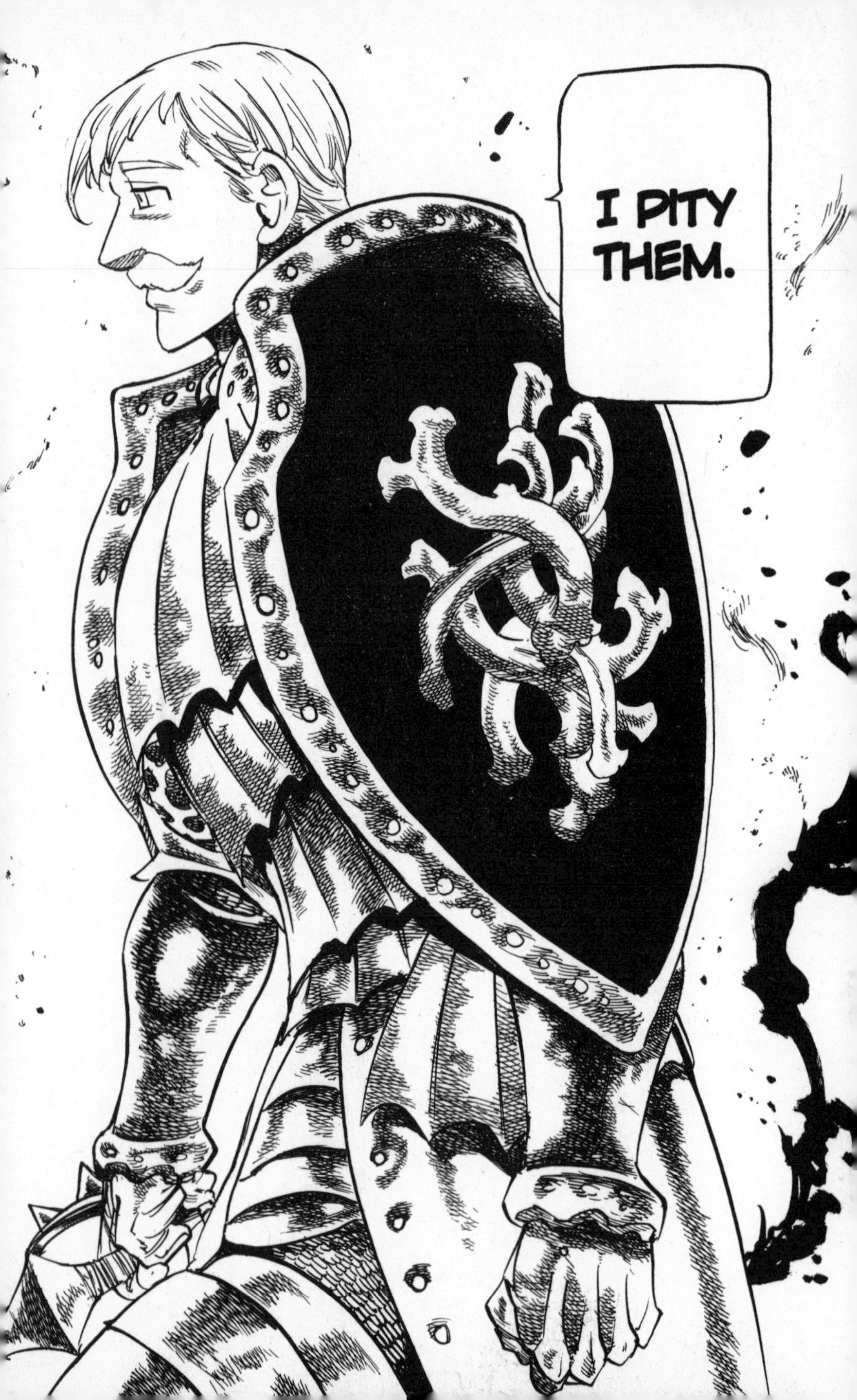
I PITY THEM.

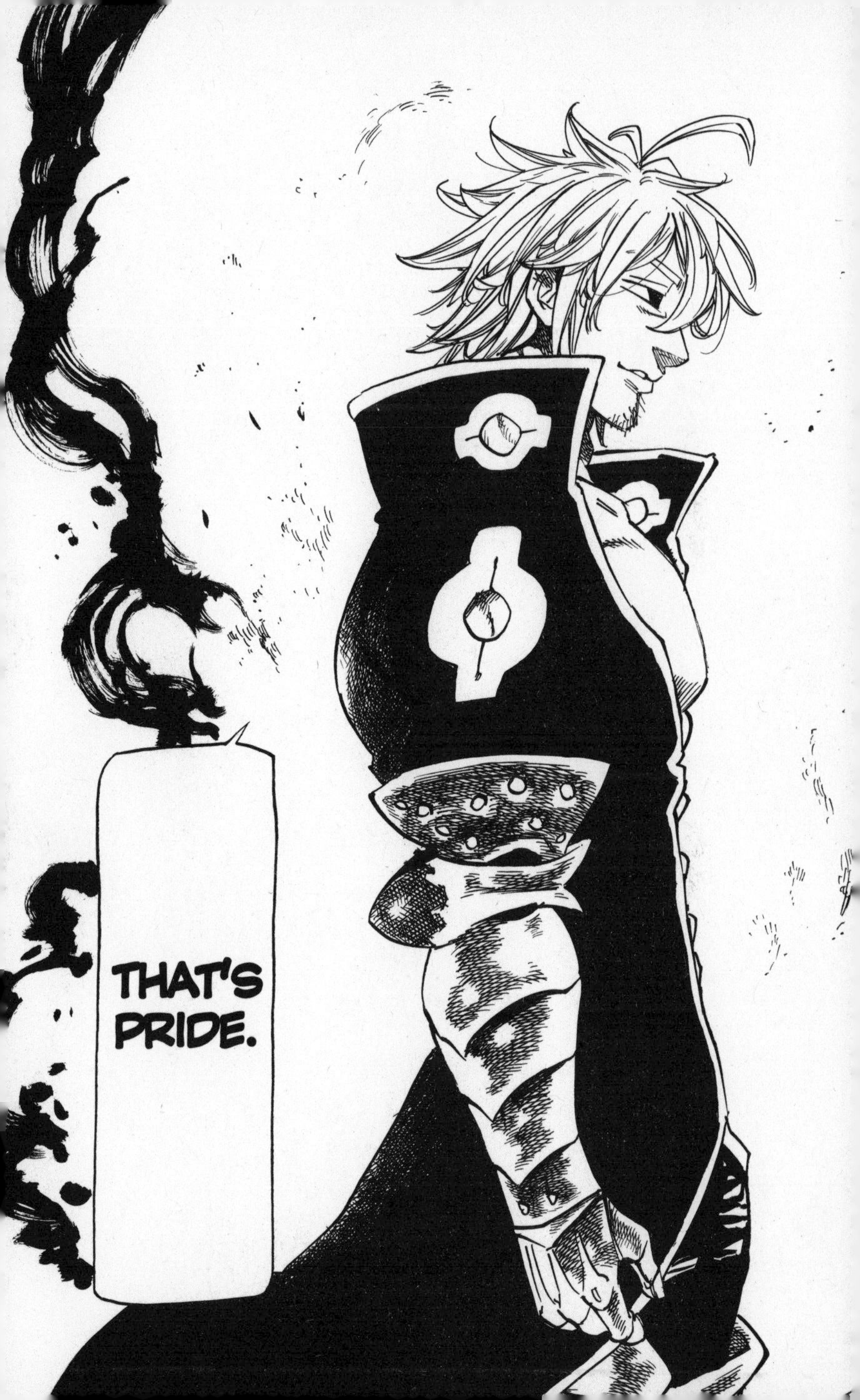
THAT'S PRIDE.

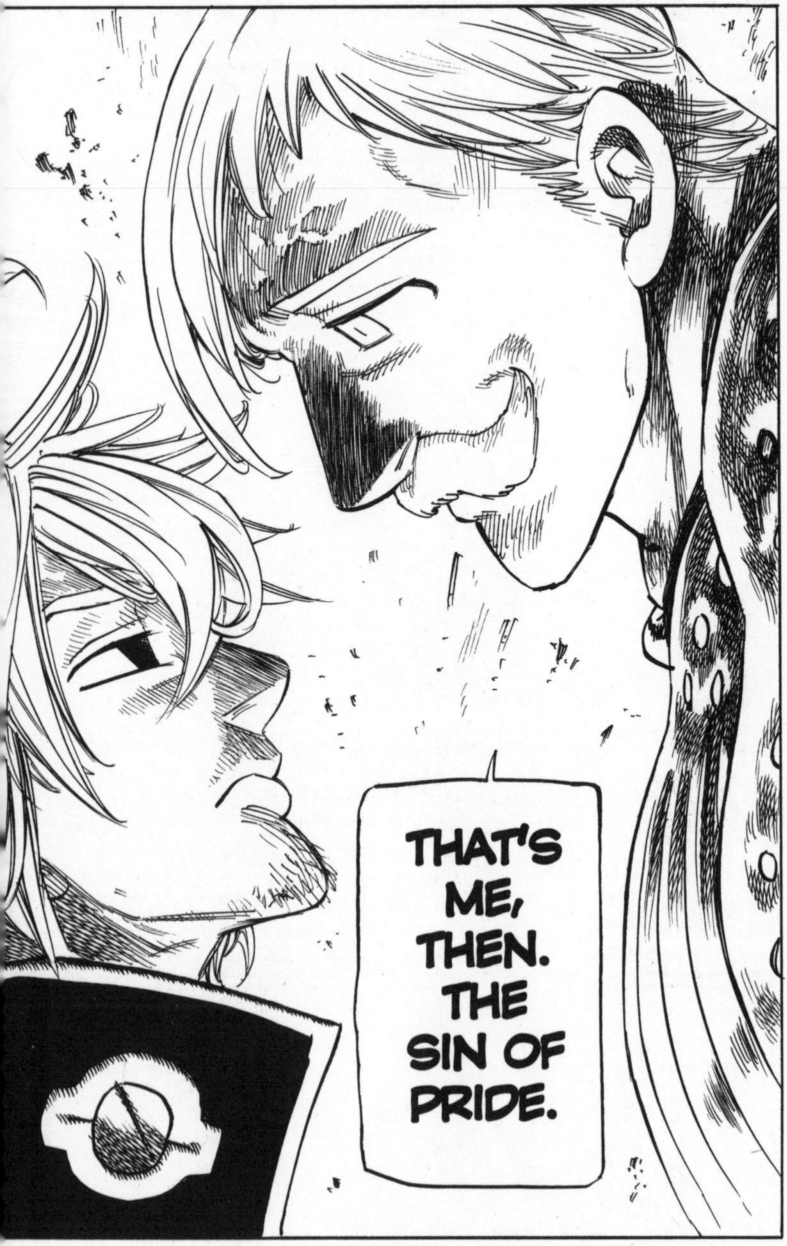
THAT'S ME, THEN. THE SIN OF PRIDE.

Chapter 184 - Mega Clash!

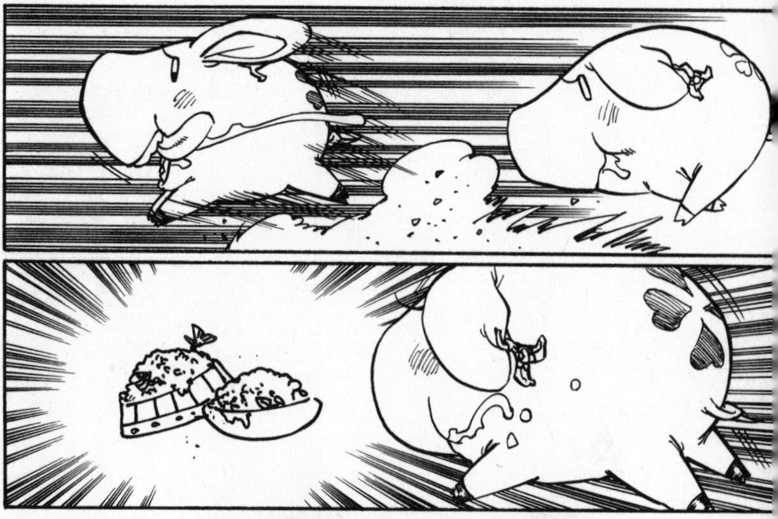

THE SEVEN DEADLY SINS

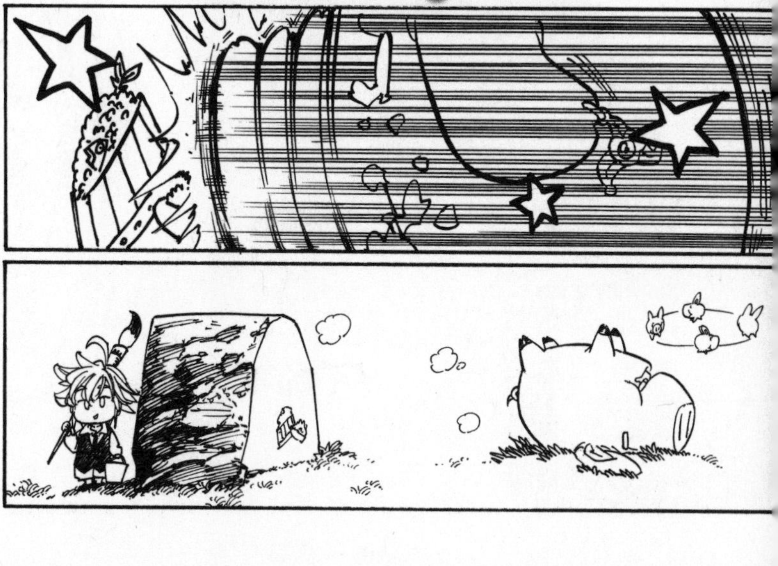

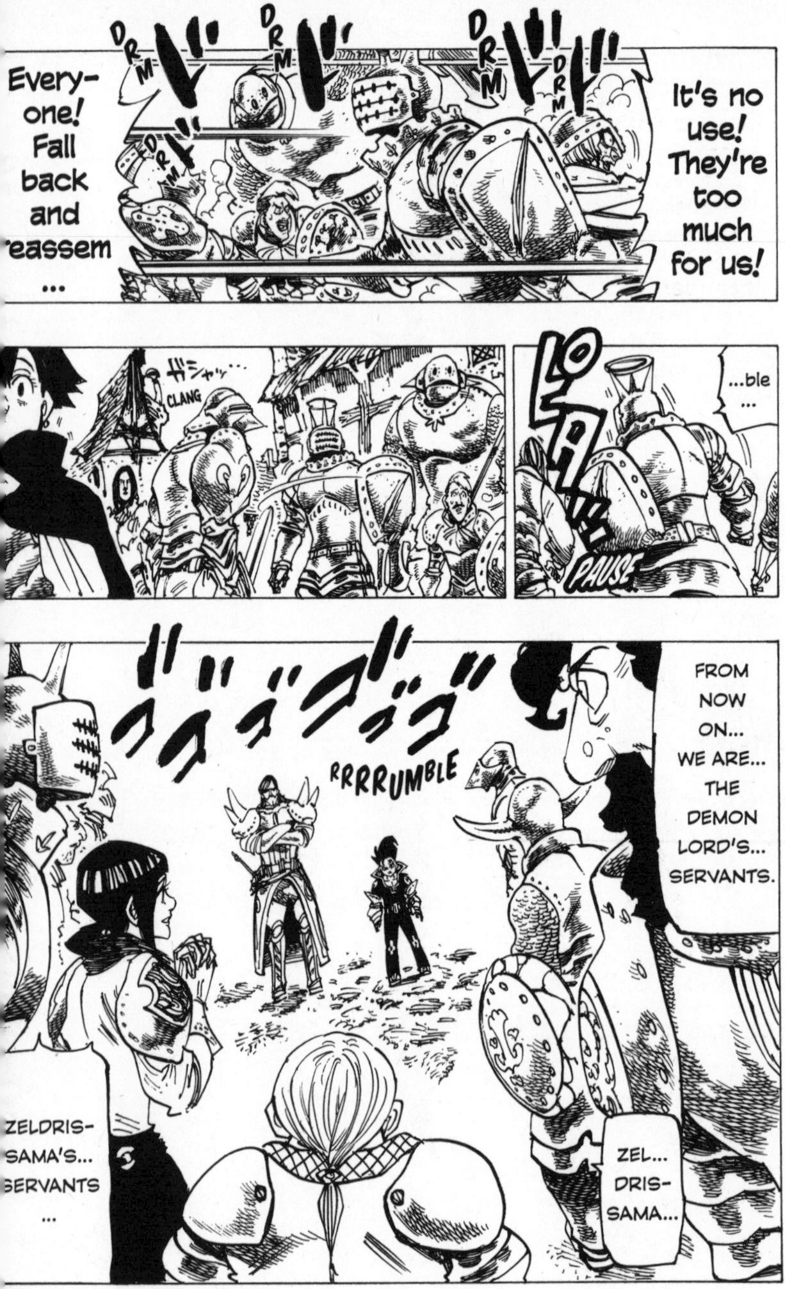
DRM
DRM
DRM
DRM
DRM
It's no use! They're too much for us!
Every- one! Fall back and reassem...
...ble...
PAUSE
ガシャッ
CLANG
FROM NOW ON... WE ARE... THE DEMON LORD'S... SERVANTS.
RRRRUMBLE
ZEL... DRIS- SAMA...
ZELDRIS- SAMA'S... SERVANTS...

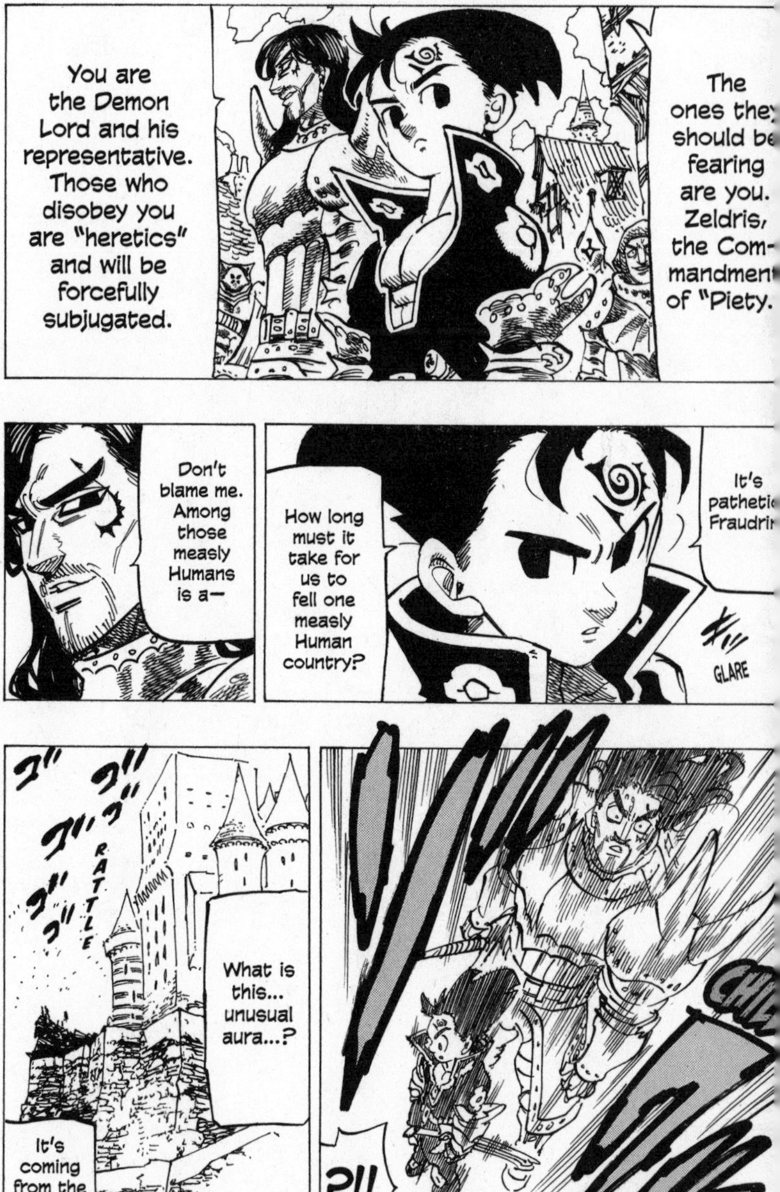
The ones the
should be
fearing are you. Zeldris, the Com-mandmen
of "Piety.
You are the Demon Lord and his representative. Those who disobey you are "heretics" and will be forcefully subjugated.
It's patheti
Fraudri
How long must it take for us to fell one measly Human country?
GLARE
Don't blame me. Among those measly Humans is a—
CHI
?!!
RATTLE
What is this... unusual aura...?
It's coming from the castle.

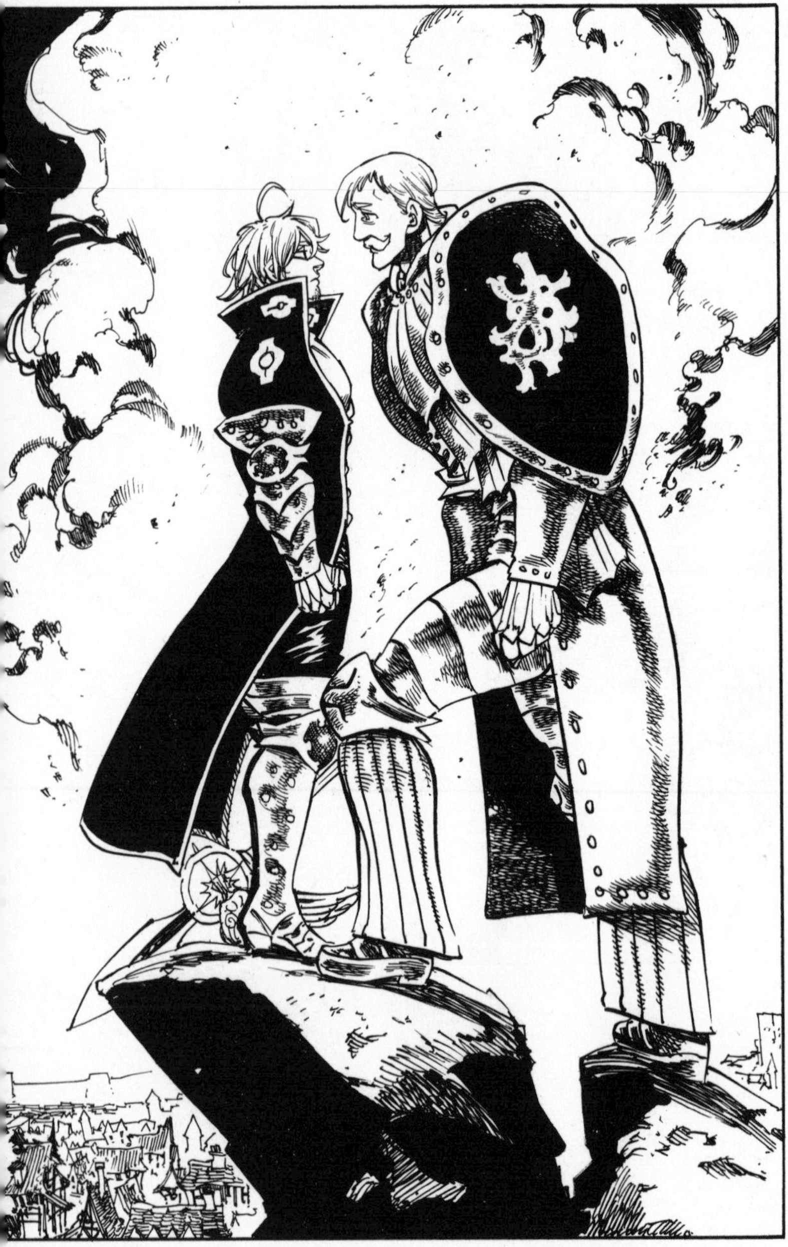

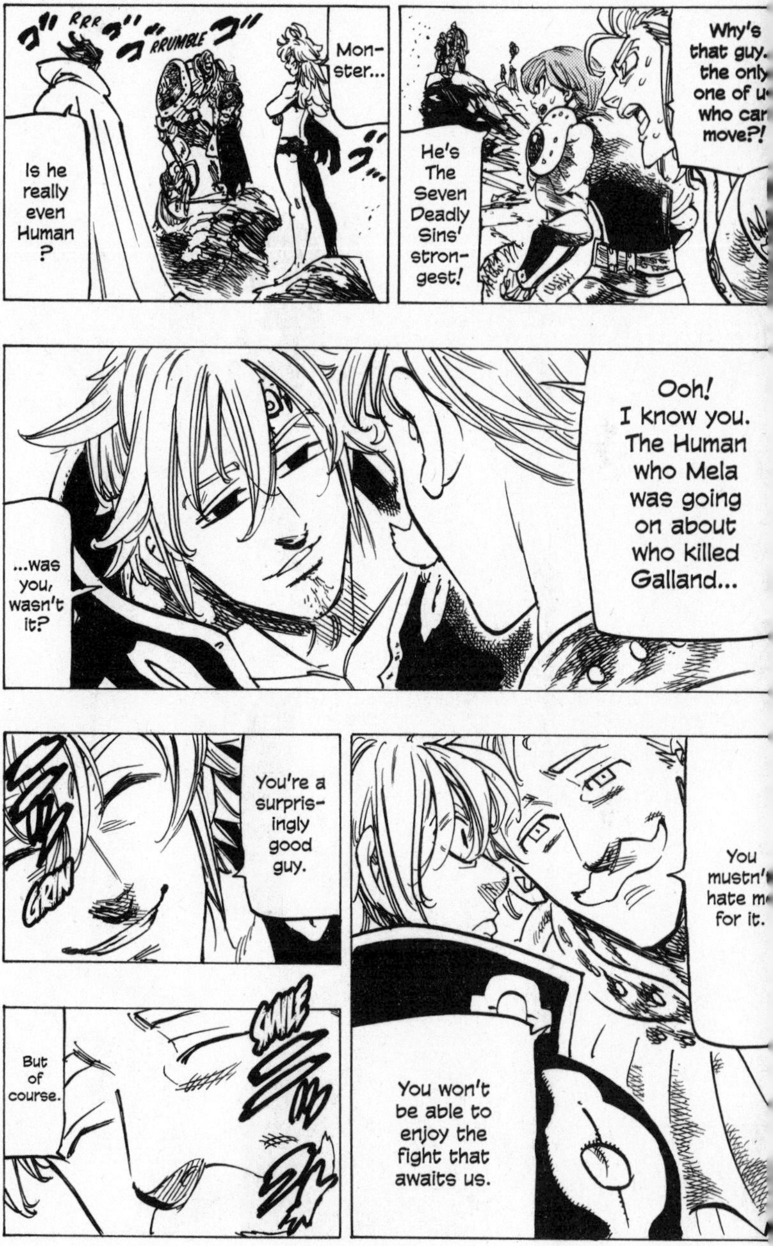
Why's that guy... the only one of u who ca move?!
He's The Seven Deadly Sins' strongest!
RRR
RRUMBLE
Monster...
Is he really even Human?
Ooh! I know you. The Human who Mela was going on about who killed Galland...
...was you, wasn't it?
You mustn' hate m for it.
You won't be able to enjoy the fight that awaits us.
You're a surprisingly good guy.
GRIN
SMILE
But of course.

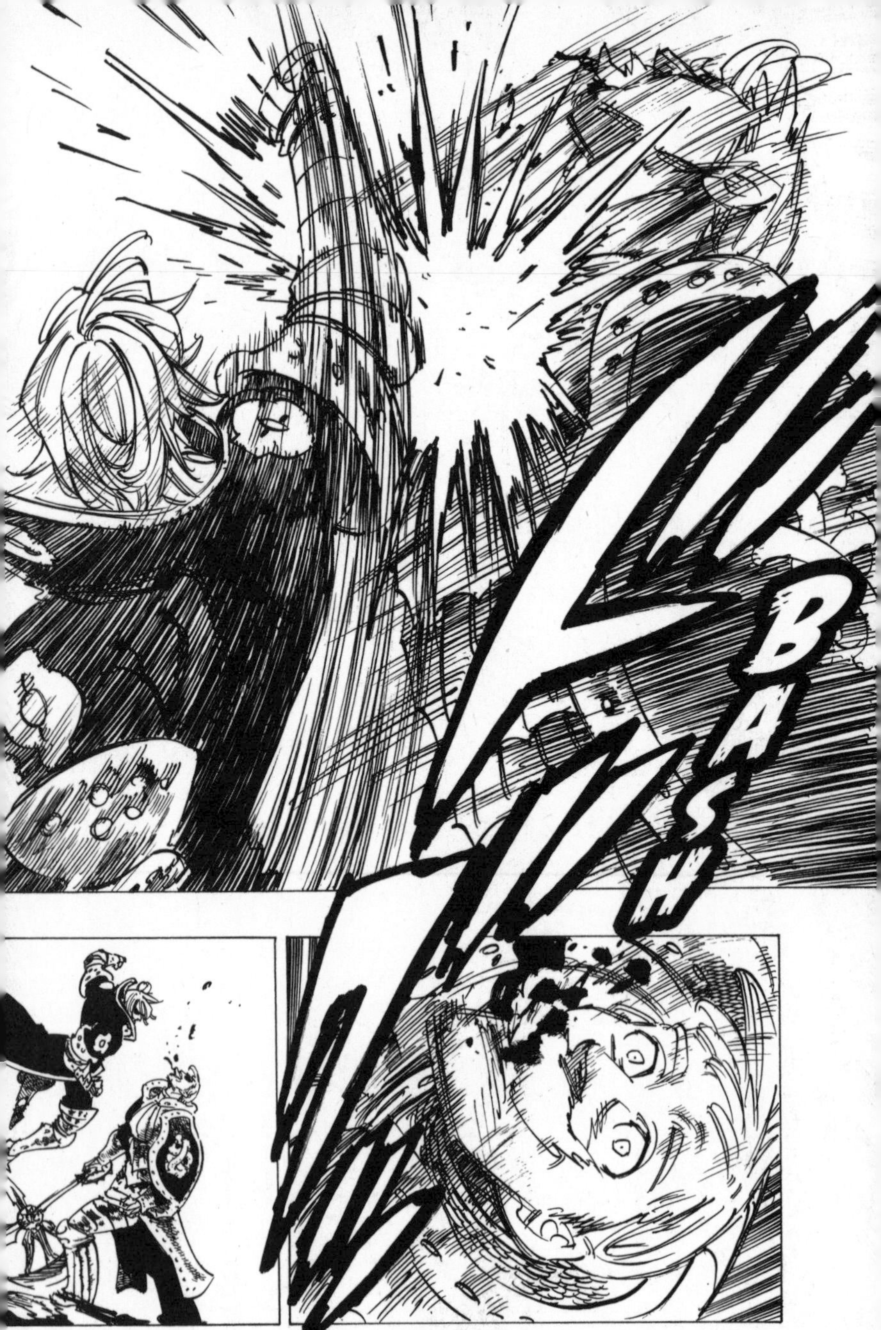
BASH

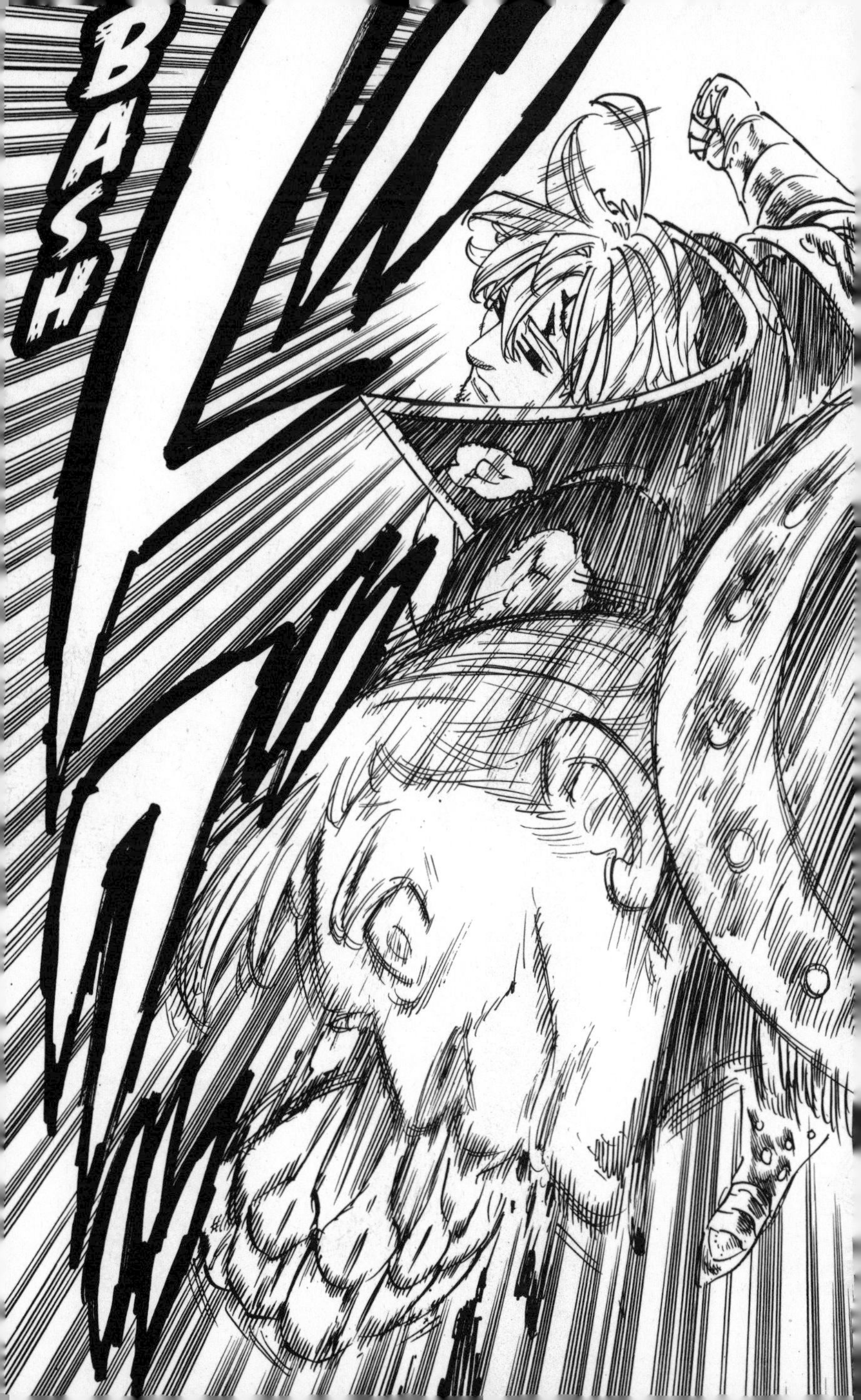
BASH

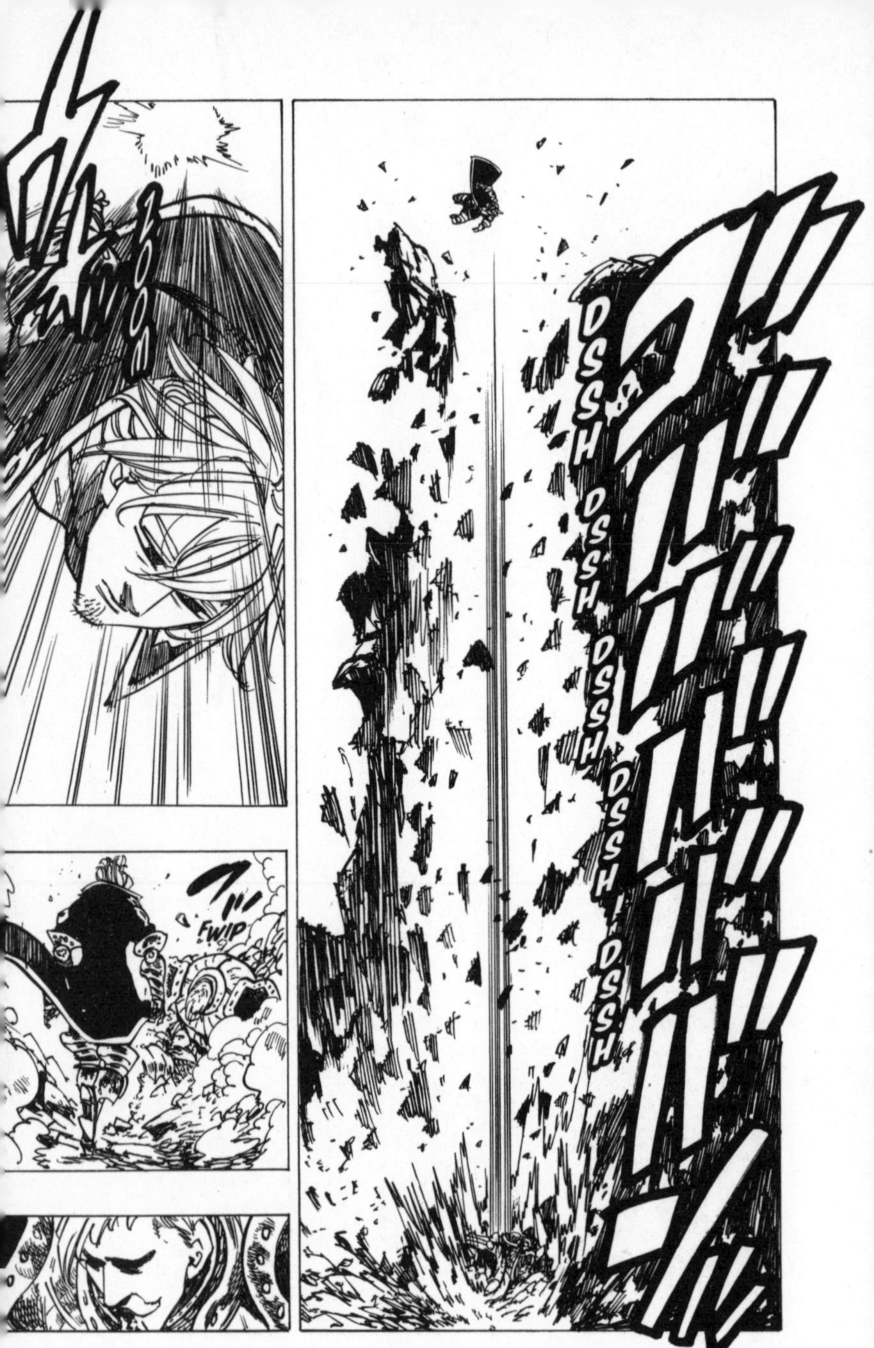
DSSH DSSH DSSH DSSH DSSH
ZOOOM
FWIP

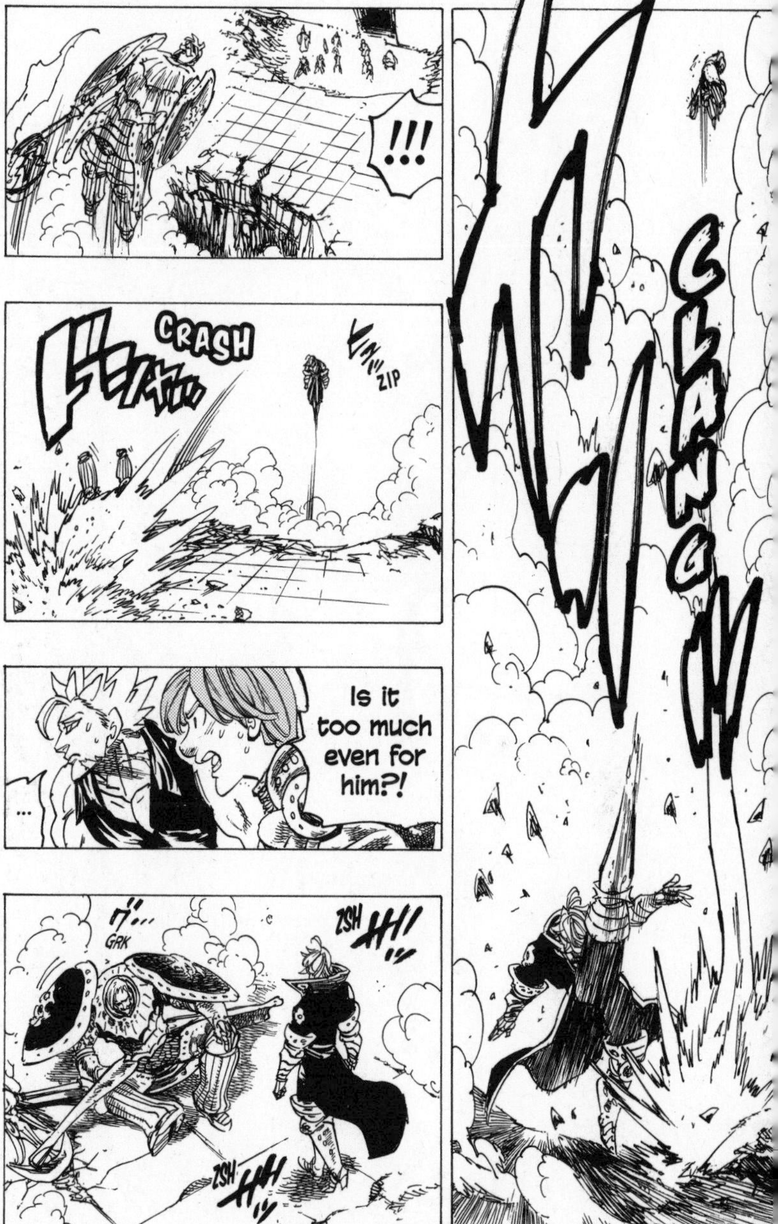
CLANG
!!!
ZIP
CRASH
Is it too much even for him?!
...
ZSH
GRK
ZSH

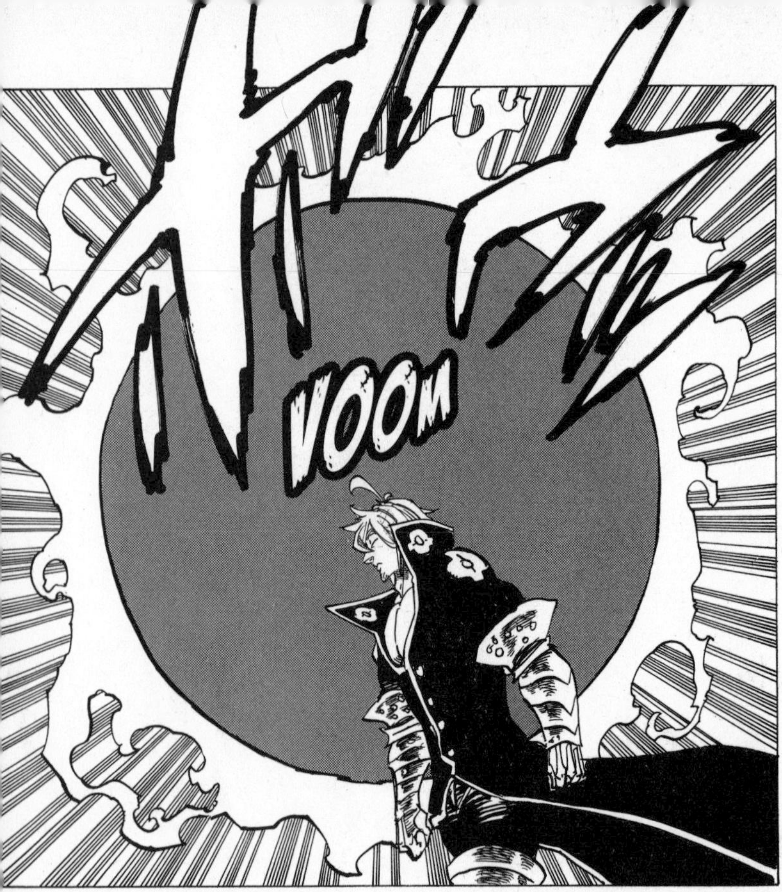
VOOM
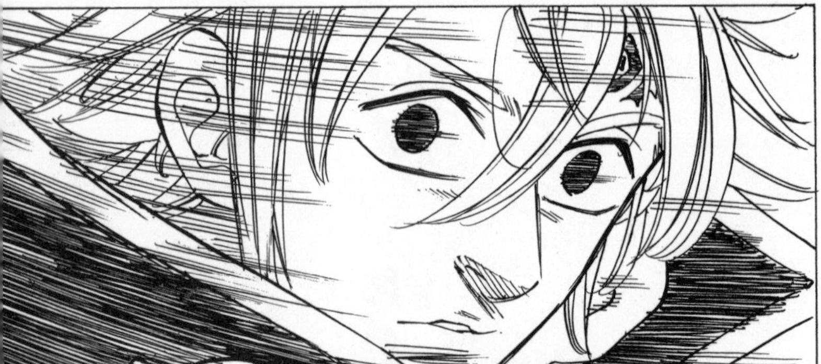

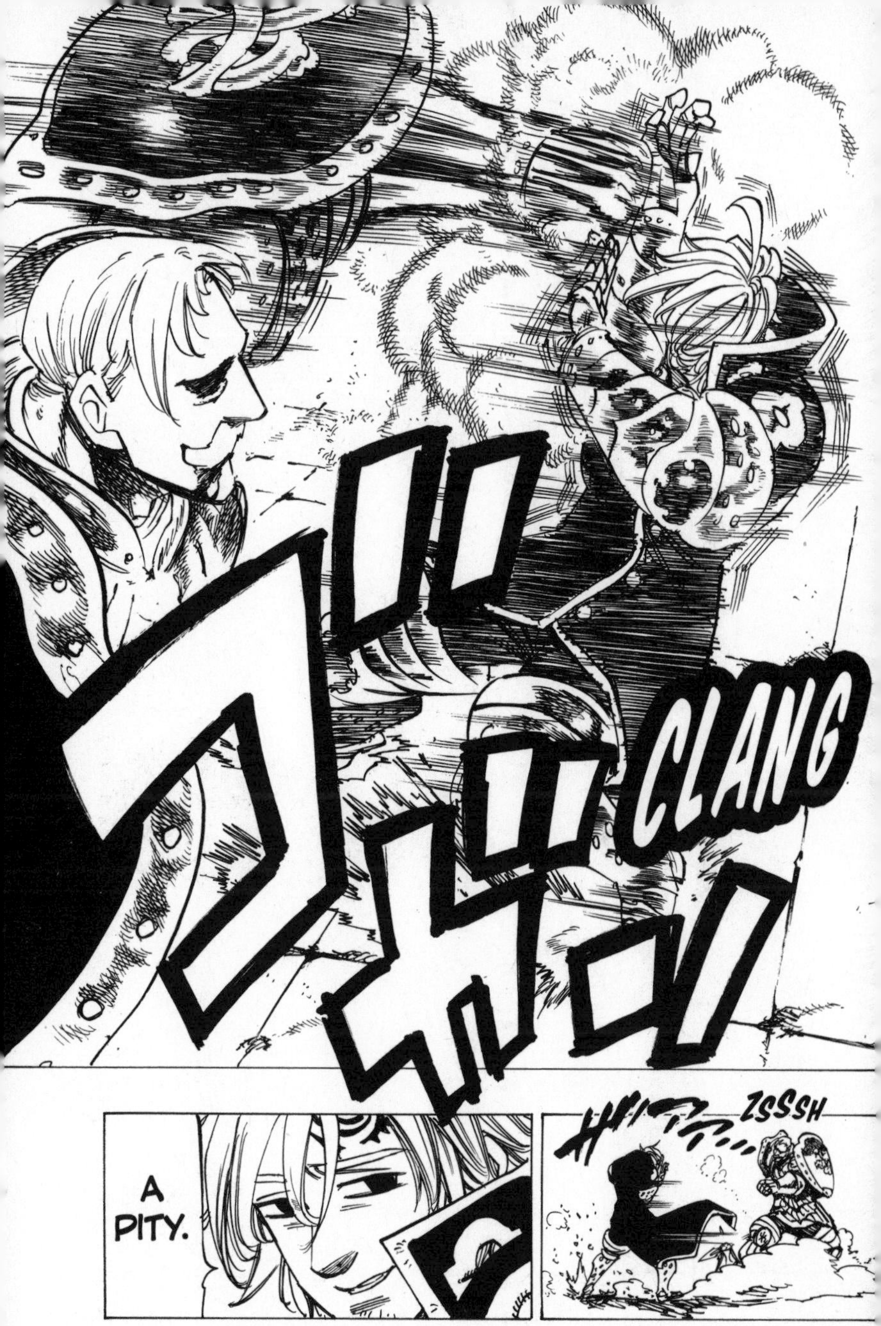
CLANG
ZSSSH
A PITY.

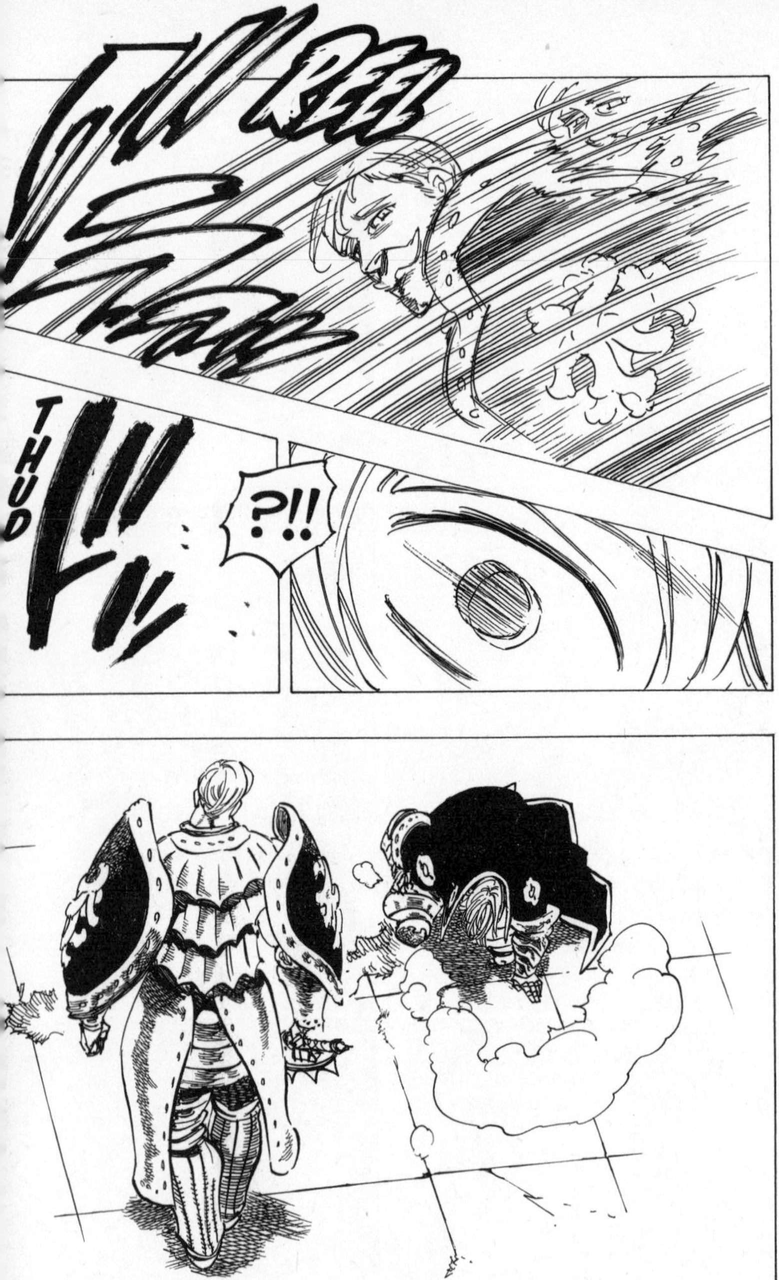
?!!
THUD

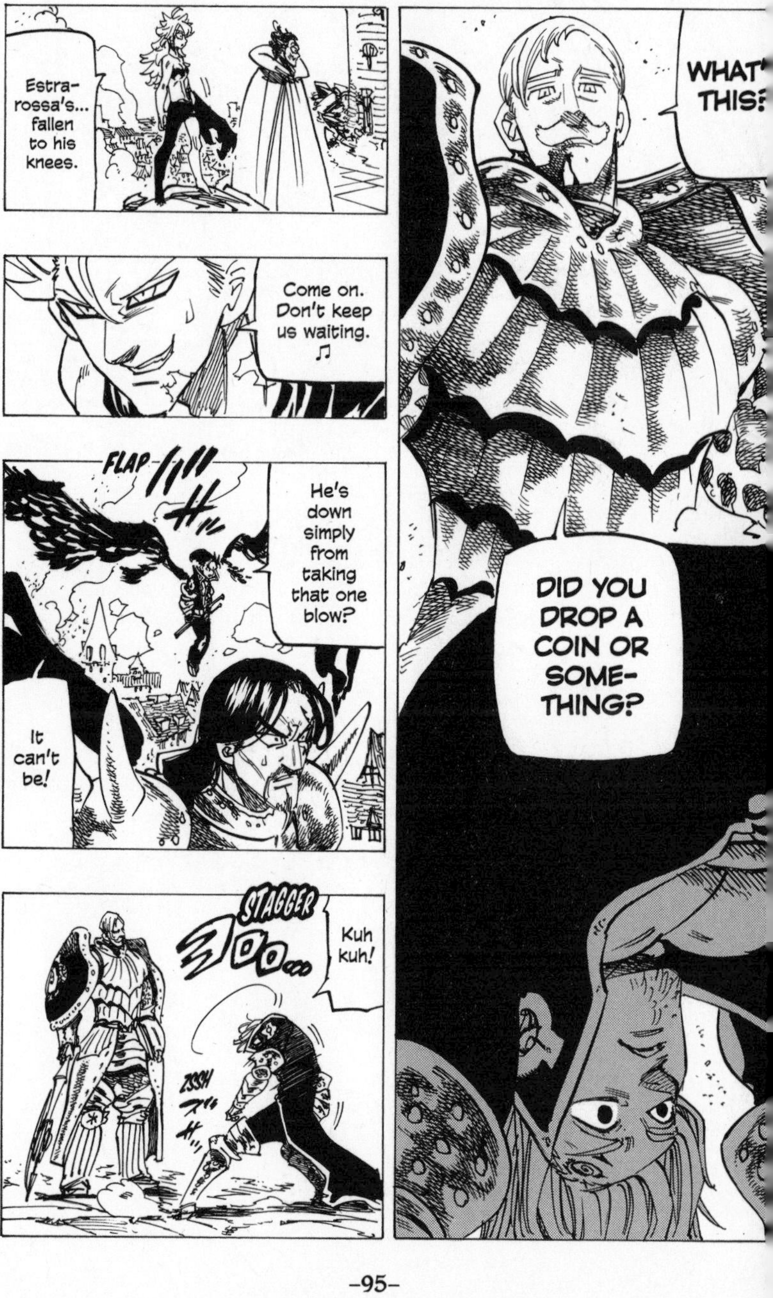
WHAT' THIS?
DID YOU DROP A COIN OR SOME-THING?
Estra-rossa's... fallen to his knees.
Come on. Don't keep us waiting. ♫
FLAP
He's down simply from taking that one blow?
It can't be!
STAGGER
Kuh kuh!
ZSSH

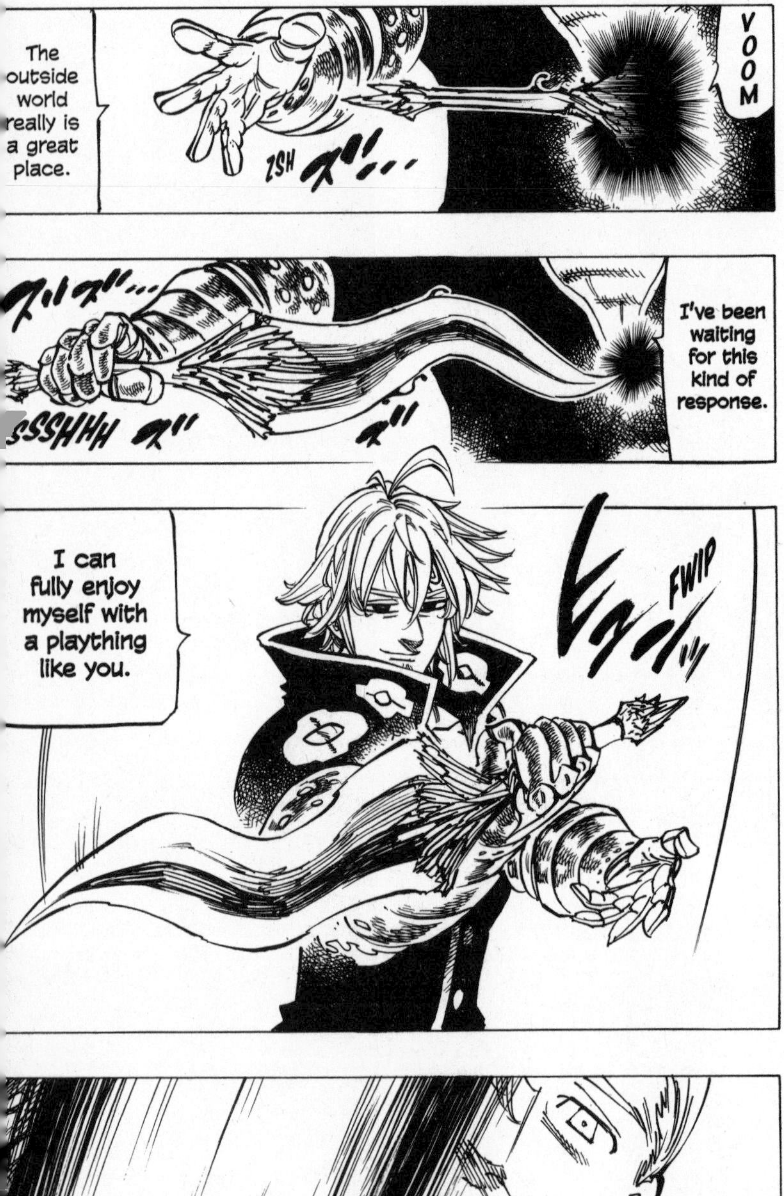
VOOM
The outside world really is a great place.
ZSH
I've been waiting for this kind of response.
SSSHHH
FWIP
I can fully enjoy myself with a plaything like you.

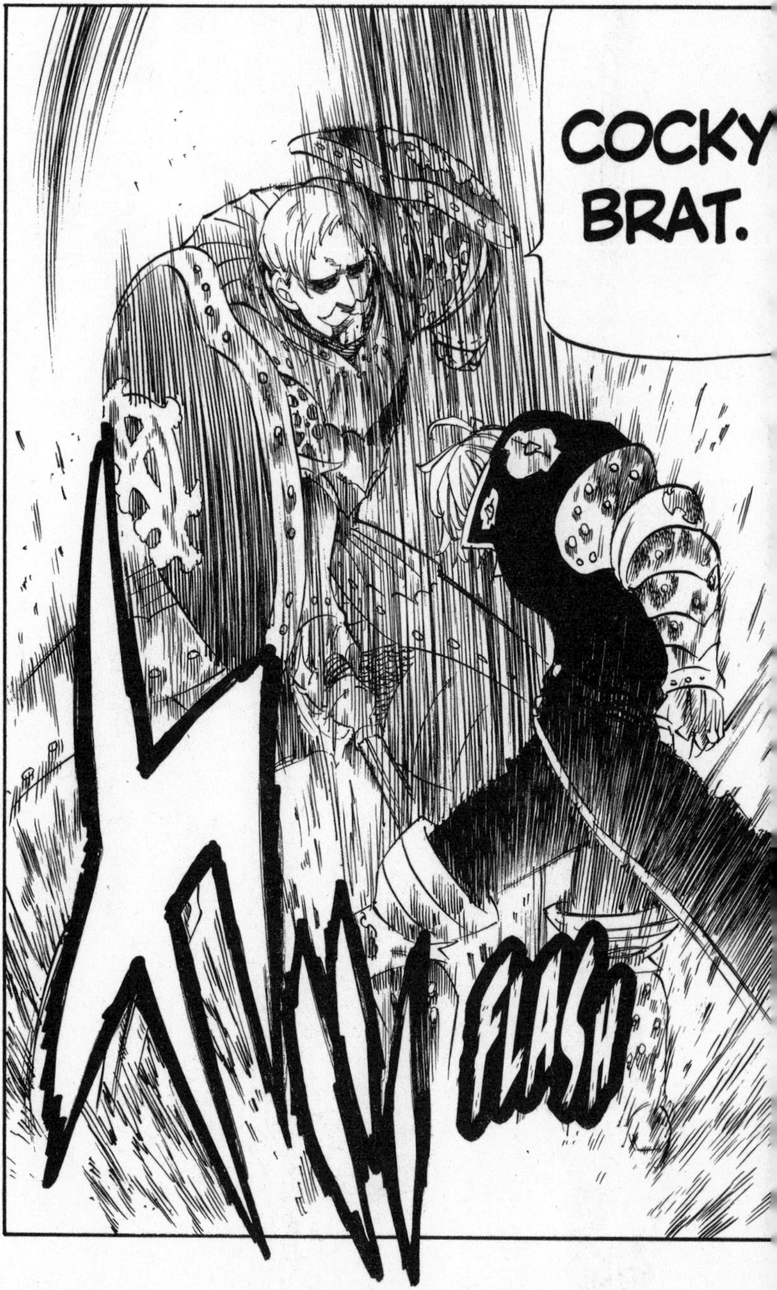
COCKY BRAT.
FLASH

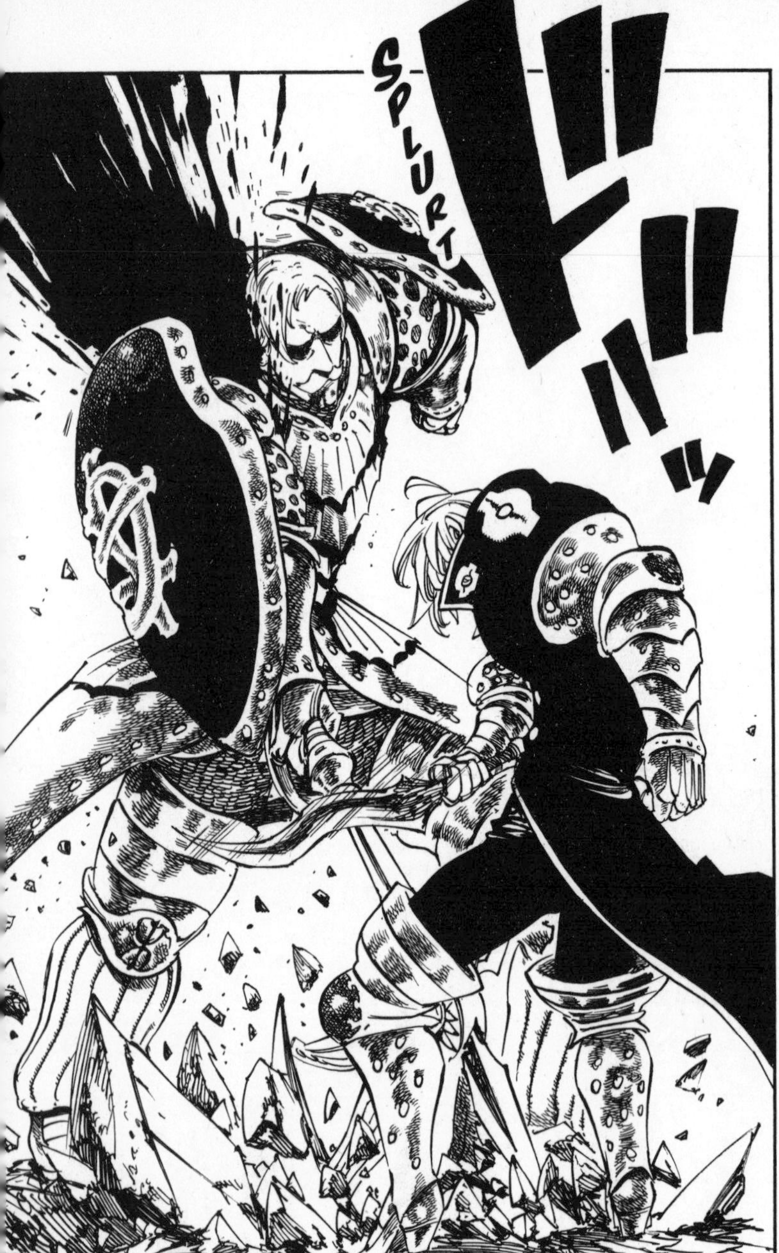
SPLURT
ドゴゴッ

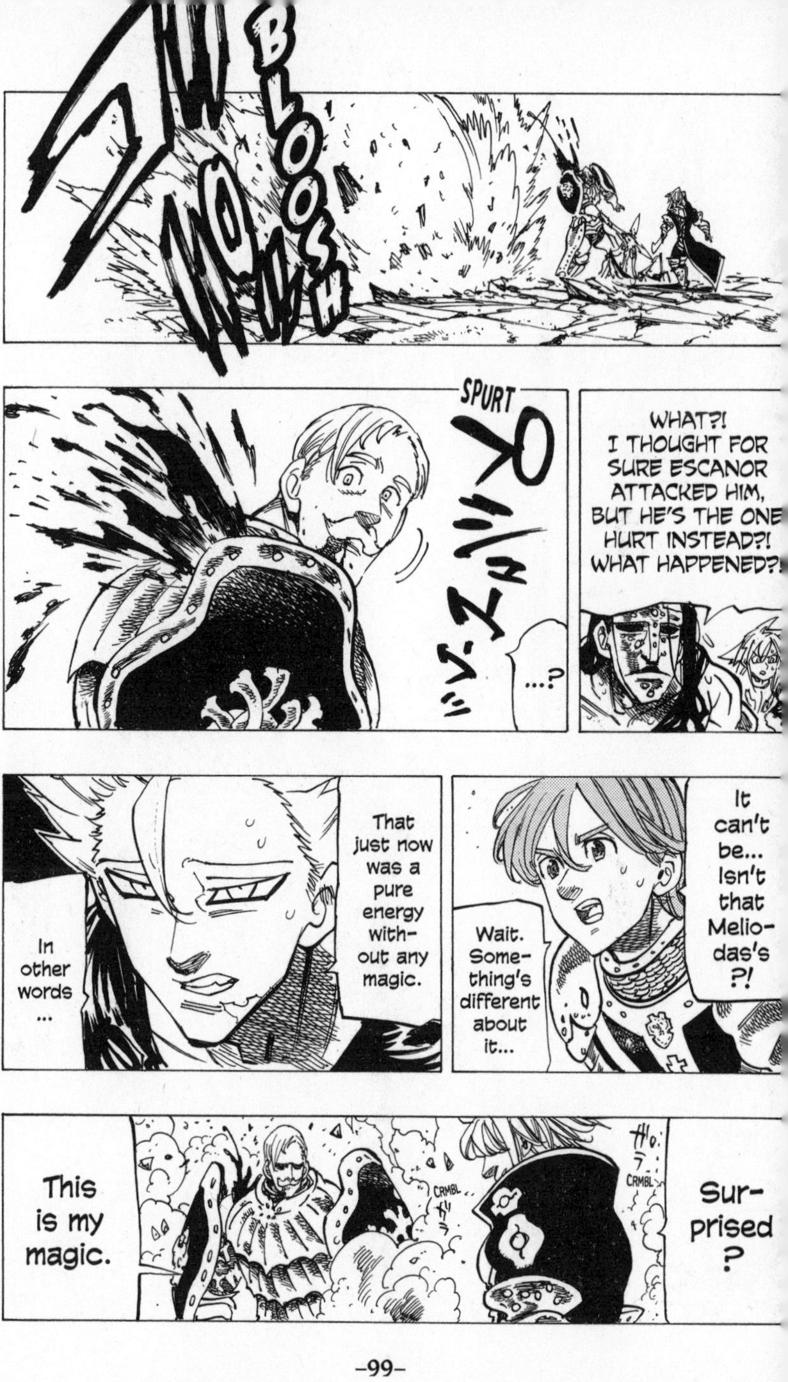
BLOOSH
WHAT?! I THOUGHT FOR SURE ESCANOR ATTACKED HIM, BUT HE'S THE ONE HURT INSTEAD?! WHAT HAPPENED?!
SPURT
...?
It can't be... Isn't that Meliodas's ?!
Wait. Something's different about it...
That just now was a pure energy without any magic.
In other words ...
Surprised ?
CRMBL
CRMBL
This is my magic.

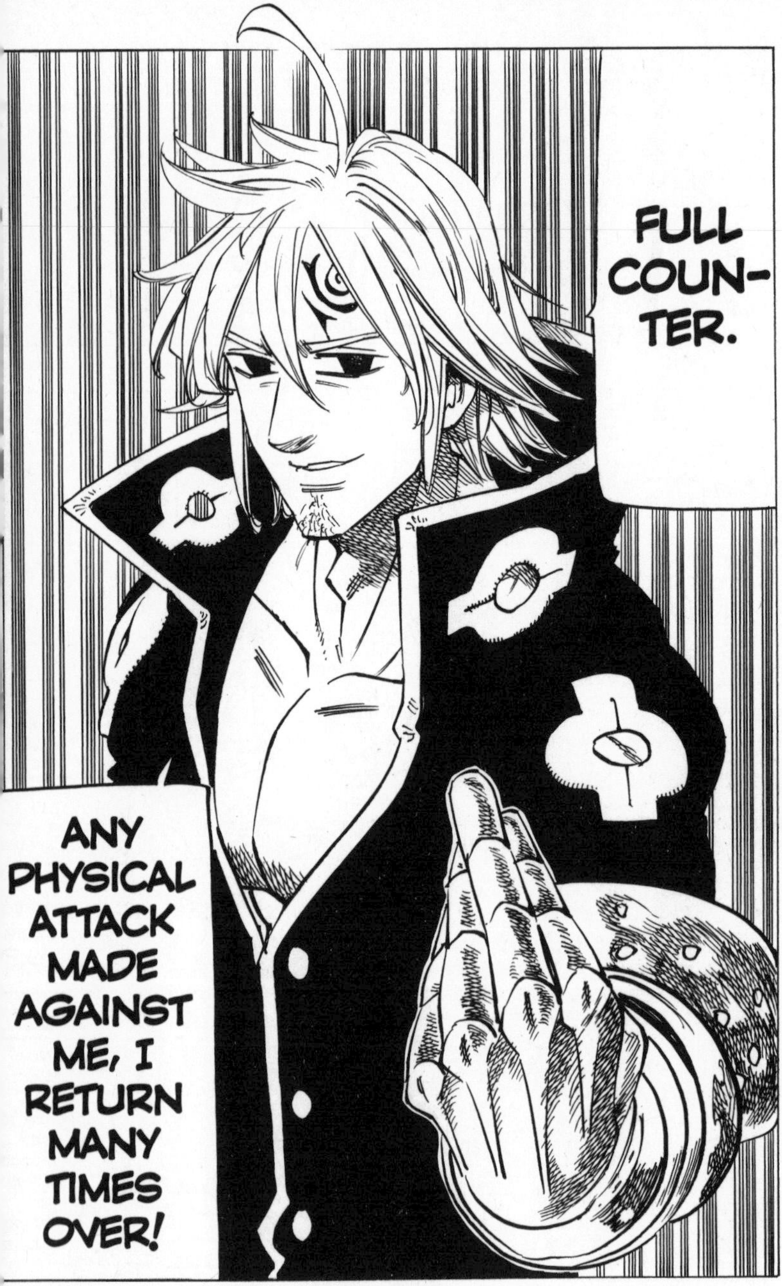
FULL COUN-TER.
ANY PHYSICAL ATTACK MADE AGAINST ME, I RETURN MANY TIMES OVER!

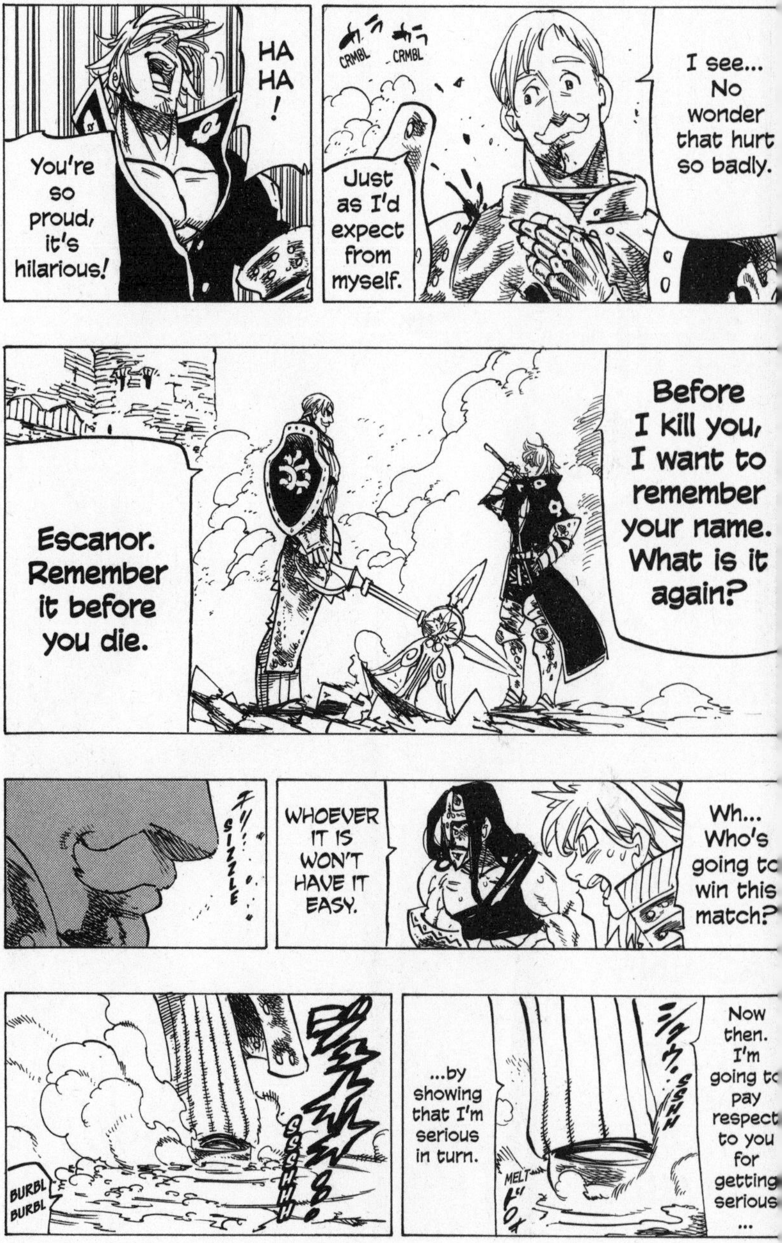
I see... No wonder that hurt so badly.
CRMBL CRMBL
Just as I'd expect from myself.
HA HA !
You're so proud, it's hilarious!
Before I kill you, I want to remember your name. What is it again?
Escanor. Remember it before you die.
Wh... Who's going to win this match?
WHOEVER IT IS WON'T HAVE IT EASY.
SIZZLE
Now then. I'm going to pay respect to you for getting serious...
SSHH
...by showing that I'm serious in turn.
MELT
SSSHHH
BURBL BURBL

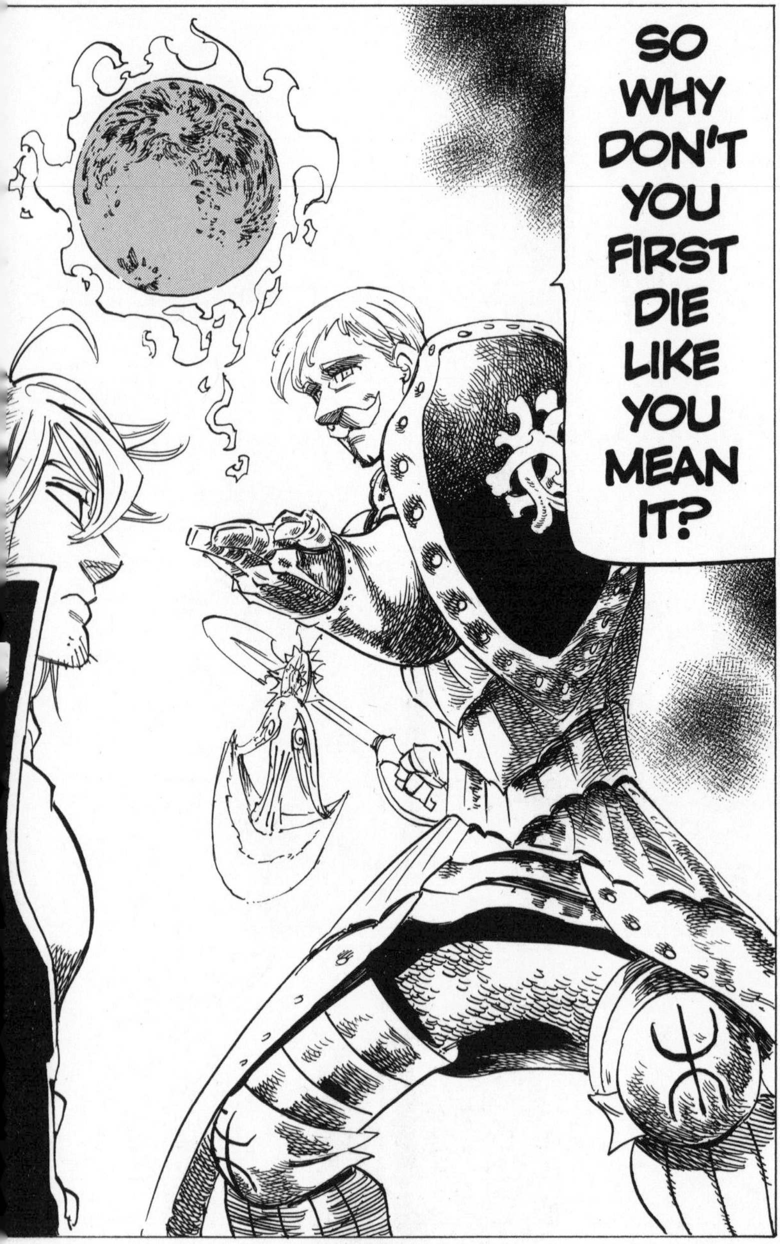
SO WHY DON'T YOU FIRST DIE LIKE YOU MEAN IT?

Chapter 185 - Pride vs. Love

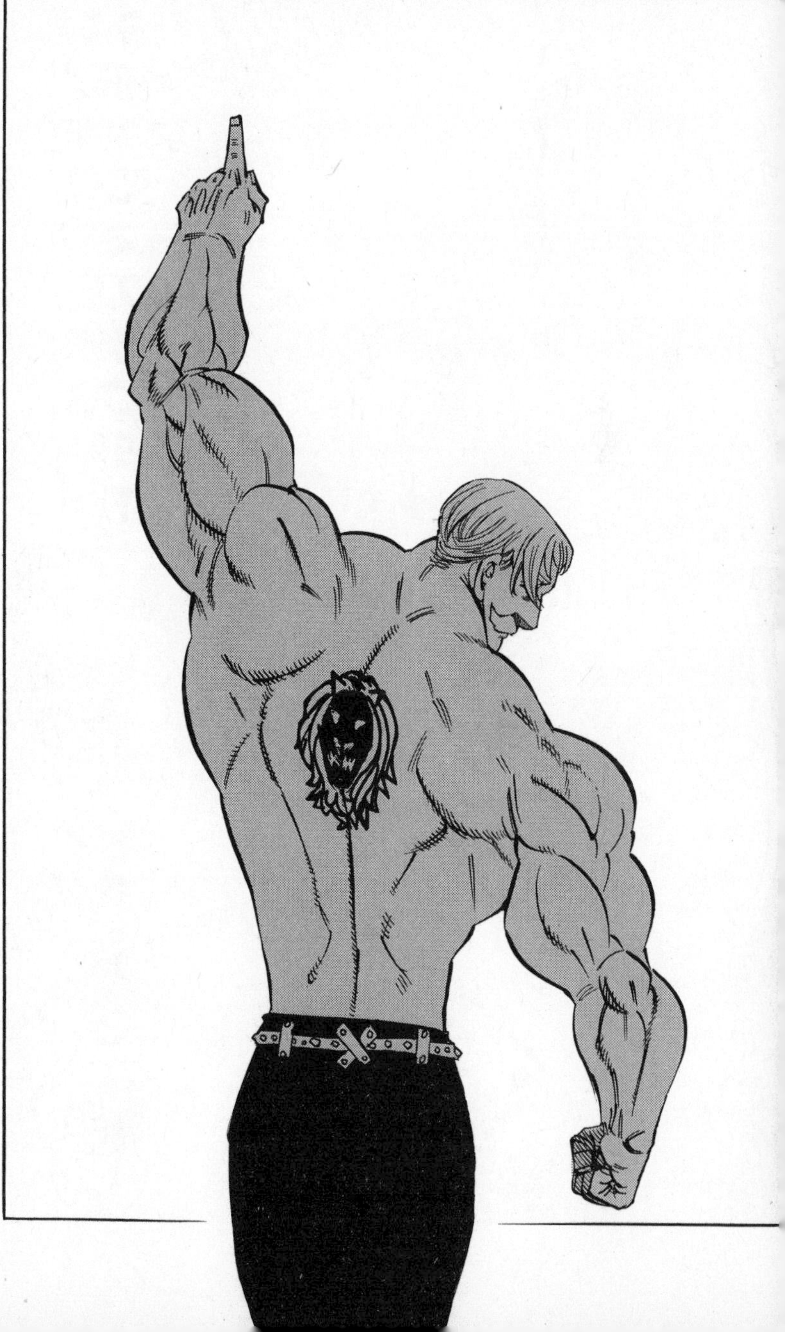

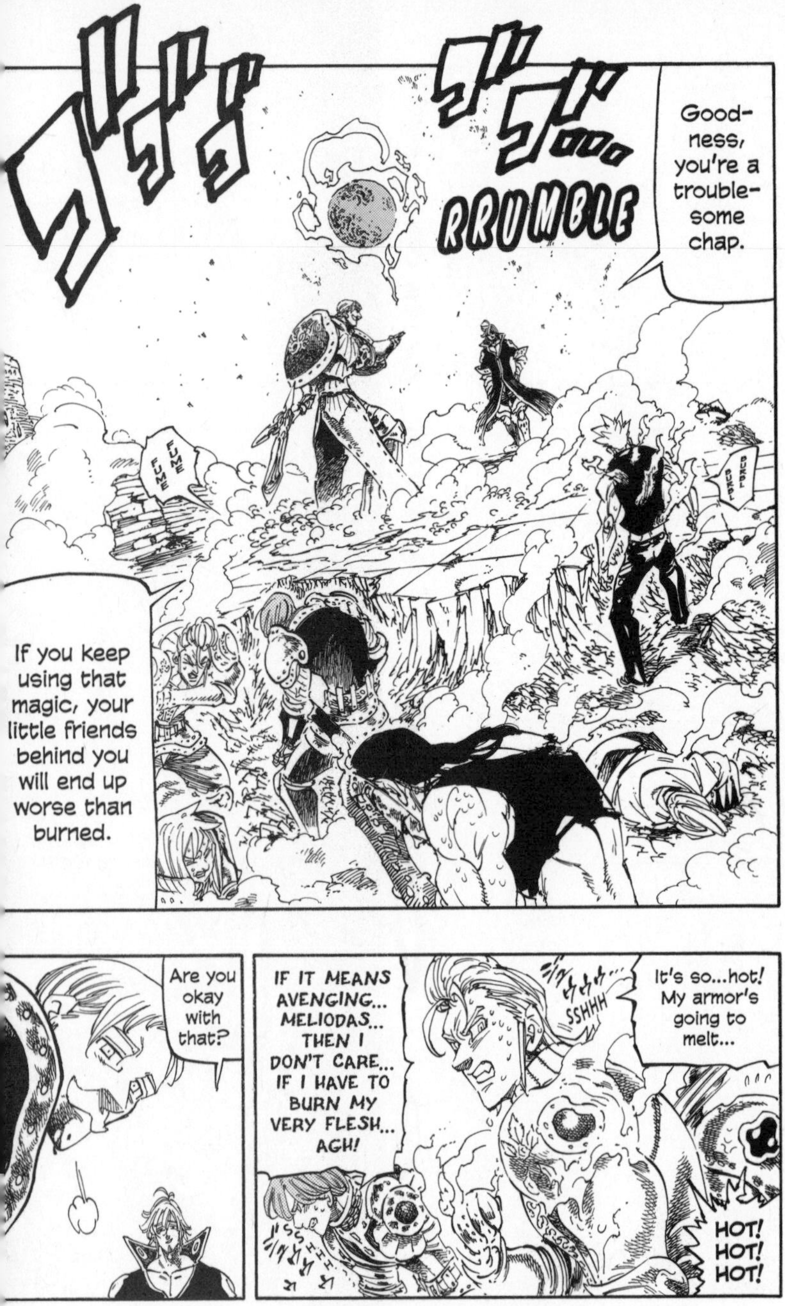
RRUMBLE
Goodness, you're a troublesome chap.
FUME FUME
BURBL BURBL
If you keep using that magic, your little friends behind you will end up worse than burned.
It's so...hot! My armor's going to melt...
SSHHH
IF IT MEANS AVENGING... MELIODAS... THEN I DON'T CARE... IF I HAVE TO BURN MY VERY FLESH... AGH!
HOT! HOT! HOT!
Are you okay with that?

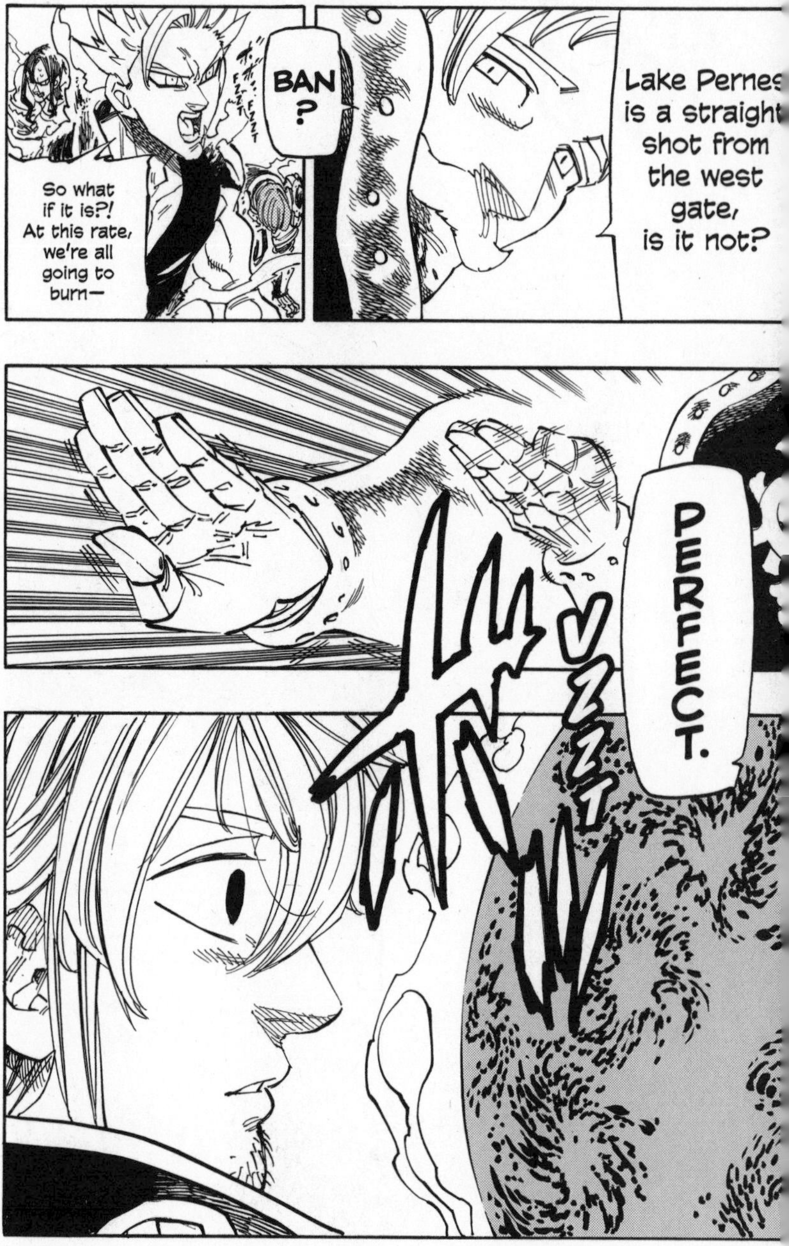
Lake Pernes is a straight shot from the west gate, is it not?
BAN?
FZZT FZZT
So what if it is?! At this rate, we're all going to burn—
PERFECT.
VZZZT

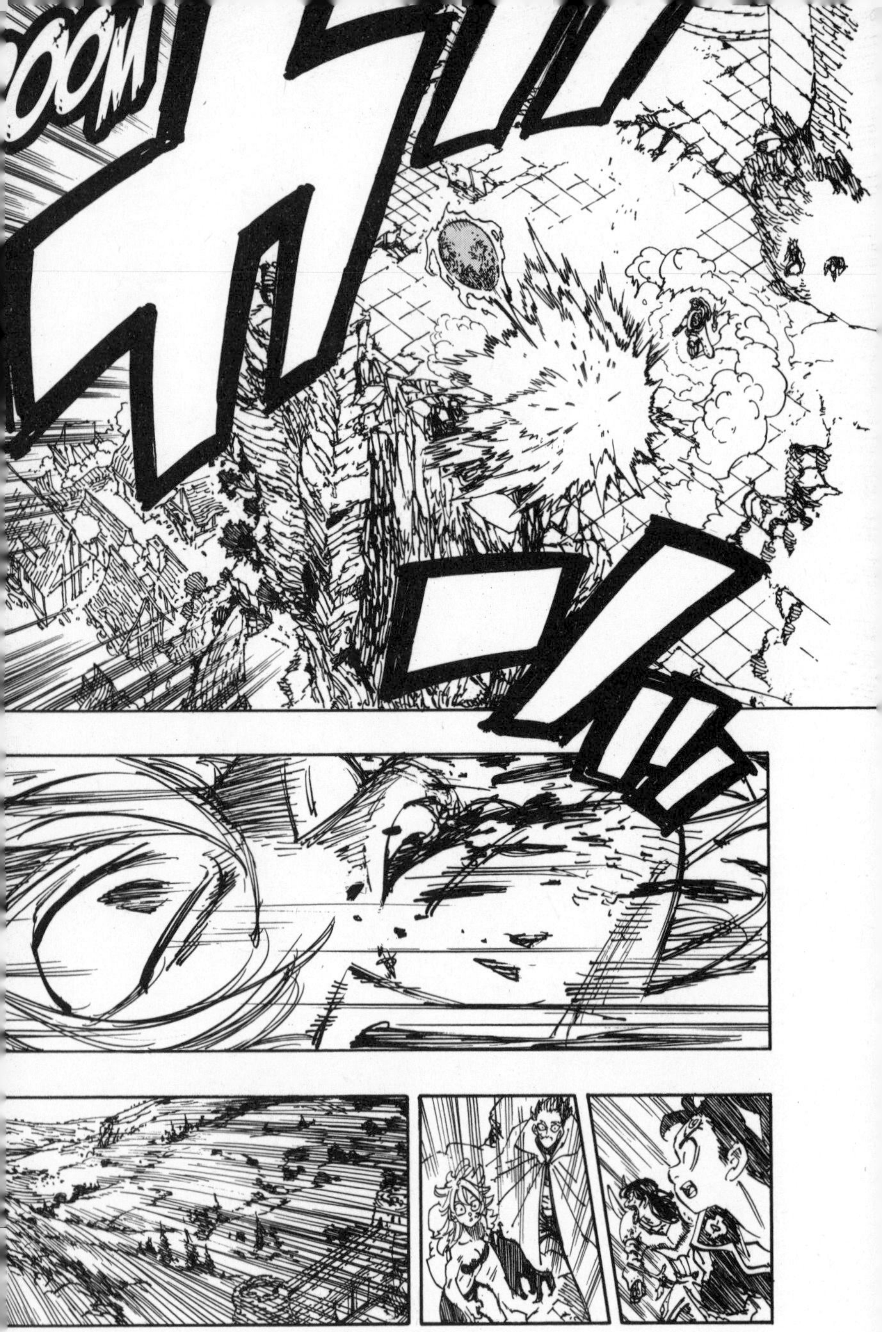
OOM

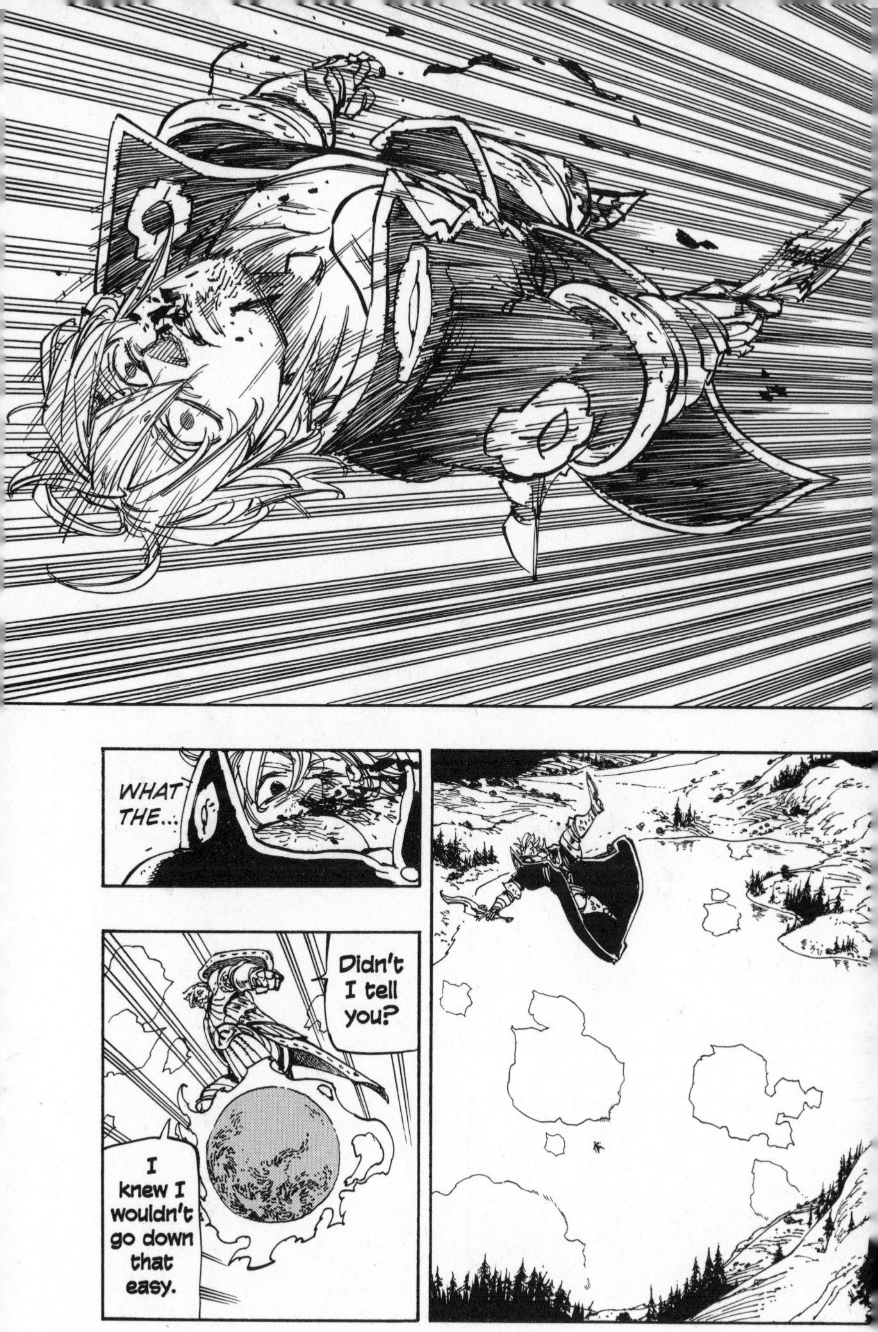
WHAT THE...
Didn't I tell you?
I knew I wouldn't go down that easy.

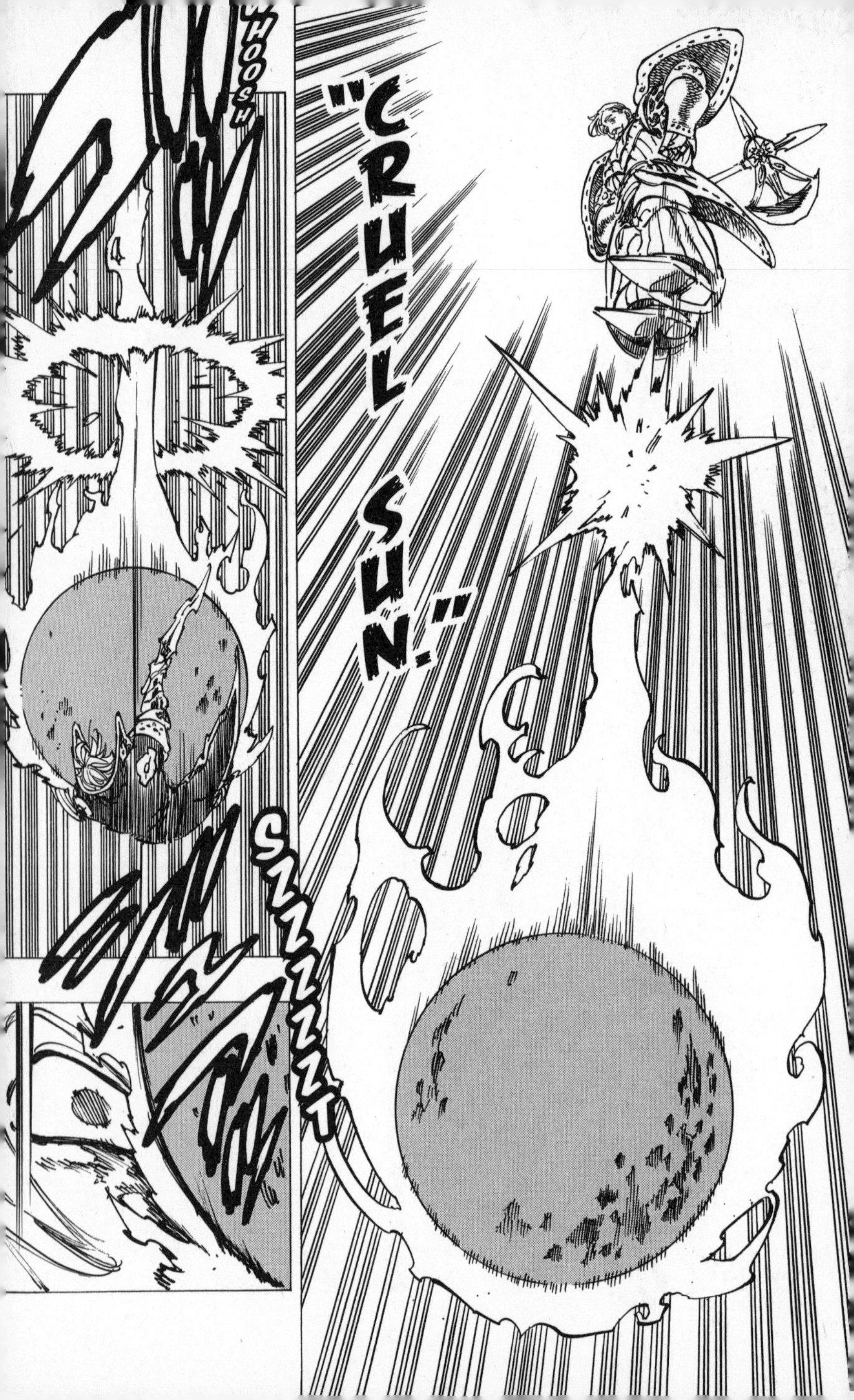
"CRUEL SUN."
WHOOSH
SNNNNNNT

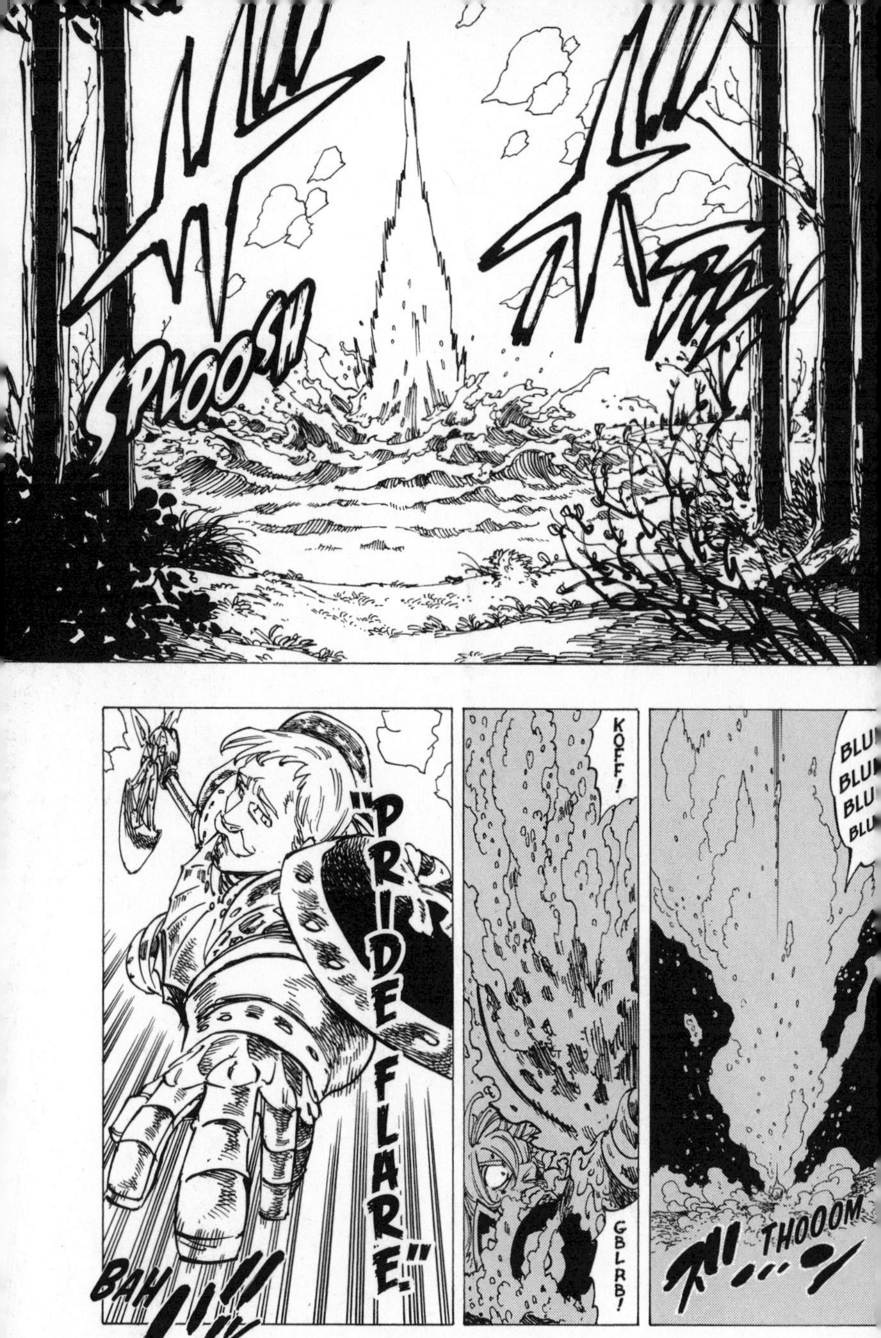
SPLOOSH
BLU BLU BLU BLU
THOOOM
KOFF!
GBLRB!
"PRIDE FLARE."
BAH!!!

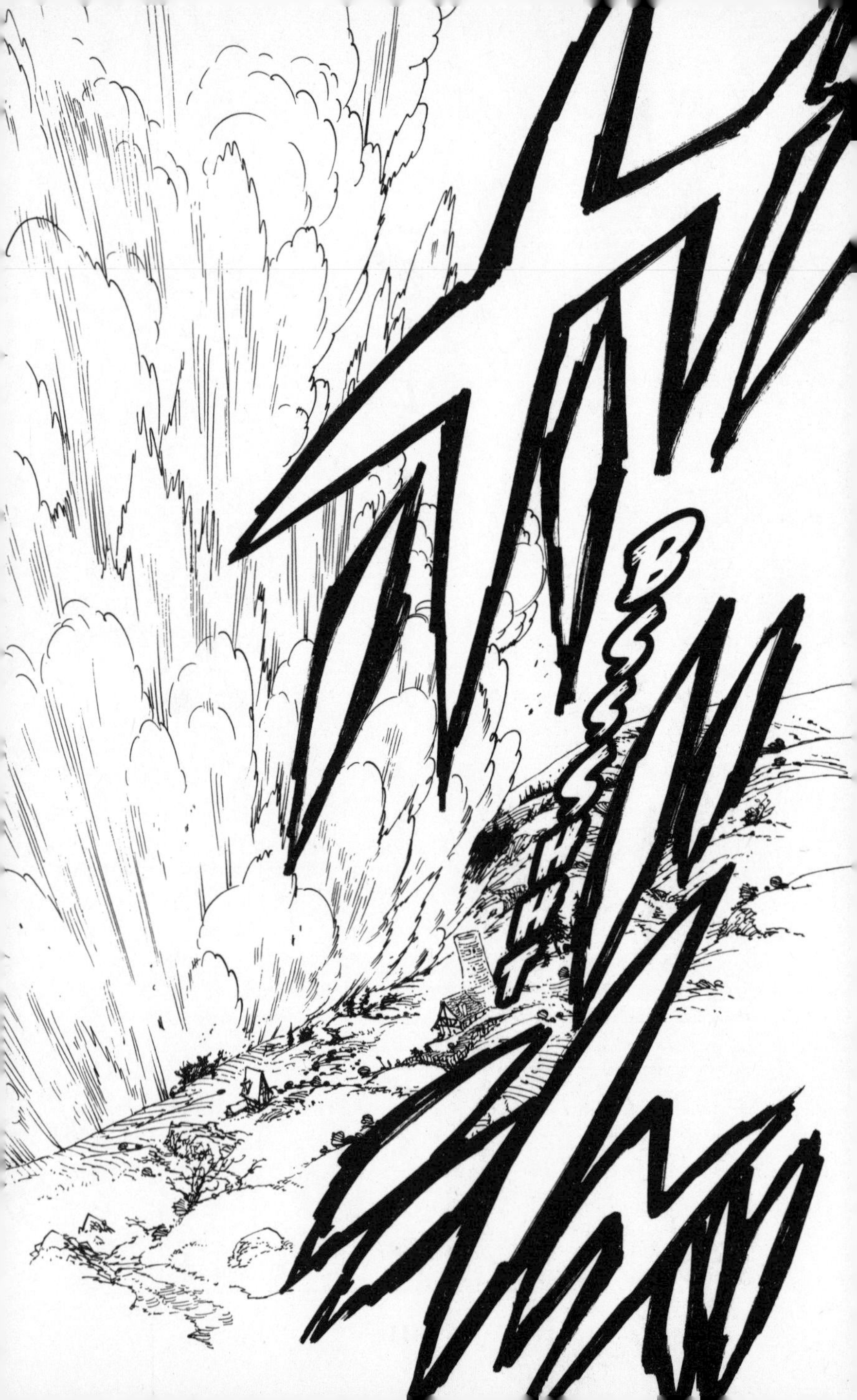
BSSSHHT

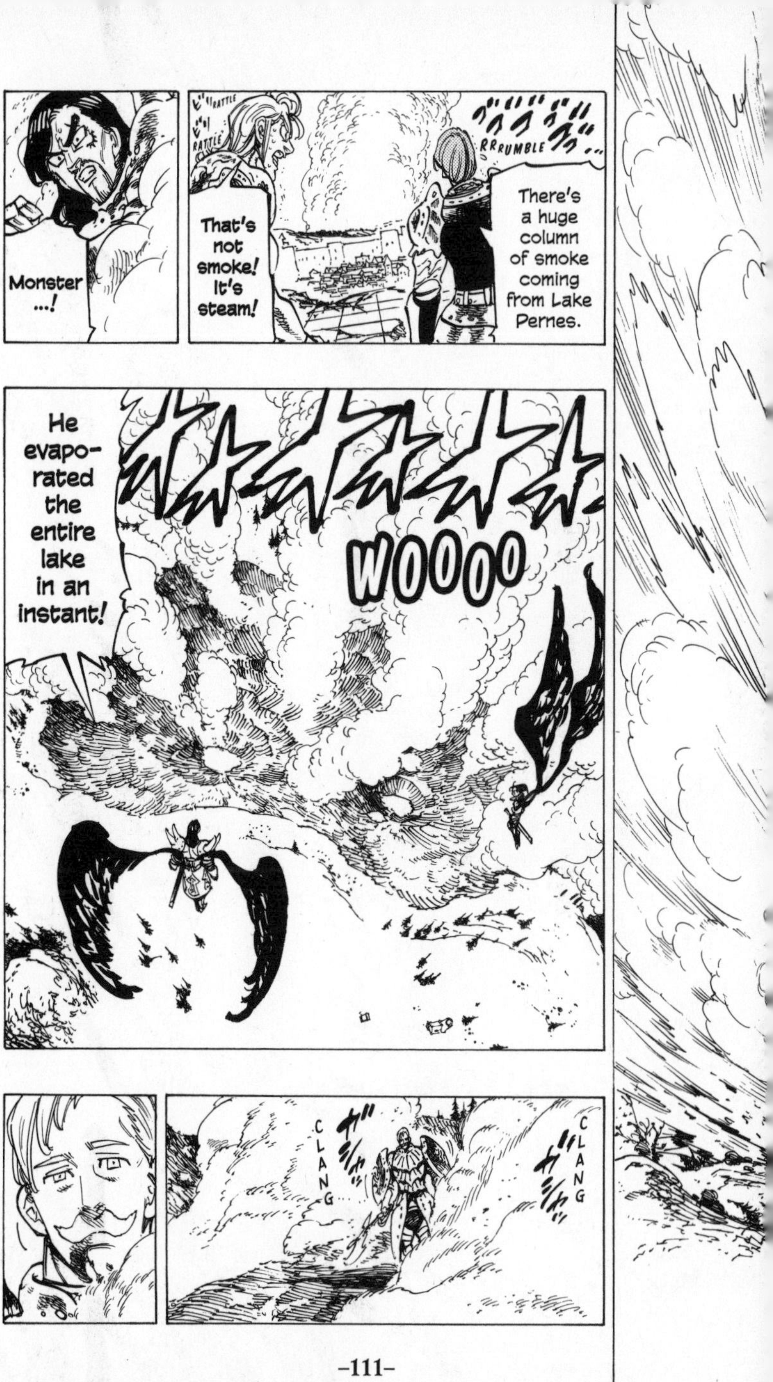
RRRUMBLE
There's a huge column of smoke coming from Lake Pernes.
RATTLE
RATTLE
That's not smoke! It's steam!
Monster ...!
WOOOO
He evapo-rated the entire lake in an instant!
CLANG
CLANG

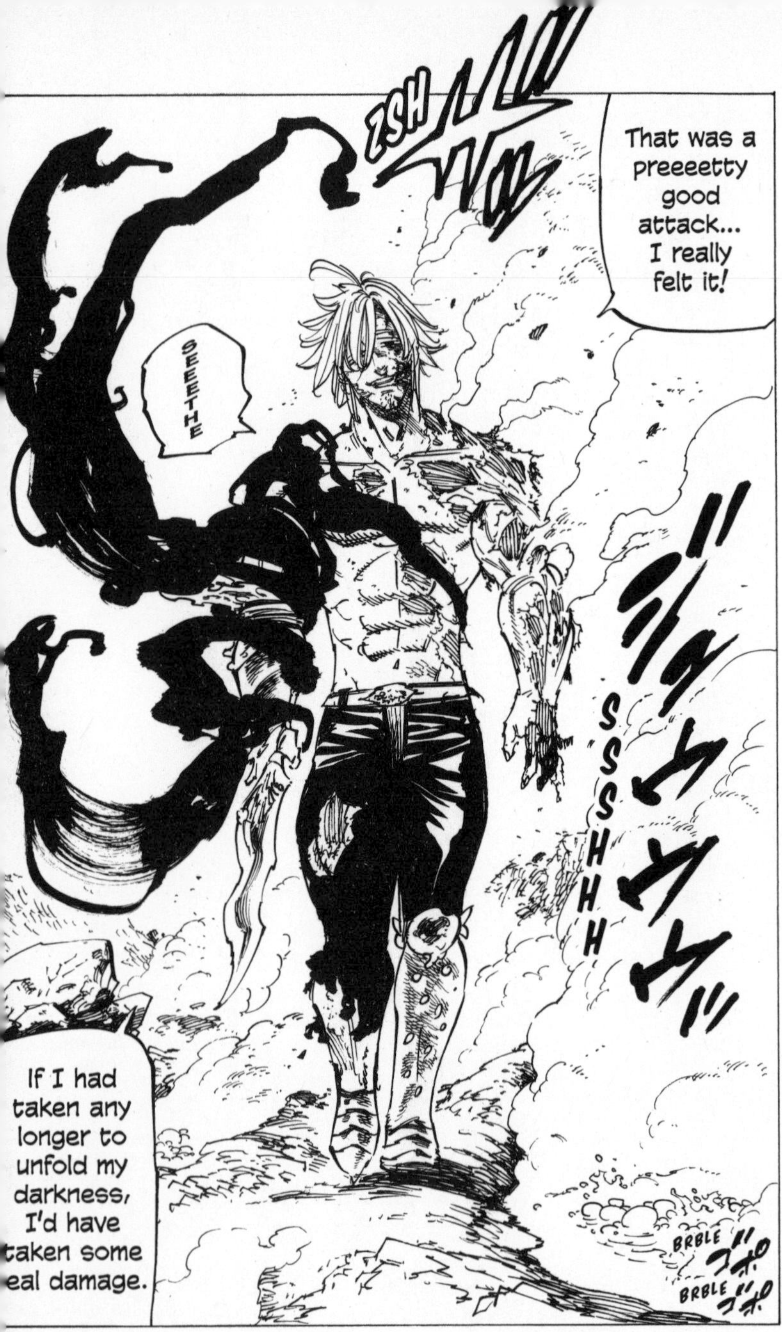
That was a preeeetty good attack... I really felt it!
ZSH
SEEETHE
SSSHHH
BRBLE
BRBLE
If I had taken any longer to unfold my darkness, I'd have taken some eal damage.

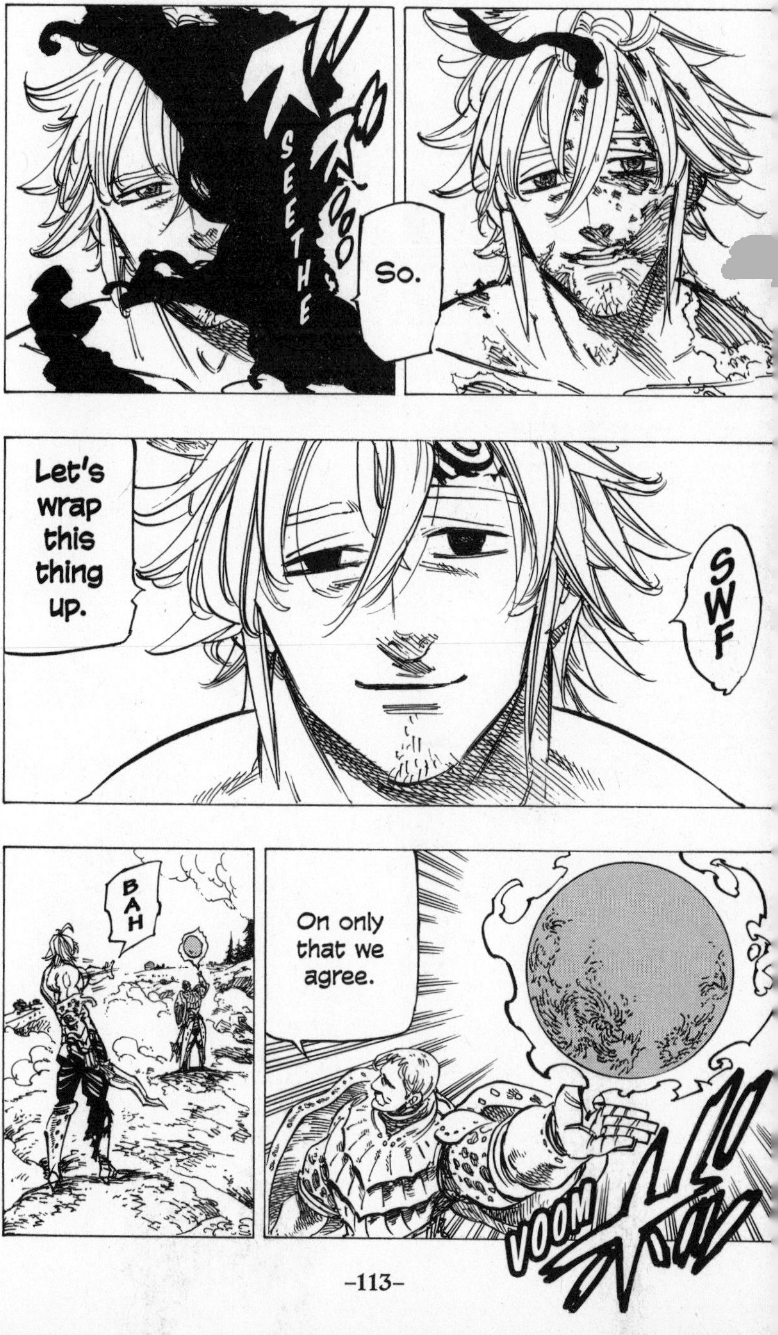
So.
SEETHE
SWF
Let's wrap this thing up.
On only that we agree.
VOOM
BAH

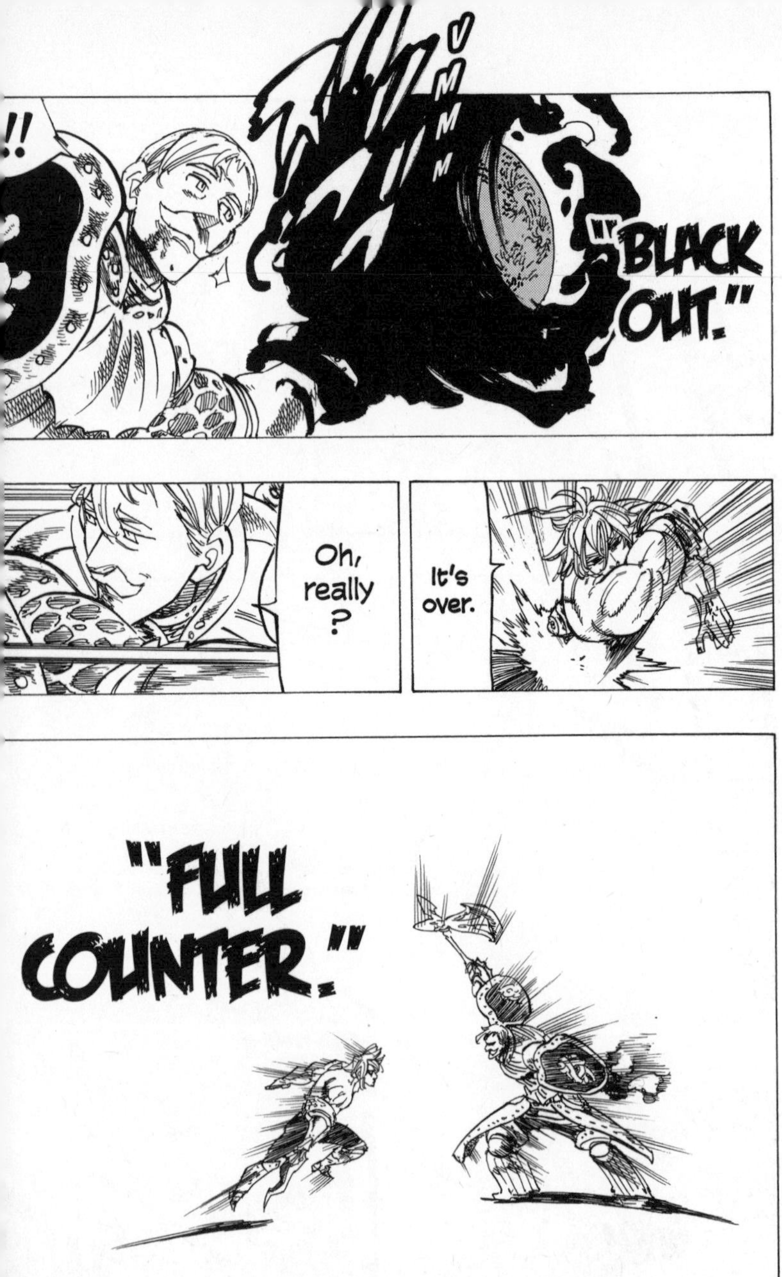
"BLACK OUT."
VMMMM
!!
It's over.
Oh, really?
"FULL COUNTER."

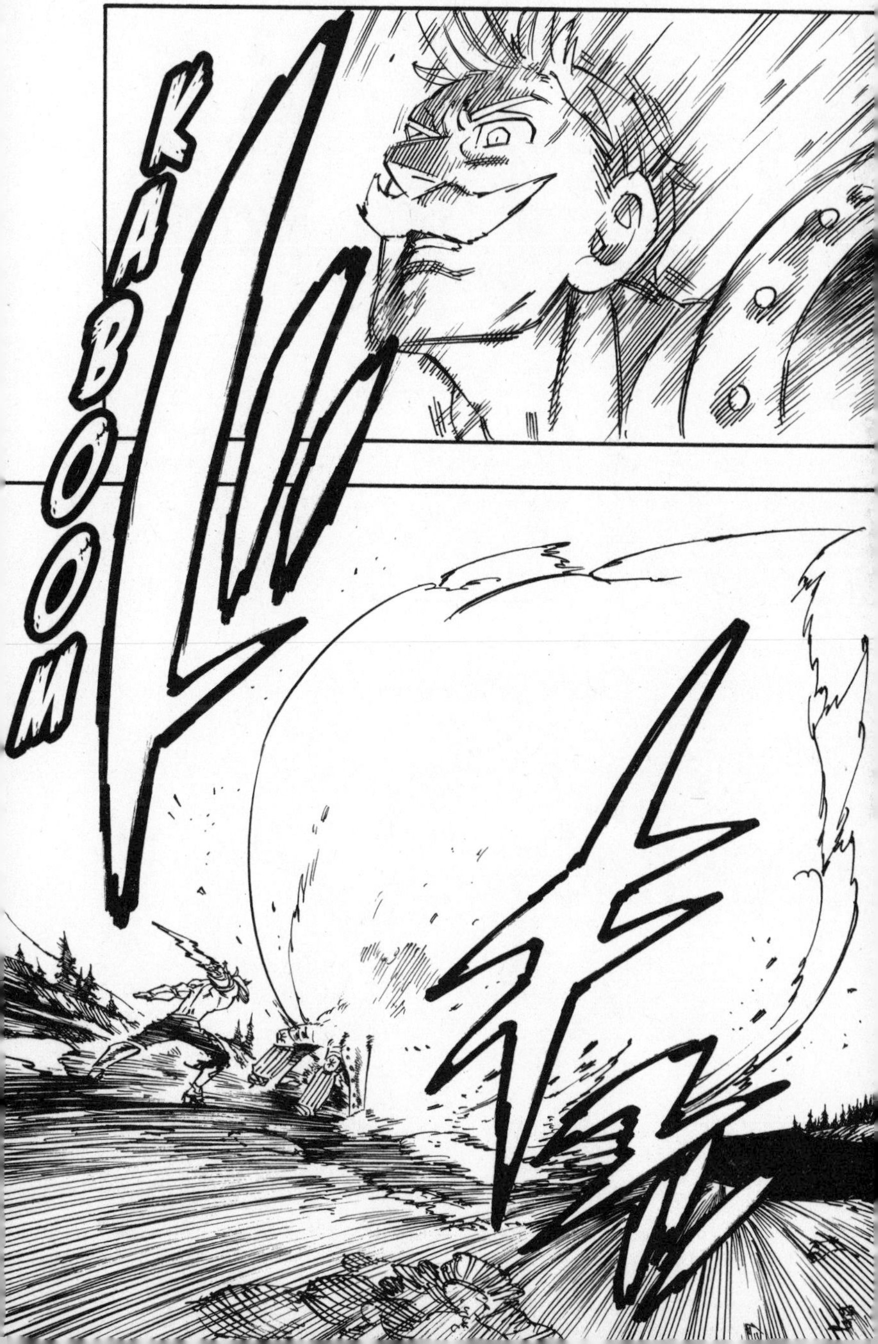
KABOOOM

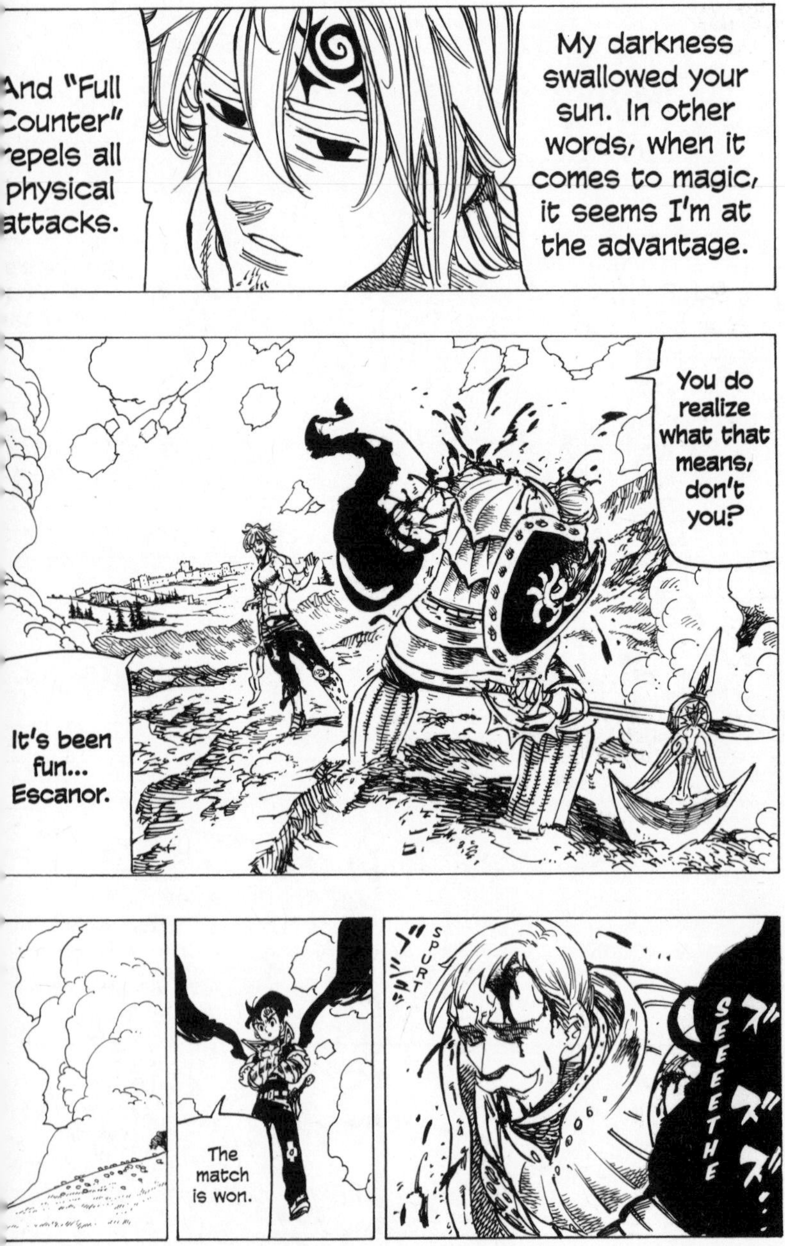
My darkness swallowed your sun. In other words, when it comes to magic, it seems I'm at the advantage.
And "Full Counter" repels all physical attacks.
You do realize what that means, don't you?
It's been fun... Escanor.
SPURT
SEEEETHE
...
The match is won.

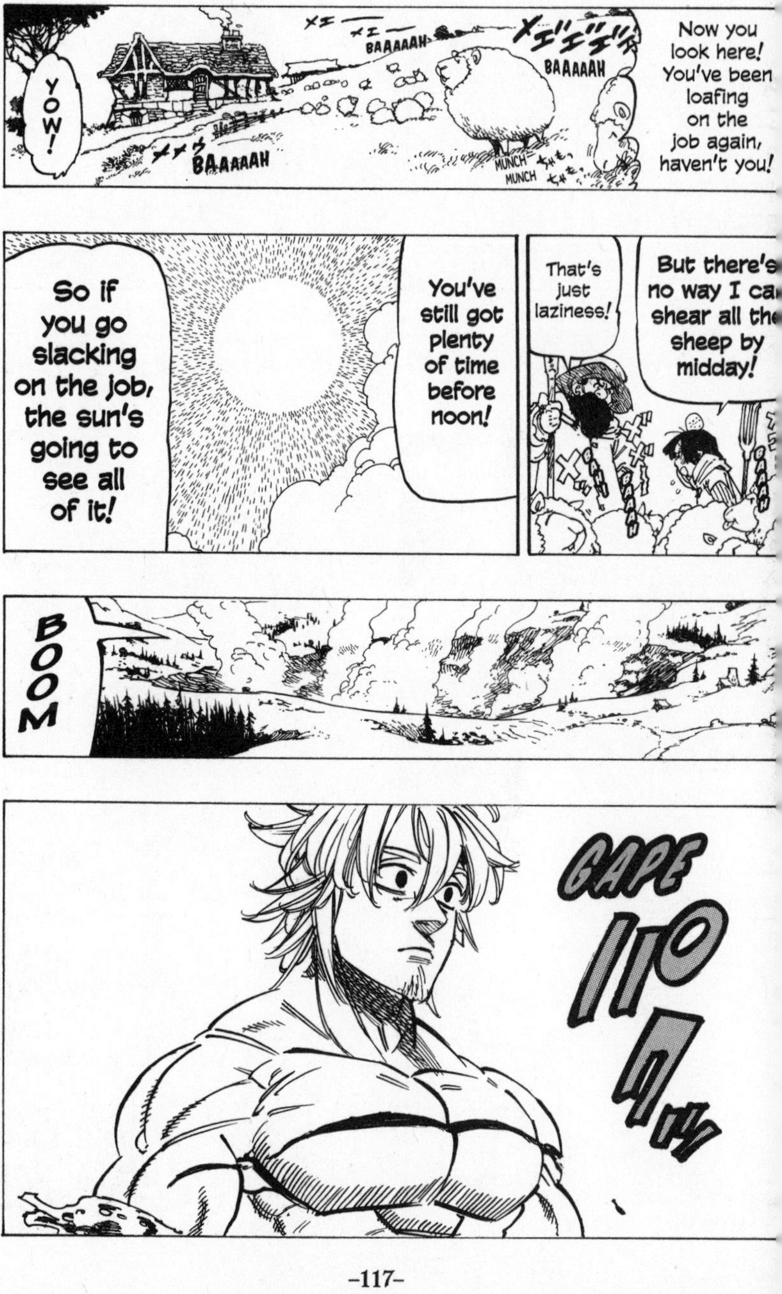
Now you look here! You've been loafing on the job again, haven't you!
BAAAAAH
MUNCH MUNCH
BAAAAAH
BAAAAAH
YOW!
But there's no way I ca shear all the sheep by midday!
BAAAH
That's just laziness!
BAAAH
BAH!
You've still got plenty of time before noon!
So if you go slacking on the job, the sun's going to see all of it!
BOOM
GAPE

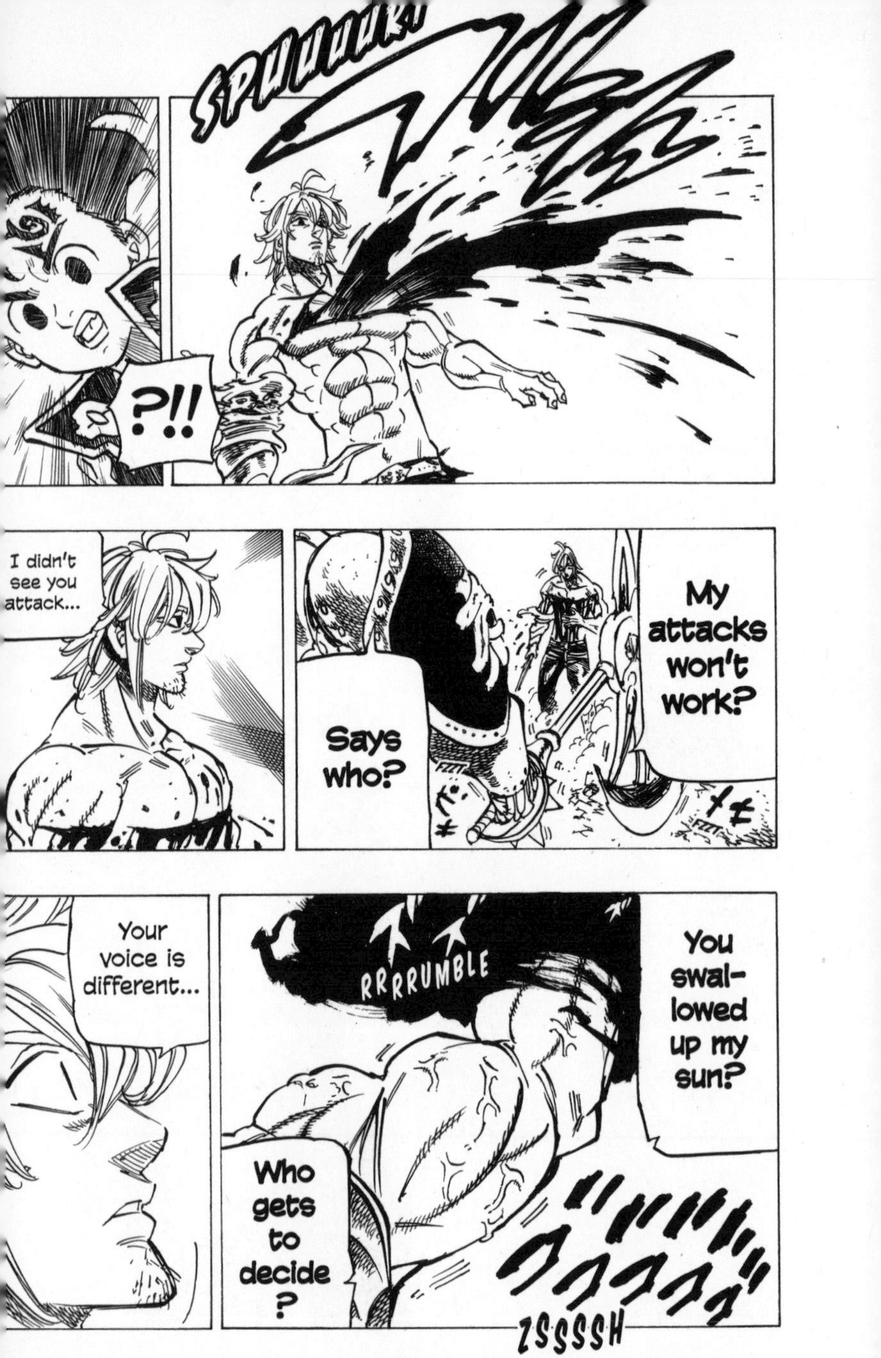
SPUUUUR!
?!!
My attacks won't work?
Says who?
FZZT
FZZT
I didn't see you attack...
You swal-lowed up my sun?
RRRRUMBLE
Who gets to decide?
ZSSSSH
Your voice is different...

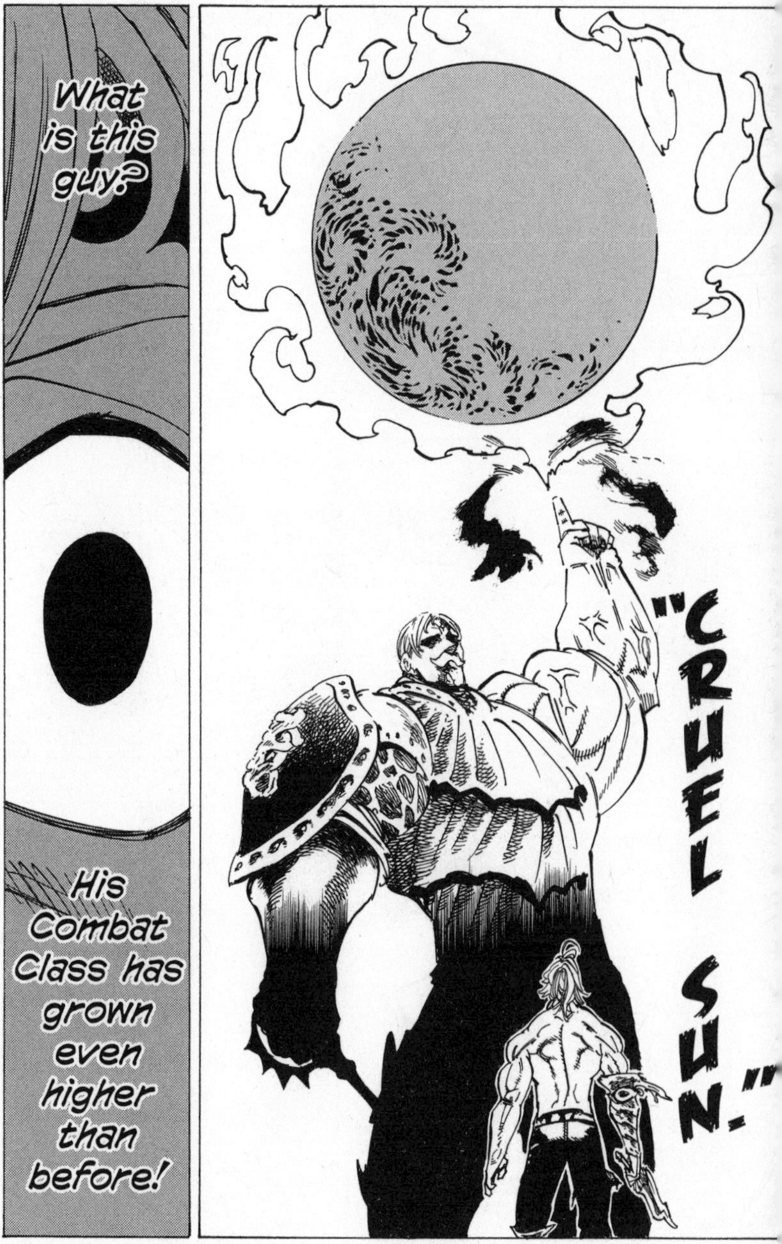
"CRUEL SUN."
What is this guy?
His Combat Class has grown even higher than before!

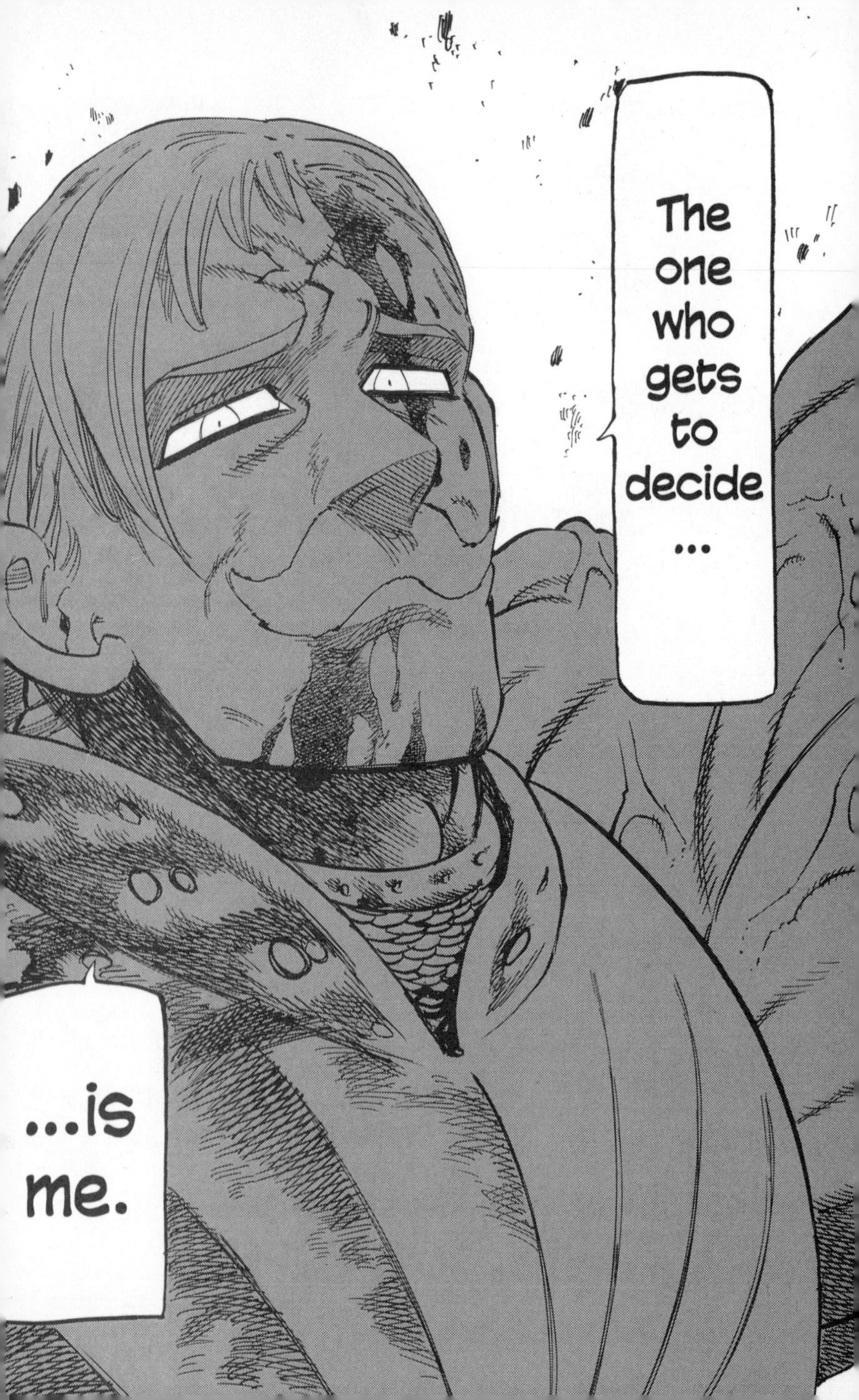
The one who gets to decide...
...is me.

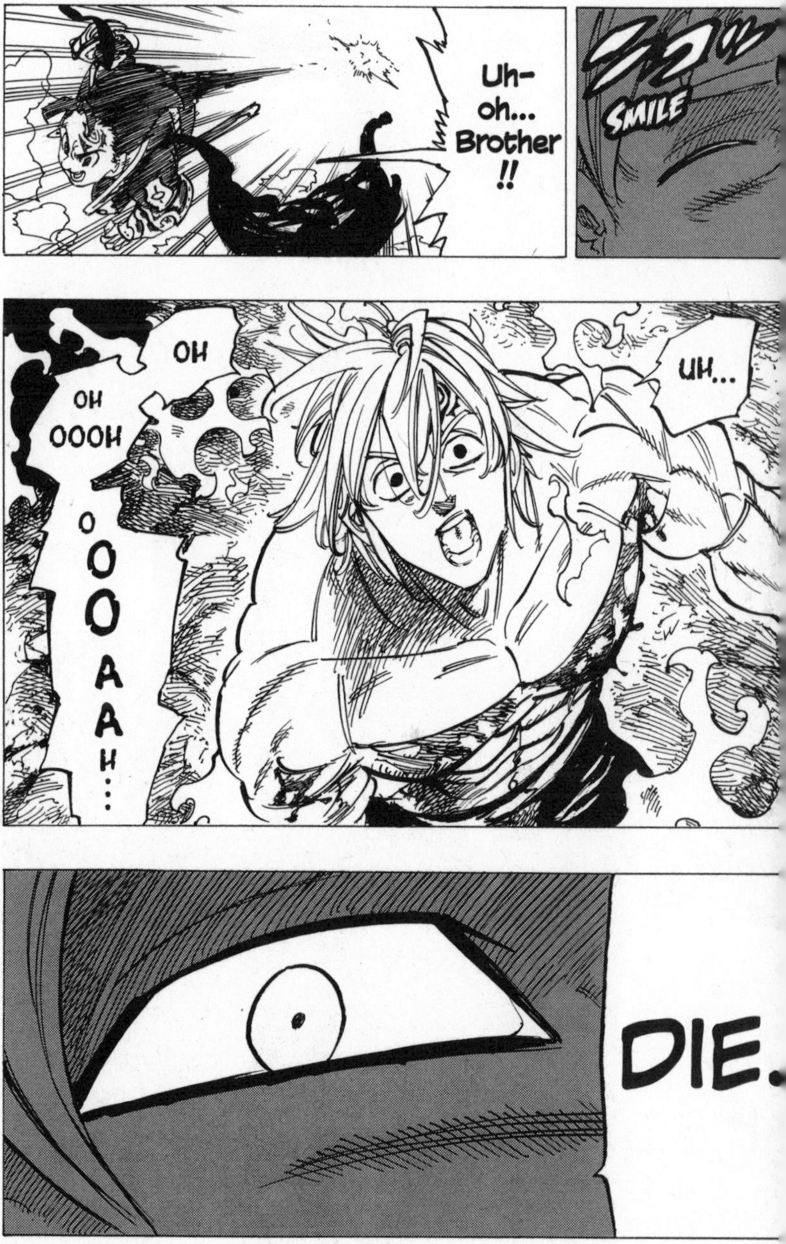
SMILE
Uh-oh... Brother!!
UH...
OH
OH OOOH
OOOAAH...
DIE.

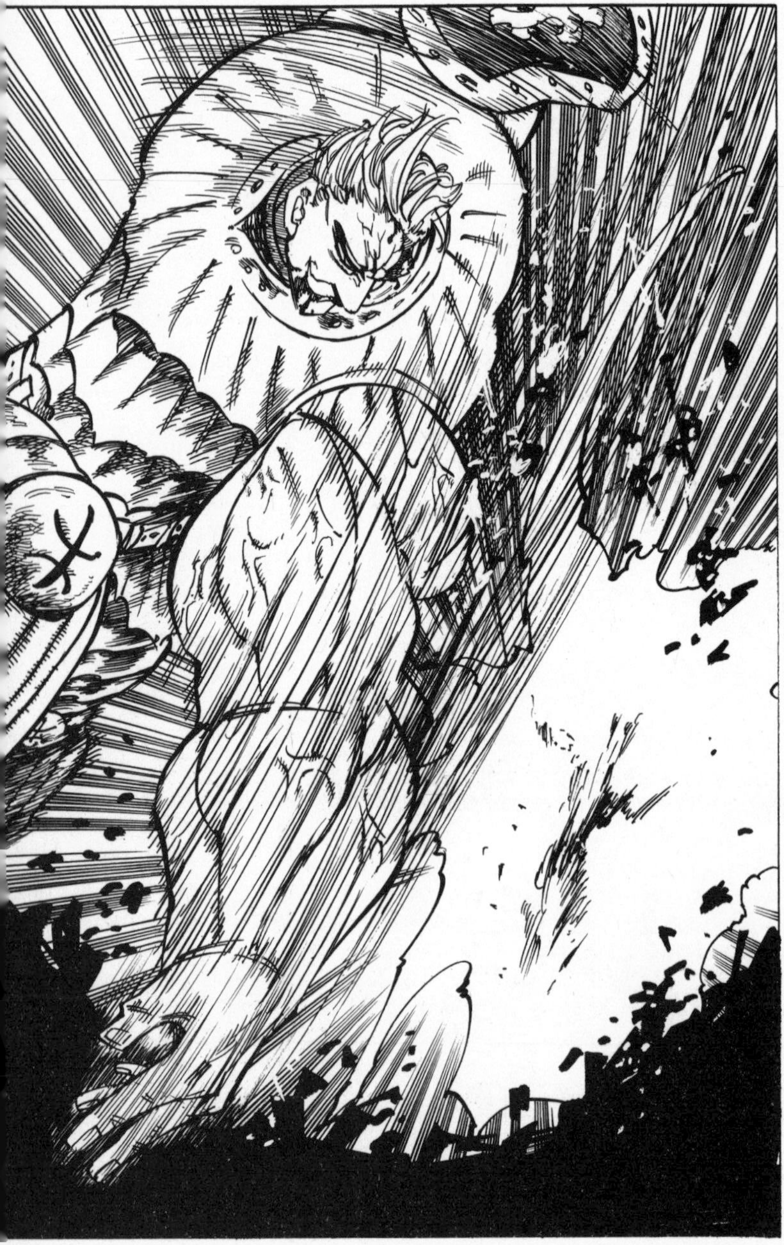

Chapter 186 - Defensive War in Liones

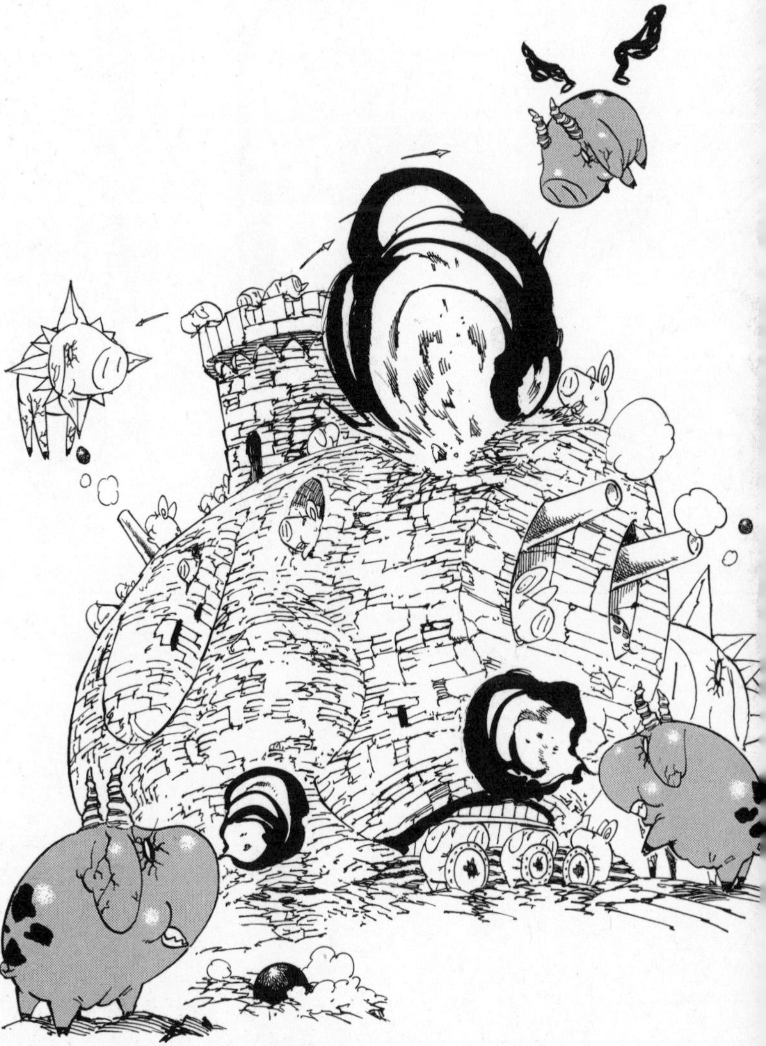

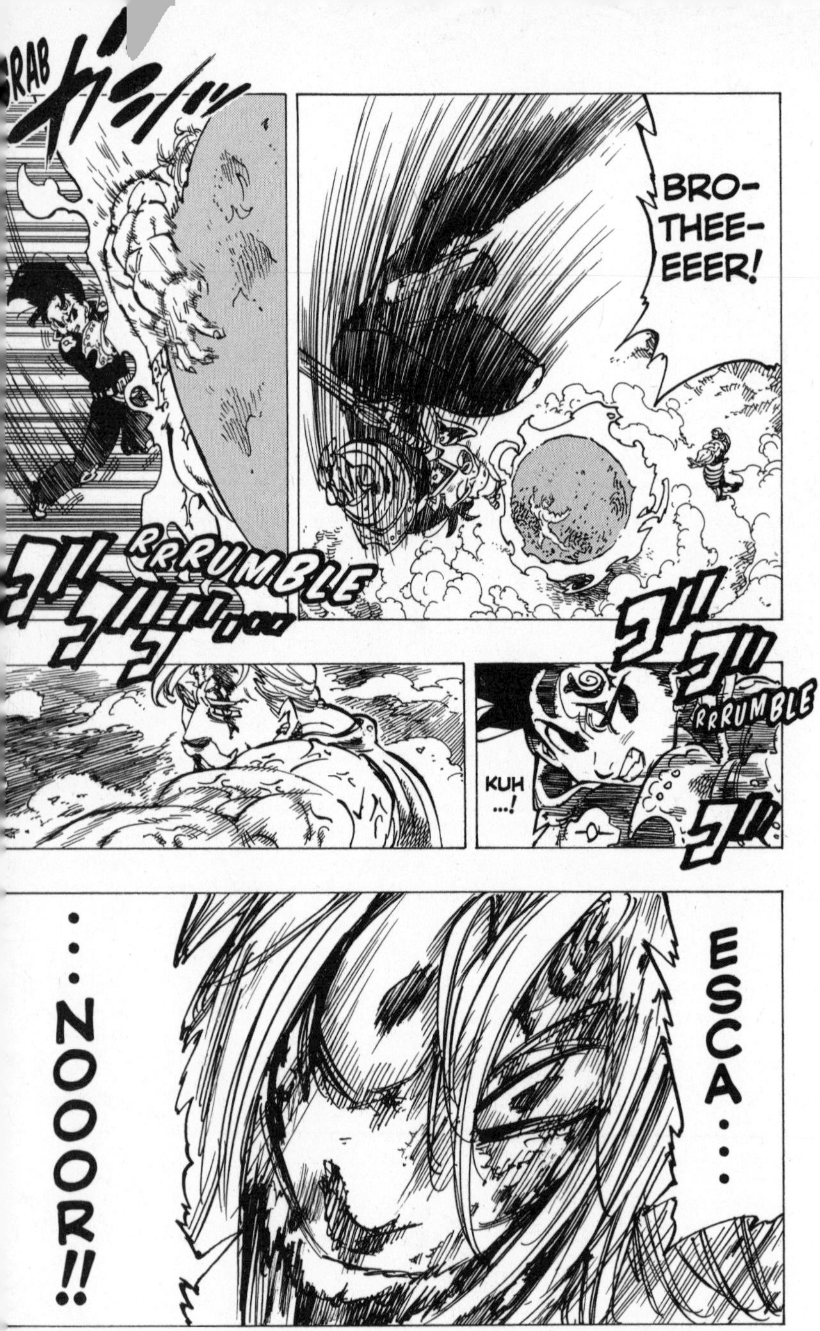
BRO-
THEEE-
EEER!
GRAB
RRRUMBLE
RRRUMBLE
KUH
...!
ESCA...
...NOOOR!!

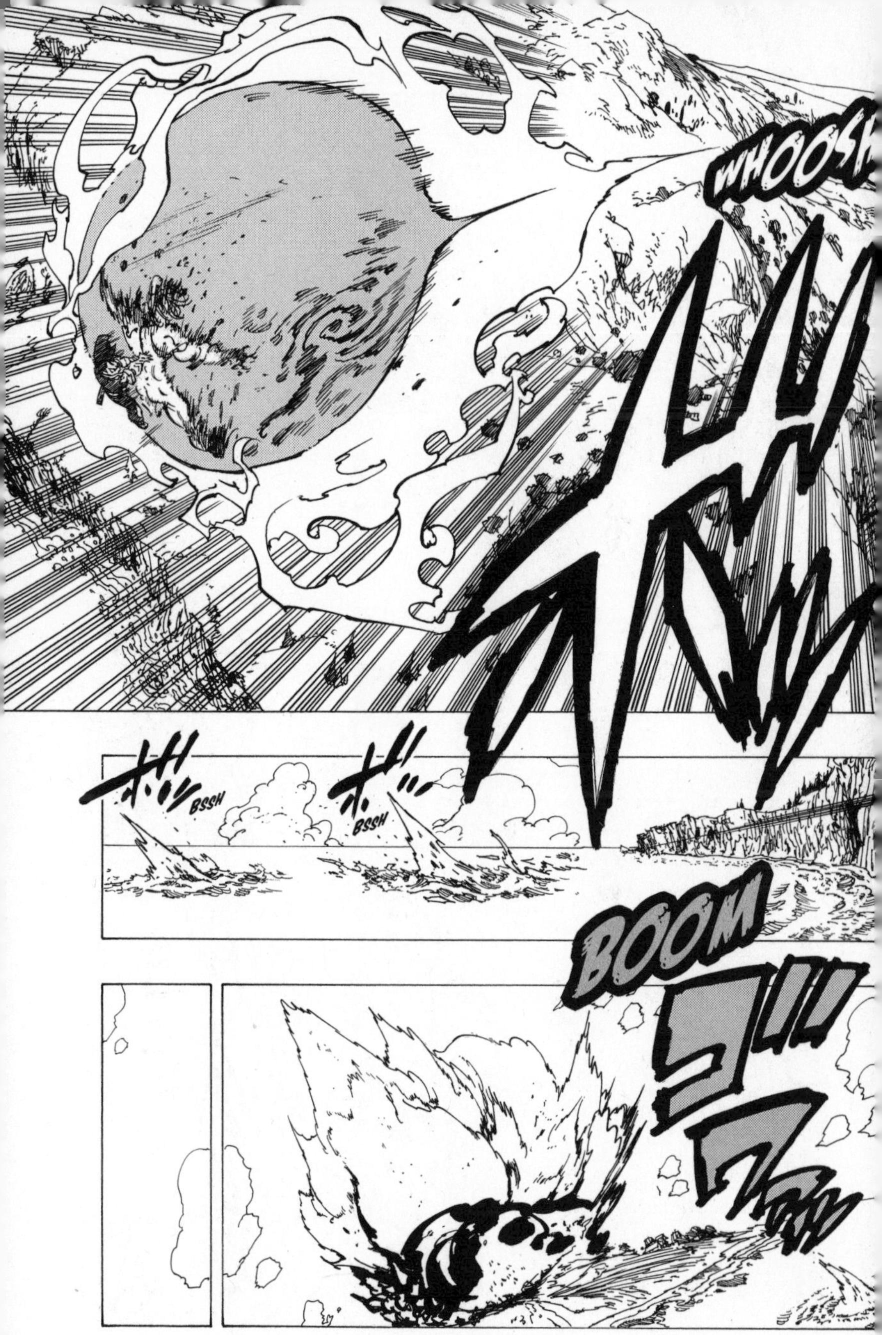
WHOOS
BSSH
BSSH
BOOM

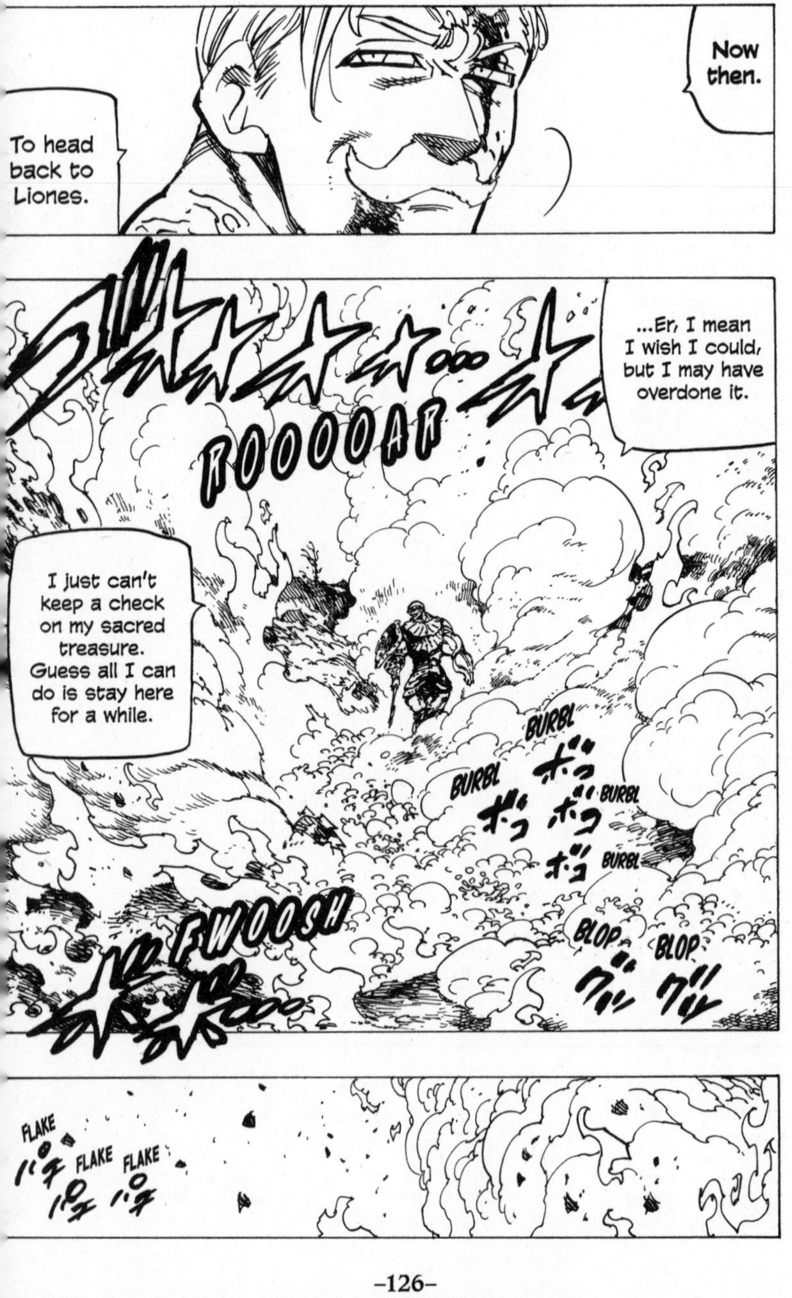
Now then.
To head back to Liones.
...Er, I mean I wish I could, but I may have overdone it.
ROOOOAR
I just can't keep a check on my sacred treasure. Guess all I can do is stay here for a while.
BURBL
BURBL
BURBL
BURBL
BLOP
BLOP
FWOOSH
FLAKE
FLAKE
FLAKE

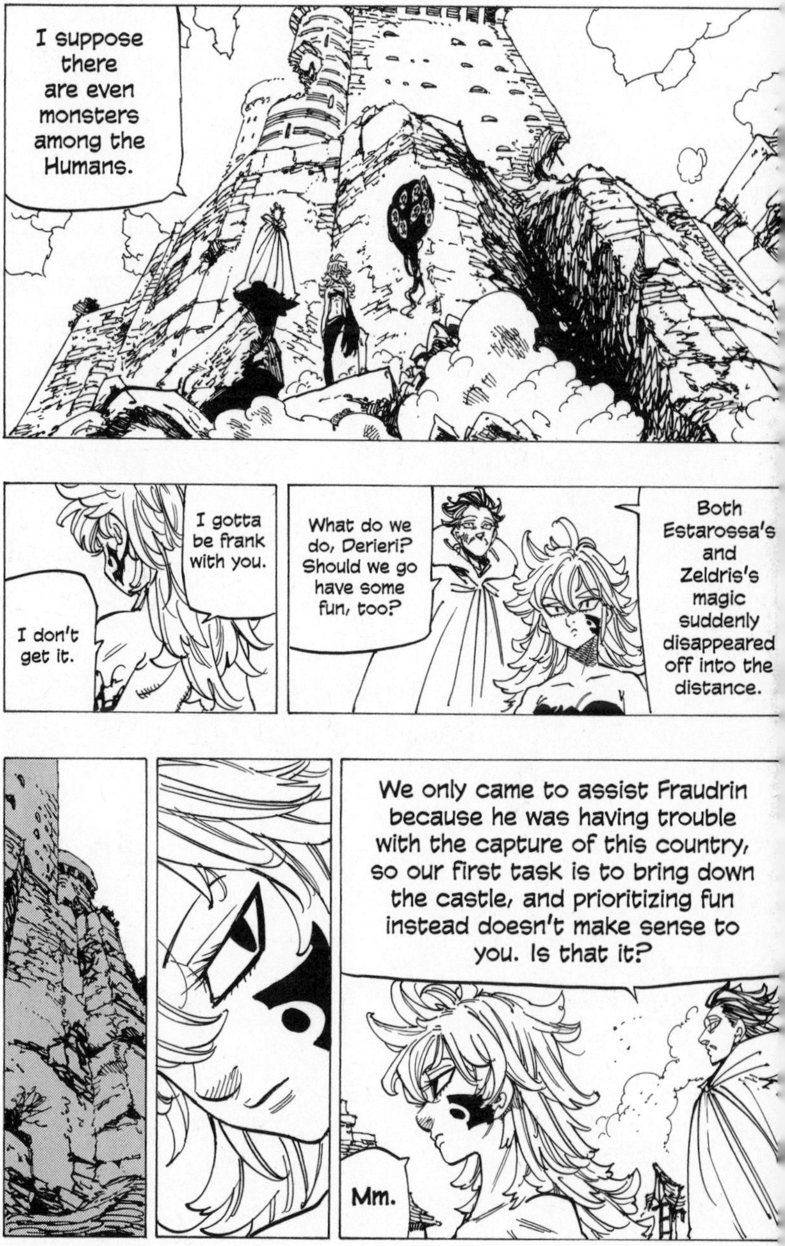
I suppose there are even monsters among the Humans.
Both Estarossa's and Zeldris's magic suddenly disappeared off into the distance.
What do we do, Derieri? Should we go have some fun, too?
I gotta be frank with you.
I don't get it.
We only came to assist Fraudrin because he was having trouble with the capture of this country, so our first task is to bring down the castle, and prioritizing fun instead doesn't make sense to you. Is that it?
Mm.

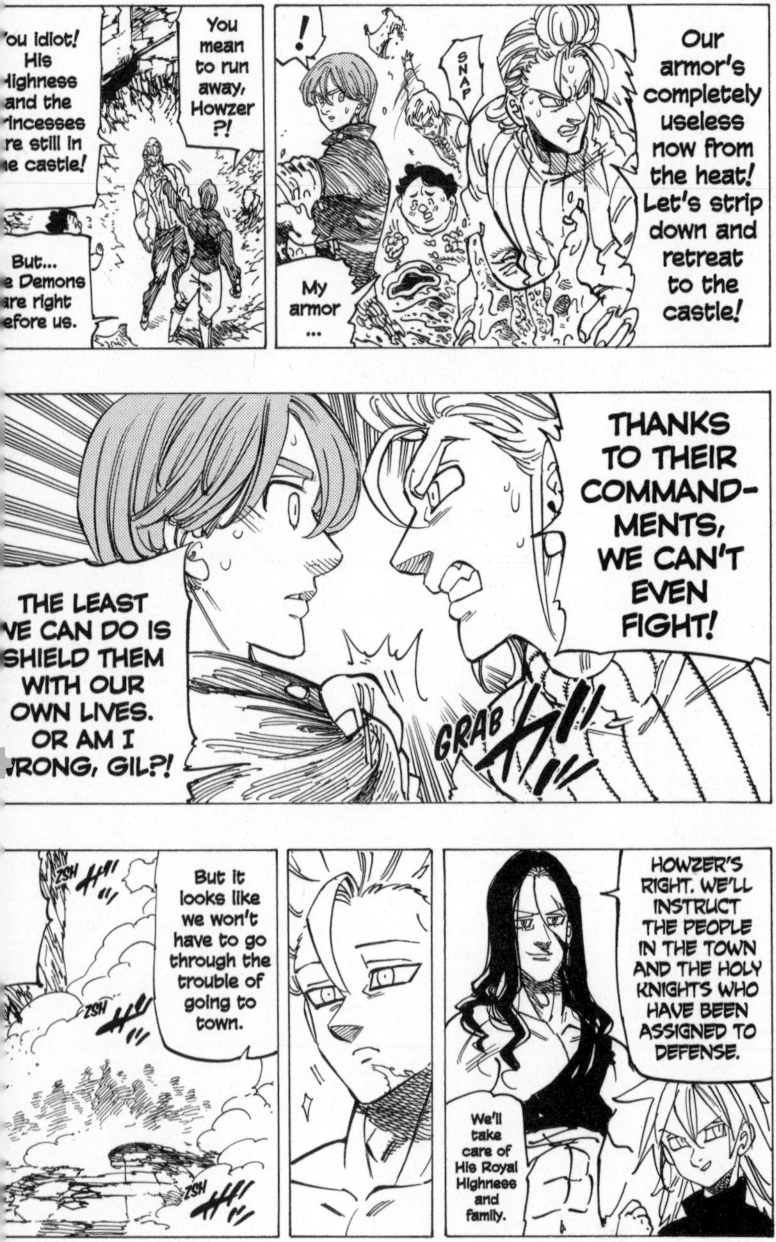
Our armor's completely useless now from the heat! Let's strip down and retreat to the castle!
SNAP
!
My armor ...
You mean to run away, Howzer?!
'ou idiot! His Highness and the rincesses re still in e castle!
But... e Demons are right efore us.
THANKS TO THEIR COMMAND-MENTS, WE CAN'T EVEN FIGHT!
GRAB
THE LEAST VE CAN DO IS SHIELD THEM WITH OUR OWN LIVES. OR AM I VRONG, GIL?!
HOWZER'S RIGHT. WE'LL INSTRUCT THE PEOPLE IN THE TOWN AND THE HOLY KNIGHTS WHO HAVE BEEN ASSIGNED TO DEFENSE.
We'll take care of His Royal Highness and family.
But it looks like we won't have to go through the trouble of going to town.
ZSH
ZSH
ZSH

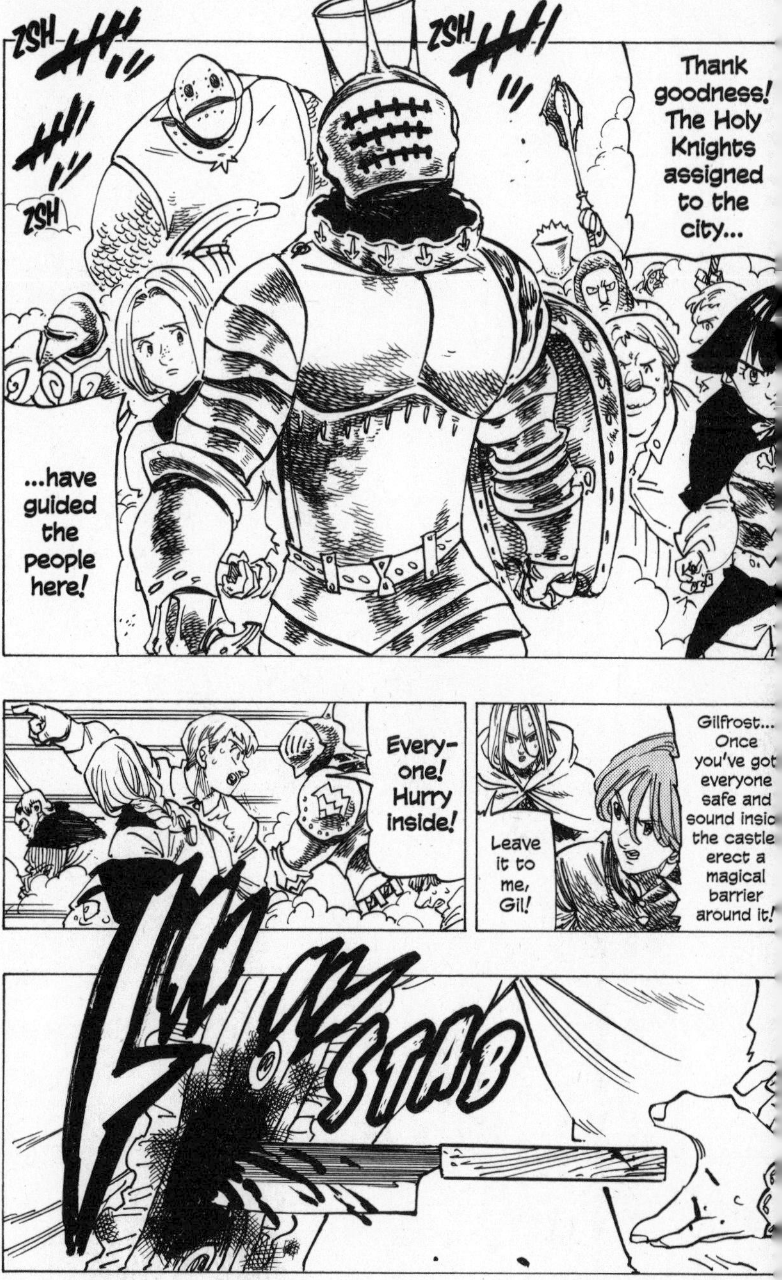
ZSH
ZSH
ZSH
Thank goodness! The Holy Knights assigned to the city...
...have guided the people here!
Gilfrost... Once you've got everyone safe and sound insi the castle erect a magical barrier around it!
Leave it to me, Gil!
Everyone! Hurry inside!
STAB

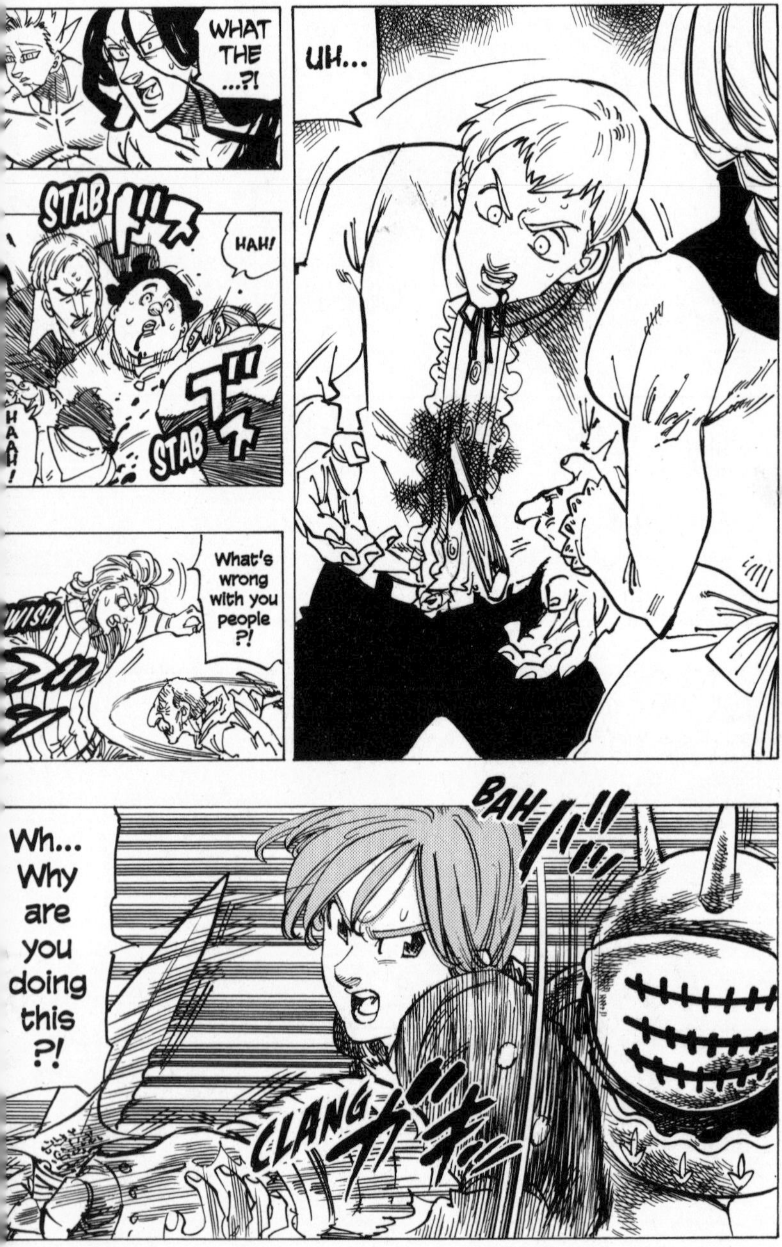
UH...
WHAT THE ...?!
STAB
HAH!
HAAH!
STAB
What's wrong with you people ?!
WISH
BAH
Wh... Why are you doing this ?!
CLANG

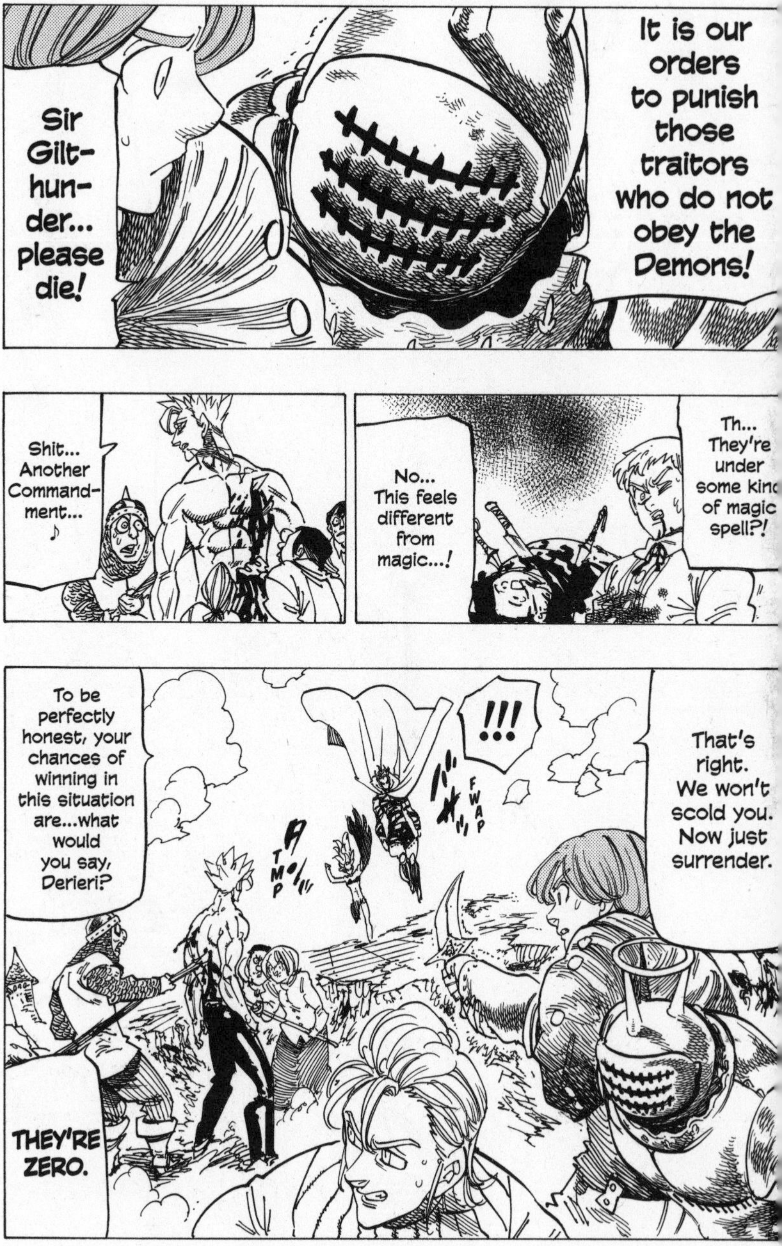
It is our orders to punish those traitors who do not obey the Demons!
Sir Gilthunder... please die!
Th... They're under some kind of magic spell?!
No... This feels different from magic...!
Shit... Another Commandment... ♪
That's right. We won't scold you. Now just surrender.
!!!
FWAP
TMP
To be perfectly honest, your chances of winning in this situation are...what would you say, Derieri?
THEY'RE ZERO.

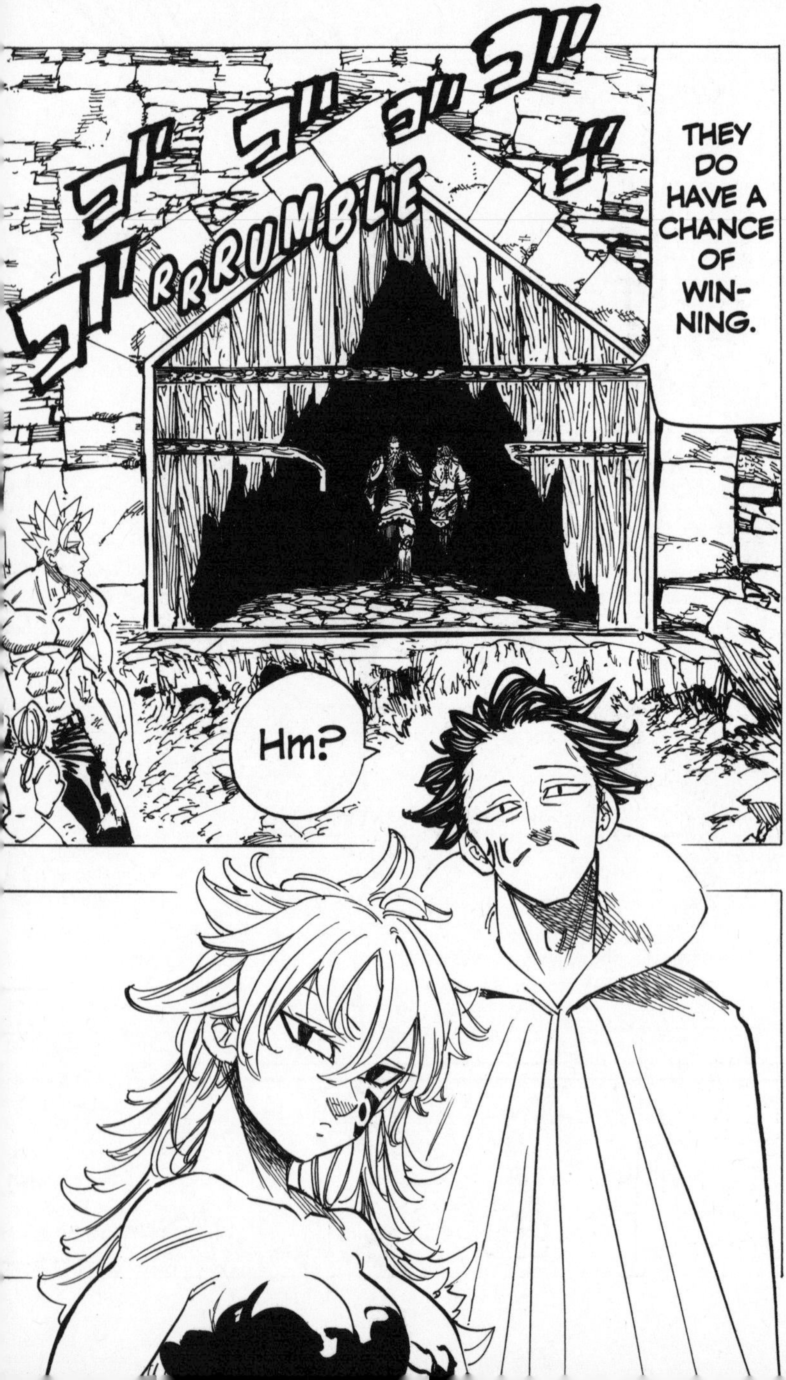
THEY DO HAVE A CHANCE OF WIN-NING.
RRRUMBLE
Hm?

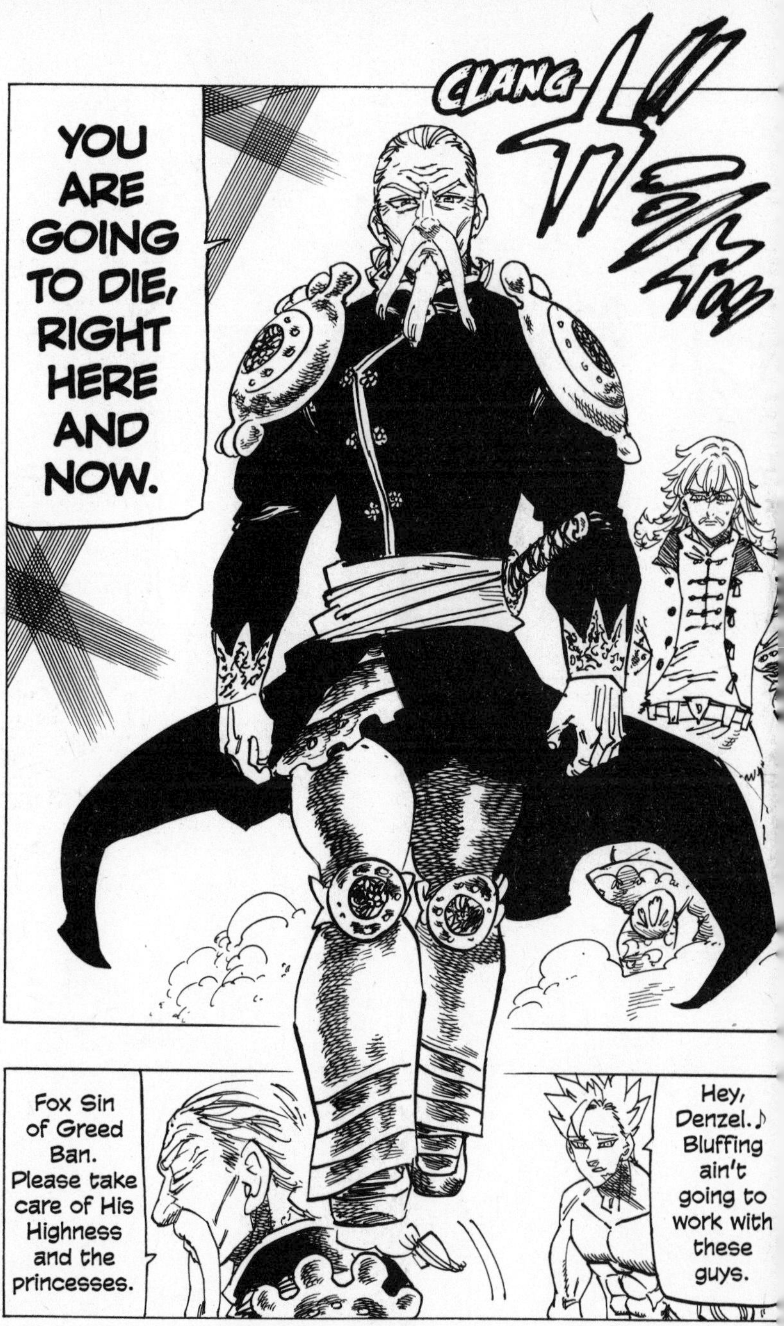
CLANG
YOU ARE GOING TO DIE, RIGHT HERE AND NOW.
Hey, Denzel.♪ Bluffing ain't going to work with these guys.
Fox Sin of Greed Ban. Please take care of His Highness and the princesses.

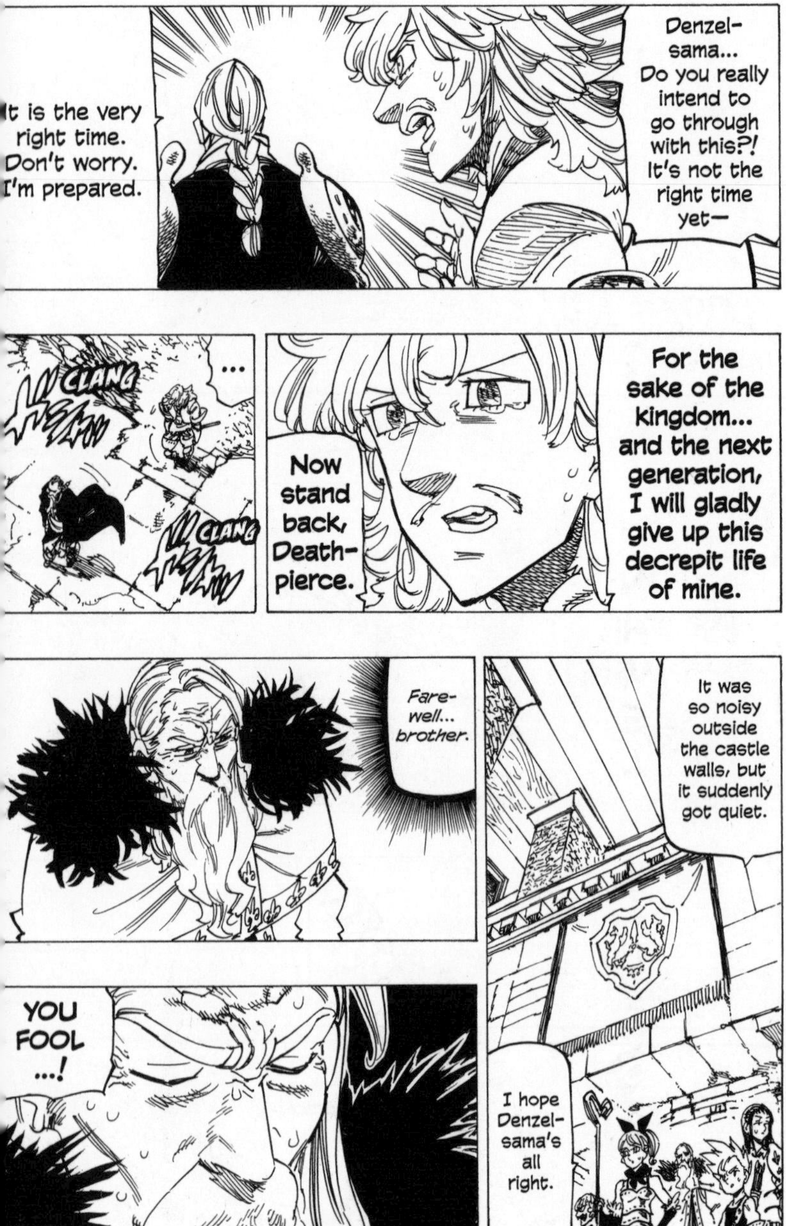
Denzel-sama... Do you really intend to go through with this?! It's not the right time yet—
It is the very right time. Don't worry. I'm prepared.
For the sake of the kingdom... and the next generation, I will gladly give up this decrepit life of mine.
Now stand back, Death-pierce.
...
CLANG
CLANG
It was so noisy outside the castle walls, but it suddenly got quiet.
I hope Denzel-sama's all right.
Fare-well... brother.
YOU FOOL ...!

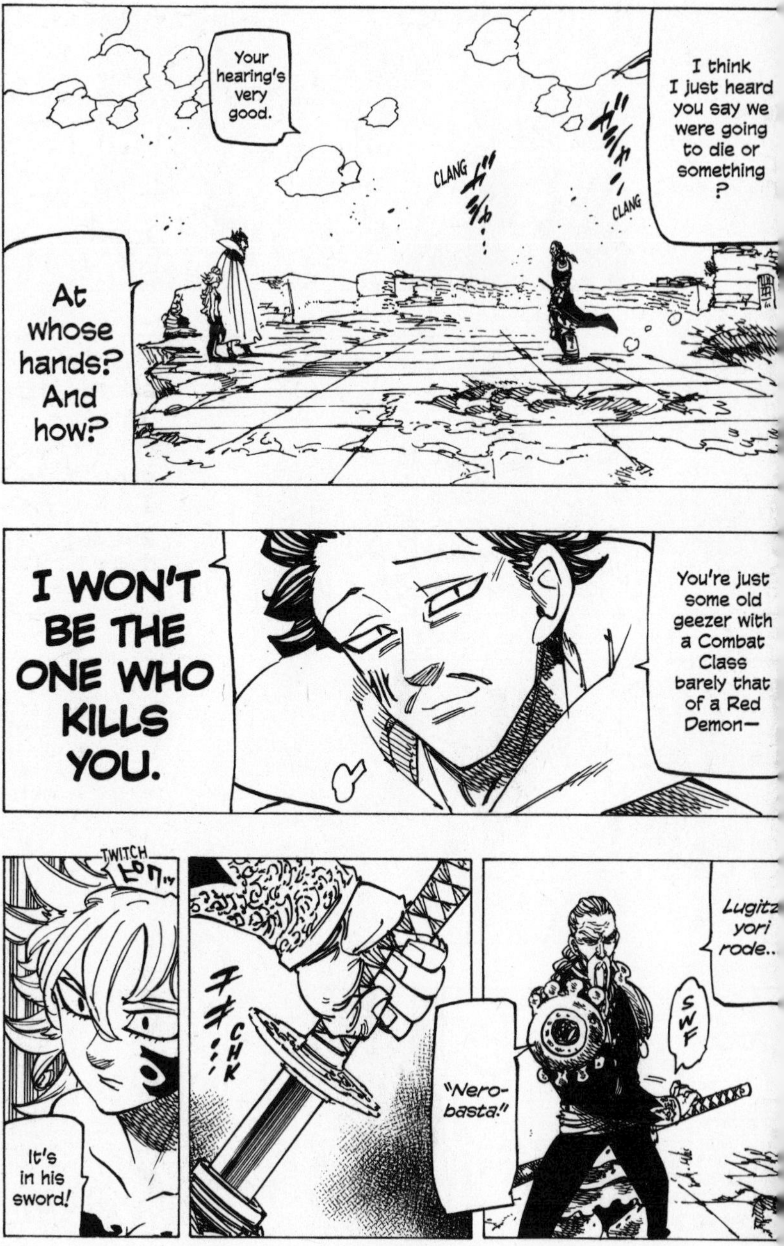
I think I just heard you say we were going to die or something?
CLANG
CLANG
Your hearing's very good.
At whose hands? And how?
You're just some old geezer with a Combat Class barely that of a Red Demon—
I WON'T BE THE ONE WHO KILLS YOU.
Lugitz yori rode..
SWF
"Nero-basta!"
CHK
TWITCH
It's in his sword!

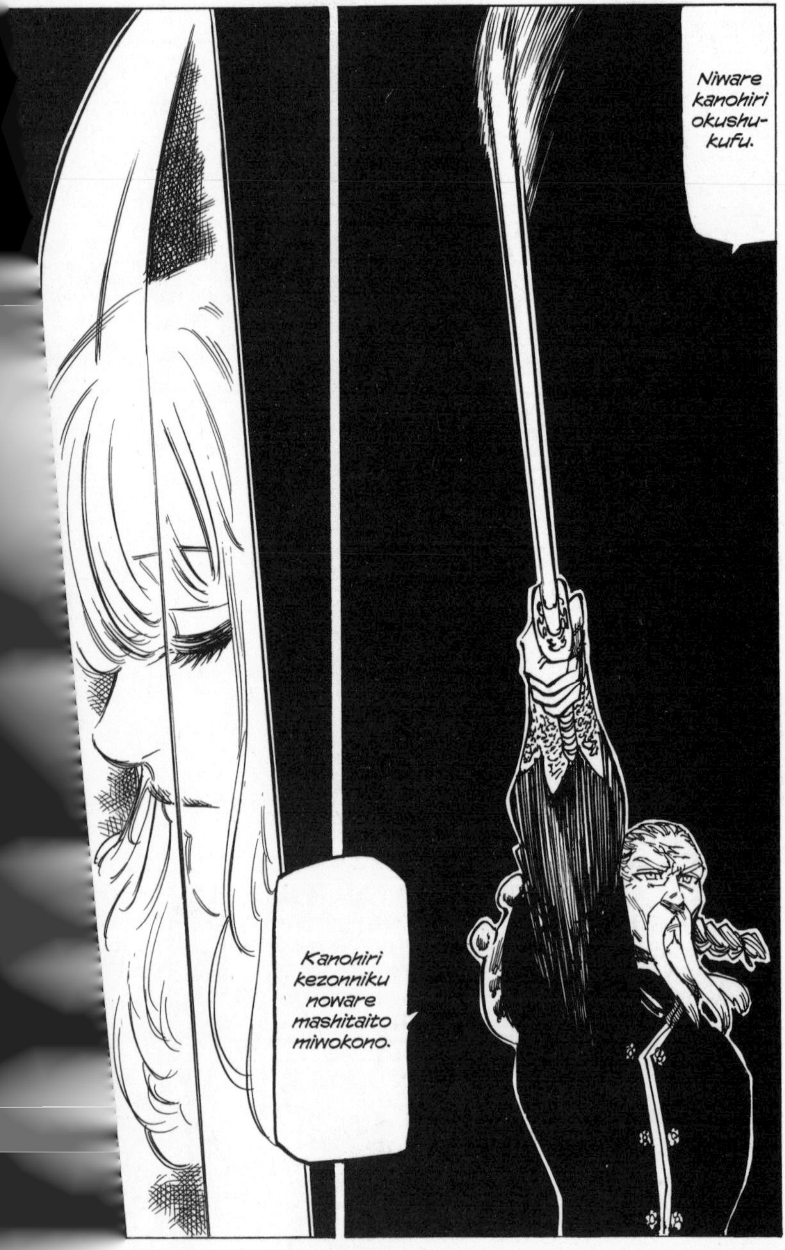
Niware kanohiri okushu-kufu.
Kanohiri kezonniku noware mashitaito miwokono.

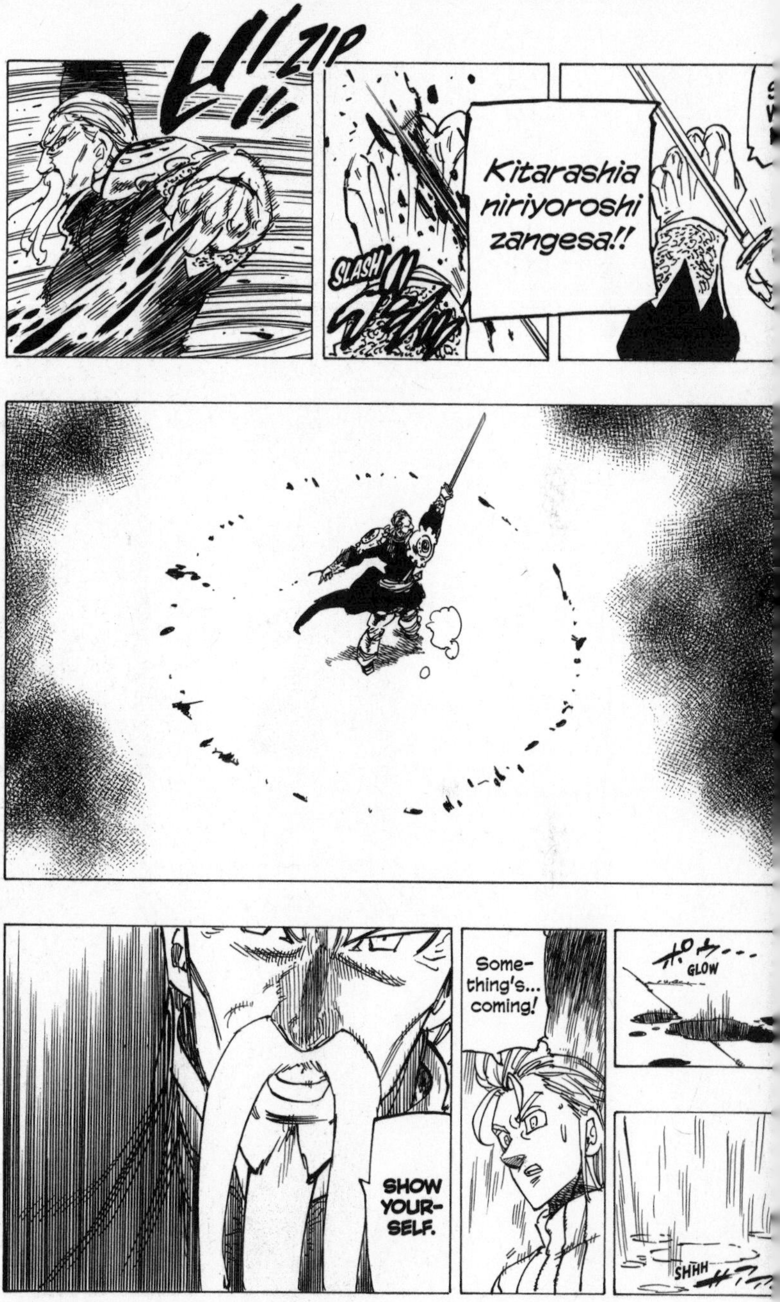
Kitarashia niriyoroshi zangesa!!
SLASH
ZIP
GLOW
SHHH
Something's... coming!
SHOW YOURSELF.

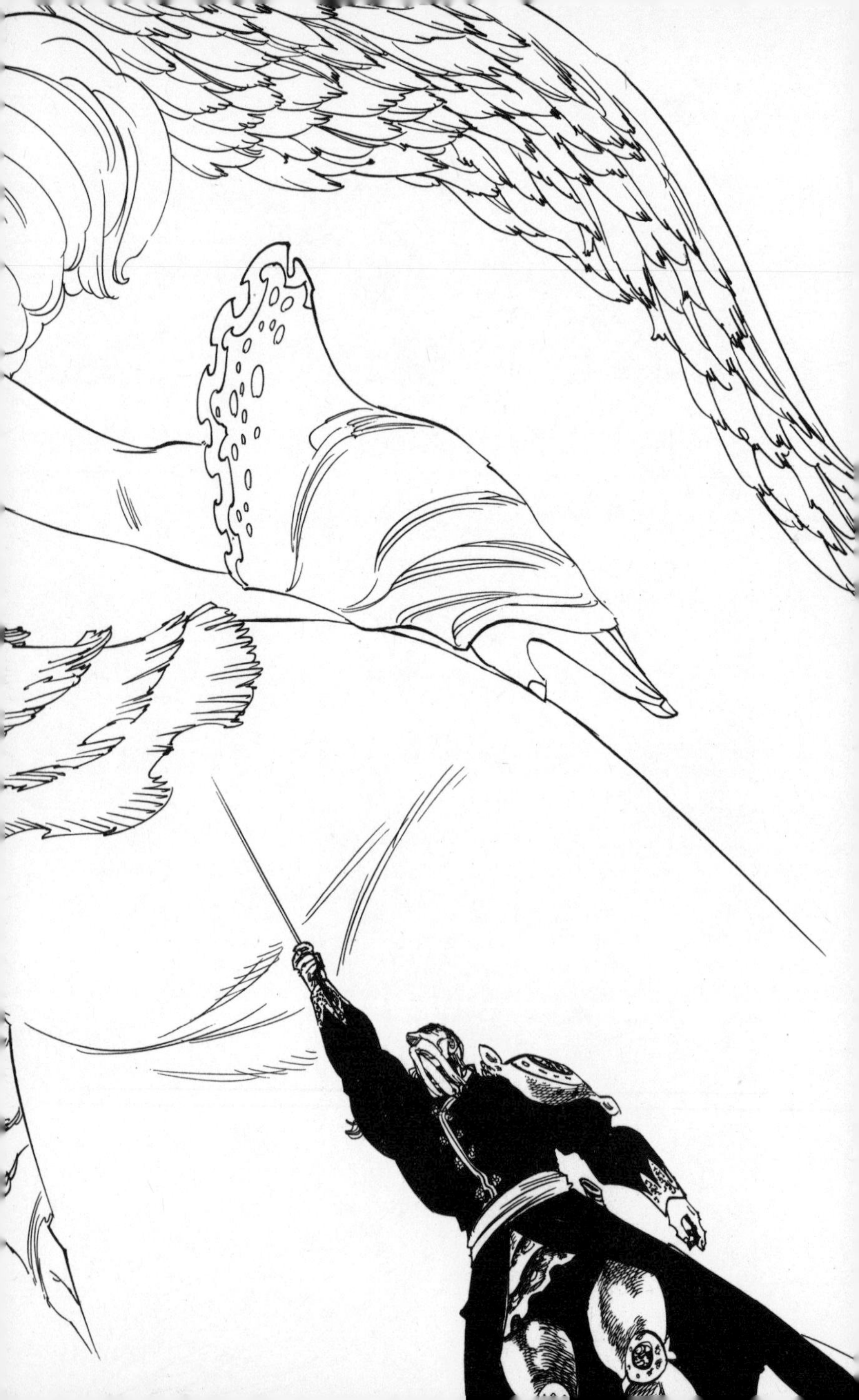

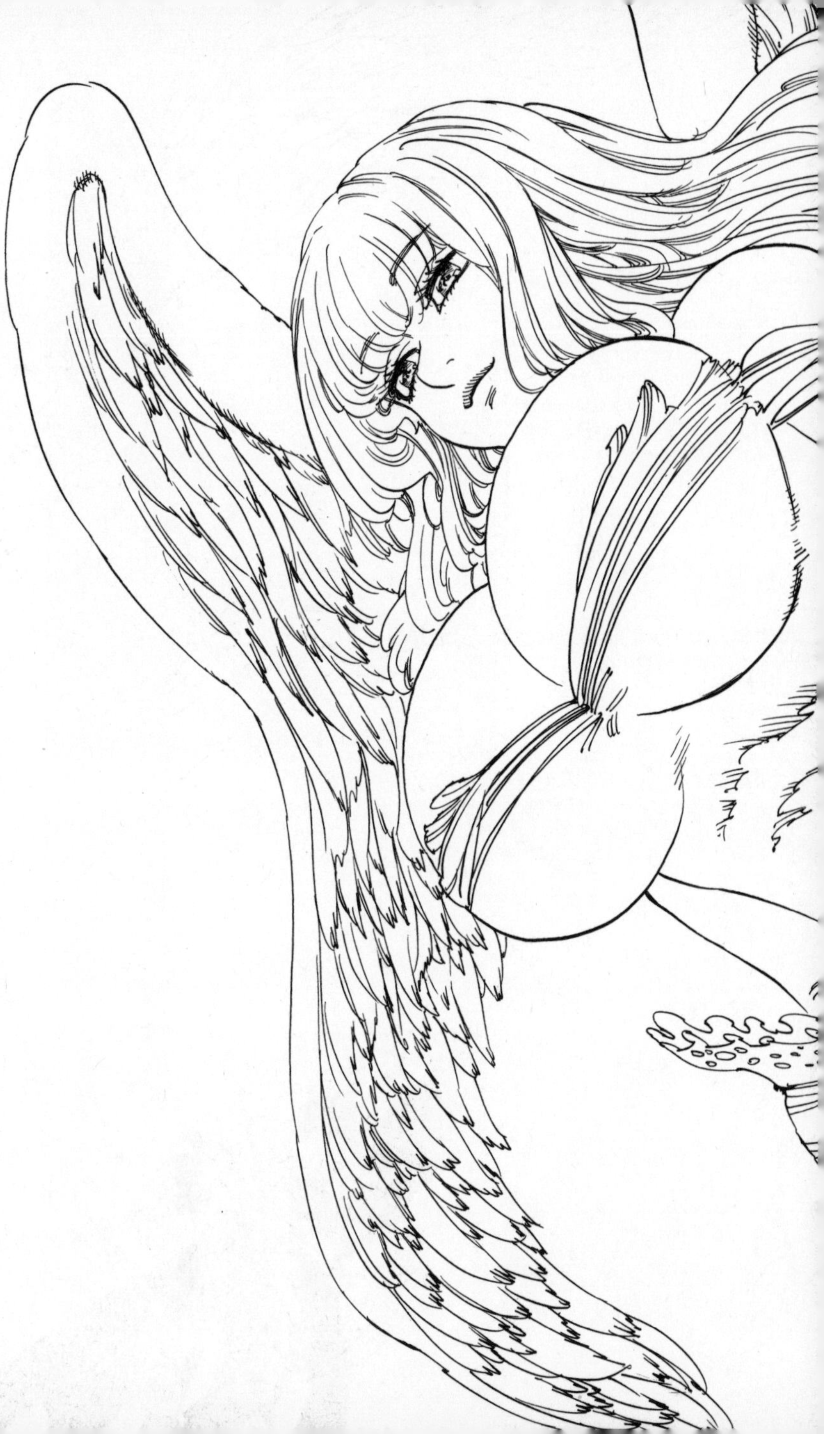

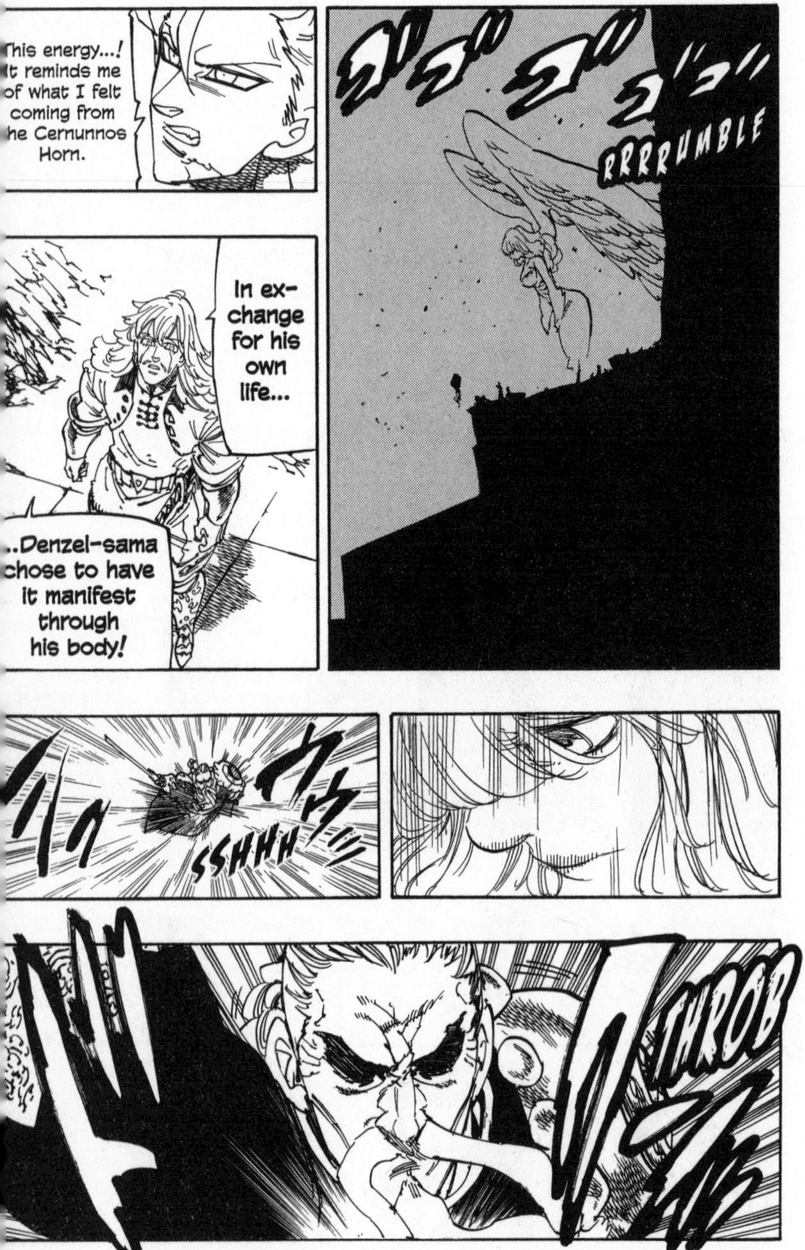
RRRRUMBLE
This energy...! It reminds me of what I felt coming from the Cernunnos Horn.
In exchange for his own life...
...Denzel-sama chose to have it manifest through his body!
SSHHH
THROB

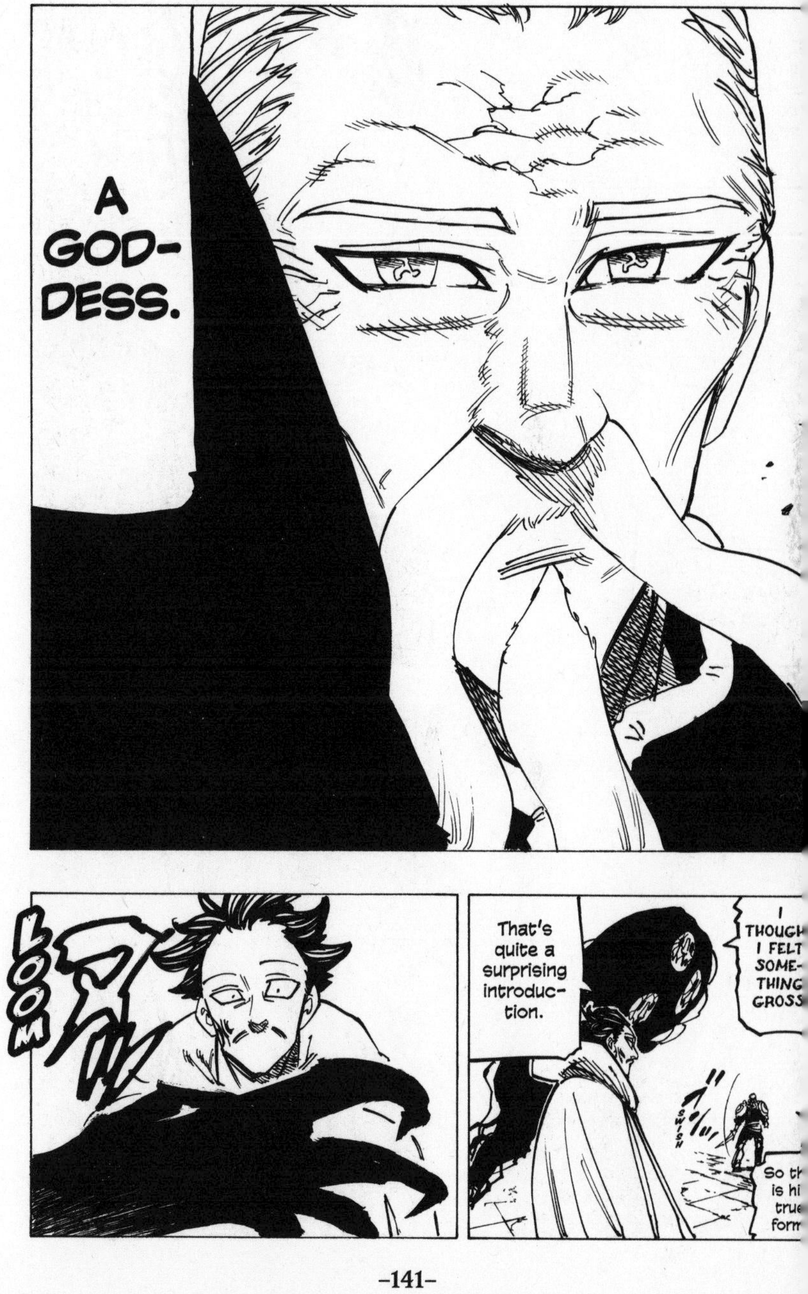
A GOD-DESS.
I THOUGH I FELT SOME- THING GROSS
That's quite a surprising introduc- tion.
SWISH
So th is hi true form
LOOM

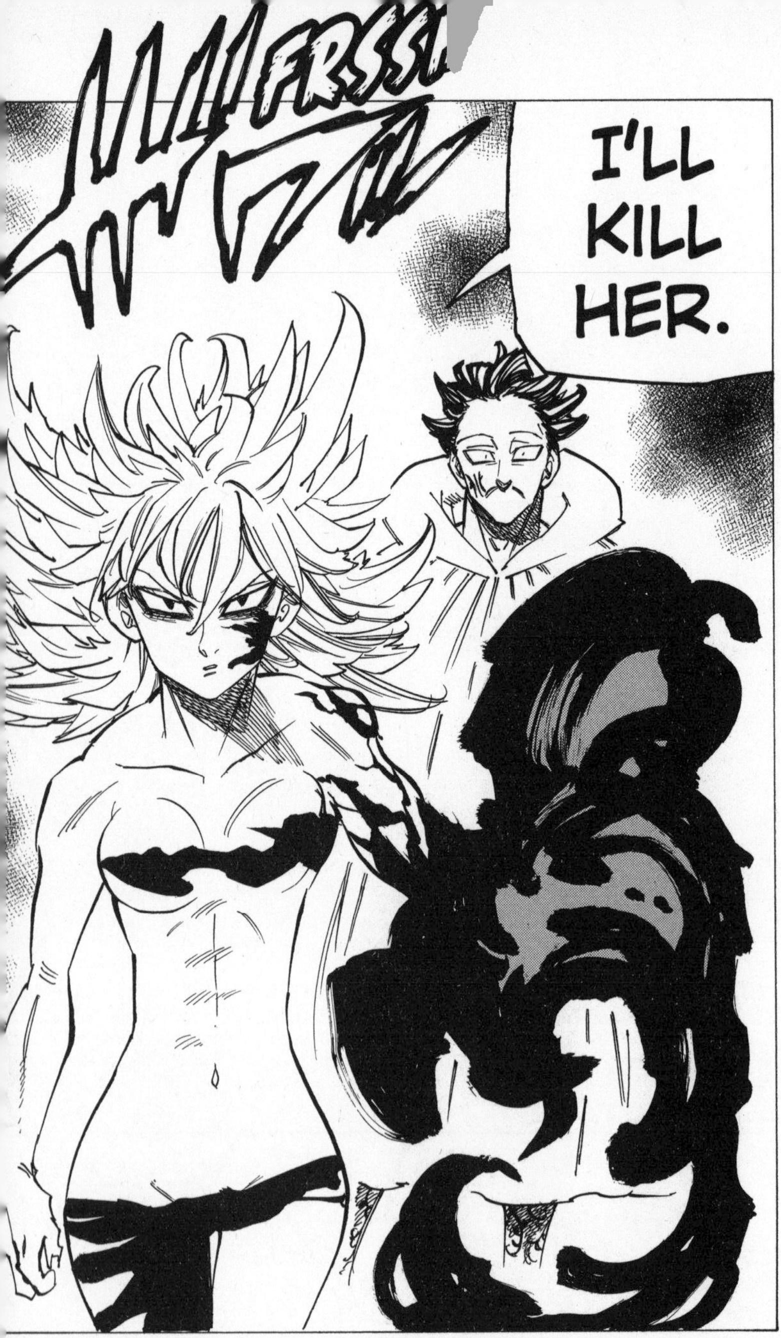
I'LL KILL HER.

Chapter 187 - Die, All You Wicke

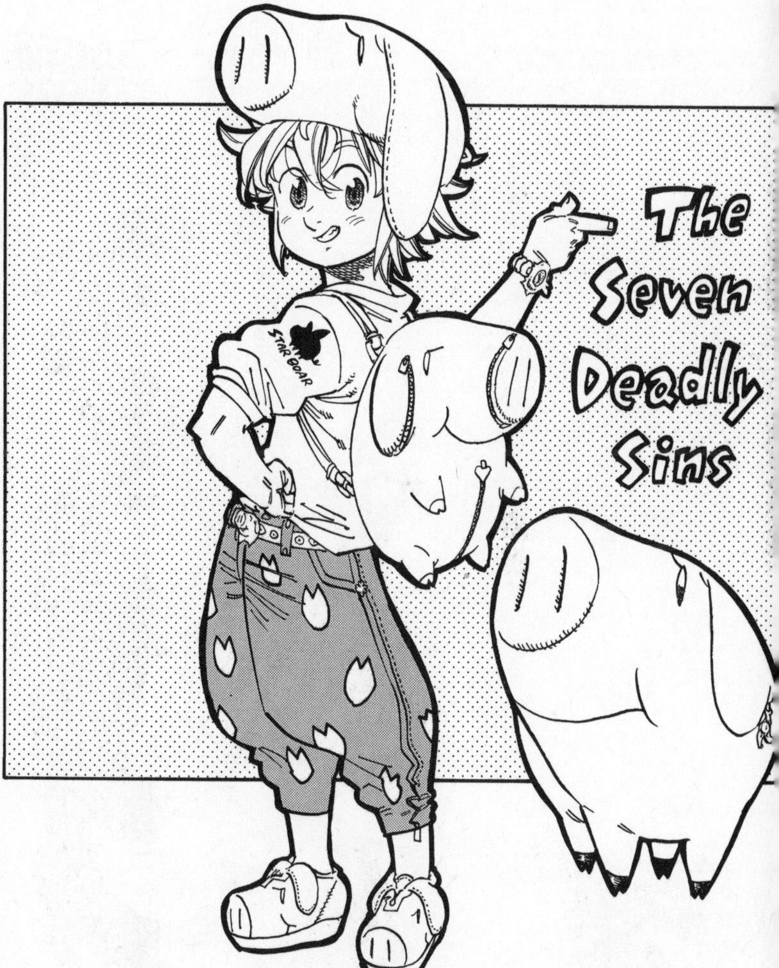
The Seven Deadly Sins
STAR BOAR

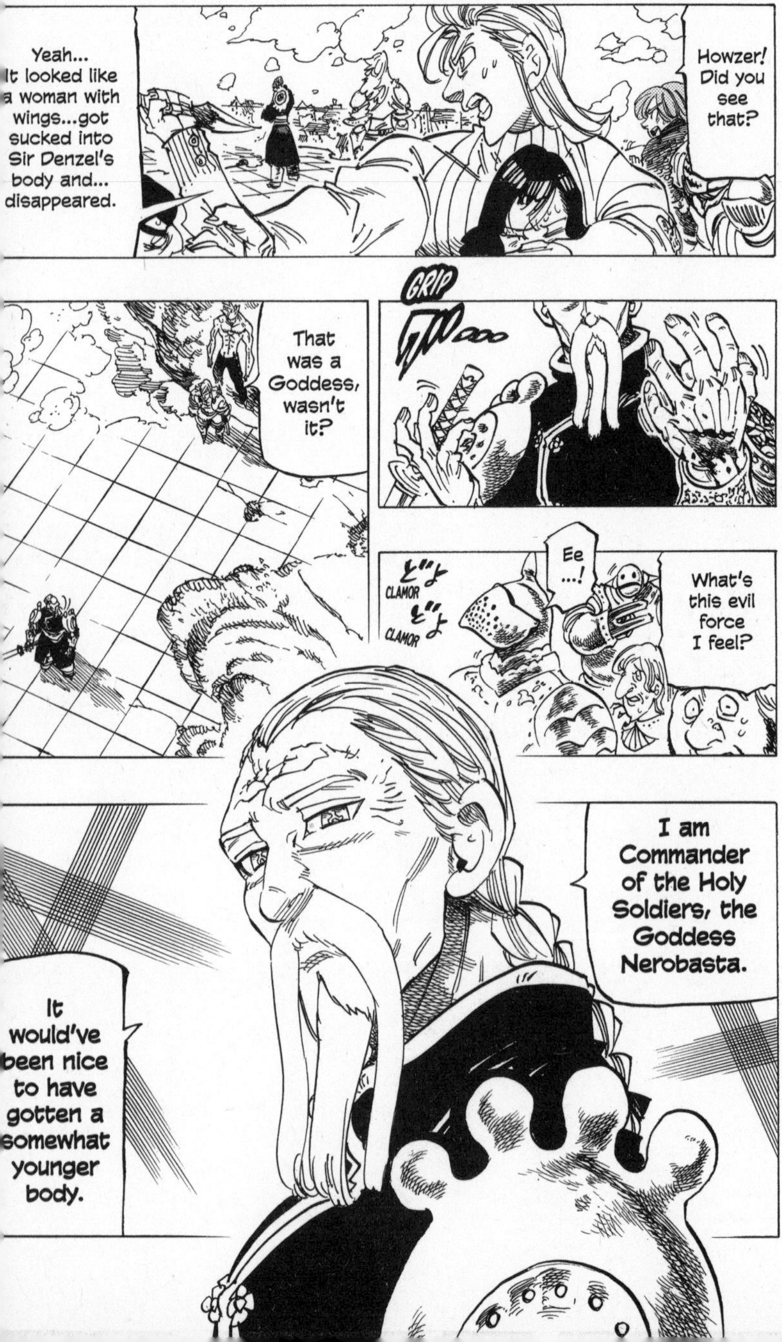
Howzer! Did you see that?
Yeah... It looked like a woman with wings...got sucked into Sir Denzel's body and... disappeared.
GRIP
What's this evil force I feel?
Ee ...!
どよ CLAMOR
どよ CLAMOR
That was a Goddess, wasn't it?
I am Commander of the Holy Soldiers, the Goddess Nerobasta.
It would've been nice to have gotten a somewhat younger body.

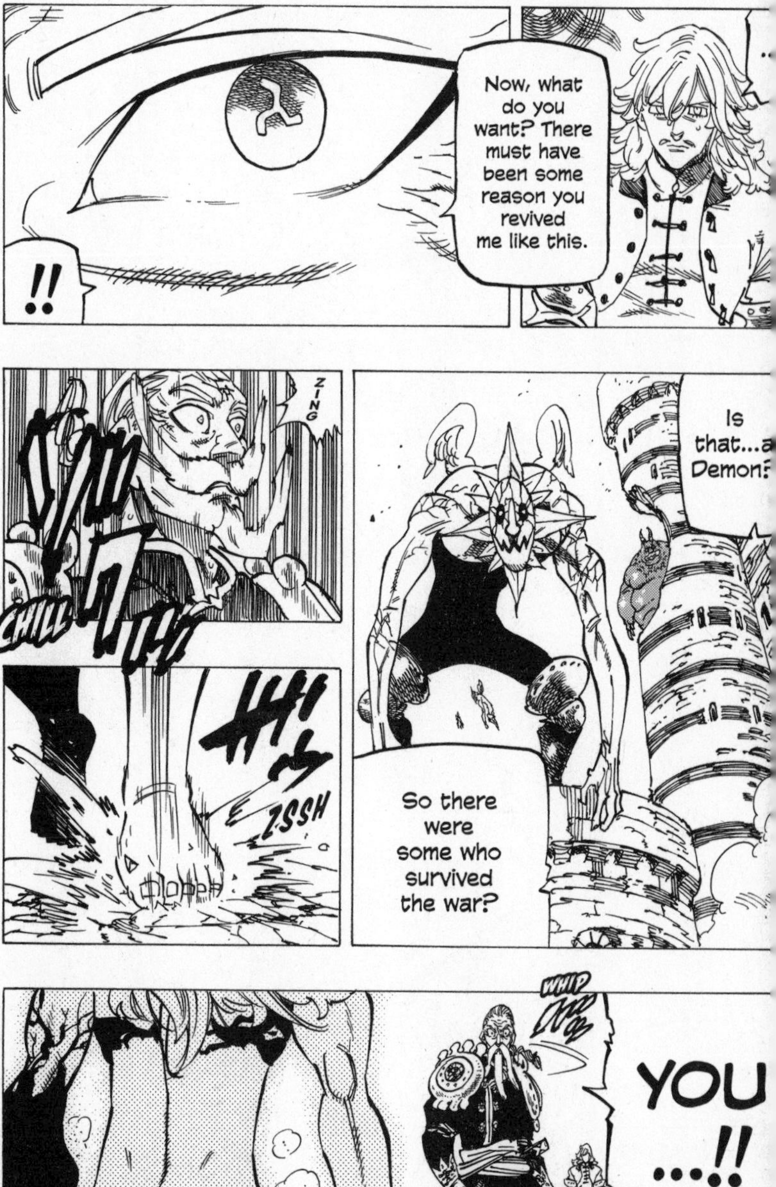
Now, what do you want? There must have been some reason you revived me like this.
!!
Is that...a Demon?
So there were some who survived the war?
ZING
CHILL
ZSSH
WHIP
YOU ...!!

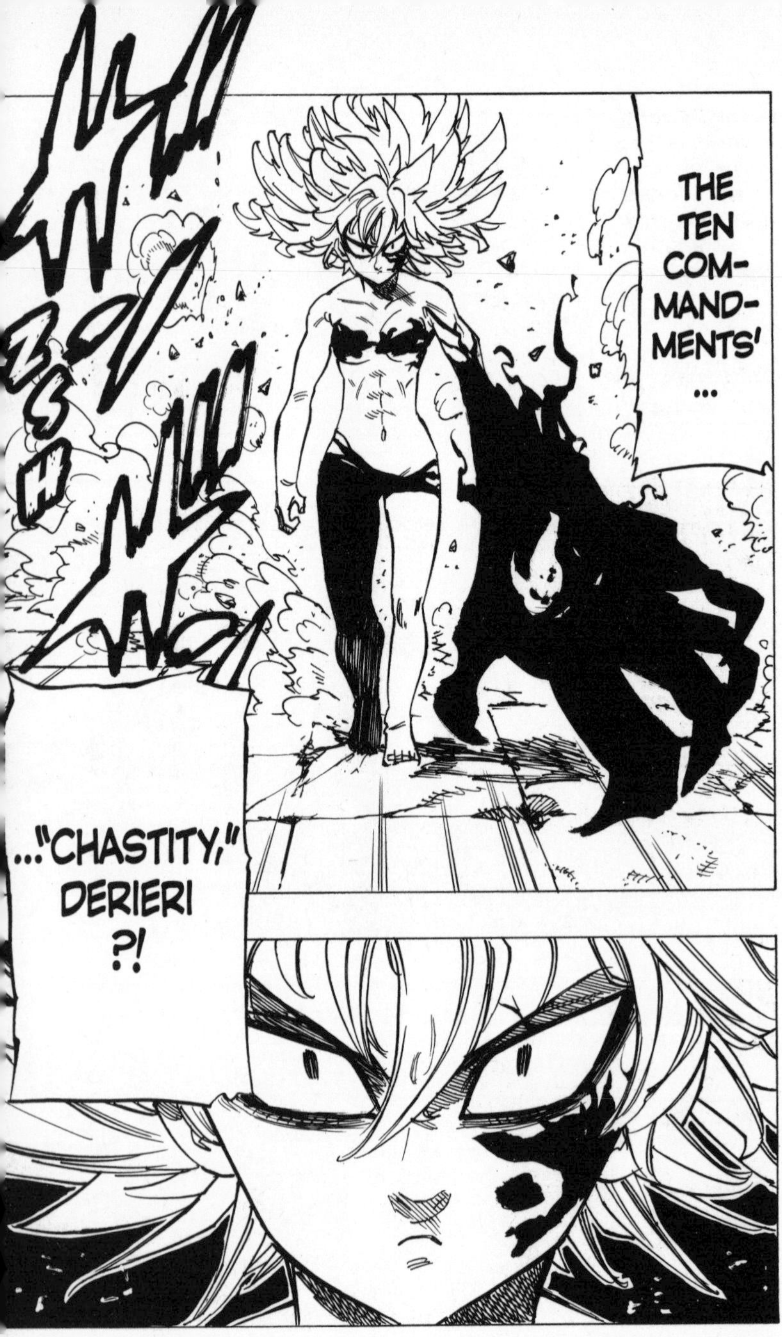
THE TEN COMMANDMENTS'...
..."CHASTITY," DERIERI ?!

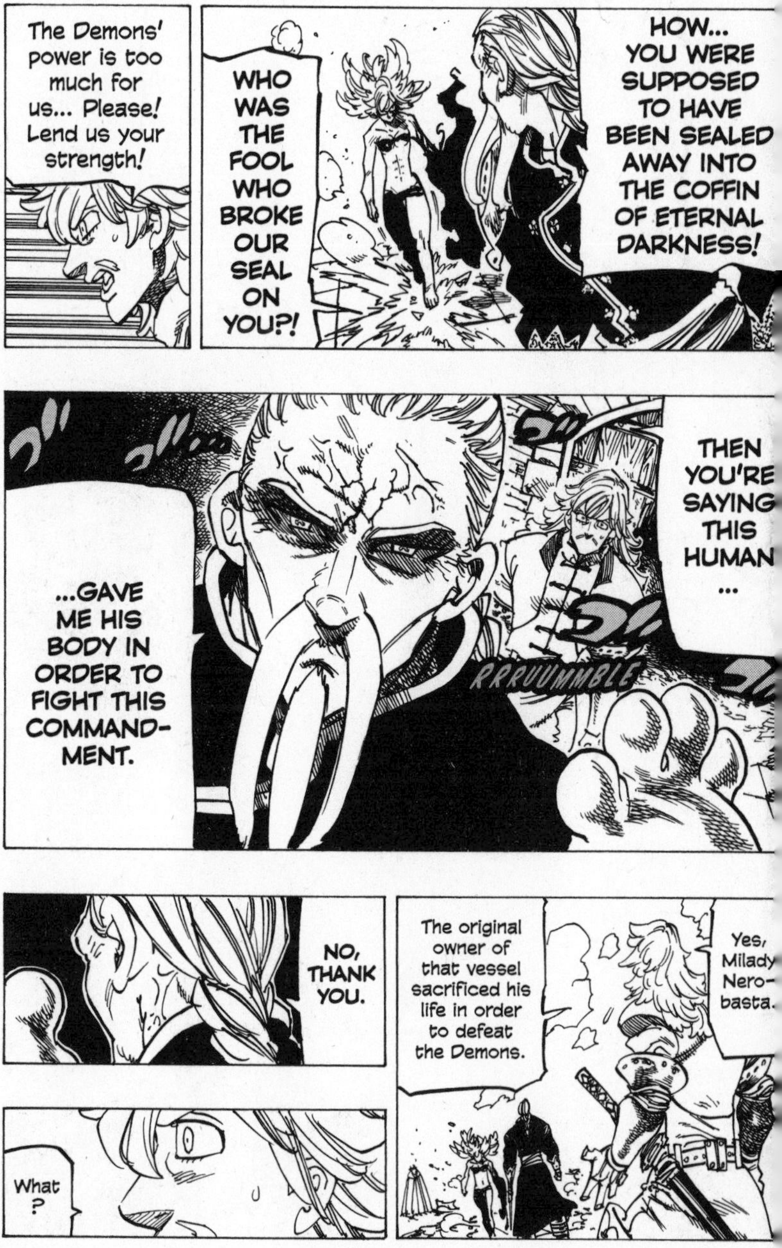
HOW... YOU WERE SUPPOSED TO HAVE BEEN SEALED AWAY INTO THE COFFIN OF ETERNAL DARKNESS!
WHO WAS THE FOOL WHO BROKE OUR SEAL ON YOU?!
The Demons' power is too much for us... Please! Lend us your strength!
THEN YOU'RE SAYING THIS HUMAN ...
RRRUUMMBLE
...GAVE ME HIS BODY IN ORDER TO FIGHT THIS COMMAND-MENT.
Yes, Milady Nero-basta.
The original owner of that vessel sacrificed his life in order to defeat the Demons.
NO, THANK YOU.
What ?

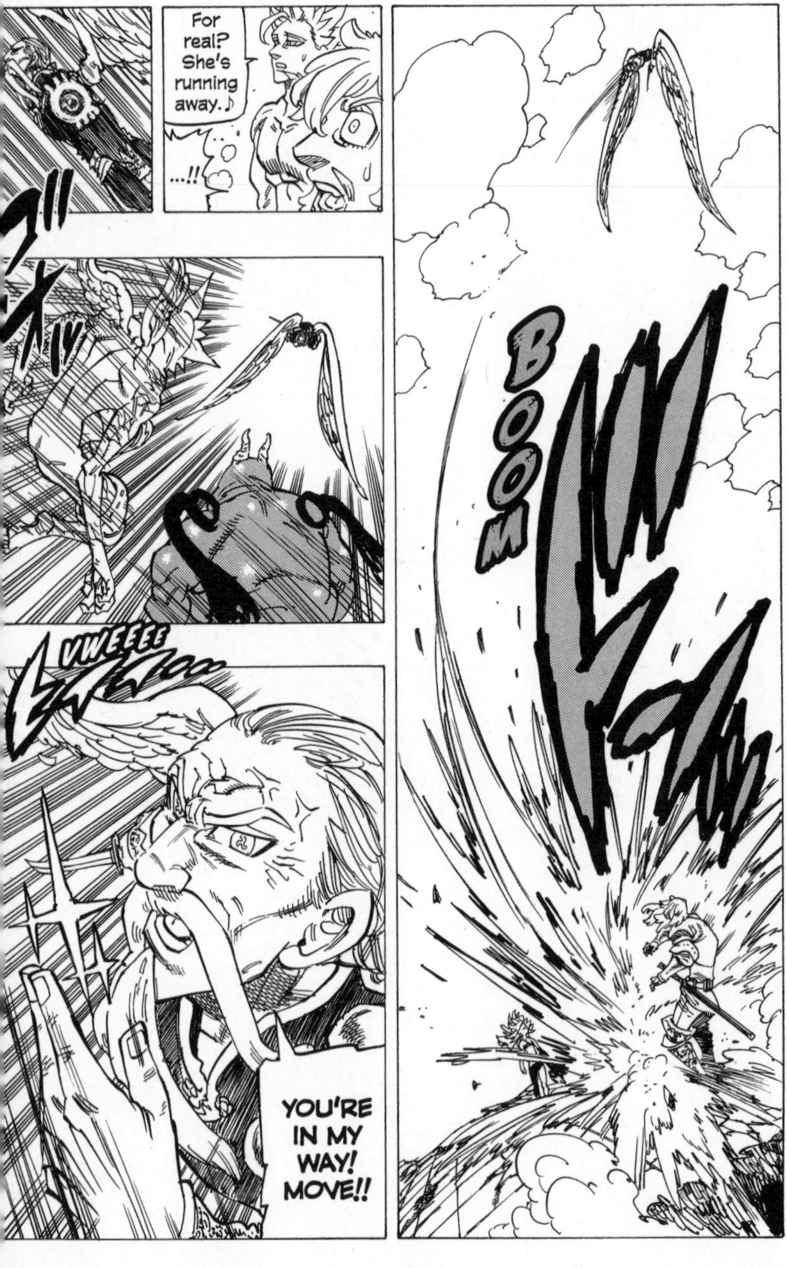
BOOOM
For real? She's running away.♪
...!!
VWEEEE
YOU'RE IN MY WAY! MOVE!!

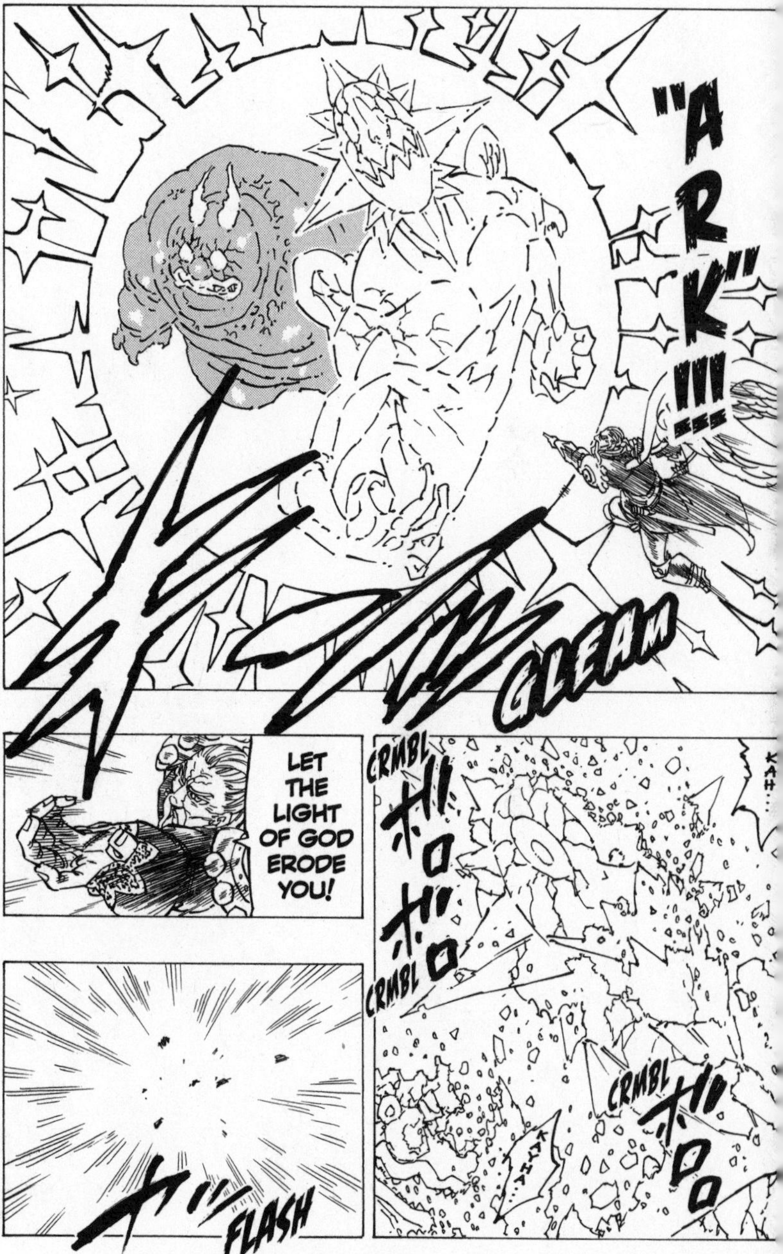
"ARK"!!!
GLEAM
KAH...
CRMBL
CRMBL
CRMBL
KAHA...
LET THE LIGHT OF GOD ERODE YOU!
FLASH

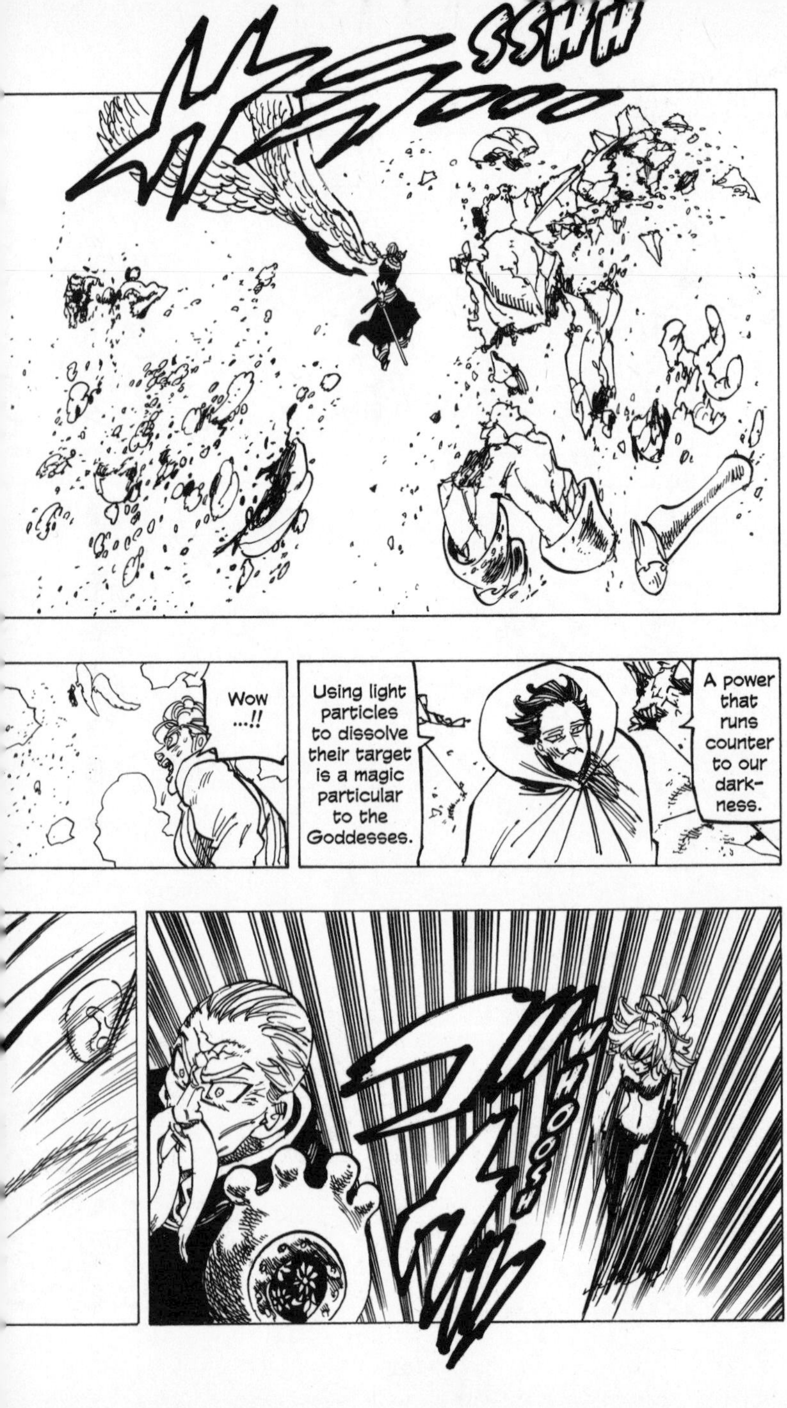
A power that runs counter to our dark-ness.
Using light particles to dissolve their target is a magic particular to the Goddesses.
Wow ...!!

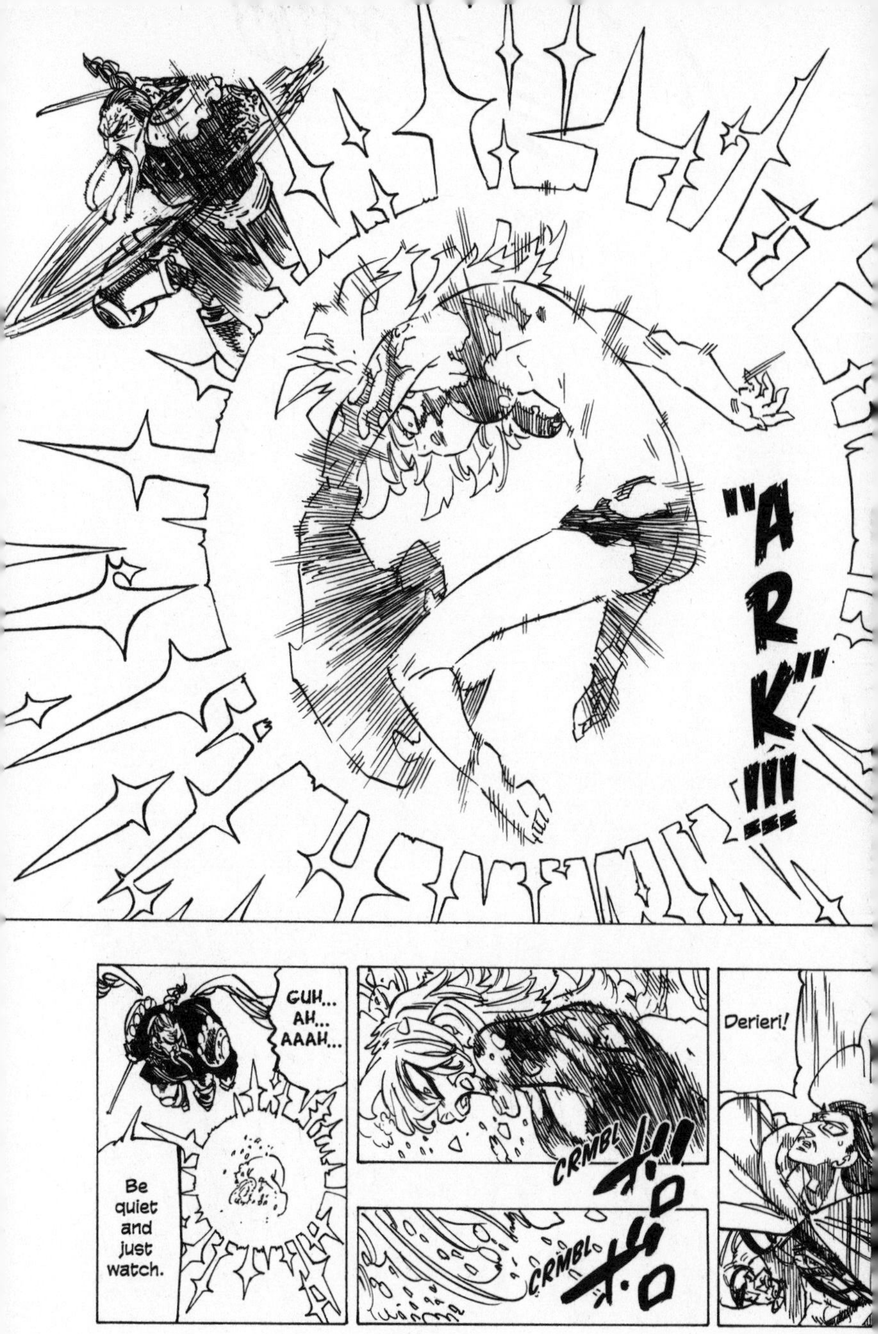
"ARK"!!!
Derieri!
CRMBL
CRMBL
GUH... AH... AAAH...
Be quiet and just watch.

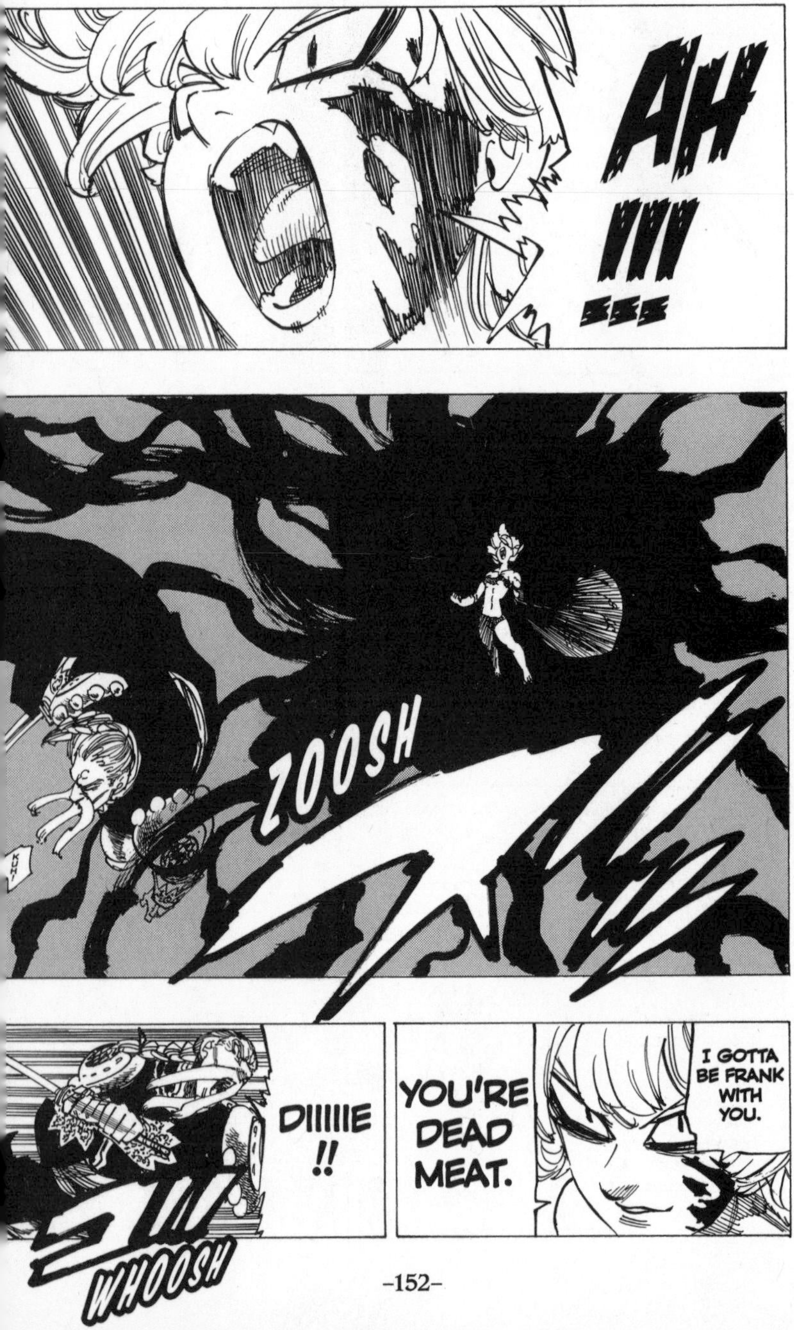
AH!!!
ZOOSH
KUH!
I GOTTA BE FRANK WITH YOU.
YOU'RE DEAD MEAT.
DIIIIIE!!
WHOOSH

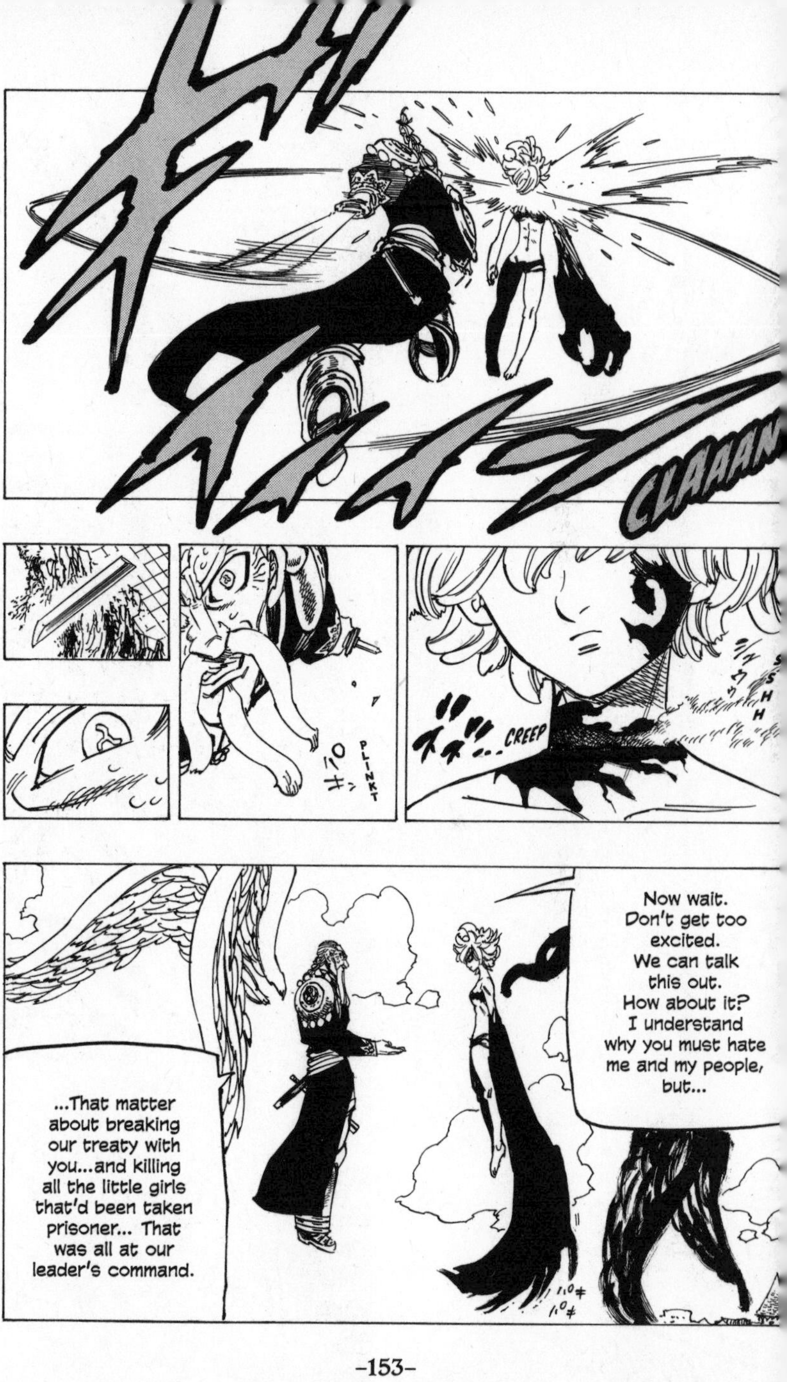
CLAAAN
SHHH
CREEP
PLINKT
Now wait. Don't get too excited. We can talk this out. How about it? I understand why you must hate me and my people, but...
...That matter about breaking our treaty with you...and killing all the little girls that'd been taken prisoner... That was all at our leader's command.

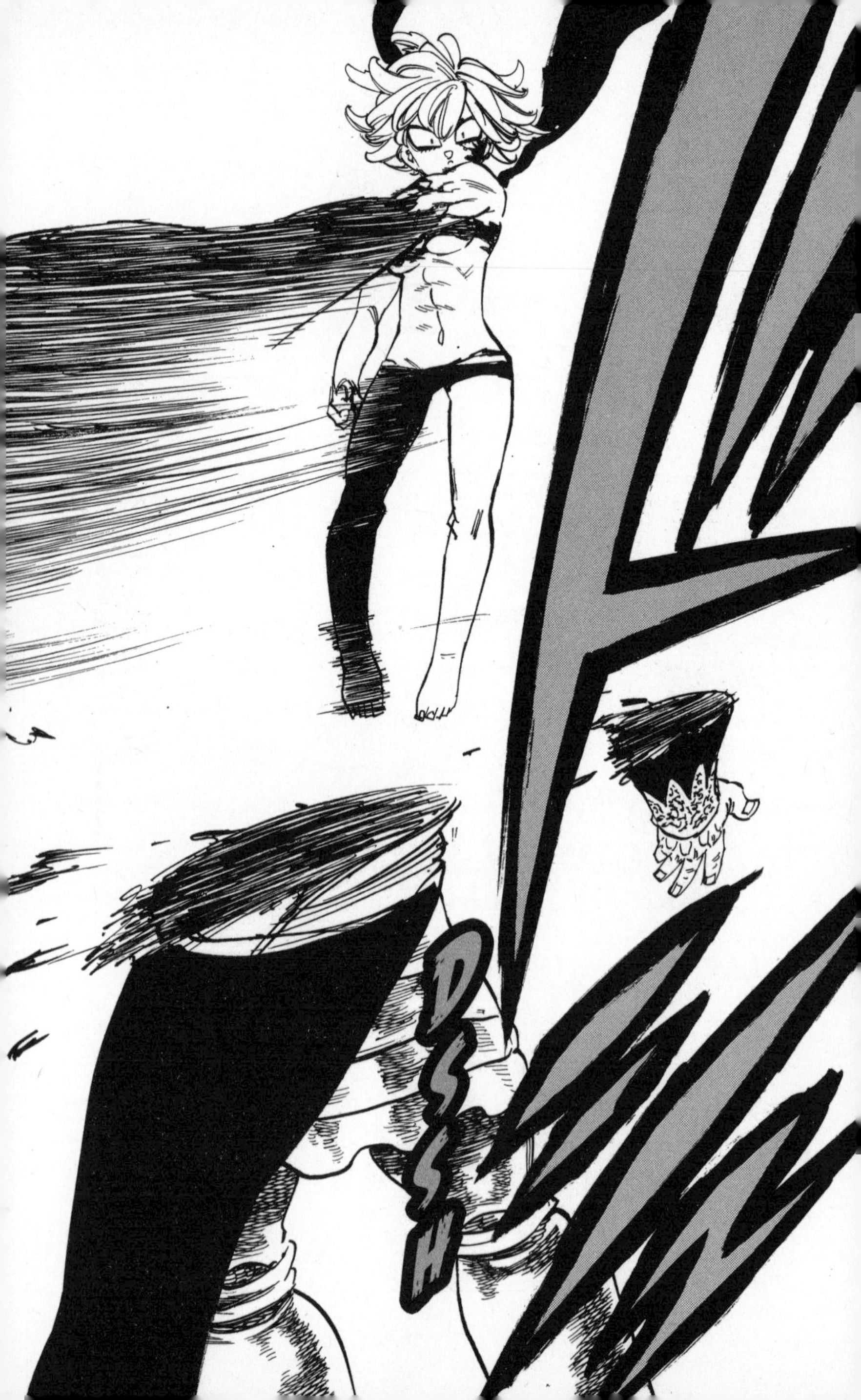
!!
DASH

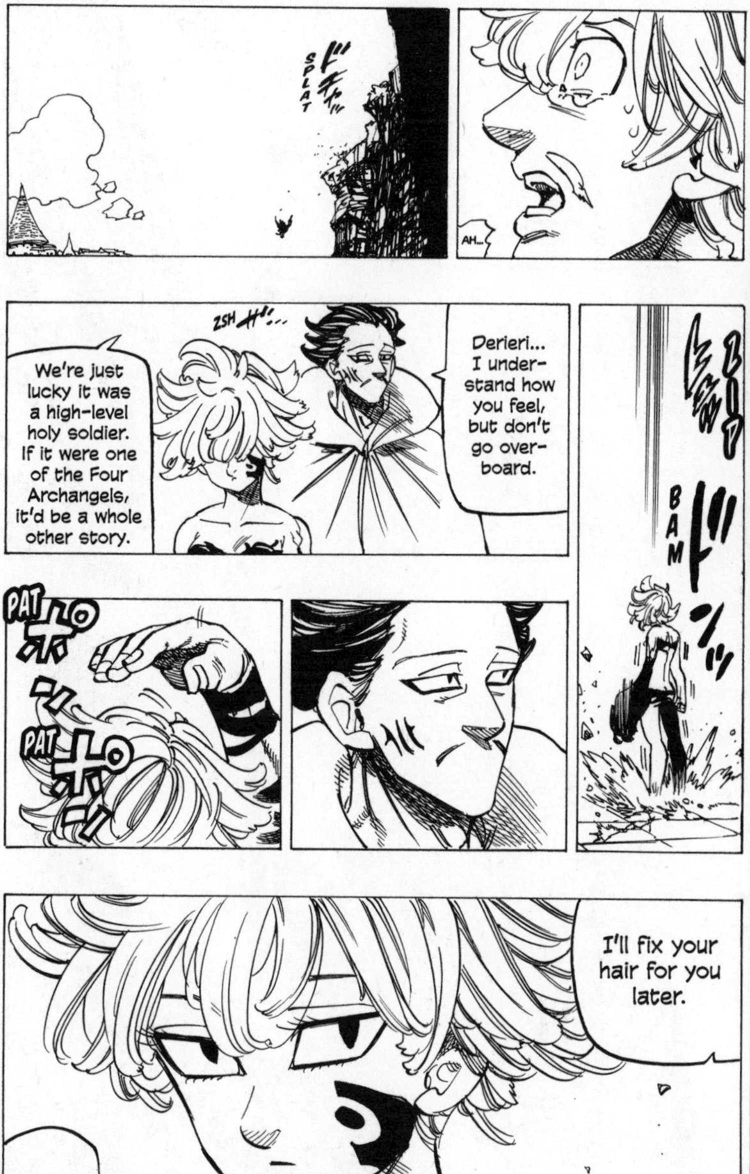
AH...
SPLAT
BOD
BAM
Derieri... I understand how you feel, but don't go overboard.
ZSH
We're just lucky it was a high-level holy soldier. If it were one of the Four Archangels, it'd be a whole other story.
PAT
PAT
I'll fix your hair for you later.
Mm.

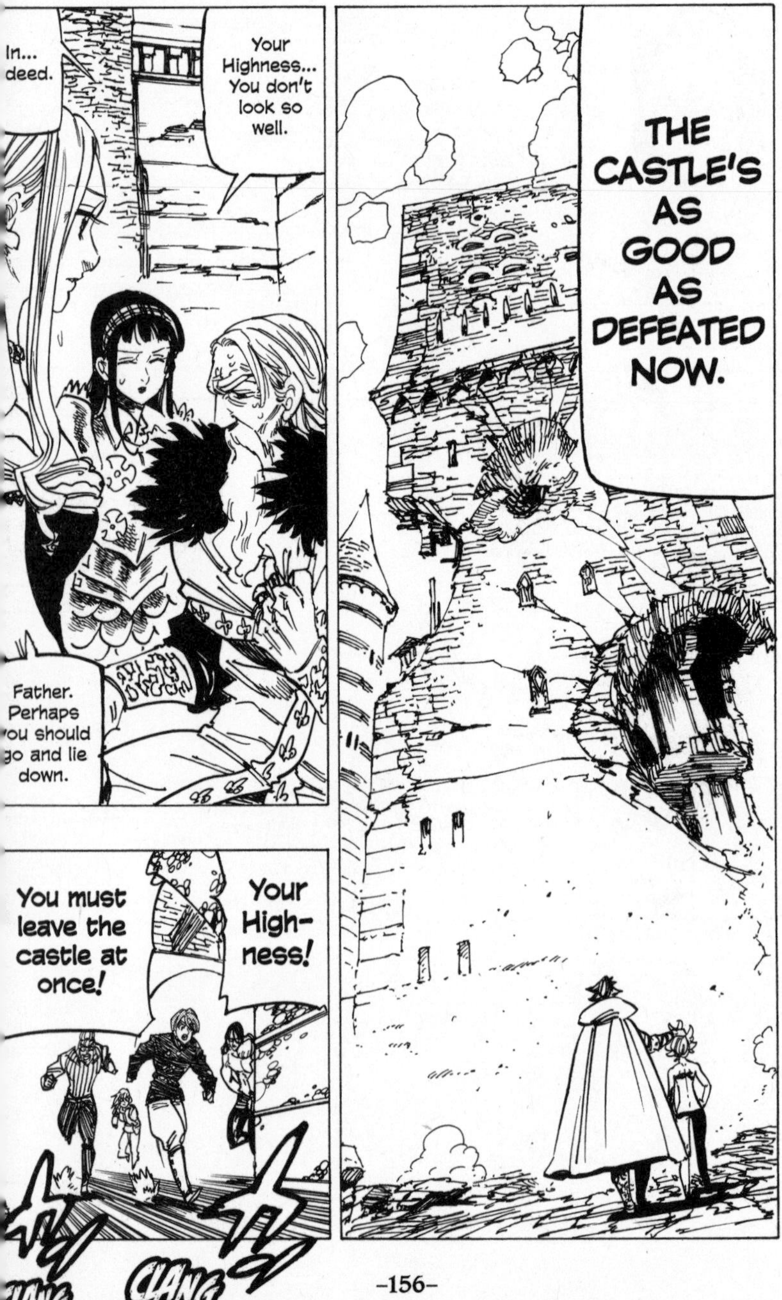
THE CASTLE'S AS GOOD AS DEFEATED NOW.
Your Highness... You don't look so well.
In... deed.
Father. Perhaps you should go and lie down.
Your High-ness!
You must leave the castle at once!
CLANG
CLANG

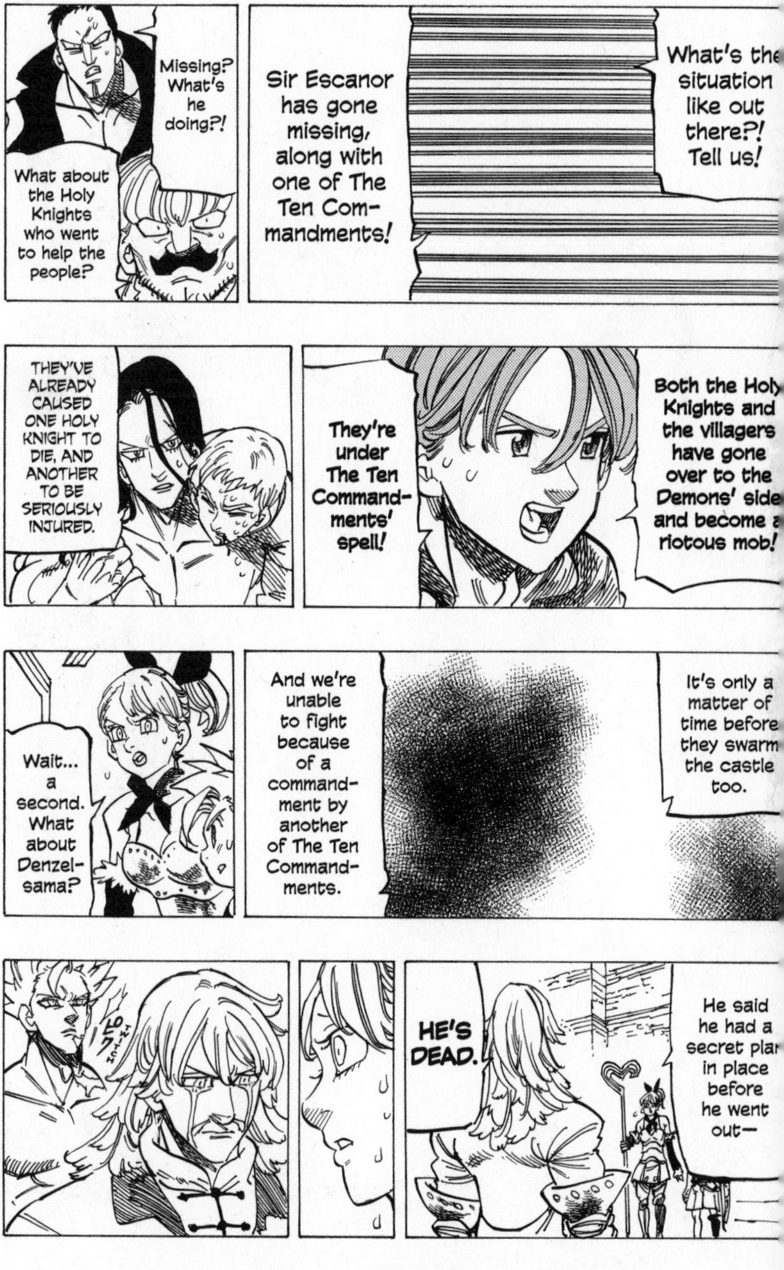
What's the situation like out there?! Tell us!
Sir Escanor has gone missing, along with one of The Ten Commandments!
Missing? What's he doing?!
What about the Holy Knights who went to help the people?
Both the Holy Knights and the villagers have gone over to the Demons' side and become a riotous mob!
They're under The Ten Commandments' spell!
THEY'VE ALREADY CAUSED ONE HOLY KNIGHT TO DIE, AND ANOTHER TO BE SERIOUSLY INJURED.
It's only a matter of time before they swarm the castle too.
And we're unable to fight because of a commandment by another of The Ten Commandments.
Wait... a second. What about Denzel-sama?
He said he had a secret plan in place before he went out—
HE'S DEAD.

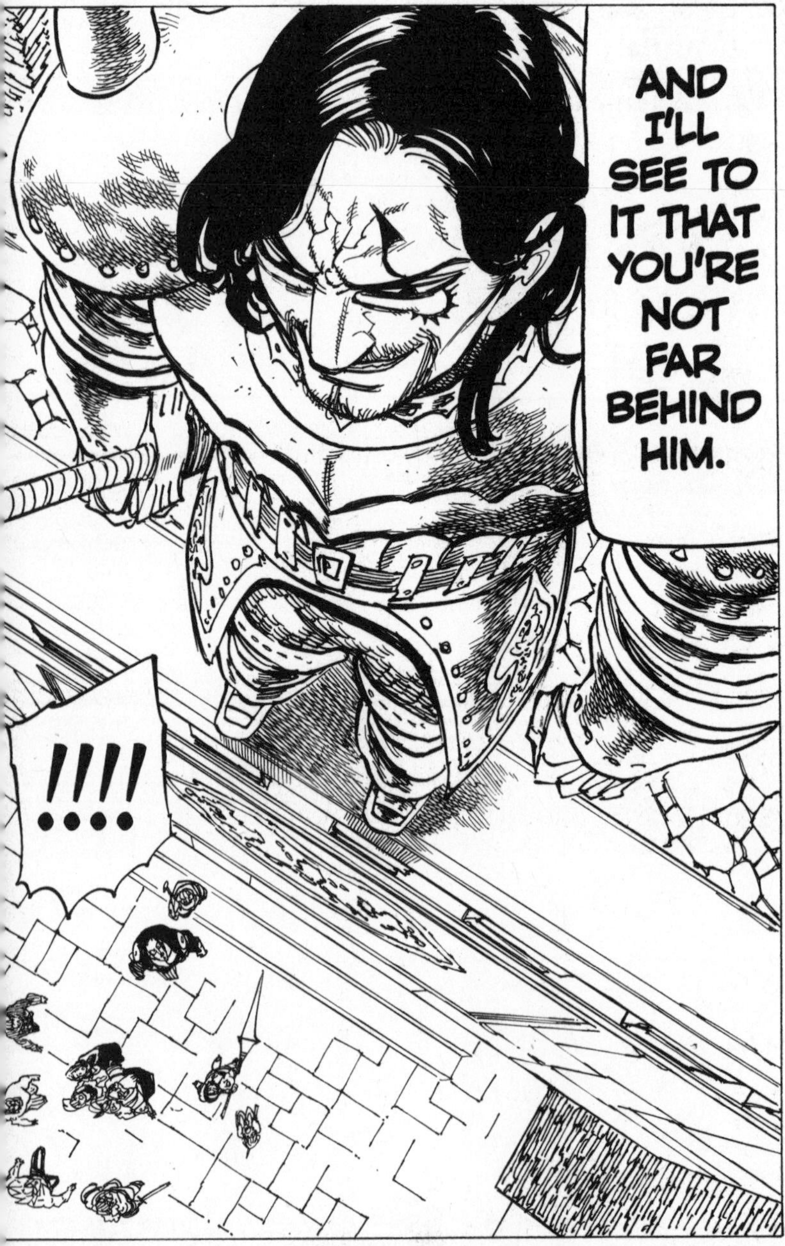

AND I'LL SEE TO IT THAT YOU'RE NOT FAR BEHIND HIM.
!!!!

"THE SEVEN DEADLY SINS" Q&A CORNER

"CHATTING KNIGHTHOOD"

Be sure to include your name and location with your submission!!

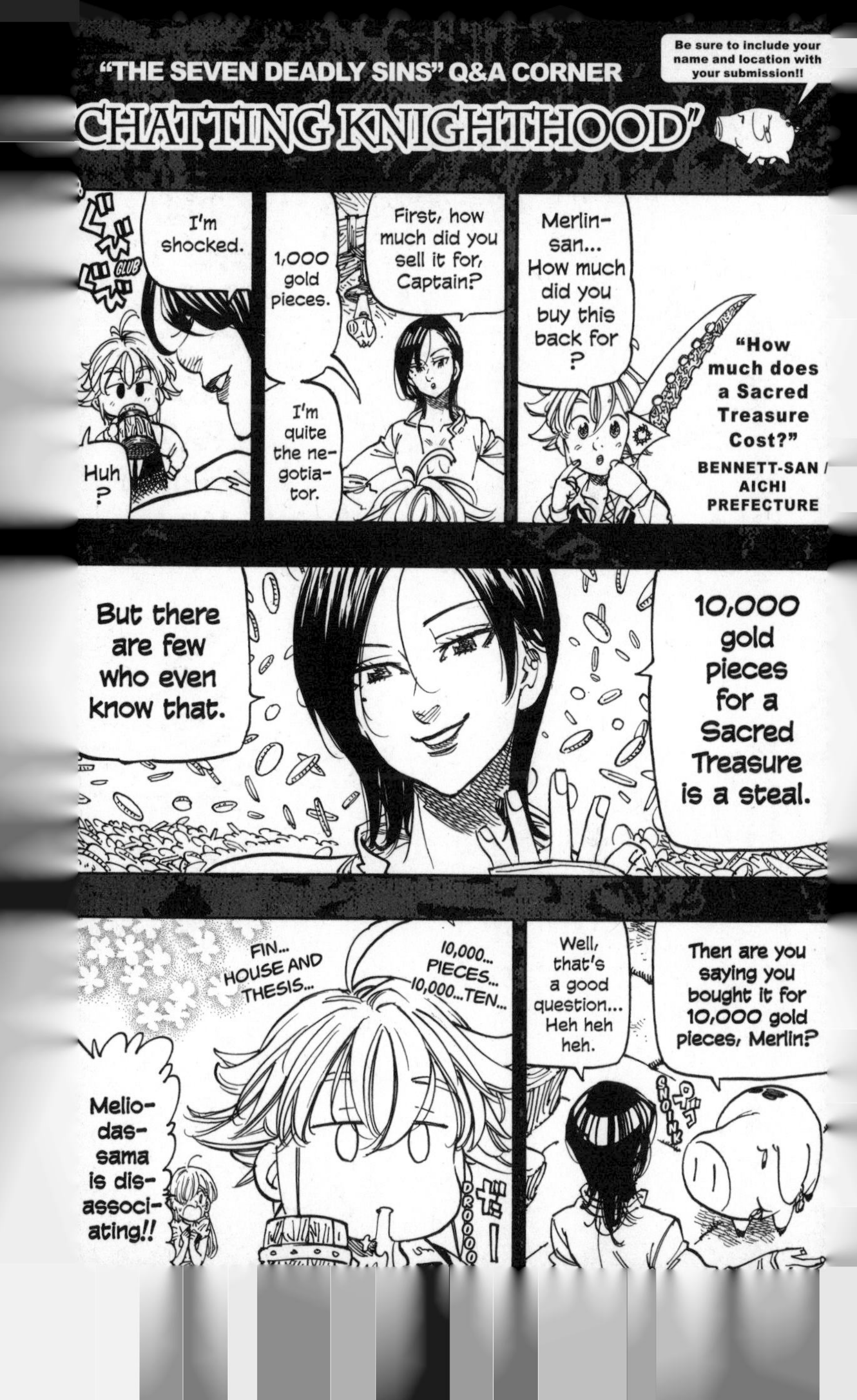
"How much does a Sacred Treasure Cost?"
BENNETT-SAN / AICHI PREFECTURE
Merlin-san... How much did you buy this back for?
First, how much did you sell it for, Captain?
1,000 gold pieces.
I'm quite the negotiator.
I'm shocked.
GLUB
Huh?
10,000 gold pieces for a Sacred Treasure is a steal.
But there are few who even know that.
Then are you saying you bought it for 10,000 gold pieces, Merlin?
SNOINK
Well, that's a good question... Heh heh heh.
10,000... PIECES... 10,000...TEN...
FIN... HOUSE AND THESIS...
DROOOOO
Melio-das-sama is dis-associ-ating!!

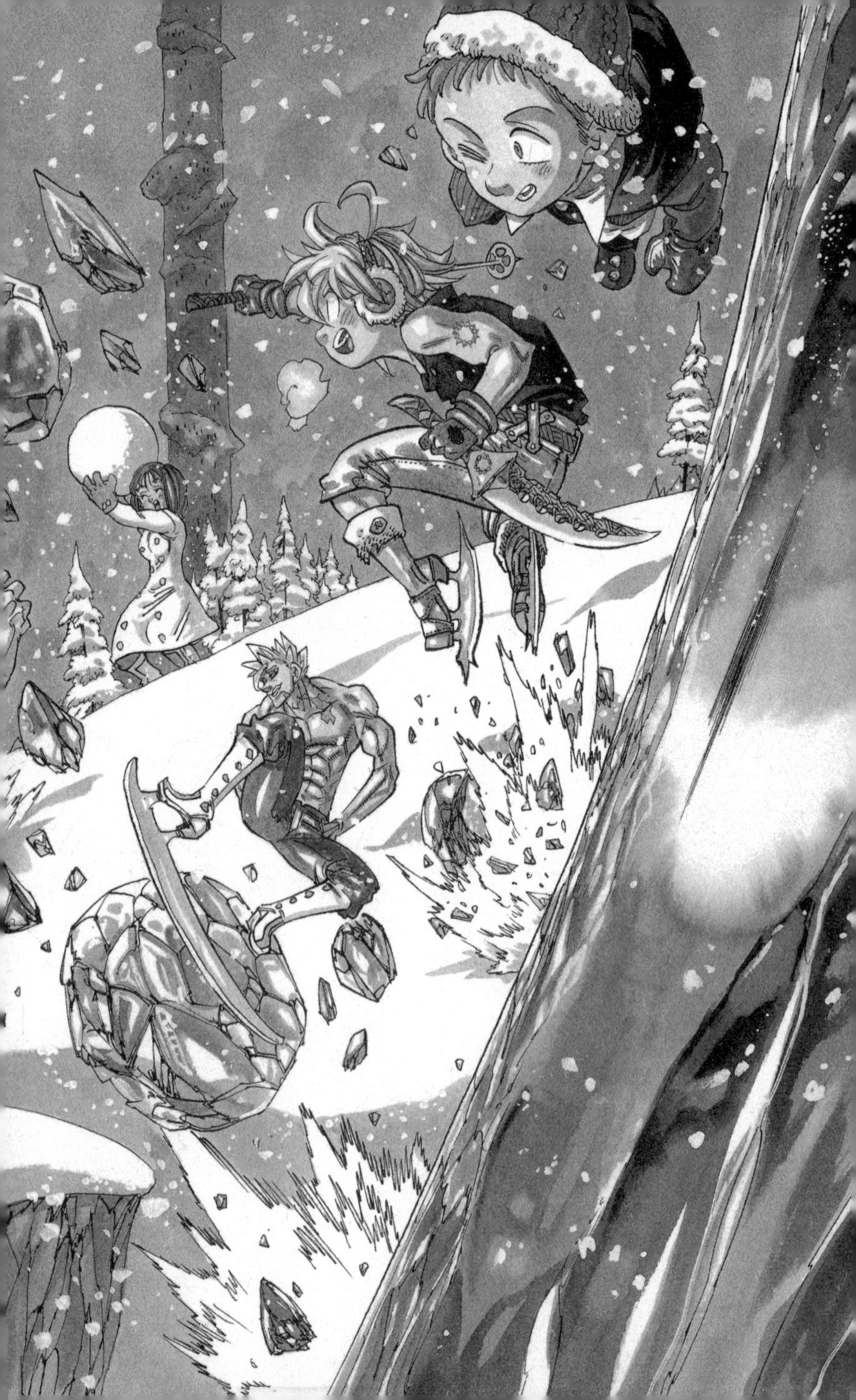

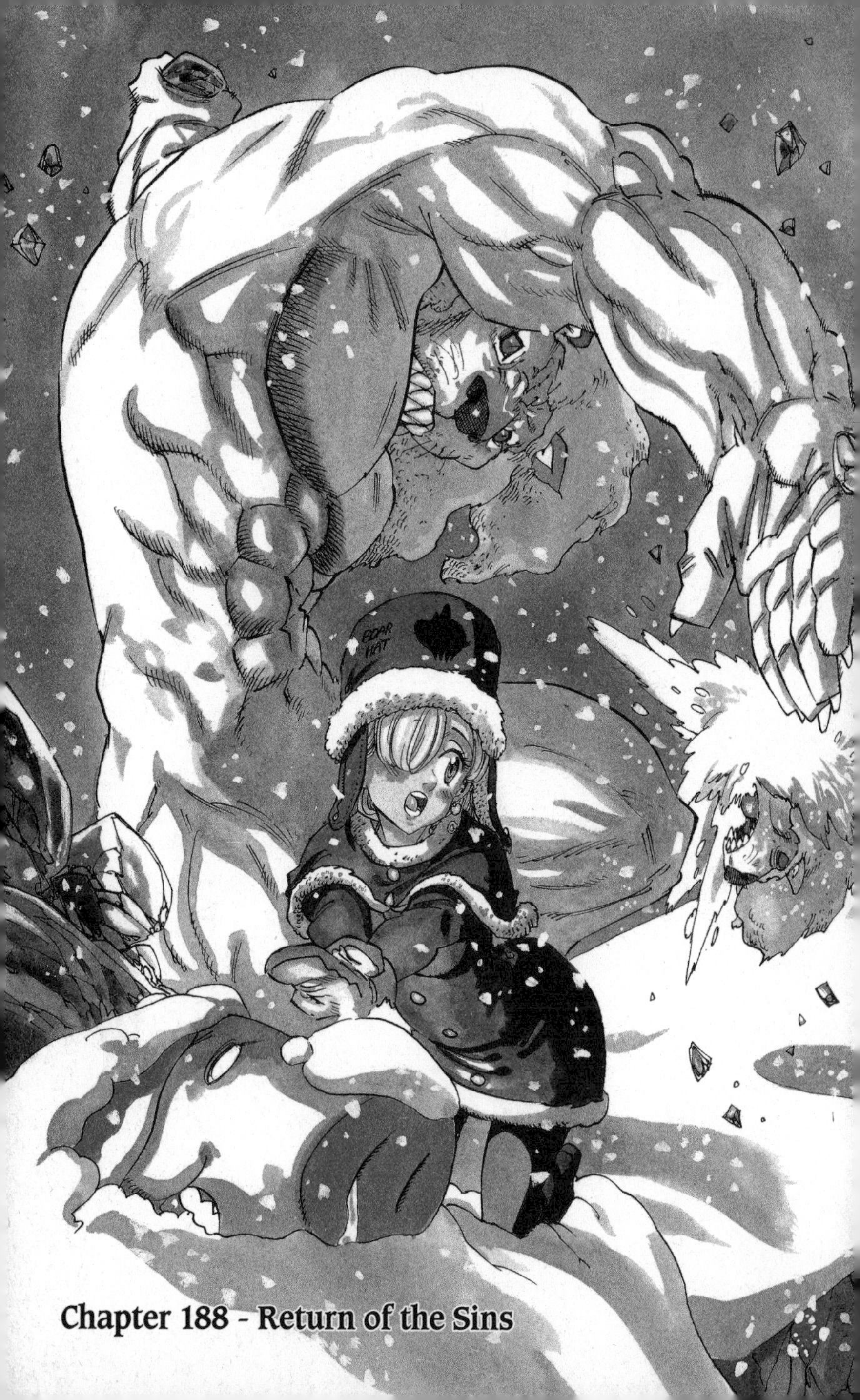
BOAR HAT

Chapter 188 - Return of the Sins

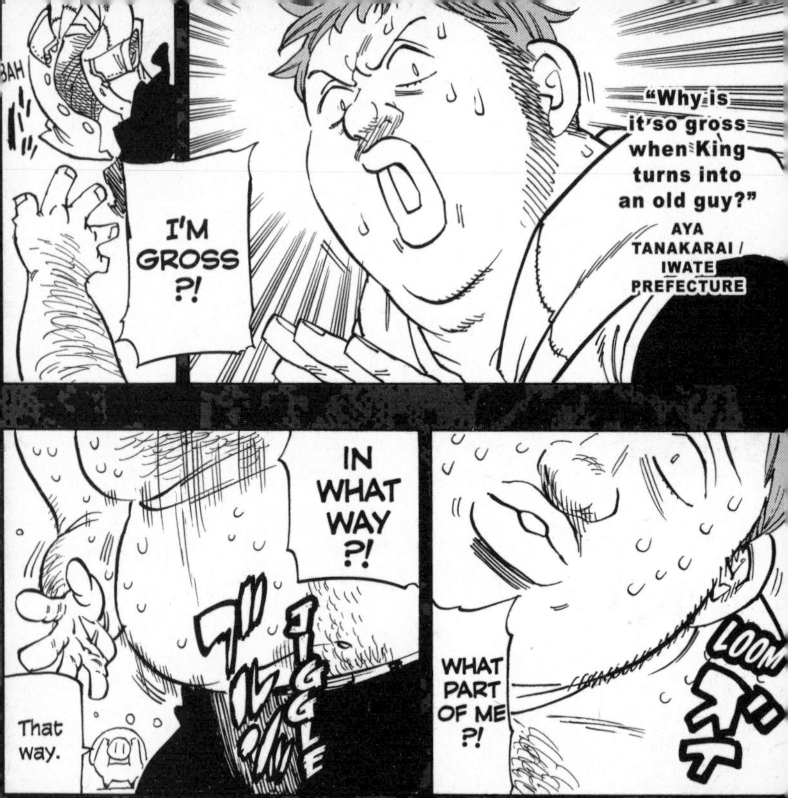
"Why is it so gross when King turns into an old guy?"
AYA TANAKARAI / IWATE PREFECTURE
I'M GROSS ?!
BAH
WHAT PART OF ME ?!
LOOM
IN WHAT WAY ?!
JIGGLE
That way.

Now Accepting Applicants for the Chatting Knighthood!

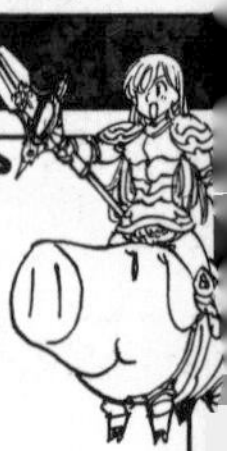

- Write your question on a postcard and send it in!
- Write as many questions as you like on your postcard!
- Don't forget to write your name and location on the back of your postcard!
- The "Chatting Knights" who are particularly noteworthy and run in the print edition will be gifted with a signed specially made pencil board!

Send to:
The Seven Deadly Sins Chatting Knighthood
c/o Kodansha Comics
451 Park Ave. South, 7th floor,
New York, NY 10016

- Submitted letters and postcards will be given to the artist. Please be aware that your name, address, and other personal information included will be given as well.

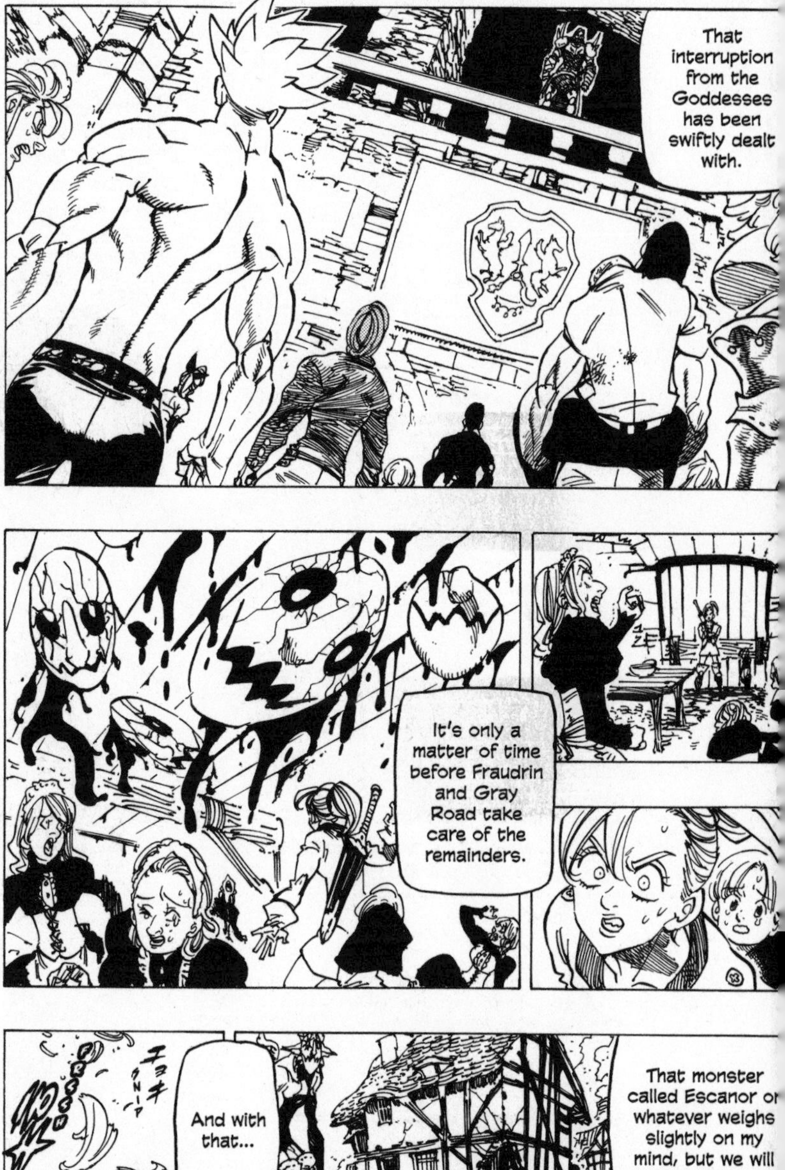
That interruption from the Goddesses has been swiftly dealt with.
It's only a matter of time before Fraudrin and Gray Road take care of the remainders.
That monster called Escanor or whatever weighs slightly on my mind, but we will be on standby until he's back.
And with that...

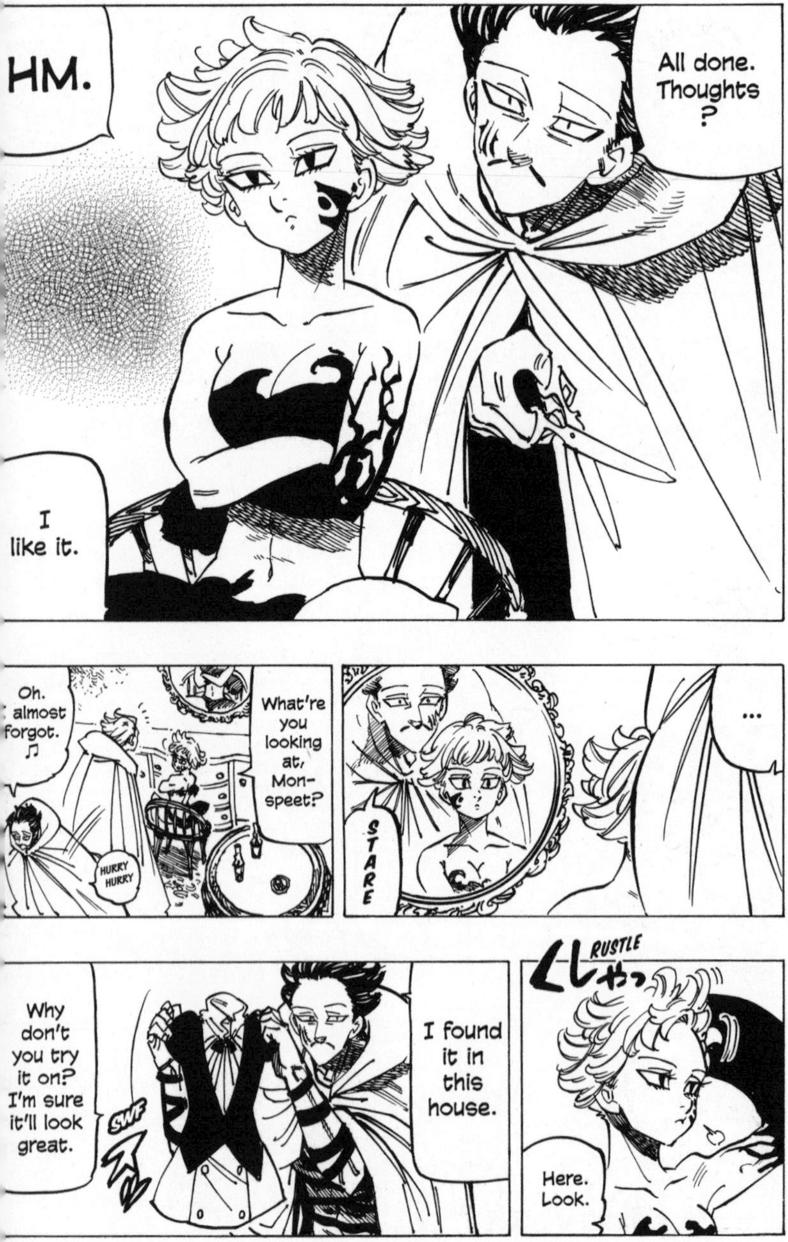
All done. Thoughts?
HM.
I like it.
...
STARE
What're you looking at, Monspeet?
Oh. almost forgot. ♫
HURRY HURRY
RUSTLE
Here. Look.
I found it in this house.
Why don't you try it on? I'm sure it'll look great.
SWF

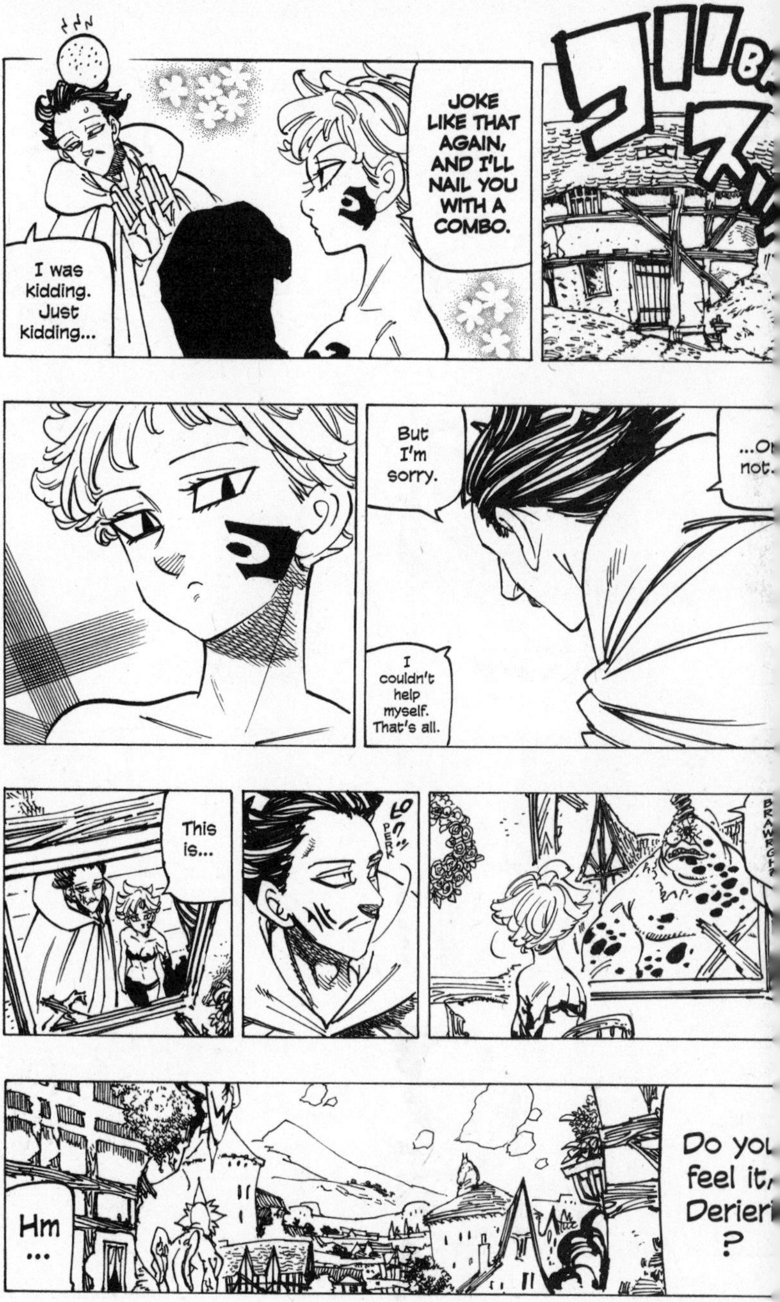
BA
JOKE LIKE THAT AGAIN, AND I'LL NAIL YOU WITH A COMBO.
I was kidding. Just kidding...
...O not.
But I'm sorry.
I couldn't help myself. That's all.
BRAWRGH
PERK
This is...
Do yo feel it, Derier ?
Hm ...

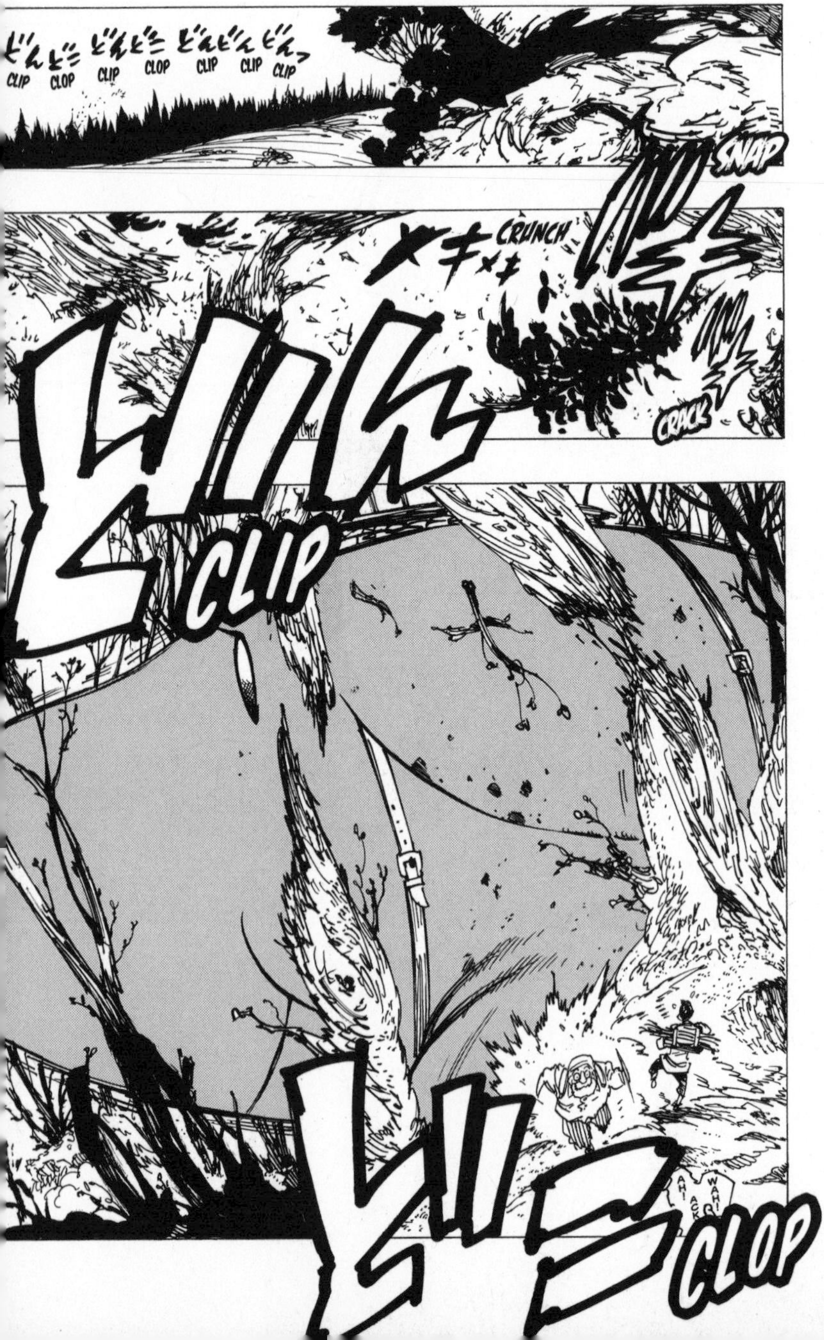
CLIP CLOP CLIP CLOP CLIP CLIP CLIP
SNAP
CRUNCH
CRACK
CLIP
CLOP
WAH!
ACK
AH!

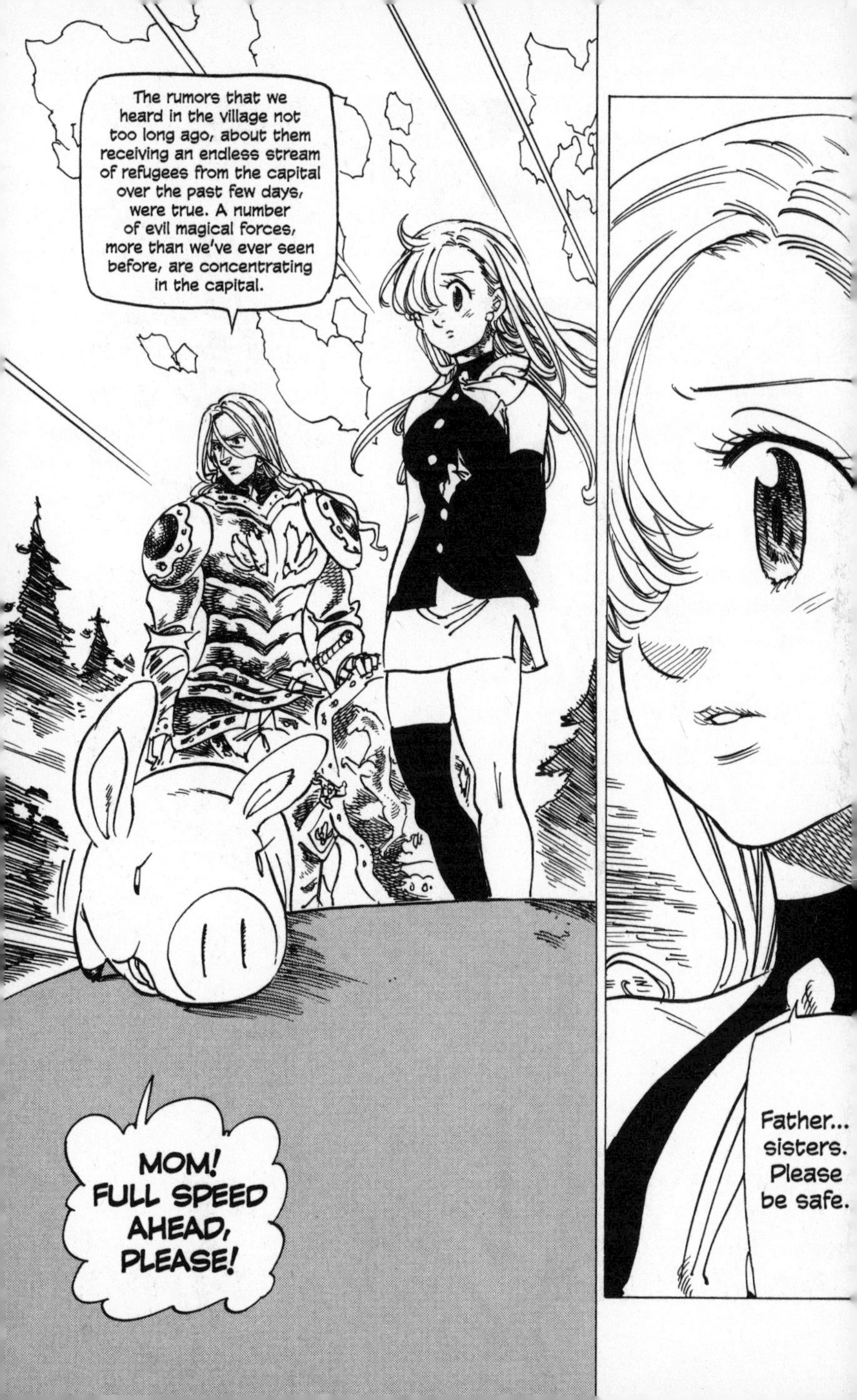
Father... sisters. Please be safe.
The rumors that we heard in the village not too long ago, about them receiving an endless stream of refugees from the capital over the past few days, were true. A number of evil magical forces, more than we've ever seen before, are concentrating in the capital.
MOM! FULL SPEED AHEAD, PLEASE!

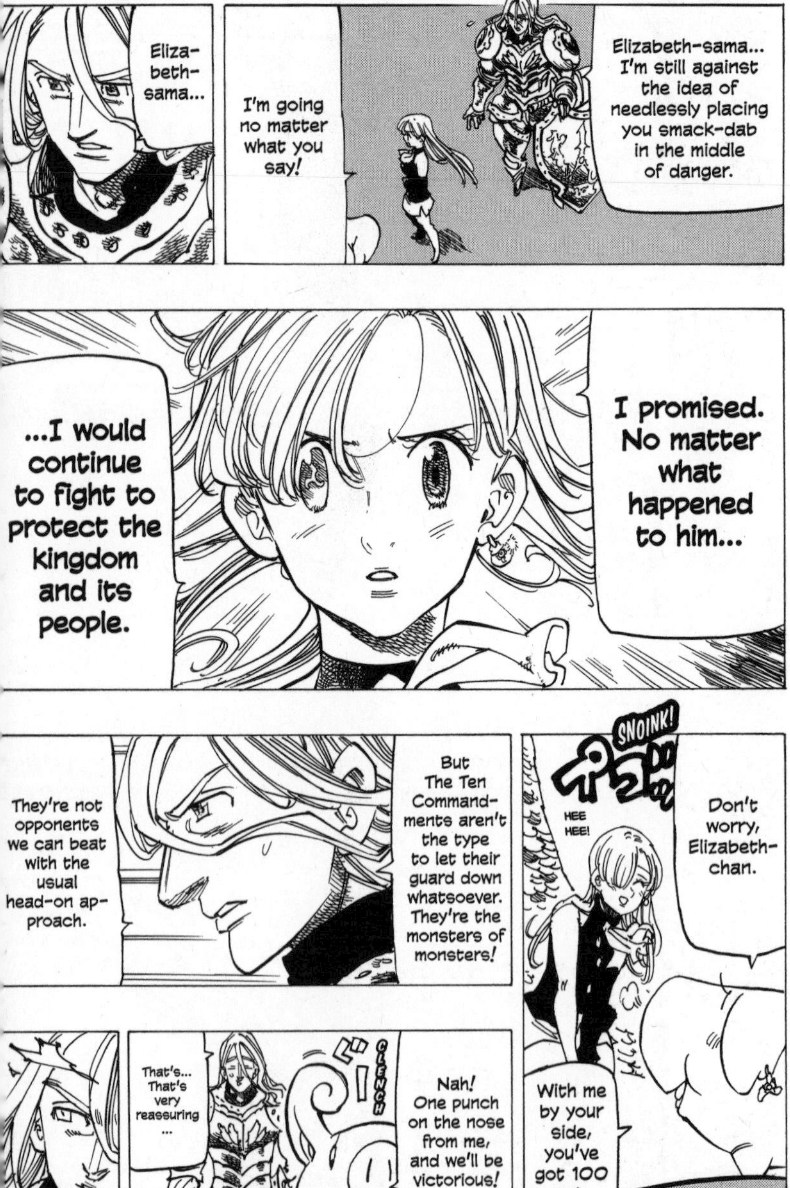
Elizabeth-sama... I'm still against the idea of needlessly placing you smack-dab in the middle of danger.
I'm going no matter what you say!
Eliza-beth-sama...
I promised. No matter what happened to him...
...I would continue to fight to protect the kingdom and its people.
SNOINK!
HEE HEE!
Don't worry, Elizabeth-chan.
With me by your side, you've got 100 pork-power!
But The Ten Commandments aren't the type to let their guard down whatsoever. They're the monsters of monsters!
They're not opponents we can beat with the usual head-on approach.
CLENCH
Nah! One punch on the nose from me, and we'll be victorious!
That's... That's very reassuring ...

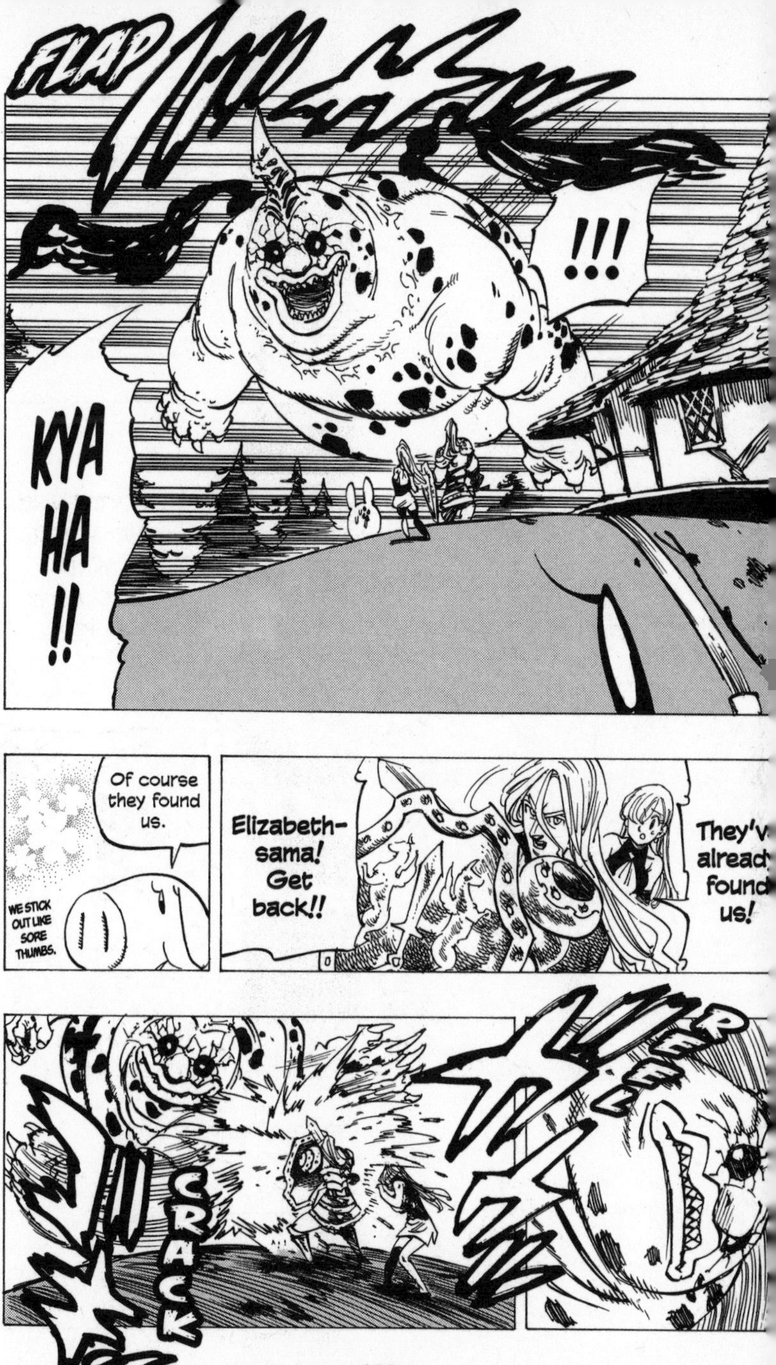
FLAP
!!!
KYA HA HA!!
They'v alread found us!
Elizabeth-sama! Get back!!
Of course they found us.
WE STICK OUT LIKE SORE THUMBS.
CRACK

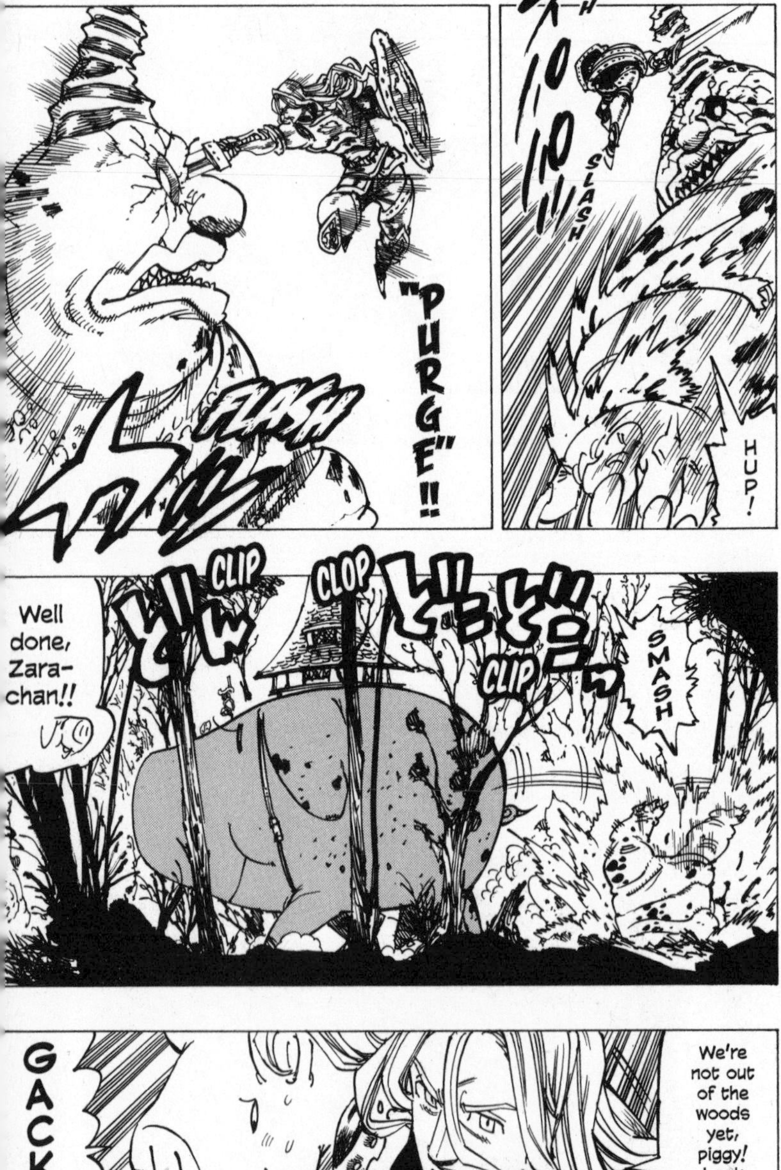
SLASH
SLASH
HUP!
"PURGE"!!
FLASH
SMASH
CLIP
CLOP
CLIP
Well done, Zara-chan!!
We're not out of the woods yet, piggy! Look what's up ahead!
GACK!!

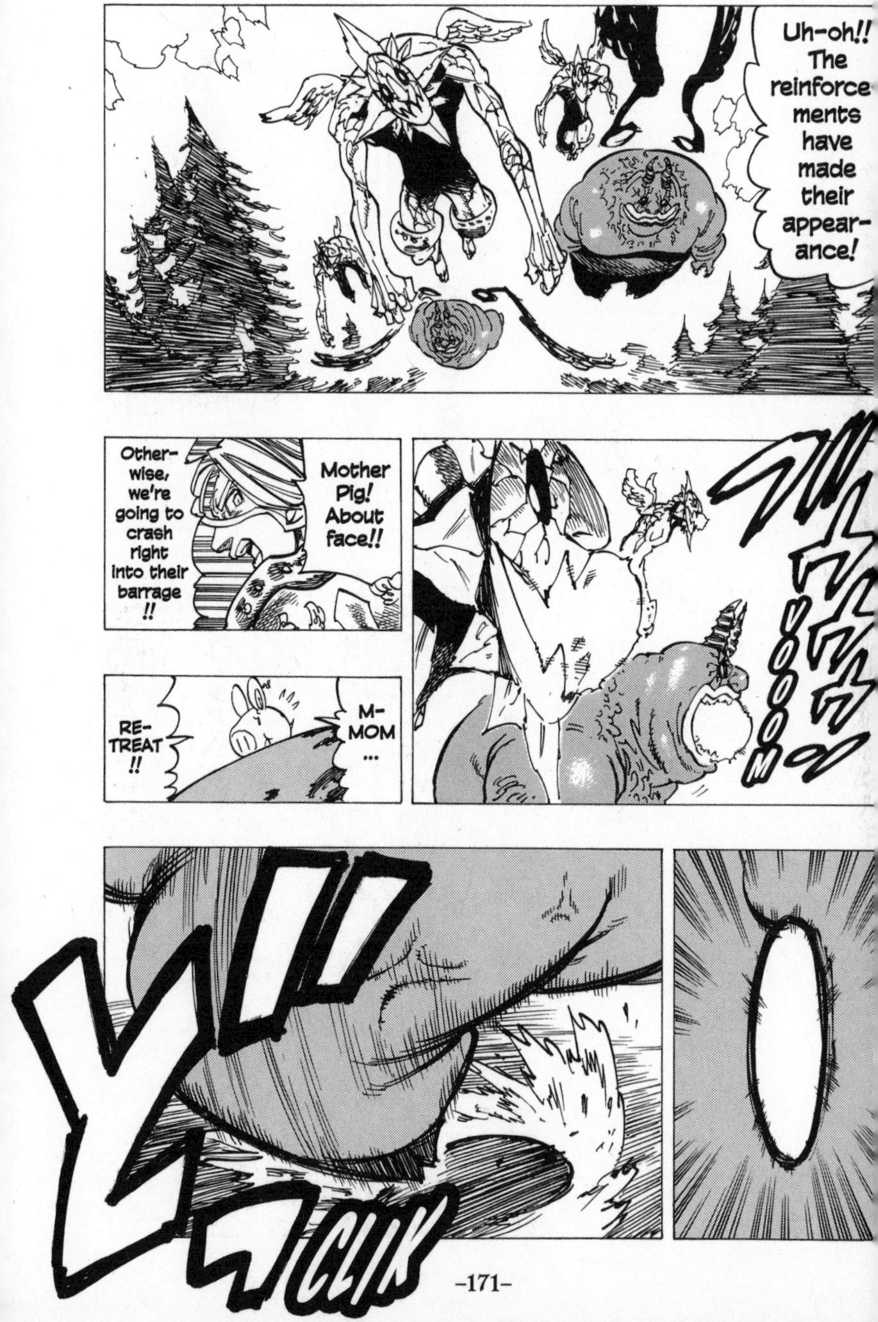
Uh-oh!! The reinforcements have made their appearance!
VVOOOOM
Mother Pig! About face!!
Otherwise, we're going to crash right into their barrage!!
M-MOM...
RE-TREAT!!
CLIK

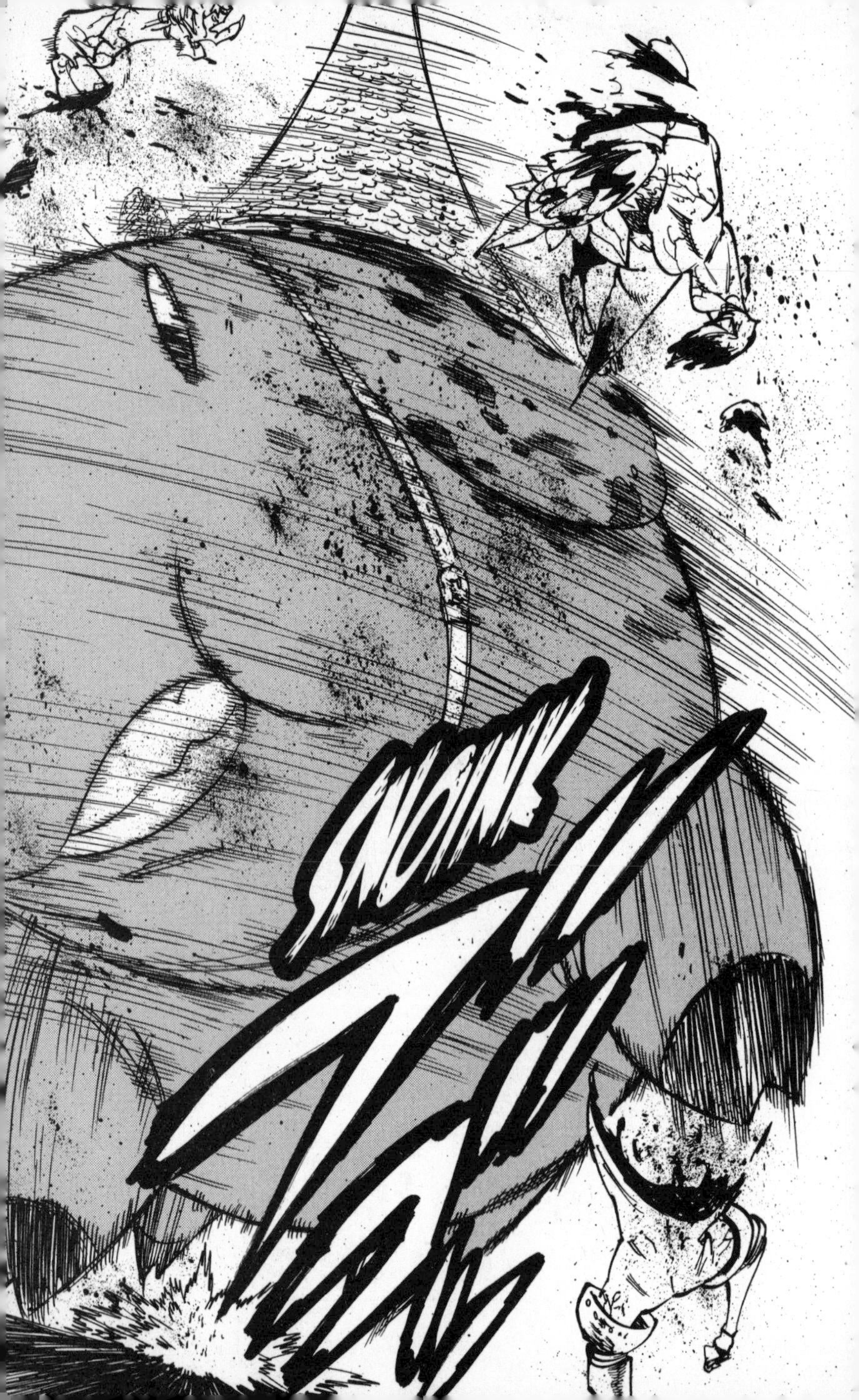

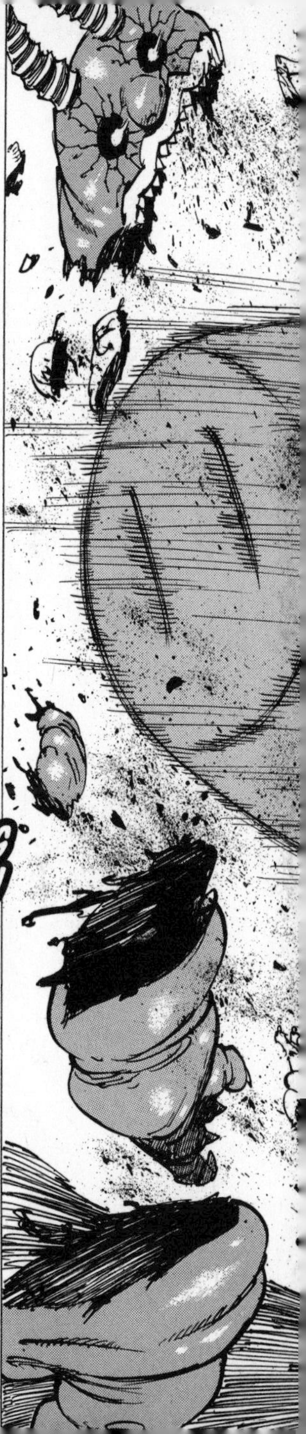

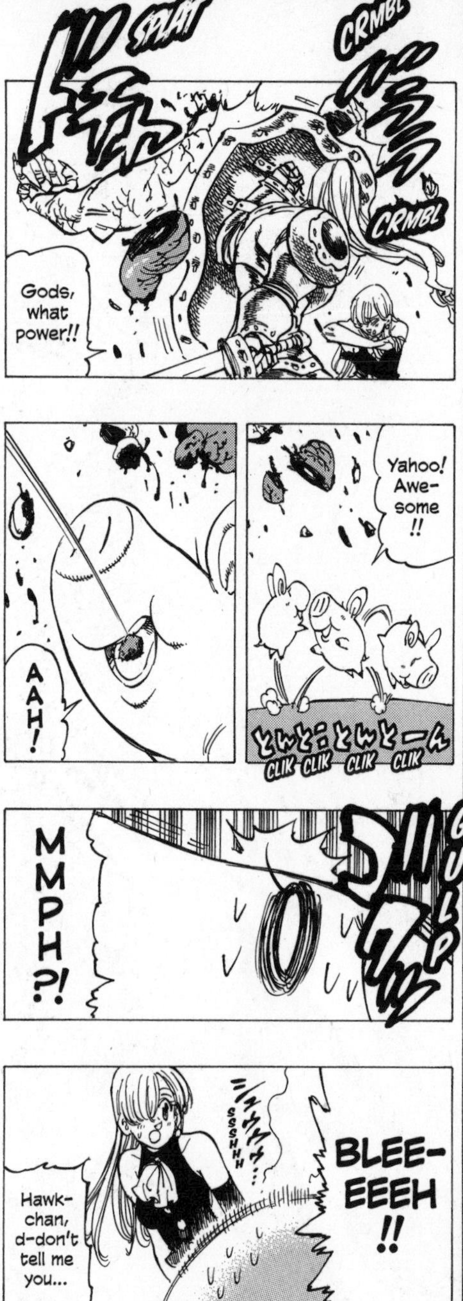
CRMBL
CRMBL
SPLAT
Gods, what power!!
Yahoo! Awesome!!
CLIK CLIK CLIK CLIK
AAH!
GULP
MMPH?!
BLEEEEEH!!
SSSHHH
Hawk-chan, d-don't tell me you...

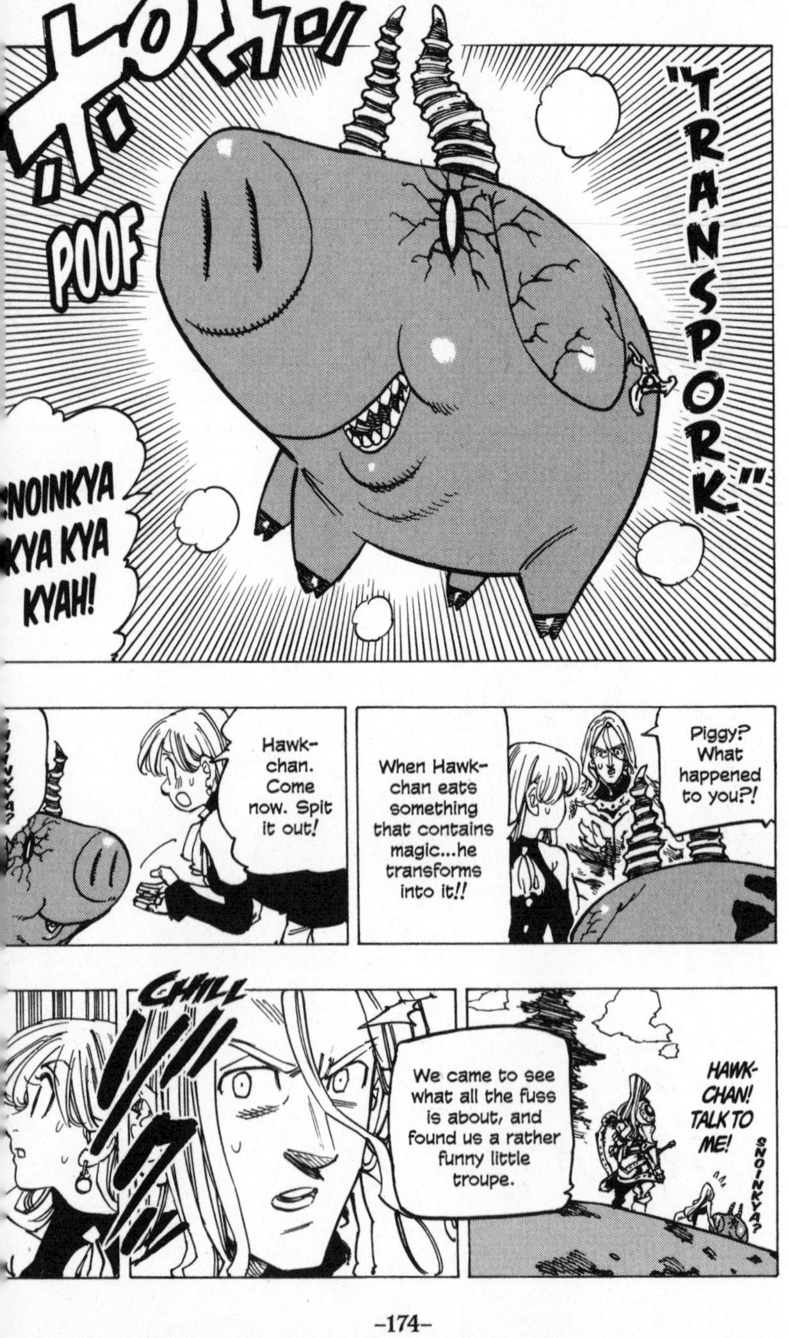
"TRANSPORK"
POOF
SNOINKYA KYA KYA KYAH!
Piggy? What happened to you?!
When Hawk-chan eats something that contains magic...he transforms into it!!
Hawk-chan. Come now. Spit it out!
SNOINKYA?
HAWK-CHAN! TALK TO ME!
SNOINKYA?
We came to see what all the fuss is about, and found us a rather funny little troupe.
CHILL

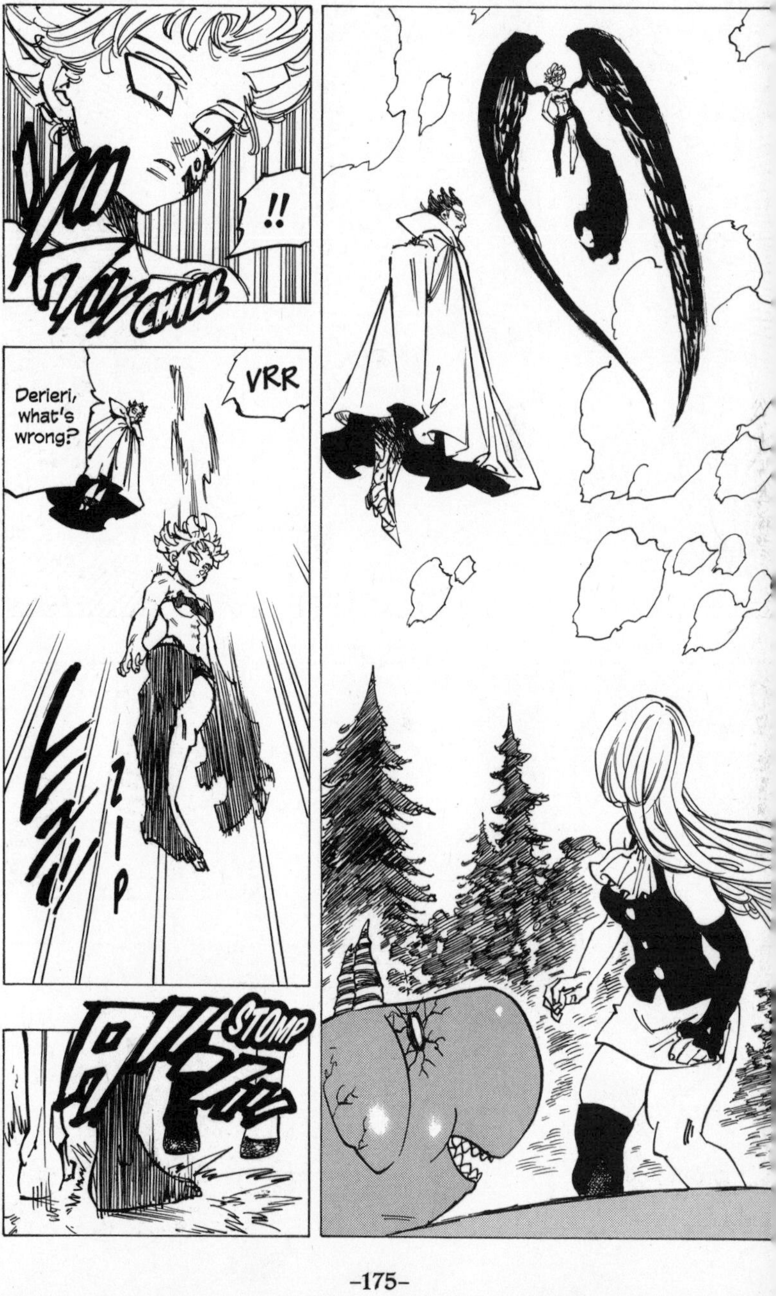
!!
CHILL
VRR
Derieri, what's wrong?
ZIP
STOMP

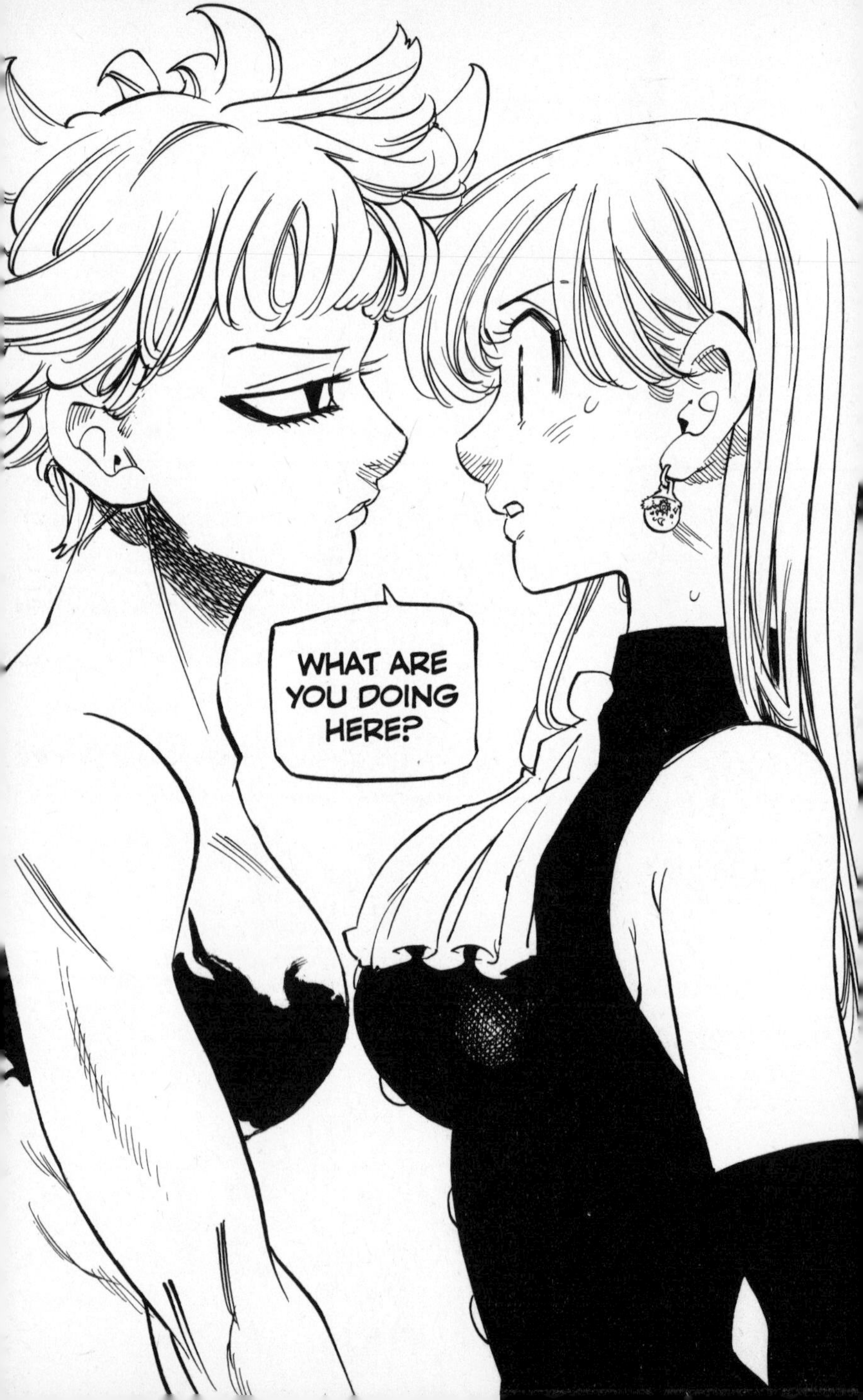
WHAT ARE YOU DOING HERE?

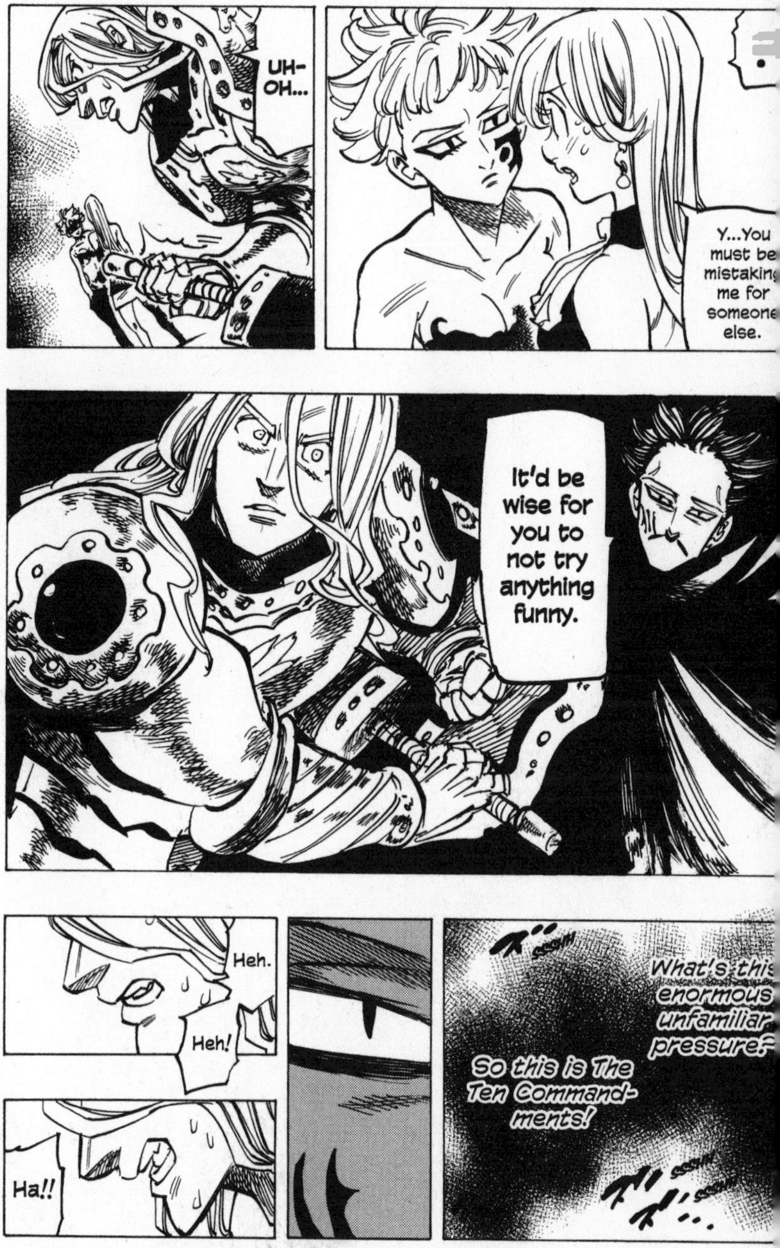
...
Y...You must be mistaking me for someone else.
UH-OH...
It'd be wise for you to not try anything funny.
SSSHH
What's this enormous unfamiliar pressure?
So this is The Ten Commandments!
SSSHH
SSSHH
Heh.
Heh!
Ha!!

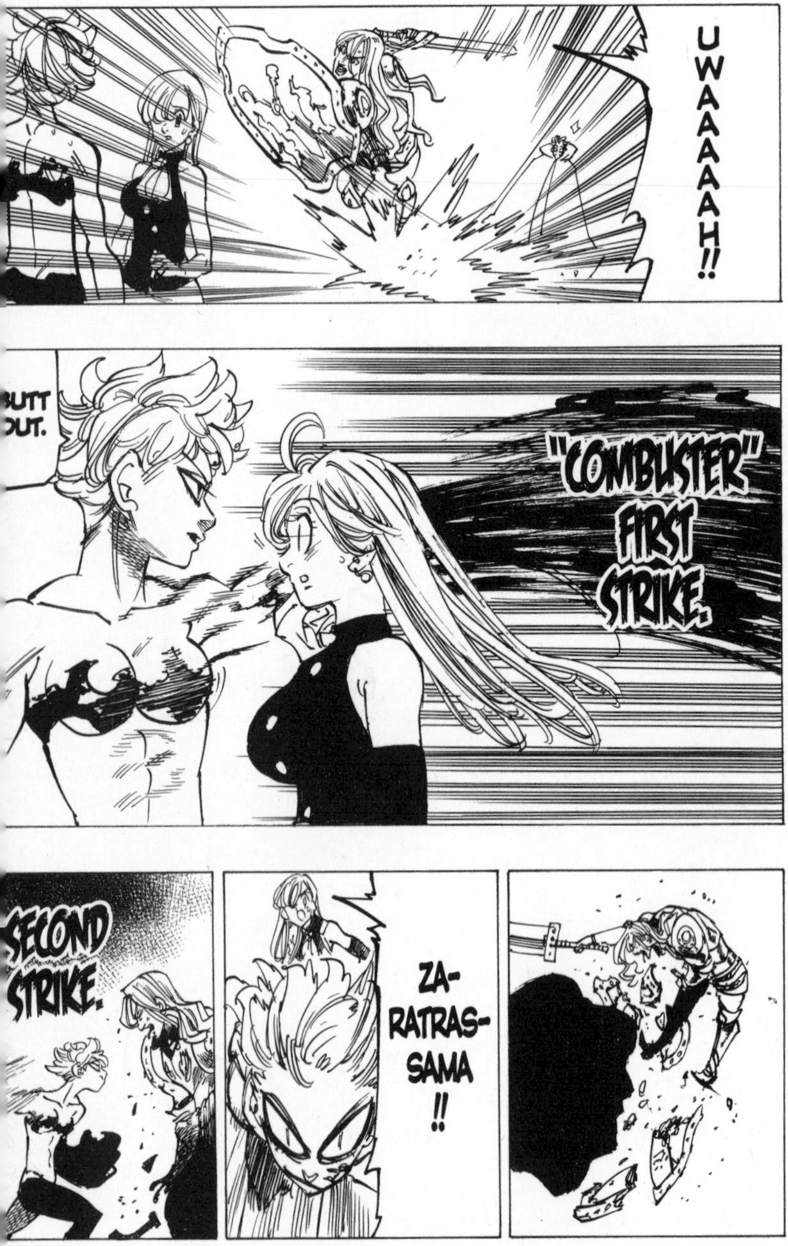
UWAAAAAH!!
BUTT OUT.
"COMBUSTER" FIRST STRIKE.
SECOND STRIKE.
ZA-RATRAS-SAMA !!

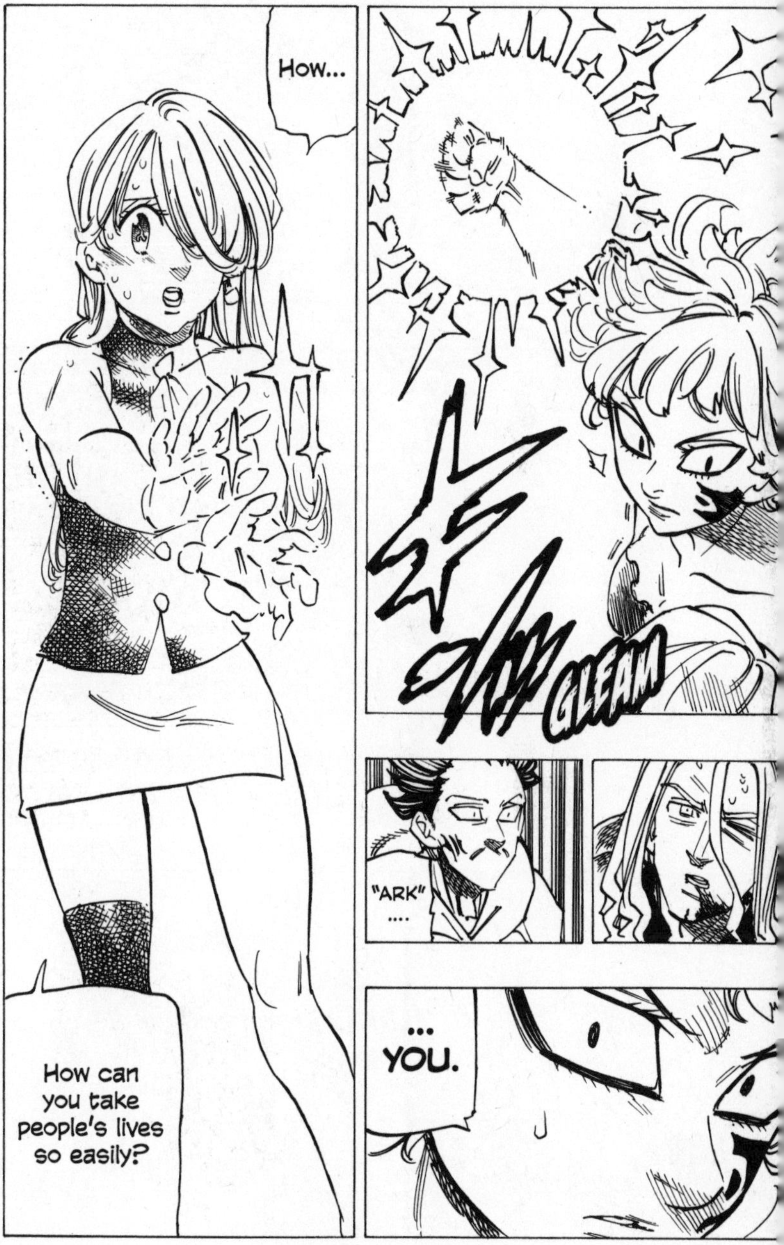
GLEAM
"ARK"
....
... YOU.
How...
How can you take people's lives so easily?

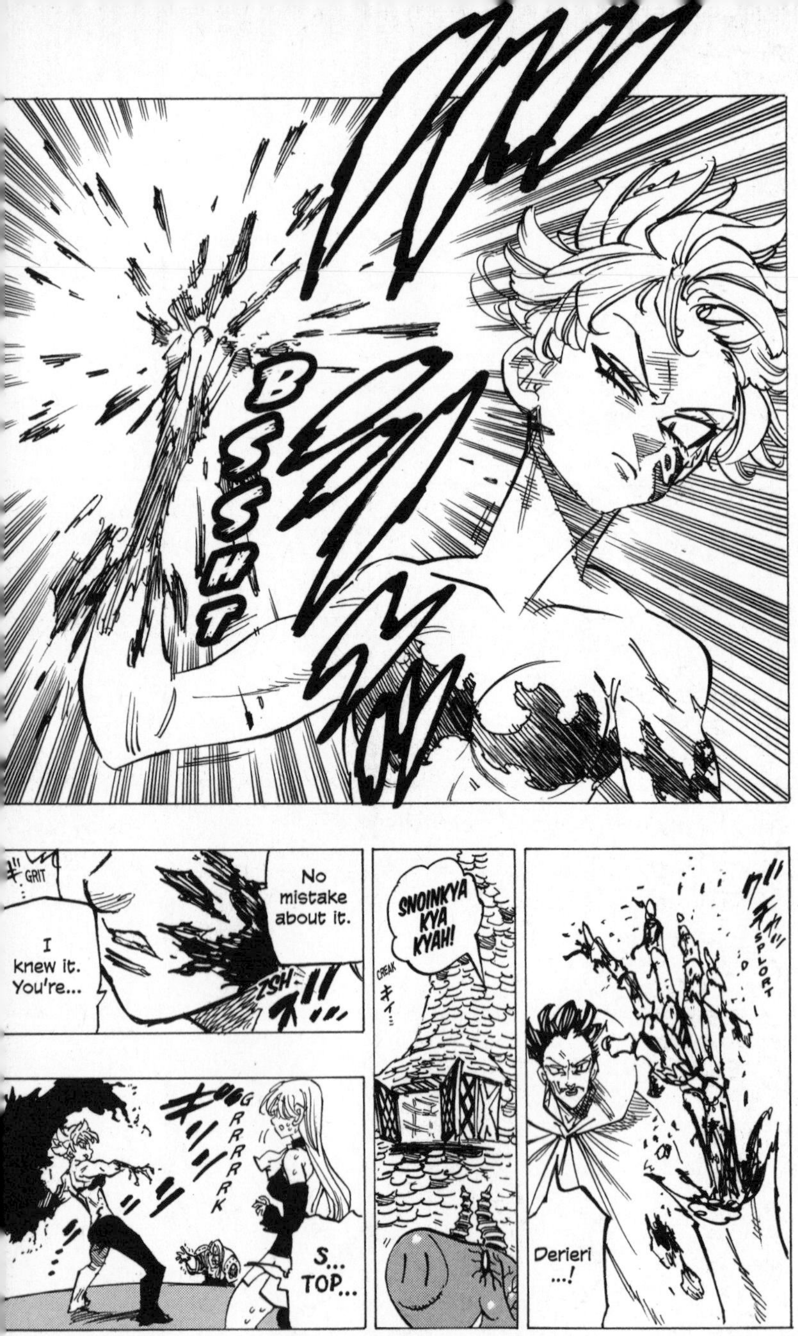
BSSHT
SPLORT
Derieri ...!
CREAK
SNOINKYA KYA KYAH!
No mistake about it.
GRIT
ZSH
I knew it. You're...
GRRRRRK
S... TOP...

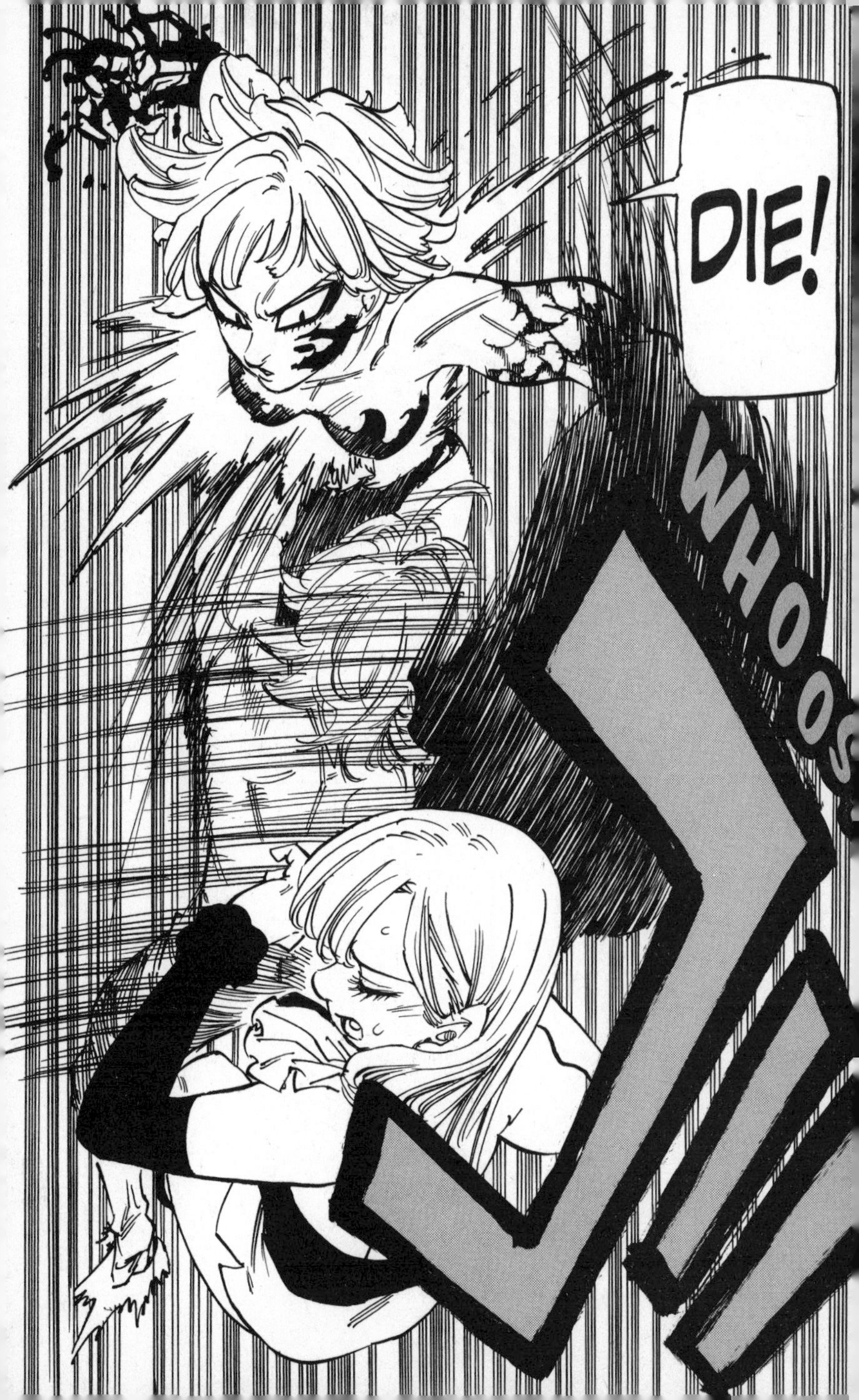
DIE!
WHOOS

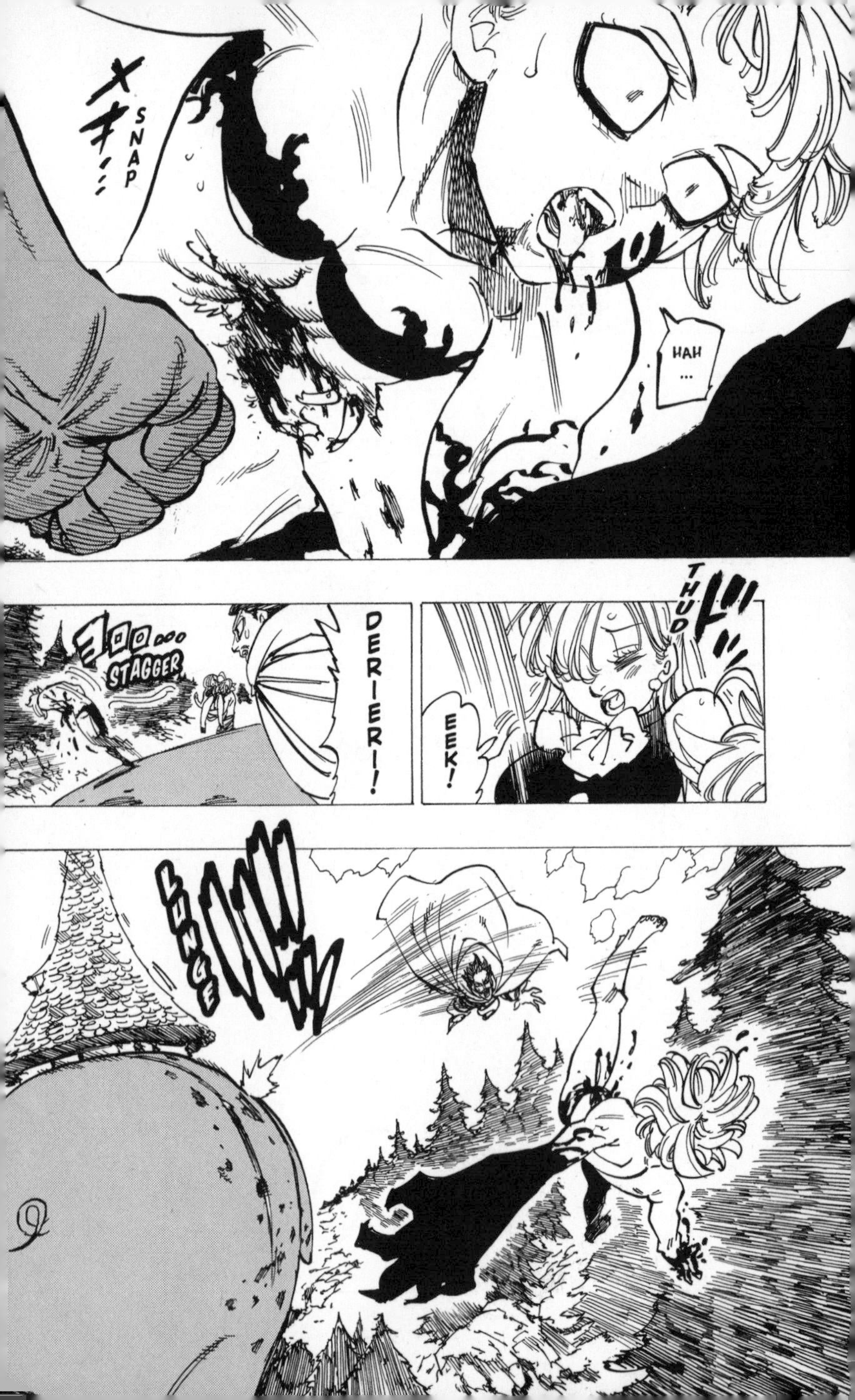
SNAP
HAH ...
THUD
EEK!
DERIERI!
STAGGER
LUNGE

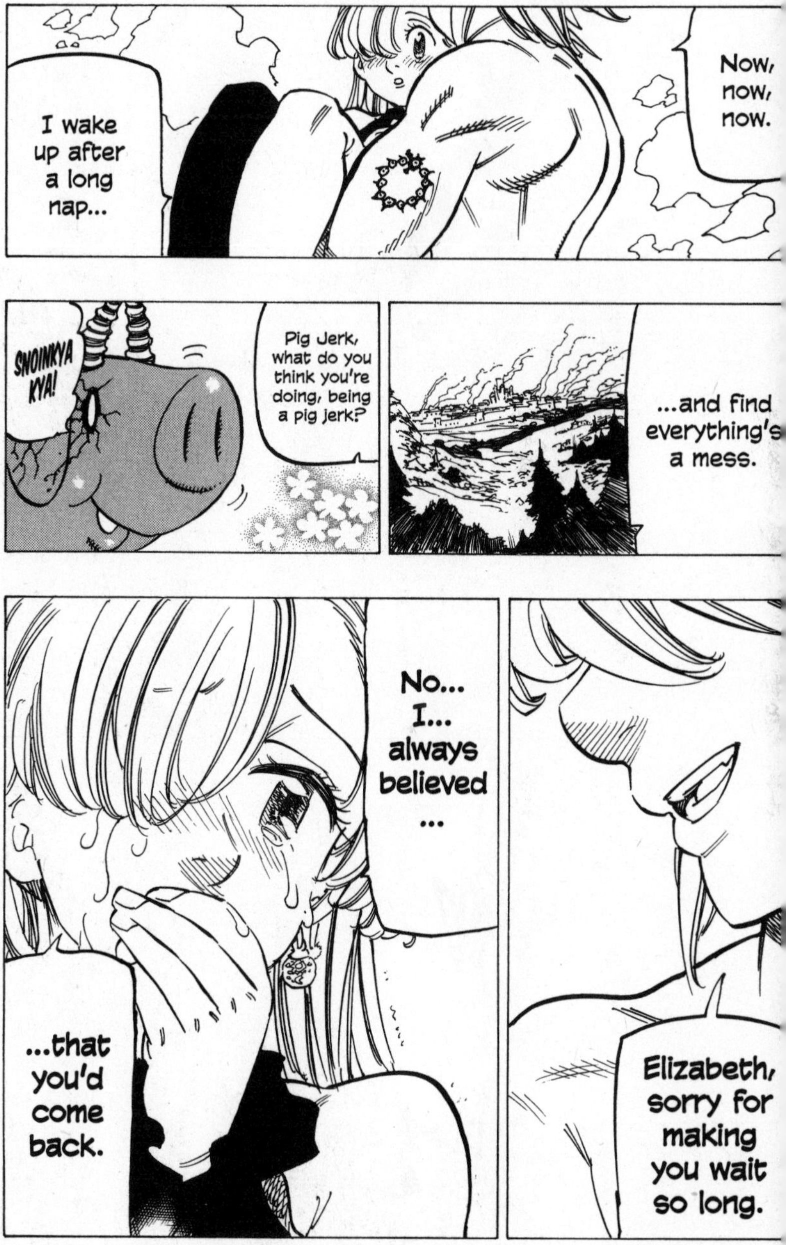
Now, now, now.
I wake up after a long nap...
...and find everything's a mess.
Pig Jerk, what do you think you're doing, being a pig jerk?
SNOINKYA KYA!
Elizabeth, sorry for making you wait so long.
No... I... always believed...
...that you'd come back.

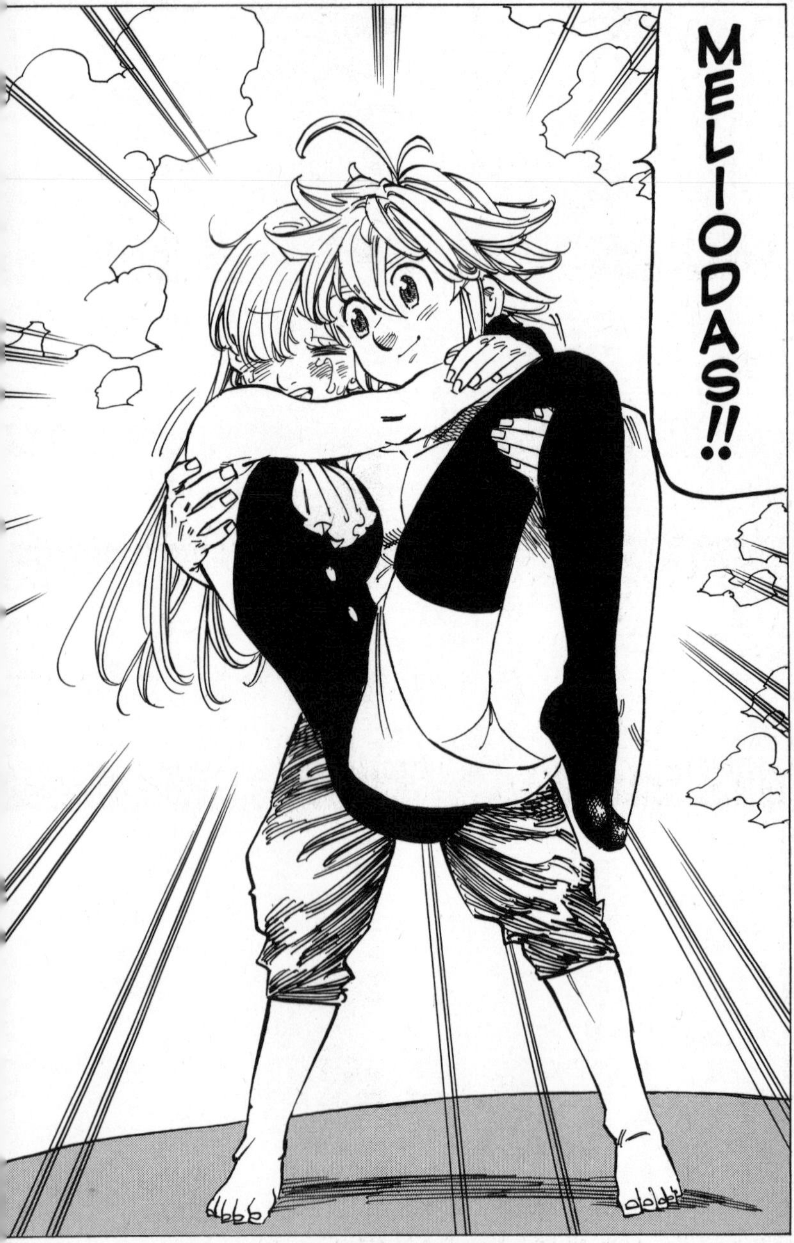
MELIODAS!!

To Be Continued in Volume 24...

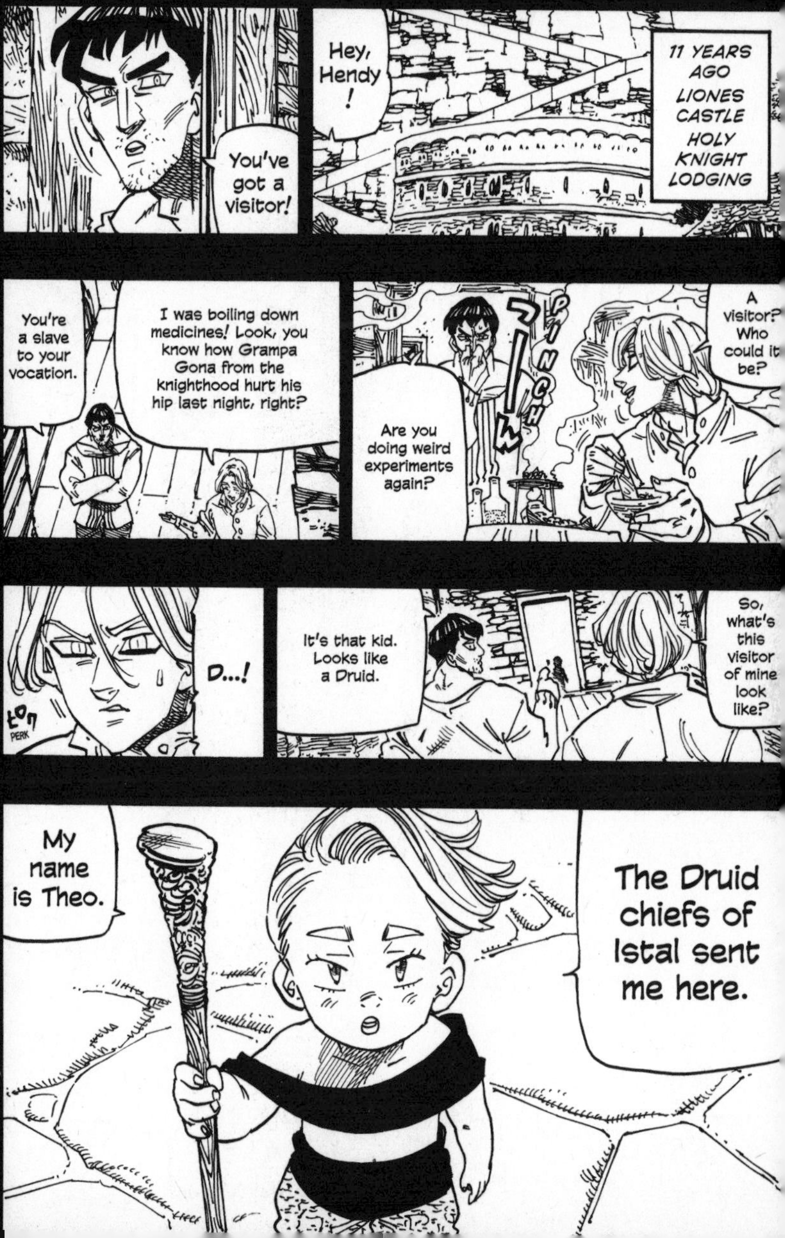
11 YEARS AGO LIONES CASTLE HOLY KNIGHT LODGING
Hey, Hendy!
You've got a visitor!
A visitor? Who could it be?
PINCH
Are you doing weird experiments again?
I was boiling down medicines! Look, you know how Grampa Gona from the knighthood hurt his hip last night, right?
You're a slave to your vocation.
So, what's this visitor of mine look like?
It's that kid. Looks like a Druid.
D...!
PERK
The Druid chiefs of Istal sent me here.
My name is Theo.

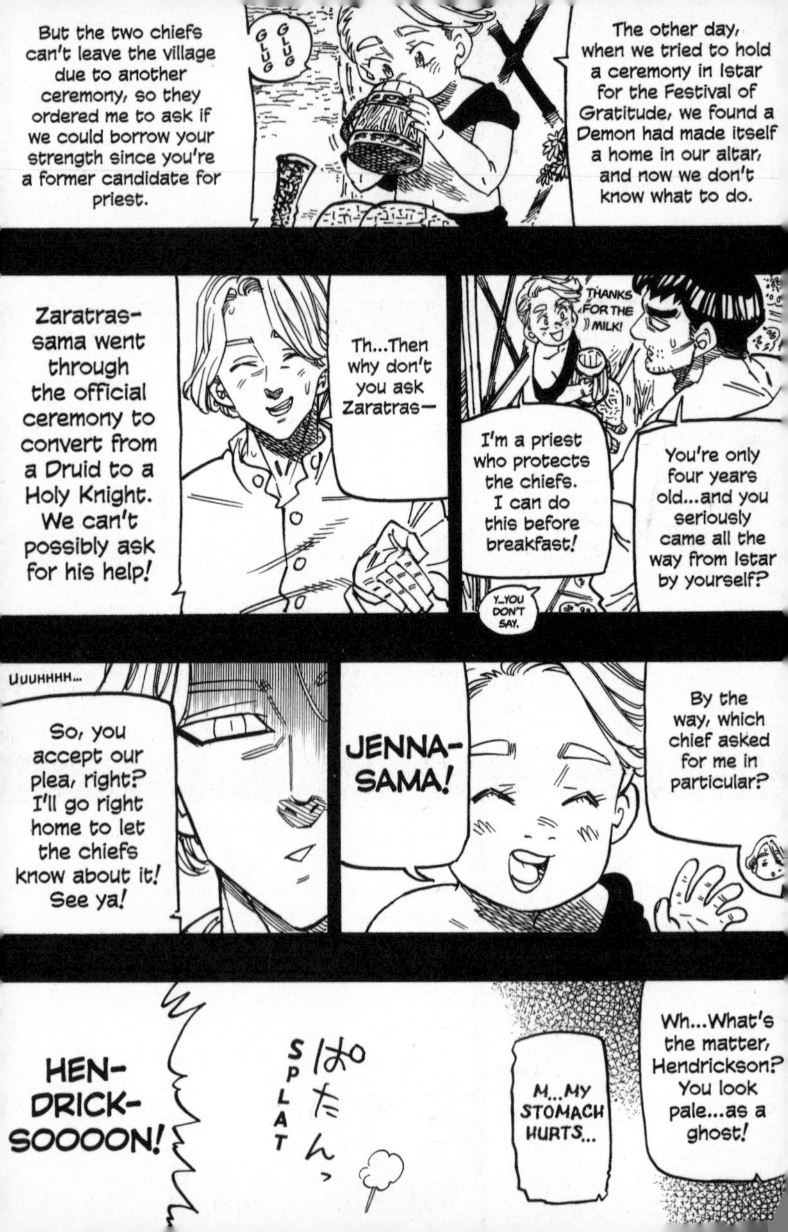
The other day, when we tried to hold a ceremony in Istar for the Festival of Gratitude, we found a Demon had made itself a home in our altar, and now we don't know what to do.
GLUG GLUG
But the two chiefs can't leave the village due to another ceremony, so they ordered me to ask if we could borrow your strength since you're a former candidate for priest.
THANKS FOR THE MILK!
You're only four years old...and you seriously came all the way from Istar by yourself?
I'm a priest who protects the chiefs. I can do this before breakfast!
Y...YOU DON'T SAY.
Th...Then why don't you ask Zaratras—
Zaratras-sama went through the official ceremony to convert from a Druid to a Holy Knight. We can't possibly ask for his help!
By the way, which chief asked for me in particular?
JENNA-SAMA!
UUUHHHH...
So, you accept our plea, right? I'll go right home to let the chiefs know about it! See ya!
Wh...What's the matter, Hendrickson? You look pale...as a ghost!
M...MY STOMACH HURTS...
ぱたん
SPLAT
HEN-DRICK-SOOOON!

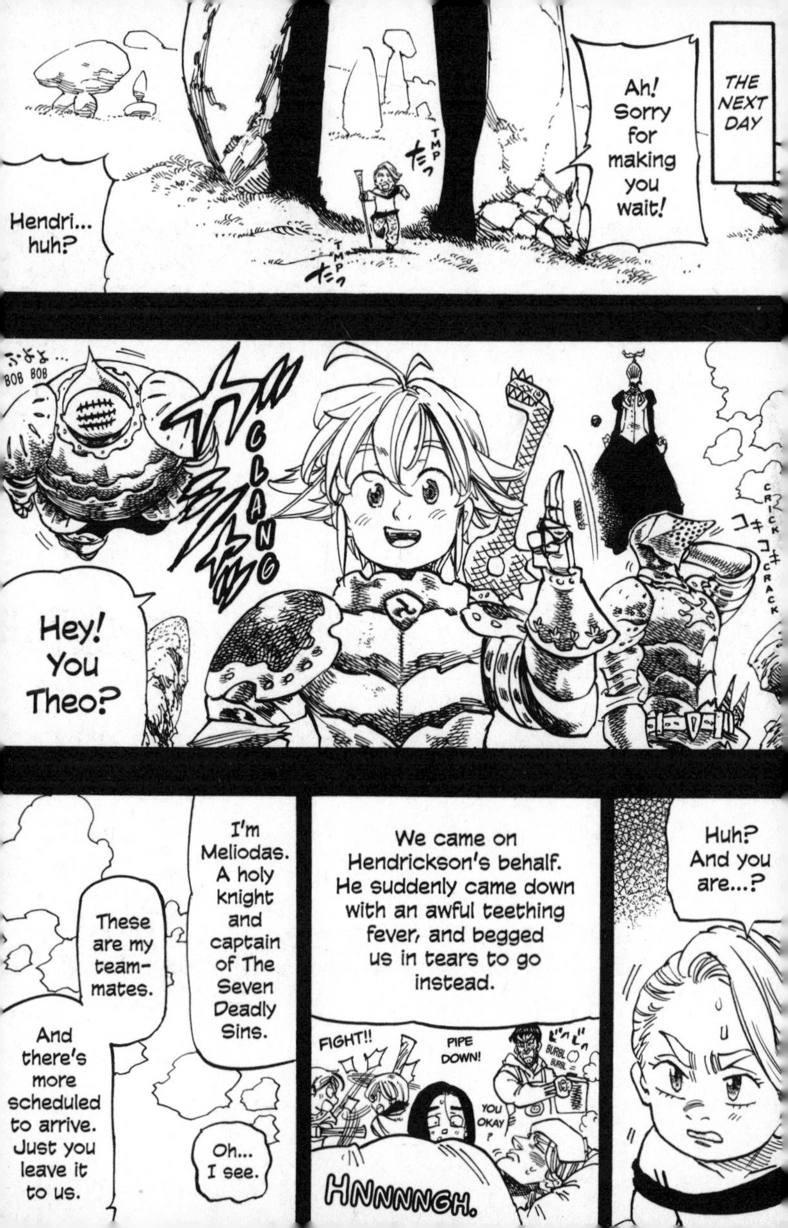
THE NEXT DAY
Ah! Sorry for making you wait!
TMP
TMP
Hendri... huh?
CRICK CRACK
CLANG
BOB BOB
Hey! You Theo?
Huh? And you are...?
We came on Hendrickson's behalf. He suddenly came down with an awful teething fever, and begged us in tears to go instead.
BURBL BURBL
PIPE DOWN!
FIGHT!!
YOU OKAY?
HNNNNGH.
I'm Meliodas. A holy knight and captain of The Seven Deadly Sins.
These are my team-mates.
And there's more scheduled to arrive. Just you leave it to us.
Oh... I see.

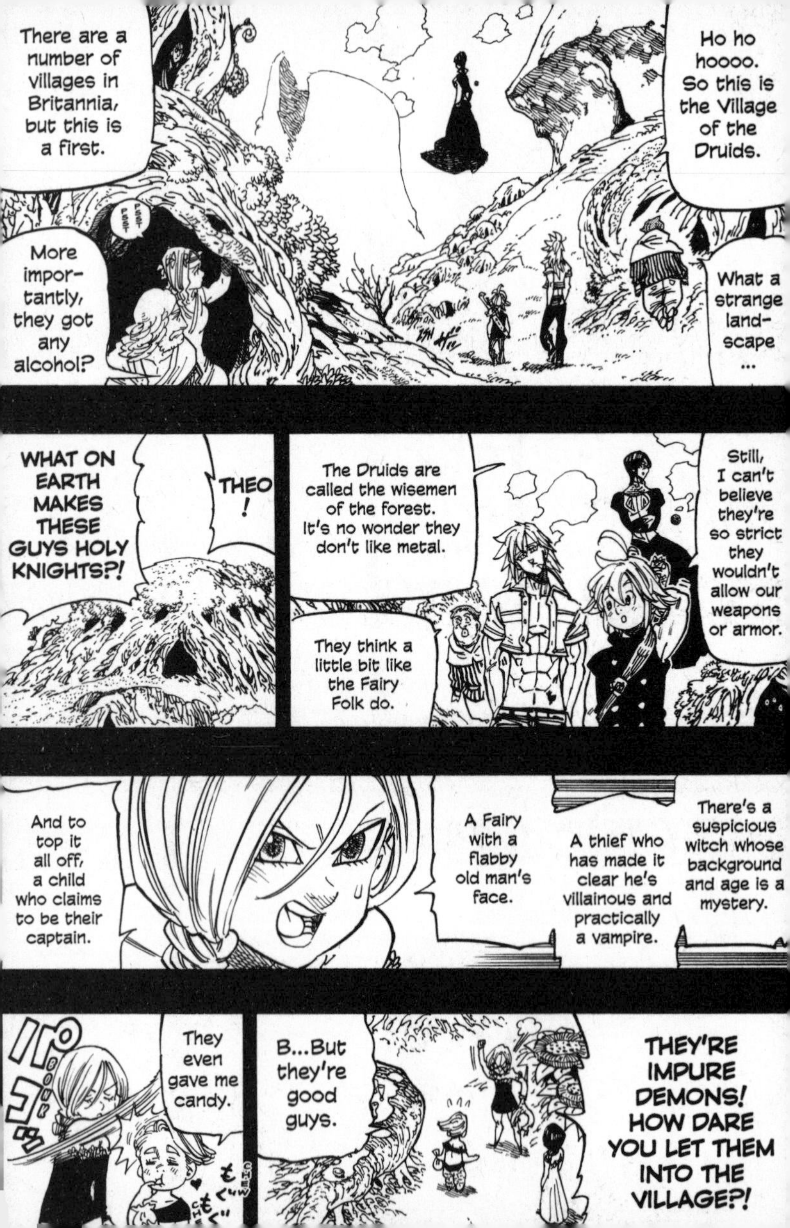
Ho ho hoooo. So this is the Village of the Druids.
There are a number of villages in Britannia, but this is a first.
What a strange landscape...
More importantly, they got any alcohol?
Still, I can't believe they're so strict they wouldn't allow our weapons or armor.
The Druids are called the wisemen of the forest. It's no wonder they don't like metal.
They think a little bit like the Fairy Folk do.
THEO!
WHAT ON EARTH MAKES THESE GUYS HOLY KNIGHTS?!
There's a suspicious witch whose background and age is a mystery.
A thief who has made it clear he's villainous and practically a vampire.
A Fairy with a flabby old man's face.
And to top it all off, a child who claims to be their captain.
THEY'RE IMPURE DEMONS! HOW DARE YOU LET THEM INTO THE VILLAGE?!
B...But they're good guys.
They even gave me candy.
CHEW CHEW

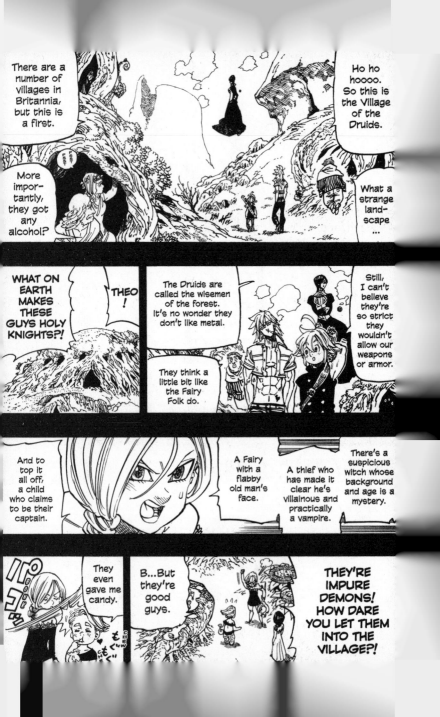

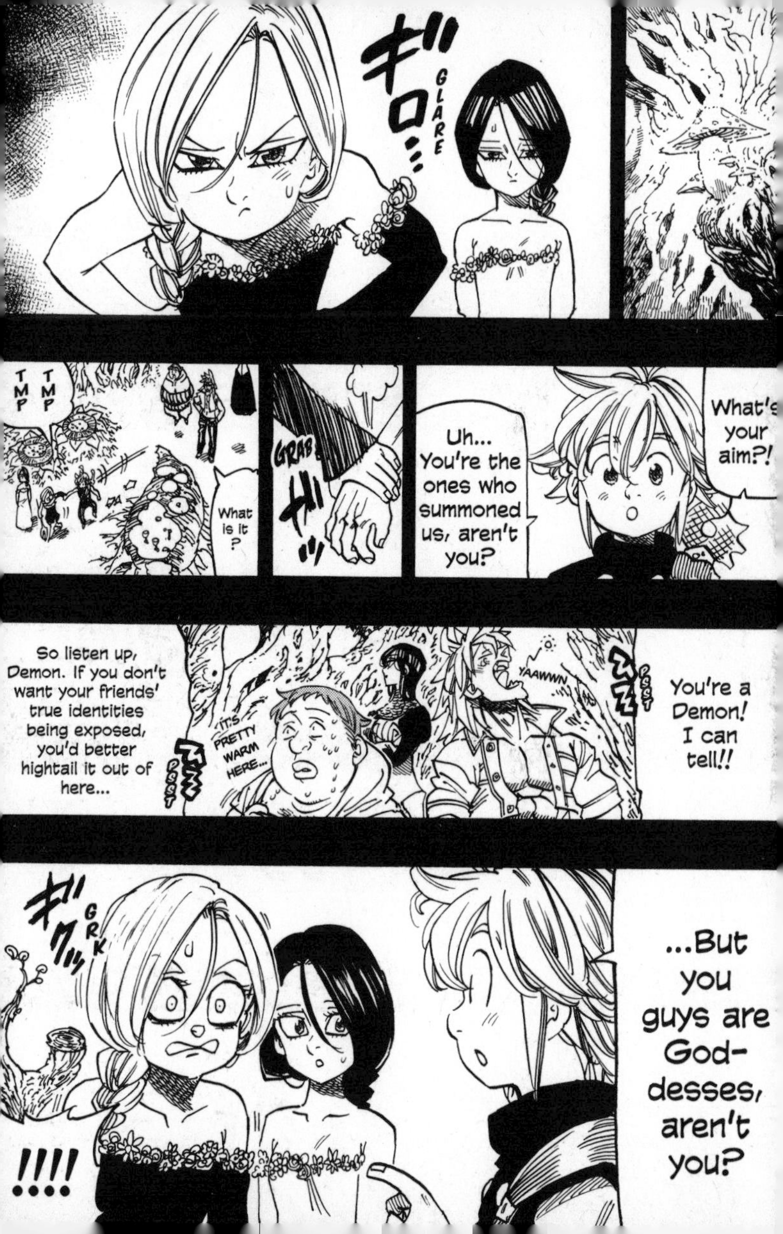
GLARE
What's your aim?!
Uh... You're the ones who summoned us, aren't you?
GRAB
What is it?
TMP TMP
You're a Demon! I can tell!!
PSST
YAAWWN
IT'S PRETTY WARM HERE...
PSST
So listen up, Demon. If you don't want your friends' true identities being exposed, you'd better hightail it out of here...
...But you guys are God-desses, aren't you?
GRK
!!!!

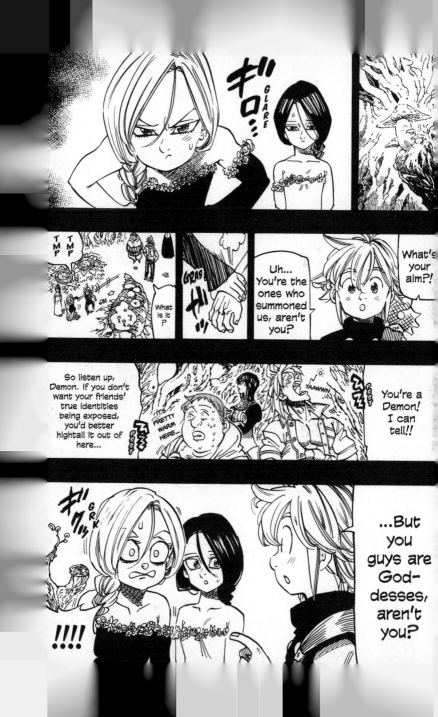

KODANSHA
COMICS

new
ries
m the
eator
Soul
ter, the
egahit
anga and
ime seen
Toonami!

un and lively...
great start!"
-Adventures in
Poor Taste

FIRE FORCE

By Atsushi Ohkubo

e city of Tokyo is plagued by a deadly phenomenon: spontaneous
uman combustion! Luckily, a special team is there to quench the
ferno: The Fire Force! The fire soldiers at Special Fire Cathedral 8
e about to get a unique addition. Enter Shinra, a boy who possesses
e power to run at the speed of a rocket, leaving behind the famous
levil's footprints" (and destroying his shoes in the process).
an Shinra and his colleagues discover the source of this strange
pidemic before the city burns to ashes?

Atsushi Ohkubo/Kodansha Ltd. All rights reserved.

KC
KODANSHA COMICS

Japan's most powerful spirit medium delves into the ghost world's greatest mysteries!

Story by Kyo Shirodaira, famed author of mystery fiction and creator of *Spiral*, *Blast of Tempest*, and *The Record of a Fallen Vampire*.

Both touched by spirits called yôka Kotoko and Kurô have gained uniqu superhuman powers. But to gain he powers Kotoko has given up an ey and a leg, and Kurô's person life is in shambles. S when Kotoko sugges they team up to de with renegades fro the spirit world, Kur doesn't have many othe choices, but Kotoko might ju: have a few ulterior motives...

IN/SPECTRE

STORY BY **KYO SHIRODAIR**
ART BY **CHASHIBA KATAS**

© Kyo Shirodaira, Chashiba Katase/Kodansha Ltd. All rights reserve

The Seven Deadly Sins volume 23 is a work of fiction. Names, characters, places, and incidents are the products of the author's imagination or are used fictitiously. Any resemblance to actual events, locales, or persons, living or dead, is entirely coincidental.

A Kodansha Comics Trade Paperback Original.

The Seven Deadly Sins volume 23 copyright © 2016 Nakaba Suzuki
English translation copyright © 2017 Nakaba Suzuki

All rights reserved.

Published in the United States by Kodansha Comics, an imprint of Kodansha USA Publishing, LLC, New York.

Publication rights for this English edition arranged through Kodansha Ltd., Tokyo.

First published in Japan in 2016 by Kodansha Ltd., Tokyo.

ISBN 978-1-63236-514-9

Printed in the United States of America.

www.kodanshacomics.com

9 8 7 6 5 4 3 2 1

Translation: Christine Dashiell
Lettering: James Dashiell
Editing: Lauren Scanlan
Kodansha Comics edition cover design: Phil Balsman